Franco Corelli

A MAN, A VOICE

Selections on CD*

Great Voices, Volume 5

1. PAGLIACCI (Leoncavallo) "No, pagliaccio non son" – Milan (RAI), 1954 [2:44]
2. WERTHER (Massenet) "Ah, non mi ridestar" – RAI Concert 1955 [2:50]
3. LA FANCIULLA DEL WEST (Puccini) "Ch'ella mi creda" (with Tito Gobbi) – Milan, La Scala, 1956 [2:39]
4. I LOMBARDI (Verdi) "La mia letizia infondere" – RAI, 1957 [2:27]
5. MADAMA BUTTERFLY (Puccini) "Addio, fiorito asil" – RAI, 1957 [1:41]
6. ANDREA CHÉNIER (Giordano) "Come un bel dì di maggio" – Naples, Teatro di San Carlo, 1958 [2:50]
7. ADRIANA LECOUVREUR (Cilea) "Le dolcissime effigie" – Naples, Teatro di San Carlo, 1959 [4:36]
8. ADRIANA LECOUVREUR (Cilea) "L'anima ho stanca" – Naples, Teatro di San Carlo, 1959 [1:52]
9. TOSCA (Puccini) "Recondita armonia" – Livorno, Teatro la Gran Guardia, 1959 [2:47]
10. CARMEN (Bizet) "Il fior che avevi a me tu dato" – Palermo, Teatro Massimo, 1959 [3:46]
11. POLIUTO (Donizetti) "Sfolgorò divino raggio" –Milan, La Scala, 1960 [4:12]
12. ANDREA CHÉNIER (Giordano)"Un dì all'azzurro spazio" – Vienna, Staatsoper, 1960 [5:04]
13. IL TROVATORE (Verdi) "Ah! sì, ben mio" (with Antonietta Stella) – Milan, La Scala, 1962 [4:26]
14. IL TROVATORE (Verdi) "Di quella pira" (with Antonietta Stella and Piero De Palma) – Milan, La Scala, 1962 [2:54]
15. LES HUGUENOTS [GLI UGONOTTI] (Meyerbeer) Love duet from Act IV (with Giulietta Simionato) – Milan, La Scala, 1962 [11:36]
16. TURANDOT (Puccini) "Gli enigmi sono tre" (with Birgit Nilsson) – Milan, La Scala, 1964 [1:07]
17. TURANDOT (Puccini) "No, no, principessa altera!" (with Birgit Nilsson) – Milan, La Scala, 1964 [:58]
18. TURANDOT (Puccini) "Nessun dorma" – Milan, La Scala, 1964 [3:12]

*All performances "live."

19. LA FORZA DEL DESTINO (Verdi) "O tu che in seno agli angeli" – Philadelphia, Academy of Art, 1965 [6:11]

20. TOSCA (Puccini) "E lucevan le stelle" – Parma, Teatro Regio, 1967 [3:20]

21. LE CID (Massenet) "Ô souverain" – New York, Philharmonic Hall 1968 [5:01]

1. Orchestra and Chorus of the Radiotelevisione Italiana directed by Alfredo Simonetto. 2. Orchestra conducted by Mario Rossi. 3. and 11. Orchestra of Teatro alla Scala of Milan conducted by Antonino Votto. 4. and 5. RAI Symphonic Orchestra. 6. Orchestra of the Teatro di San Carlo of Naples conducted by Franco Capuana. 7. and 8. Orchestra of the Teatro di San Carlo of Naples conducted by Mario Rossi. 9. Orchestra of the Teatro la Gran Guardia of Livorno conducted by Mario Parenti. 10. Orchestra of the Teatro Massimo of Palermo conducted by Pierre Dervaux. 12. Orchestra of the Vienna State Opera (Wiener Staatsoper) conducted by Lovro von Matacic. 13. through 18. Orchestra of Teatro alla Scala of Milan conducted by Gianandrea Gavazzeni. 19. Orchestra conducted by Anton Guadagno. 20. Orchestra of the Teatro Regio of Parma conducted by Giuseppe Morelli. 21. Orchestra conducted by Alfredo Silipigni.

GREAT VOICES

Volumes published in this series:

Franco Corelli

A MAN, A VOICE

by
Marina Boagno
with
Gilberto Starone

translated by
Teresa Brentegani and Samuel Chase

chronology by
Gilberto Starone

discography by
Gilberto Starone

tapography by
Federico Rota

videography and filmography by
Gilberto Starone, Mark Schiavone and Stephen R. Leopold

compact disc compiled by
Mark Schiavone

GREAT VOICES

5

BASKERVILLE
PUBLISHERS, INC.

Baskerville Publishers, Inc.
7616 LBJ Freeway, Suite 510, Dallas, TX 75251-1008

Library of Congress Cataloging-in-Publication Data

Boagno, Marina.
    [Franco Corelli. English]
    Franco Corelli : a man, a voice / by Marina Boagno, with Gilberto Starone ; translated by Teresa Brentegani and Samuel Chase ; chronology by Gilberto Starone ; discography by Gilberto Starone ; tapography by Federico Rota ; videography and filmography by Gilberto Starone, Mark Schiavone, and Stephen R. Leopold ; compact disc compiled by Mark Schiavone.
       p. cm. -- (Great voices ; 5)
    Translation of: Franco Corelli : un uomo, una voce.
    Includes bibliographical references and index.
    ISBN 1-880909-50-2
    1. Corelli, Franco. 2. Tenors (Singers)--Italy--Biography.
I. Starone, Gilberto. II. Title. III. Series.
ML420.C676B613 1996
782.1'092--dc21
[B]   96-50939
                                                 MN

Manufactured in the United States of America
First Printing, 1996

*"Human singing is not only a biological phenomenon.
Beneath the physical sound there is an intellectual vibration
which is the reflection of a spiritual vibration.
The sound of* ordinary voice *belongs to man's physical body
and subconscious, and it is simple automatic vibration.
The* technical voice, *which evolves from analysis
in a rational, natural process, shapes the vocal instrument.*

*"But the voice, fruit of a superior experience
linked to man's divine nature, from which inspiration flows,
is* melodic breath, spirit. "Spiritus intus alit":
it breathes in the vibration and transfigures it."

GIACOMO LAURI-VOLPI
(from *Misteri della voce umana*)

Introductions to the American Edition

"A voice of heroic power, yet with great beauty of tone; darkly sensuous, mysteriously melancholic... but above all, a voice of thunder and lightning, fire and blood." HERBERT VON KARAJAN on Franco Corelli (*specifically of his Manrico in the maestro's famous production of* Il trovatore *at the 1962 Salzburg Festiva*l)

Karajan's famous quote brings back the whole Corelli experience. Truly, to see and hear Corelli as Manrico (or for that matter as Calaf, Ernani, Radames, Chénier, Cavaradossi, etc.) was more than an exciting event. You were very much in the thrilling presence of vocal "thunder and lightning, fire and blood!" How long would Corelli hold the high D-flat at the end of the *Trovatore* trio? How many high Cs would he interpolate and where would he put them in *Turandot, Ernani* or *Aida*? Audiences and critics never knew because Corelli himself never knew. "The music makes your blood race, makes you alive... I like to do dangerous things, I like adventure," he would declare.

The transformation of Corelli onstage with a sword in his hand was something to behold. There was a gleam of madness in the eyes, thrills in his movement and excitement in his voice. The fact that he also looked like a warrior god to begin with made the fantastic even more real. And yet... "above all, it was the voice."

Most extraordinary, perhaps, was Corelli's ability to sing with great power yet still preserve tonal splendor. This was especially apparent in the upper register of his voice. Most other tenors (even those with great range) would "thin out" on the top. Corelli's electrifying high notes would be almost as "thick" or full as the notes in his middle voice and still have a brilliant ring. Much of this appeared miraculous because Corelli was largely self-taught and his voice was a unique combination of God-given gift and pure self-will. Explosively produced from within, through a maze of raw emotion, Harold C. Schonberg described it in "The New York Times" as "a force of nature, an act of God, the vocal equivalent of an earthquake, volcano or hurricane."

Could any "method" explain his feats of vocalism? There is no doubt that he was influenced by the teachings of Antonio Melocchi, as was the great tenor Mario Del Monaco. In recent interviews Corelli has discussed Melocchi's methods, which involved singing with a lowered larynx, and the way he adapted those methods to his own voice by learning to "float" his larynx. Words are of little help to explain the process of voice placement, which depends so much on the singer's feelings, but it's an easier matter to assess the results of his hard work. He could match Del Monaco in size and volume, but he could also do things that no other "*tenore di forza*" (including Del Monaco) would even dream of. In terms of agility and the ability to vary the color of his voice and produce dynamic effects at will throughout his range Corelli was every bit as close to the masters of the nineteenth century as his mentor, Lauri-Volpi.

In the book you are about to read terms will be used such as mezza voce, legato, vibrato, tessitura and fiato (for the singer's breath) which should be familiar to anyone with general knowledge of singing or music. In any case, the editors have chosen not to italicize them. However, few if any of the big-voiced tenors to follow Corelli have been able to manage certain effects which were fundamental to his way of singing, so in keeping with Baskerville Publishers' desire to popularize and educate, I will say a few words about them.

We will frequently hear about Corelli's *filatura*—his "filatura on the B-flat" at the end of "*Celeste Aida*," for example (from "*filare la voce*," to spin the voice) where a phrase, usually one that lies high for the voice (where all vocal effects are more difficult and impressive), is "spun out" and sustained very evenly, though there may be a very beautiful dynamic change to finish it, such as a diminuendo "to the breath," to nothing.

By the way, Corelli distinguished himself by being able to handle the very high *tessiture* of bel canto opera in spite of heroic efforts in the lower-lying, more dramatic repertory, sometimes performing operas with such different vocal requirements dangerously close together in time.

It is hard to find equivalents for terms like *smalto* and *squillo* in English. The former has been translated as "patina," for example, but that's a rather dry way to suggest the point where the metal and the velvet of the voice come together, the quicksilver edge of tone where something cool and sure is being changed into something fiery and evanescent. "Squillo" is literally "ring," but is often described as glowing, shimmering, shining. All great voices have this quality, but in this instance, there's no such thing as excess. The Corelli squillo was endlessly thrilling because it proclaimed the ease with which he produced his voice. Even his softest tones always seemed abundantly alive, almost as if they were nourished by something besides muscle and bone and breath.

The *smorzando* effect, sometimes called *morendo*, describes the diminuendo of a note (again, usually a high note) to suggest a dying away. This is the hardest of all effects for the tenor and it is very seldom heard in our time, if at all, from voices that are described as heroic or dramatic. Corelli may have been the last tenor able to make a huge, forte sound at the top of his range and bring it down to pianissimo without an apparent break in his voice. Perhaps it was possible only because of years of hard work which enabled him to do a *messa di voce* (p>f>p) on every note in his range. Perhaps it was possible because he was humble before the accomplishments of the great tenors who preceded him, and willing to keep challenging himself and going far beyond what would have been acceptable to the audiences of his day.

Much has been written about his supposed fear, and Ms. Boagno has very interesting things to say about it. Her conclusions square with my observations of Corelli onstage: there was tension when he sang, and we may have felt it as much as he did, but not fear, per se. Could it be that what was mistaken for fear was really a sense that he had gone beyond the bounds of what is possible for man? Wasn't there a precedent for this kind of thing in the art of Ancient Greece, in Homer?

Certain great singers seem to possess a sense of responsibility that balances the sense of preferment or specialness they feel for having been endowed with voices that produce rapture in those who hear them. Perhaps in Corelli that sense of responsibility was too acute because he truly understood how much was possible for the voice he had been given: that is, almost anything.

Certainly, as Ms. Boagno and others in the know have pointed out, Corelli was never afraid of audiences—he needed them to be at his best. Perhaps they were a way for him to share the responsibility, so that what was happening to him in moments of exaltation was in the nature of a human experiment, with a great many people participating, and less like the usual thing we encounter with tenors whose egos are every bit as big as their voices, and seem to be saying, "I'm the best!" when they sing. "Just listen and you'll see!"

Hearing some of what Corelli accomplished between 1951 and 1975 it is possible to make comparisons, and surely there are those who will find another tenor more to their taste, but no one who fully understands the possibilities of the human voice can deny what Corelli achieved. It is unnecessary to pile up superlatives as long as we have access to live recordings of his performances. Yet there are still those who would disparage him for ending his career too soon, or for being too difficult, for *divismo*, or who knows what nonsense, and all of us who have cared about Corelli as a man as well as a voice are grateful to Marina Boagno for setting the record straight.

Above all Franco Corelli deserves our thanks for making the effort to get the best out of himself over long years when he was virtually alone in knowing what he was trying to do, and for continuing that struggle out of respect for Truth in Art, even when it meant that he had to give more of himself than he or anyone else had the right to expect was in him. For making that effort, as well as for what he achieved with it, he stands alone, and his memory and his example are always with us.

MARK SCHIAVONE, December, 1996

To My American Readers:

I cannot begin to say how happy I am to have my book published in the United States, where it will henceforth be available to all English-speaking readers. I think all of you will recognize that this was a "labor of love," a love which I know is shared by thousands of Corelli fans all over the world. A love which, I hope, will enable you to understand a choice I made, and I feel I must briefly explain.

You will doubtless notice that in my book very few references are made to the events of Franco Corelli's private life. This was the only request Corelli—in his kind, even shy way, that some of you know from experience—made to me, and I was glad to respect his wish, all the more so since it corresponded with my original intentions. Actually, I believe you will agree that Franco Corelli's artistry is history in the annals of opera, while his privacy is quite another domain, and that he is as entitled to it as any of us.

I hope that you will not only enjoy this book, but above all that it will be of some help in better understanding the unique voice and artistry of a man who totally identified himself with his voice—whose personality is fully embodied and fulfilled in his voice, and only in it. I also hope that my book will make the new generations of opera fans feel that true art never belongs to the past, but remains a source of emotions forever alive and present, and that it will help feeding the expectations we all share for a "new wave" of really great artists able to truly revive opera, and make our dearest memories full of joy and pleasure, rather than regret.

MARINA BOAGNO, December, 1996

Contents

A Man, A Voice

*"You would do me a favor if you would write,
not that I'm a dramatic tenor or a lyric tenor, but
that I am a voice."*

FRANCO CORELLI
*(in an interview with Giuliano Ranieri
in* Epoca, *July 26th, 1970)*

The Purity of Myth

by Gustavo Marchesi

IT WOULD BE IMPOSSIBLE to speak briefly of Franco Corelli. To capture in a few words his voice, his look on the stage: it would be like trying to make a Sequoia into a Bonsai. Still, it's done today, it's necessary. To compress the music into a compact disc, the action into a videotape. We must all bow down to the written word, and it must occupy less and less space. Then when we're alone, free from the coils of microtechnology we can roll out our memories, and that which we love takes shape in our minds like the genie in Aladdin's lamp.

Turandot was the last clip of Franco's I've seen. I believe that there will never again be a Calaf like his, perhaps there never has been—not even Puccini can have imagined him so beautiful and talented. The prince that smiles no more and says everything in his song, covering with his voice the distance that separates "Pekino" (Beijing) from us. He is a creature in which the forms of the Eastern fairy tale (in which all things are beautiful, even the ogres) enrich the drama of Western man.

What is this drama? It is the unreachable, that is to say, the desire of attaining the unattainable without the hope that it will happen. In *Turandot* Puccini succeeded in giving the tension between West and East a dimension in sound. Corelli is the incarnation, the presence which demonstrated that myth isn't only an idea.

It is difficult not to rely on rhetoric when saying this kind of thing. When we celebrate great artists we tend to represent them by crowns, laurels, adoring figures, and excessive ornamentation; or by an excess of words. But we do it because we are too excited and lose our sense of shame, or what other people call self-control.

Luckily we are sincere, because we are only moved to behave this way out of gratitude.

I am very grateful to Franco Corelli because he gave me moments when reality was suspended, when I was shocked or moved beyond belief. Better, all these feelings together. I'm reminded of the meditation on missed opportunities, "*l'ora fuggita*" of Mario, the painter in *Tosca*, or the finale of *Norma*, or of *Carmen*, or his Faust, or his Alvaro, and once again I don't know when I will hear or see something like it again. But what does it matter? I had this luck, and that should be enough.

Then, I am grateful to Franco for a walk we took together once. Franco was singing in my city, where I was a critic. I wasn't supposed to meet him privately—it was my policy with all artists. It was Giuseppe Pugliese who insisted I meet Corelli, and he succeeded in persuading me, for the idea attracted me a lot. So I went with Franco and other friends to visit some monuments as one does partly for cultural enrichment, but even more for touristic reasons, to take the air and wander about.

Franco was a person who moved me. He was a boy in his spirit and didn't hide his sincere wonder at great things. He was amazed that men like us could have done so much: to think, to build, to imagine. His sensitivity was revealed so openly, without artifice, in a way that seemed impossible in a man of the theater, whose profession requires him to pretend, and to overcome spontaneity in order to express it.

How did the singer and man relate to each other? How did they get along?

In a word, I thought: purity. I am still convinced. There are the self-proclaimed *savants* of consummate experience—maybe they were born this way, already experts—with all the tricks of the profession; and there are the pure, those who go before the public fearful of failure, even if they've studied hard, because they feel inferior to their task.

Corelli, who we can say was born with the responsibility of someone who had a God-given voice and a blinding presence, never went onstage without the scruples, fear and devotion of a beginner. Every time he had to start again from the beginning—he who had been given the most precious gifts by Apollo himself.

Today we all owe him our gratitude for his sincerity.

For Franco Corelli

by GIANANDREA GAVAZZENI

IN TALKING ABOUT ART in general, and musical execution in particular, I never use the formulaic expression "the greatest," "the most illustrious," "the most exceptional," etc. These are vulgar expressions to leave to zealots and low-class flatterers.

I prefer, when speaking of interpreters whose experience has covered a vast artistic territory and taken them to the most important musical and theatrical centers, to stress characteristics, peculiarities, the *je ne sais quoi* that have differentiated one artist from the other at the highest levels.

This is the case with Franco Corelli.

I listened to him for the first time at the Sperimentale of Spoleto, and right after, in the following season, at the Rome Opera in the *Giulietta e Romeo* of Zandonai.

Guido Sampaoli was the artistic director. Right at the debut he had immediate faith in Corelli's possibilities. There were, as always, skeptics, those who said that Sampaoli was wrong to entrust to the debut artist a part with such a forbidding tessitura. A tense, dramatic part such as the part of Zandonai's Romeo.

Sampaoli had no doubts. He insisted on his idea and he wasn't wrong. Corelli's first steps on the path of operatic melodrama were prompted by that *Giulietta e Romeo* (which I heard). Then he kept on one step at at time (which is always a sign of continuing and lasting progress), on both sides of the Atlantic... Until he became one of the top performers for a few decades of operatic life.

His heroic squillo, his power—exactly what is meant by the "metal" of the voice—his stage presence, quickly asserted themselves and lit the fuse...

I have memories of particular performances of his that were very committed. Above all at La Scala during very happy times for him and for me...

The exceptional *Turandot* of the 1964 season premiere at La Scala with him and Birgit Nilsson, with the Riddle Scene, that nobody had ever heard sung that way till then. Almost certainly it will never be sung that way again.

Together with this performance was his *Trovatore*, a Manrico desperate in his passion and his inescapable fate; then, still at La Scala, *Andrea Chénier, Fanciulla del West, La battaglia di Legnano* at the 1961 season premiere, *Fedora* with Maria Callas (who will ever again hear such a second act?)... All the way to the unforeseen and explosive success of *Les Huguenots* in 1962.

Corelli and Simionato, Cossotto as the page, Ghiaurov as Marcello, Sutherland as Margherita di Navarra: the cast that only Francesco Siciliani could gather when bringing forgotten operas to light.

The first night subscription audience thought they would be listening to a big bore: *The Huguenots?* Who were they? *What* were they?

The audience of Milanese high society found an amazing cast arrayed before them. The duet between Corelli and Giulietta at the finale of the fourth act brought down the house. Raoul's famous phrase and Valentina's reply had the Scala audience in a frenzy.

These are my memories of Franco Corelli. He was a true pillar of my success during the happiest days of my life in the theater.

Dear Franco, only the memory remains. We must have patience: life, art, music, theater—all require it. There's no going back.

Bergamo, July 6, 1990

Strange Letters

by Marina Boagno

Milan, March 6, 1988

"Da tempo mi pervengono strane lettere..."
I think you remember the line.
Somehow the decision to write you was made like that:
while listening to your *Andrea Chénier*...

THIS WAS THE BEGINNING of the first letter I sent to Franco
Corelli—and perhaps it really was quite strange—announcing
that I was going to write a book about him.

At the time I had been thinking of such a book for about a
year. Since then, two more have gone by before my book took
its final form. Two years full of coincidences, meetings and
occurrences, all of which (big or small) were decisive to the
accomplishment of my project.

In all over three years of research. Not only in theater archives and libraries, but also into the "mystique" beyond the
facts.

Because in addition to the information, which of course is
necessary in the chronicling of Franco Corelli's career (and here
my meeting with Gilberto Starone was of the greatest importance), my aim was to find a personality, if at all possible. Better said, a *person*. Hence the necessity of following two different
paths of research (apart from the traditional collection of reviews, articles and anecdotes).

First of all, the listening. I think I have listened to every existing (or at least, every available) live tape performance and recording of Franco Corelli's voice. Not only with the purpose (obviously indispensable) of getting a deep technical knowledge of his voice, but also, and in a way above all, to catch the traces (I would say the clues) of his personality. Because I believe—and I told him as much during one of our telephone conversations—a singer does not sing only with his (or her) voice, not only with technique, not if he is a great artist. He puts all of himself into his singing: his sensitivity, his personality, even his life experiences.

And, by the way, I also believe this is the reason why each one of us either "likes" or "dislikes" a singer independent (to a certain extent, of course) of his technical ability. Because our "meeting" with a voice is, in the first place, a matter of sensitivity, a matter of *feeling*. And I have *loved* Franco Corelli's voice and artistry long before I fully appreciated his exceptional technical qualities.

The next step (logically, if not chronologically) was to get nearer to Franco Corelli's personality through a long series of meetings and conversations with people who knew him more or less well. His colleagues first of all, but also friends, fans, mere members of the audience. Here again, trying to find not only (and not mainly) information but rather nuances, feelings, perceptions of how these people felt about Corelli, of their relationships with him.

In the end I wanted to go to Ancona, if only for a couple of hours. And so I did, in a rush (in between two trains) on my way from Spoleto, where I had checked the Centro Lirico Sperimentale archives.

I did not know the city. I had little time and I did not even know for sure what I was looking for: an impression, a feeling, an atmosphere, maybe a ghost... But I felt that I would find something, I would find Franco sooner or later.

I looked for him near the place where he was born. In the small corners the war did not destroy. The ones which were doubtless unchanged: the old arcades with their shabby stone pavements, the small squares now full of cars, a little triangular meadow just in front of the place where his home was, squeezed between the highway and the narrow canal, a picturesque shelter for little boats surrounding the Mole Vanvitelliana.

There and then I understood what I was looking for. Something—anything—we might have in common: a shared experience, a sensation, a feeling (even a short-lived one) which could help me overstep rationality, documentation, the aseptic accumulation of facts and scraps of history.

I found it—or I thought I did—on the stone bridge crossing to the impressive pentagonal building of the Mole (entirely surrounded by the sea) on whose walls an imaginative child could easily see "in his mind's eye" wandering knights and pirates, princes and troubadours.

Closing my eyes, I savored the salt scent of the sea, the smells of pitch, of boats, of seaweed floating in the low water. Little by little I felt myself being swept up into another dimension, beyond space and time.

For a moment it was as if I had met Franco as a child. It was as if we had dreamed the same dreams. The space-hungry dreams of children born in front of the sea, to which the curve of the horizon is not a limit, but the beginning of an immense, unexplored world, full of fabulous allurements. A fantastic border: you can throw dreams over and follow them crossing a rainbow bridge.

For a moment I felt him at my side. And our ages were the ones when everything is feasible, and we shared the same need to be "others"—the same yearning for the infinite.

It was in the moment, in that flashing, fleeting encounter, that I believed (for the first time) the dream I had thrown over the horizon, which was this book, could become a reality.

Nevertheless the main leg of my journey is still missing.

At the moment I am writing these lines, my book is (apart from some final touches) finished, but I have never (as yet) met Franco Corelli personally.

I think we began to know each other a little, step by step. First by letter, then by telephone. It was by those letters and the half-dozen phone conversations (which were the sum total of our direct acquaintance) that I, above all, got from him an impression of great kindness: an inborn, natural kindness, very different from cold, formal politeness.

We will meet for the first time (I hope) at the end of August. But that will be another story. Who knows—another book?

Milan, June 21, 1990

I WROTE THE ABOVE PREFACE to my work about six years ago. Of course, since then I have met Franco Corelli a number of times, and also our telephone conversations have become longer and easier. But I do not feel I must change a single word of what I have written about him, about his artistry, and above all, about his personality. He is exactly as I imagined he was, as I expected he was. Maybe even nicer, more charming, more unassuming...

Now that I have begun to know him as a person, I am all the more glad and proud to have given him the gift of this book.

Milan, September 22, 1996

PART ONE

Under His Pillow

"Corelli (...) became aware of the countless pitfalls
which were waiting at every turn in the road
for tenors who relied principally on their natural gift,
the voice that they found in their cradles
by the grace of God, under their pillows, as the
Dauphin of France found his sceptre."

RODOLFO CELLETTI

Spoleto

I T WAS A BEAUTIFUL SPRING NIGHT...
Surely there are many other ways to start a biography, but most of them are academic, and I feel I am entitled to begin Franco Corelli's story as if it were a fairy tale.

Actually, an artist's biography is also a sort of fairy tale to a certain extent because a true artist—whatever the art form—has the power to transport the observer (in our case, the member of an audience) to a dimension which is different, larger, more complex and more complete than everyday reality, and the artist himself must therefore be able to experience and "live" this dimension in the first place.

Anyway, it probably *was* a beautiful spring night when Franco Corelli was born in Ancona, in a house just a stone's throw from the Adriatic Sea.

Born in Le Marche, then. A country whose inhabitants are traditionally known as very private people, and serious, sober, and strong-minded hard workers. A country, too, where music is in the very air people breathe. Not only is it Rossini's birthplace, but also Beniamino Gigli's and many other great singers' from Renata Tebaldi to Sesto Bruscantini and Anita Cerquetti. A country where singing is the rule more than the exception.

Young Franco, nevertheless, had no artistic ambition. When he sang it was only amateur singing. His interests were different: he studied, finished high school, went to university, and above all he enthusiastically practiced a number of sports: boat-racing, swimming, boxing. After some time he got a job as a surveyor in the Ancona municipal administration. Plainly none of these activities had anything to do with singing.

Furthermore, at home his singing exhibitions were not much appreciated. On the contrary, he was often asked to shut up, and for a very good reason. Franco's voice was not suitable to small places. Even if it was still a bit rough and harsh—he had given it no musical training—it was an explosion of sound whose impressive power could only have been meant to ex-pand in great theaters and great arenas.

Of course someone finally noticed it. A friend of his, bari-tone Carlo Scaravelli, prompted him to study, persuaded him to go to Pesaro for an audition. The result was good, but actu-ally young Franco would never attend regular classes in Pesaro Conservatory. For some time he traveled back and forth from Ancona to Pesaro two or three times a week with a small group of friends (among them Scaravelli and Carlo Perucci, another baritone, who would later become the artistic director in Macerata and in the Verona Lyric Opera). Then Corelli con-tinued his studies in a very special way: Scaravelli kept study-ing in Pesaro and, back in Ancona, he "passed" his lessons to his friend.

But even in those early days Corelli studied mostly by him-self: obstinately, tentatively, listening to records of great sing-ers past and present, trying and trying again to find, not the same sound, but the position in which the sound should be uttered; getting angry, despairing; then in the end, conquering a phrase, a note, a nuance—and above all, conquering him-self. This was a method that Corelli would amend and perfect over the years, but never abandon throughout his career.

In 1950 Corelli took part in tests for admission to post-graduate courses in the Florence Teatro Comunale. He was enrolled in a three-month course, but he felt ill at ease and, above all, he was not satisfied with the teaching method.

At that time Maestro Guido Sampaoli, who afterwards

would take a major role in launching Corelli's career, prompted him to compete in the Spoleto "Centro Lirico Sperimentale" contest.

Many people were favorably impressed by the young tenor, but in the end he was not admitted. When the Florence experience was over he went back home to Ancona.

The real, decisive turn in Franco Corelli's career—and in his life as well—would come the following year, again in Spoleto.

In January 1951 he again competed in the "Centro Sperimentale" contest, which was already in its fifth year.

Selections were made in Rome, at the Teatro Argentina. The applicants numbered more than two hundred, and the judges had to be very strict. Maestro Ottavio Ziino—conductor, but also, as he himself put it, "general dogsbody" of the contest—ran into Corelli in Argentina Square, where he was about to step into the theater. Maestro Ziino had already appreciated Corelli's voice the previous year, and obviously he believed the young tenor deserved a little encouragement.

"Corelli," he said, "if you are not admitted this year, I will go away, I will resign!"[1]

However Franco, until the very last moment, was rather keen not to show up at all. He had left Ancona running a temperature, and on his filing card (which is still kept in the contest records, in Spoleto) it is noted that he "retired due to illness." Later the note was erased with a stroke of a pen (at the time, filing cards were not computerized, but still written with pen and ink).

After that Corelli felt obviously better... or else had second thoughts. He went before the judges—they were Maestro Alessandro Bustini, from Santa Cecilia Conservatory, Maestro Giuseppe Bertelli, for Rome Teatro dell'Opera, Mario Rinaldi and Fernando Lunghi, music critics, Maestro Attilio Brasiello, representing the Italian government, which granted its support to the contest, and a sixth member, probably the chairman, whose name I could not find in the documents—and sang *"Celeste Aida."*

Maybe it was Maestro Ziino's encouragement, maybe the judges' kinder mood, or, more likely, a bit of good luck... the fact is that, as Corelli himself remembers, the romanza "came out" with extraordinary ease.

"I had never succeeded in singing the aria like that before," he says. "The B-flat came out so well, I held it for so long, that I was almost ashamed of myself!"

This time—finally—he was admitted with a not sensational but high enough mark (7.75 of 10. Anita Cerquetti, for instance, got an 8), to the "Corso di Avviamento" (preliminary course).

Anyway, the judges' notes are more interesting than the mark itself. They are summarized on his filing card, and I think it right to quote them.

Bustini: *Good voice, how come he did not sing in a theater yet?*
Rinaldi: *He has good material, but not everything is beautiful.*
Bertelli: *Big generous voice, good volume.*
Lunghi: *Good, ringing, loud, sure.*
Brasiello: *Good material, how come he is not in a career yet?*

The most evident feature, in these notes (apart from Maestro Bertelli's favorable opinion, which was especially relevant, because the conductor would be in charge of the young singers' training, with their debut in view) was the question two judges asked themselves: "Why does this applicant not sing in a theater yet?"

It does not seem daring to infer from such comments that the applicant's performance must already have achieved a rather high professional level.

The training course, which took place in Rome as well, was divided into two sections, one concerning vocal aspects, the other acting. From May to August, for four months, every day, the young singers studied and rehearsed.

The Centro Sperimentale management was still rather short of money. "In those first years we even had no housing," Maestro Ziino relates. "Often we rehearsed at my place, or at Professor Picozzi's—he taught the Art of Acting at the Santa Cecilia Conservatory and was the Centro Sperimentale stage director."

What was not missing, however, was enthusiasm on the one hand and professionalism on the other. Young applicants were strictly trained. Those who were deficient in dedication or in actual personal qualities were unrelentingly rejected. Only twenty-eight out of the original two hundred applicants were chosen for the debut... and this was not the final number.[2]

Corelli was scheduled to sing *Aida* opposite Anita Cerquetti. He started studying the Radames role, the first rehearsals were on... and then the troubles began.

At this point we can let Corelli himself speak. During a meeting in his honor in Ancona, on October 25, 1981, many years after, he told about that difficult start of his career.

I was scheduled to sing Aida, *and at first the opera, which had seemed to me so easy, was moving along. Then I realized that the more I studied, the more the opera eluded me... I can't say I could not make it out, but... I was not able to find a way to face it without worrying, to finish it in a good voice. At that point, obviously, the theater management reacted by telling me: "Corelli, if you cannot sing* Aida, *you must give up." But one day a maestro sostituto* [assistant conductor] *of the theater, who was coaching another tenor in* Carmen, *told me, "Corelli, try this aria." I sang the aria so well that the conductor hastily went to the manager and said, "Look, Sampaoli,"—he was the general manager of the Rome Opera, and I owe him a lot in my career—"look, Corelli in* Carmen *is really good."*

With these simple, unassuming words, Corelli summed up, after thirty years—twenty-five of which constituted the most brilliant career—the incidents of his debut.

In the following years a number of legends flourished about this debut (maybe that cannot be helped when a singer becomes a "divo"). That is why I think it all the more right to tell, here, the true and very simple story.

After the decision to include *Carmen* in the schedule, the day of the debut finally arrived. The "historic date" is August 26, 1951, a Sunday.

That *Carmen* opposite Lucia Danieli (whose debut took place the previous year), Ofelia diMarco (Micaela) and Emanuele Spatafora (Escamillo), conducted by Maestro Ottavio Ziino, gained the young singers, and particularly Corelli as Don José, a triumphant welcome from the audience and very good reviews from the press.

We can get an idea of the audience's reaction from the newspaper "L'Unità" (August 28, 1951). The headline is: CARMEN *TRIUMPHS AT THE TEATRO NUOVO, AMONG CHEERS FOR THE FRESHMEN*. And the article proceeds thus:

> *The season of the Spoleto "Teatro Lirico Sperimentale" opened on Sunday evening with Bizet's* Carmen. *The public, which crowded the theater, welcomed the young artists, most of whom were singing for the first time on any stage, with warm applause and several curtain calls. In the role of Don José, Franco Corelli, at his debut, too, was up to expectations. His singing was a magnificent crescendo from the first act duet to the "romanza del fiore" [Flower Song], which he was able to render with the requisite expressiveness, creating a real frenzy among the public, who demanded an encore...*

The encore was not granted, as would be the case countless times in the ensuing twenty-five years.

The critics, too, were unanimous in their positive judgment about the young tenor, and predicted an exciting future for him.

The Rome daily newspaper "Il Messaggero," under the title,

TRIUMPH OF CARMEN *AT SPOLETO "TEATRO SPERIMENTALE,"* called Corelli's Don José "impassioned," and said that he "had proved himself a singer of uncommon vocal gifts." The review ended tersely with: "He is a tenor we will soon hear about."

Some days after, commenting on the second performance, the same newspaper added:

> *About Franco Corelli, we can say again that, if he wants it, he has already opened the doors of the most important theaters for future triumphs.*[3]

Obviously, the farsighted optimism of these judgments was also tempered, now and then, by some negative comment.

For example the critic of the Rome "Il Tempo" wrote:

> *A tenor with exceptional vocal resources, which are still somewhat too physical.*[4]

It comes as no surprise that such a stern critic as Giuseppe Pugliese—who arrived at Spoleto, as he himself wrote many years after,[5] "preceded by the fame of being a merciless fault-finder"—on several later occasions noted marked limitations in the young Corelli's voice, and above all in his technique, even if they were fully understandable in a mostly self-taught singer at his debut.

However, it is rather surprising to read the same critic's immediate, off-the-cuff reaction: proof of a first impression he would later define as absolutely "unforgettable."

On August 28, commenting on the Spoleto season in its entirety, he promised readers another article with reviews of the individual operas, and couldn't help mentioning the name Franco Corelli. A few days later, in the promised article, he traced a singularly accurate profile of the young tenor.

> *Tenor Franco Corelli's Don José in* Carmen *will doubtless remain one of the best successes of the present season. A*

dragoon who is physically fit and athletic, Corelli is also an artist by nature, gifted with an exceptional musical sensitivity. His voice is uncommonly rich—it is beautiful, rangy, strong and intense. His phrasing, the lyric or dramatic accents, are already those of a mature singer. His interpretation proceeded step by step. But no one, till the second act, would have believed this young singer capable of expressing the character's dramatic development as he did in the following two acts with such a sure, native ability, so humanly moved and so moving in his humanity, with the dramatic and psychological insight of a true artist. And a true artist he will be, without doubt, when he learns to control his voice better and mends some faults in his placement, which sometimes jeopardize the emission and the beauty of the sound.[6]

Of course these comments seem obvious, nowadays: it is easy to be wise after the event! But I think it correct to recognize the farsightedness of the critic who made them in the first place.

It is also very interesting to report, besides these first comments, the ones that he made about the same performance nearly forty years later, from threads of memory.

The imposing physical gracefulness of a true 'sportsman' [in English in the original text. Ed.] *came through radiantly in spite of a degree of uneasiness onstage. The difference between the 'video' and the 'audio'—as we would say nowadays—grew in the dull duet with Micaela and even, with important exceptions, in the last part of the opera. From the third act onwards, with an impressive 'crescendo,' the young tenor transformed himself. The more wild the accent became, the more he identified with his character. In the fourth act, in the tragic ups and downs of anger and desperate pleading, the disparity had disappeared and the seen and heard were completely in tune.*[7]

There is yet another, more recent memory, something Giuseppe Pugliese told me in March, 1990, during a fleeting meeting in Venice, when we were thrown together at a crowded buffet after the Maria Callas singing contest. On the spur of the moment I asked him to make a comparison with another singer at his debut: Franco Corelli. And the critic answered with these words, more or less:

> *He was already a great artist, even then. Maybe he never again sang the fourth act of* Carmen *as I saw it there and then, in Spoleto.*

Perhaps this is not entirely true. Perhaps we were still feeling the effect a disappointing evening, when the audience had applauded the judges for having the courage to say that not a single male voice was worth an award. But it does not matter if the memory is not correct, if the Spoleto Don José was not really the best Corelli sang in his career (and probably it wasn't, in fact, since he sang an impressive number of magnificent *Carmen*s). What is important is that, thirty-nine years afterward, a witness—and such an important witness—remembers it that way.

Returning to the moment of Corelli's debut, I cannot help observing that the prospect of a brilliant artistic future and the admission of the young tenor's obvious faults, actually are two sides of the same coin.

On August 26, 1951, Franco Corelli was "potentially" a great tenor. Becoming a great tenor *tout court* would be a tiring and painful enterprise. The natural qualities in evidence at his debut would only make up the basis of protracted, unceasing hard work which would carry him to the absolute pinnacle of achievement for a tenor, higher than any other in his, or our, time.

And I use the word "our" to refer my judgment to the present, to underline and to share the authoritative definition recently uttered once again by Giuseppe Pugliese himself:

A career and a model artist, with whom, as I see it, none of today's singers can possibly be compared.[8]

A River of Voice

AFTER THE HAPPY CONCLUSION of the four performances of *Carmen* the perhaps somewhat glib predictions of the press had quickly come true. The immediate result of this fortunate debut was that the doors of the Teatro dell'Opera di Roma were opened to him.

There is nothing unusual about this because, according to the ideal standards of the founder of the Spoleto Festival, Adriano Belli, and with the approval of the presiding body of the Council of Ministers, there was a special relationship with the Rome Opera in which the festival was a resource of new vocal talent. It was no accident that Guido Sampaoli, artistic director of the Rome Opera, had the same position at the Spoleto Festival.

So it was, then, armed with limited technical baggage, but also bursting with gifts of nature, the young tenor found himself projected—one might as well say, thrown—into the world of the theater.

Perhaps it would be best here, before going ahead with the story of his career, to consider his "gifts" in depth and ascertain the basis, vocal or otherwise, upon which his career was constructed.

Certainly the voice was already there. "A river of voice" as Rodolfo Celletti would say a few years later.[1] Giorgio Gualerzi would call it "a mass of sound like molten rock,"[2] even insisting, on various occasions, that this "magma" was already distinguished by an extraordinary breath control, and that the voice, most voluminous to begin with, was tremendously resonant as it expanded to fill the theater.

Beyond the apt descriptions, there is the reality of a vocal potential that was

besieged by vast limitations in the form of constraints of range, weak phrasing, uncertain cantabile *singing along with a certain shakiness, and finally high notes that were brazened out and not very convincing.*[3]

Such was the calm assessment of Giuseppe Pugliese, invaluable evidence from the day of his Roman debut, with which he will define, in the same context, "the extraordinary evolution of a voice."

This opinion does not seem to contradict what the critic expressed after the *Carmen* at Spoleto: it was one thing to judge a debut artist who had scarcely passed the level of competitive auditions, and quite another to define the limits of an artist already well on the way to a professional career.

Actually, for the most part the rest of the "great" critics discovered Corelli after his launching at La Scala in Spontini's *La vestale*, where he sang with Maria Callas to open the 1954-1955 season.

Sometimes in these first years the critical reactions were so decisively negative that it would probably be better to consider them as references to his debut performance than to those performances between 1954 and 1958, that is, those years between his debut at La Scala and the year which is generally indicated (or more or less explicitly by Rodolfo Celletti) to represent the time his career took off and Corelli had really "learned to sing."

It will be seen by what follows that, like all "historical" dates, chosen to indicate the end of one epoch and the beginning of another—such as the date for the discovery of America—these too are quite arbitrary, and that the takeoff of his career exists only in the minds of those who, not having followed his technical development step by step, suddenly discovered him all at once on some beautiful evening from a box seat at La Scala.

In reality his career didn't "take off" and there were no "historical dates." There was only a constant evolution, linear, pursued with iron will and acute intelligence, which was bound to reach the grand opera stage as a river reaches the ocean, with results which were surprising to those who had not seen or wanted to discern the signs of promise—results which, therefore, could be defined as *sudden inasmuch as they were unforeseeable.*[4]

However it is interesting to relate Celletti's judgment of how good Corelli's voice was—or wasn't—at the time of his debut.

> *Corelli (...) found himself blessed with a huge voice from the time he was born, but not one that is voluptuous, or insinuating, or elegiac, or flexible. It is a voice that is big and he doesn't sing with it so much as declaim. He lacks the first element of singing, which is the fluid movement from one sound to another, spontaneous, even, without rigidity, without strain, without harsh edges. (...) Corelli climbs forcefully into the upper register to produce high notes of ample carrying power, and gives the impression—erroneous—of being somewhat limited in his high register. Besides, he always sings full voice, with harshness and without variation of his inflections, and finally, there are irregular oscillations here and there. The timbre and color depend on the foundation in the middle voice, which results in a sound that is markedly baritonal.*[5]

To some extent it is possible for us to share these observations and criticisms, provided that, once again, we apply them to the initial endowment or "blessing" of the tenor at his debut. They become completely groundless, on the other hand, when we try to cover the years 1951-1957 *en bloc.*

They appear even more groundless in light of existing recordings which, though not numerous, are always illuminating, and permit us to dismiss a large part of those criticisms which, by dint of repetition, have become passively accepted commonplaces.

We will comment on some of these records little by little as we discuss the unfolding of Corelli's career. For now it will suffice to note, as one example, a 1953 *Norma* (I stress *1953*). The *"Meco all'altar di Venere"* has been cut, and the technical quality of the recording is very bad, but you can still hear, especially in the duet with Adalgisa and in the terzetto which closes the first act, a great variety of inflections, mezza voce notes, *smorzature*, even faint traces of agility, still far from being perfect examples, but downright surprising even for those who are not used to respecting fashionable prejudices. And in any case—if I may say so in passing—his voice remains totally beyond the reach of many of today's tenors, not debut artists but "leading tenors"—longtime, journeyman practitioners who are all too present on the stages of our great theaters.

On the other hand we will not hide the limitations (and why should we?) that noboby, starting with Corelli himself, has ever thought of denying. However, it would be very difficult to justify the arc of Corelli's career during the years between 1951 and 1957, marked by so much critical and public acclaim, if we accept as entirely valid the description of his disastrous vocal means and technique as reported above.

Common sense is enough to enable us to realize that public and critics alike must have found *something* in his interpretations above and beyond his undeniable gaps in technique, gaps that he was filling in bit by bit, performance by performance.

In this regard consider the joke of this same Celletti:

The worst was that people applauded him, maybe because he was a handsome boy; I couldn't explain this to myself otherwise.[6]

This cannot be considered anything more than a joke, because if it were taken as an explanation it would be a very poor one.

Perhaps it's best to return yet again to Corelli's own simple words. In the book by the American bass Jerome Hines, where he gathers opinions from his most important colleagues about vocal technique, there is also a very long interview with Franco Corelli in which the tenor remembers problems he faced in the first period of his career.

> *When I sang at the beginning I never thought where to place a note; I opened my mouth and I sang.* And this deficiency of technique at the beginning, he goes on to say, revealed itself also in a certain exaggerated vibrato which was present during his first period: *I am convinced that this* caprino *is caused by breath that has not found its proper point* [of placement]. *I was not using my breath well, it was somewhat dispersed. When the breath was taught to go to the right place, the voice became steady.*[7]

These were defects that would totally disappear during the next phase of his evolution, an evolution that, as Pugliese will point out without fixing any date, was *accomplished entirely within the span of a few years, and then only deepened and consolidated.*[8]

I must stress the fact that here, as elsewhere, I consider Giuseppe Pugliese's testimony particularly precious and trustworthy, not only because of a fundamental affinity with his judgment and respect for his well known competence, but also because, as I have reminded the reader already, he was not only a witness but a participant in the evolution of Corelli's early career.

Many years afterward the critic will still remember *long hours of the night always talking about singing—voice, emission, interpretation, phrasing, repertory.*[9]

And Corelli himself, at the peak of his career, will not have any difficulty in admitting publicly that he benefited from Mr.

Pugliese's advice. Asked in an interview if critical opinion in general was ever of any use to him Corelli would not hestitate to cite Pugliese as one of those who, by "tormenting" him, had contributed to his artistic development.[10]

In any case, no matter how you want to chronicle the evolution, Corelli's voice at the beginning of his career does not let one predict that the young tenor would be destined to excel in the heroic repertory.

Most people would have predicted for him, at best, a limited future as an important exponent of the verismo repertory. As an example it is enough to remember that Angelo Sguerzi went so far as to tar Celletti with the epithet "facile" for legitimizing Corelli's inclusion of *Carmen* in his repertory.[11]

Instead, in less than ten years, Corelli would graduate from *Carmen* to *Poliuto*, refute all the skeptics, and finish by conquering most, if not all, who had been against him when he debuted.

Franco Corelli reopened the cycle of tenors really able to sing, as singing presupposes, first of all, a soft sound, even when you reach the highest levels of dramatization, and it also means to give a continuity and a consistency to vocal speech, passing from one note to the other without breaks or jolts, without tonal inequalities or distortions, without contraction of the throat. To sing means also to look for the expression, not only in the vocal opening, which can be violent and sharp, but also in the modulation of sounds, in the variety of chiaroscuri, in the contraposition of fortissimi and of pianissimi, of bright colors and mezza voce notes, and lastly, especially for a tenor described as of the spinto kind, it also means to climb to the extreme high notes without fatigue. You have to give, oh yes, the impression of being able to grasp these ardent notes with strength and make them fly like bolts of thunder and lightning from one end to the other of a theater or an arena—but also of being able to manage them, being able to value their risks, to hold them tightly within your fist with a glove that appears to be made of steel but in reality is made of velvet. All these things Corelli learned how to do and the result is something to inscribe once and for all in the annals of voice for our age.[12]

These are the words of Rodolfo Celletti, who was a late convert—who "fell on the way to Damascus," as he would say himself during a radio broadcast with the irony which distinguished him.[13] Clearly this is not praise of little value.

Looking the Part

Franco Corelli, who made his 1961 Metropolitan debut in Il trovatore *seems possessed of just about every quality one could wish for the fabled species of the "ideal" Italian tenor. His voice has been compared to Caruso's; his appearance has not been compared to anybody's, and I would guess that competition in this quarter is negligible.*[1]

THIS IS THE BEGINNING of the first article about Corelli which appeared in the American magazine *High Fidelity*, and this is the sentence that perfectly serves to frame my prior description of the bases, "vocal and otherwise," upon which the debuting tenor will later build his career.

In fact a certain nonvocal element has no doubt played a very important role in Corelli's career, even if it has yet to be wholly and precisely defined. Obviously I am referring to his "pleasing physical aspect," as it was called not too many years ago by the host of a television show dedicated to Franco Corelli—with a little smile as he spoke that I might wrongly interpret as embarrassed.[2]

I am not quoting this little episode at random. Actually, from reading the abundant material that has been written on the topic one ends with the impression that Corelli's pleasing physical look has rarely been treated for what it really is: an element of his total personality which should not have become a source either of shameful embarrassment or of heavy irony, as it has all too often.

It is still true that there have been many balanced judgments, and I will quote them, but it is also true that, in the years following Corelli's first appearances onstage, and above all on television, the myth of the beautiful tenor would pass the boundaries of the world of opera to reach a female public which was scarcely expert about opera, but would besiege him before and after every performance. These crowds of "out-of-control girls" (as Pier Maria Paoletti remembers, maybe exaggerating a bit)[3] would demand his presence in the tabloids, and would even push him to appear in a pair of photo-comic books.[4]

Inasmuch as this phenomenon may be unique in operatic history, at least as far as male leads are concerned, it is quite natural to ask to what extent it influenced Corelli's career, especially in the beginning. Without doubt, as Corelli himself will say on different occasions: "A pleasing physical aspect is useful in the theater." But in light of the open sarcasm of certain commentary, even that of some critics, one cannot help but think of preconceptions formed out of envy or hostility.

"Decorative." "The hunk of the opera world" (or even the *"singing hunk"*), or for the more exacting, the *"Marlon Brando of opera stars,"* (or alternatively *"the Gary Cooper," "the Rock Hudson," "the Robert Taylor"* and so on); *"the tenor who has taken dancers, choristers and large sections of his female audience to the brink of a crisis of hysterical love."*

This is a selected list of quotations, but it could be carried on for several pages. In all of them one can feel the author's half-smile, vaguely ironic.[5]

When it isn't verging on the venomous. In the British magazine *Opera* one might read the following in a review:

...If he can substitute complete interest in the part he is por-

traying for his enthusiasm at being a handsome matinee idol, he will undoubtedly attain the top of today's tenor tree.[6]

Or in another issue of the same magazine:

Enghien's Andrea Chénier *was dominated by the dimples, legs and giant tenorial gurgle of Franco Corelli. This glamorous potpourri scored a great success, especially with the ladies. If it's a virile Jayne Mansfield as Chénier you want, Corelli's your man.*[7]

Certainly not all the critics, and not even the greatest part of them, luckily, stooped to such a level, but sometimes even those who were completely serious, and professional in judging an artistic performance, let themselves be a little bit distracted by the aesthetic impact of the tenor. This, it is important to say, was true not only at the start but throughout his career.

Take Giuseppe Pugliese, who remembered Corelli's very first appearance onstage: *a dragoon so tall, beautiful, athletic— I'd never seen anything like it.*[8] Thirty years later, Robert Connolly, the critic for *Opera*, was reviewing a performance in 1981. Corelli had reappeared in the theater after an absence of some years, and the first observation of the critic after seeing him again was: *still handsome.*[9]

Perhaps I insist on the English word specifically because "handsome" is a word that is absolutely not translatable in Italian: it is not "*bello*" (and not even "*aitante*" which is the best Italian approximation) but has more compass, referring to male beauty in its totality. It may be better translated with the words of Rodolfo Celletti, another critic whom I don't suspect of trying to sell newspapers with his writing: *A beautiful face and a statuesque figure.*[10]

Between these two chronological extremes there is an almost endless series of observations of the same kind. Here, too, you may pick at random. After a *Pirata* at La Scala in 1958 Claudio Sartori wrote that he moved about the stage with the perfection of a statue come to life.[11] In 1966, with typical British coldbloodedness, Harold Rosenthal wrote that he was *...blessed with good looks above the average...*[12] *The most handsome Romeo since Jean de Reszke*, commented Harold Schonberg of "The New York Times" after Corelli's debut in this role at the Metropolitan Opera in 1967.[13] *He looks like a tenor should*, stated Joseph Wechsberg, talking about *Don Carlo* in 1970.[14]

It will be seen that we have come a long way from the "matinee idol" both in terms of the names that have been cited and the tone of reviewers' remarks. Still, we don't have to go out on a limb to say that what was commonly defined as stage presence was an important component in Franco Corelli's artistic personality.

It remains to ask ourselves if it is true, as it was believed, and as many still believe, that [between 1951 and 1957] *Corelli gave the impression of owing his fame more to an exceptional physical presence than to outstanding qualities as a singer.*[15]

If we look at the problem closely we cannot but conclude that such a simple explanation really doesn't explain anything.

To begin with we might observe that, all things considered, the importance given to physical appearance is a rather curious phenomenon.

It is undeniable that at the moment of his debut the impact of the young tenor on the public was first of all aesthetic, and to prove this the testimony of Giuseppe Pugliese quoted above is quite sufficient. Even so, one has only to look through the pictures of any musical magazine of the time to realize that there is no shortage whatsoever of beautiful voices and handsome, beautiful men in the opera world, even if not all of them are tenors, and not all of them are *two meters and twenty centimeters tall starting from the soles of their orthopedic shoes up to the waving feathers of their helmets.*[16] The reasons for this "myth" have to be sought elsewhere.

Maybe we could even hint that it was only an advertising trick, only the brilliant thought of a smart press agent. But it is difficult to believe that at the beginning of the fifties times were ripe for such an operation.

The advertising campaigns to which we are accustomed these days that can "make" a singer or "unmake" him, at least to a certain extent, were not in fashion. In addition it's hard to believe either the advertising business or the record industry of those days capable of "hyping" an opera singer, or that they would do something like that for a singer whose future was still so uncertain.

Thanks to some precious and authoritative firsthand information I would rather believe that, although his stage presence was undoubtedly brilliant, there was something more solid and more important to justify Franco Corelli's success: an artistic personality already able to impose itself in its totality.

From this point of view the aesthetic aspect has its own role to play. It acquires a classification all its own and a just importance as part of the total dramatic coherence of the character.

It is with this in mind that I believe we should read the beautiful sentence Celletti wrote regarding the *Ernani* at La Scala:

When he appeared on the stage, robed in the black coat of the outlaw, all of a sudden the fairy-tale atmosphere of the melodrama by Verdi or Meyerbeer seemed to have been evoked, with the romantic myth of the beautiful, mysterious, gloomy man.[17]

This testifies on the spot to the correspondence between the artist and the character he is creating, and we will hear this testimony repeated very often by a variety of authoritative sources.

In this regard I would like to quote two eyewitness reports given in very different times and circumstances, yet expressed in almost the same words:

Corelli would walk onto the stage dressed in black with his turquoise foulard around his neck and he was Dick Johnson, said a great colleague, remembering a *Fanciulla del West* in which she worked with Corelli in Verona.[18]

He is the incarnation of opera—this fantastic-looking fellow who sings like that. From the moment he stepped on the stage, he was the Romantic poet... wrote Rudolf Bing in his memoirs, commenting on Corelli as Werther.[19]

It is the identical use of the verb *to be* that gives us an idea, a precise, unmistakable image—physical, I daresay—of the immediacy of the impression.

There is, obviously, a conclusion which I intend to derive from this lengthy argument, with which I have been trying to get to the bottom of the imaginative but cogent formulation of Celletti, wherein *Franco Corelli found, under the pillow in his cradle...* or if you would prefer a slightly different formulation, found himself from birth, in terms of the career that would later develop, poised for takeoff.

And the conclusion is this: even at his debut and during his very first years of experience in the theater, Corelli was never *only* a handsome man with a voice that poured from him like a river. If there had been nothing but this it wouldn't be difficult to foretell that there would have been no success waiting for him, but rather a sequence of bitter delusions. No, from the first moment he had within him—and there is no way it couldn't have been there, even if only in potential—all the signs of a great artist.

And what supports me in this conviction is the memory that when I asked a very important colleague of his (who, because of the circumstances of his career, found himself working beside Corelli for more than twenty years): from the very first meeting, could he see that Corelli was predestined to enjoy many future triumphs? I wasn't even able to finish my question. And the answer was:

Yes, one could see it. When we had the chance to sing Carmen *in Palermo* [20 February, 1953. Ed.], *it wasn't long before I had the conviction, not the impression, that he was destined to become something big, because in his voice and his personality there were already a great many elements that would guarantee him a great career.*[20]

PART TWO

Day After Day, Night After Night

"In this way, hour after hour, day after day,
night after night, performance after performance, opera
after opera, and lastly,
year after year, helped by an extraordinary spirit of
observation and by a heroic will and capacity to
sacrifice, he succeeded in giving himself
the foundation that would help him develop his voice
in range and breadth, that is, in the
vertical and horizontal dimensions—to develop
the fullness of sound that would make him absolutely
the first among the tenor voices of our age."

GIUSEPPE PUGLIESE

From Carmen to Aida

THE 31ST OF JANUARY, 1952, Franco Corelli debuted at the Rome Opera with three performances of *Giulietta e Romeo* by Riccardo Zandonai.

The passage from Don José to Romeo is perhaps a bit steep, but Maestro Sampaoli and his colleagues believed in the young tenor and the public was disposed to agree with them.

During the discussion of the program for the season, when people started talking about the *Giulietta* of Zandonai, someone objected that the problem of the tenor would arise. *But I said*, remembers Maestro Ziino, *we will never do any better than we are doing right now!*[1]

In the end, artistic management decided to take the risk. According to reliable evidence,[2] it received some criticism on artistic grounds because of the use of a clearly dramatic voice in a role that is considered lyric. Yet the stage presence of the debuting Romeo, of course, more than suited the character, and the rather middle-of-the-road *tessiture* would never cause him the slightest problem. In the audience two exceptional spectators, Giulietta Simionato and Maestro Gianandrea Gavazzeni, saw for the first time on the stage the tenor who, in the following years, they would encounter professionally on many memorable occasions. Both of them were particularly struck by him.[3]

In conclusion, even if it didn't constitute a "historical success" the experiment was received favorably.

Another thing has been noted in the performances at the opera theater, in that management was not ashamed to present fresh, young voices, even in roles that required responsibility. Nobody knew, for example, the tenor Franco Corelli, to whom was confided the part of Romeo in the Giulietta of Zandonai. Well, Mr. Corelli, who happens to have an excellent physique—which doesn't do any harm on the stage—has been much admired. Someone has noticed that it would have been better to give him a part that was easier for him to sing, something like an opera of Verdi or Donizetti. On the other hand we applaud the logic of what was done. Now the young artist will feel himself more sure and confident in other parts where comparisons are easy, having already made contact with a great stage and a demanding audience.

So wrote Mario Rinaldi in the February issue of *La Scala*. As we have seen, Rinaldi was one of the most severe judges at Spoleto.

After a few months more in the "nursery" of the Rome Opera (*We were making 40,000 lire a month and 19,000 lire a performance, when we had a performance*, Corelli will remember many years afterward, with ill-concealed amusement)[4] he finally had what could be called in a very particular sense his "great chance."

At the opera theater *Adriana Lecouvreur* was being mounted with a very prestigious cast, including Maria Caniglia and Tito Gobbi. Artistic management decided to play the young tenor's card once again in the demanding role of Maurice of Saxony.

What was at issue was only one performance, the last, a matinee which took place practically unobserved. Still, and this is the reason I spoke above of a "great chance," it represented a very important moment, maybe even the turning point for Corelli. For the first time he was proving himself in a big opera house in a leading role. To reiterate the oft-quoted words of Mario Rinaldi, *in which the comparisons are easy*. This was to be the moment in which Corelli really started to believe that he had a future in the world of opera.

From that performance on his professional career was on track. If the momentous event could be taken lightly one might say that at that matinee performance Franco decided once and for all that he wanted to be a tenor when he grew up.

That summer as well he made his debut *en plein air* at the Terme di Caracalla, once again with *Carmen*. It's fitting to open a parenthesis here because I believe that only a few if any of the singers of his technical and interpretive ability (very select company in any case) ever transgressed the careful warning of Manuel Garcia *fils* never to sing in the open with the same fearless confidence as Franco Corelli.

Ten seasons in Verona, eight at Caracalla, plus numerous appearances at the most diverse arenas and summer festivals testify, among other things, to vocal steadiness, besides physical steadiness, of the very highest order.

With *Carmen* as the debut opera, his standby, and perhaps of all the most loved, during that summer of 1952 Corelli began to lay the groundwork of his career.

As soon as he finished the performances at the Terme di Caracalla he was in Trieste, at the Castel di San Giusto, where he gave three triumphant performances.

Ten thousand people in rapture, is the way one qualified eyewitness remembers the occasion.[5] Then he was off to do *Carmen* again in San Remo, still in the open. With the same opera he finished out the month of October, in Turin.

The year 1952 ends with a return to the Rome Opera for four performances of *Boris Godunov*. This was an opera which Corelli would never take on again in the course of his career, in spite of the fact that a certain number of critics, even many years afterward, would insist on predicting for him a future as a "centralizing" tenor [that is, a dramatic tenor with baritonal qualities. Ed.], and these critics thought him particularly suited for the role of Grigori.[6]

This was to be a year of consequential choices, and it was a year that ended with a positive balance in the main, both in terms of the success he had achieved, and—perhaps more important—in terms of the experience he had acquired. The young tenor had taken his first decisive steps in the world of theater, and made his first contacts with important personalities, or even mythic personalities: Maria Caniglia, Pia Tassinari, Boris Christoff, Giulietta Simionato, Tito Gobbi... And he was becoming one of them.

In the two following years the Franco Corelli's career took off once and for all toward the most prestigious targets. First among them was his debut at La Scala.

The year 1953 was marked by an event of extraordinary importance: Corelli's debut, alongside Maria Callas, in the role of Pollione in *Norma*. It was a role that Corelli would not interpret very frequently during his career, that he would not love particularly, but in which he was destined to make an amazing, ineradicable mark. The Corelli Pollione was imposing not only for stage presence. This was a proconsul, yes, but without a belly and pink tights. This was a proconsul who also had a warm, dark voice in the middle register, which shone like a blade in the high notes.[7] This was a Pollione who came out of the shadow in which he had been traditionally enclosed by the gigantic figure of Norma, and reached his rightful dimension as a third character who could hold his own with the two priestesses. This was a powerful Pollione, but one who was at the same time particularly rich in nuances; a character that imposed himself, yes, with all the arrogance of the conqueror, but also knew how to find, when the situation required it of him, the delicate accents of Bellinian singing, technically resolved in stunning *mezze voci*.

Revolving around this debut, which we can today define as "historical" without fear of being contradicted, was a series of rather heterogeneous commitments. They began—after the umpteenth *Carmen* in Palermo—with Guerrini's *Enea* at the Rome Opera. This was an absolute novelty which critics did not welcome in the least, and which offered few chances of glory to its singers. However, Corelli found a way to make a good impression in the role of Turno, at least in terms of his stage presence, if it's true that the only really lively moments occur in the last act when the Enea (Boris Christoff) and Turno fight a Hollywood-style duel in order to get Lavinia (Antonietta Stella).[8]

Corelli then went on to take part in the inaugural performance of the season at the Maggio Musicale Fiorentino (for the record, the first of countless season premieres that will take place one after another over the course of Corelli's career, not counting the *Carmen* of Spoleto), with the first performance in Italy of the *Guerra e pace* of Prokofiev (*War and Peace*).

The opera went onstage in the midst of controversies that were more political than musical in origin, so that many critics have felt that the intrinsic merits of the score were given short shrift. The work is essentially—or wants to be—a choral opera which, for obvious reasons, can deal with only a few episodes of the monumental text of Tolstoy. The cast, although prestigious because it included some of the most illustrious names of the day, required an impressive number of solo singers—more than thirty—and obviously didn't give any one singer the chance to stand out.

Guerra e pace, though, has its own particular place in the history of Franco Corelli's career, because as far as I can tell from my research it represents the first extant recording of his voice.

At this point a curious fact is worth mentioning. The troublesome, and so far sterile, search for previous recordings has quite frankly led to a little falsehood—or perhaps to a mere mistake caused by an excess of enthusiasm. In fact, a little slip of paper which was enclosed with the record of a selection of *Carmen*, dated December 19, 1952, states that the record is the very first recording of Corelli's voice, which would be close to the truth if it weren't for the fact that the *Carmen* in question turns out to have been performed at the Teatro San Carlo of Naples exactly a year afterwards, December 19, 1953.

That being the case we need to go back and give precedence to the *Guerra e pace* at the Maggio Musicale Fiorentino as the first historically verified recording of a voice that was destined to require an important allotment of space on collector's shelves.

It is already a noteworthy voice—and indeed it was noticed in spite of the not terribly demanding tessitura and Prokofiev's rather plain, declamatory style.

An excellent Piero Besukov for his vocal impact, impetuosity and stamina in an inaccessible role was the brief but clear comment about the live record of the first performance.[9]

A small curiosity: in this historical first recording Corelli's role starts with a line that is not sung but acted—in fact, a "*Cosa accadde?*" that was neither natural nor placed, and it truly sounds as if it has been a little weakened by emotion. But then, as he will countless times in the future, the tenor becomes more sure of himself and makes a success of the performance by the end.

Anyhow, for anyone who would truly like to "go back to the beginning," the above-mentioned *Carmen* at Naples will probably give us the most precise idea of what Corelli must have been like at his debut.

About the "river of voice" we have little doubt, and even less of the passionate vehemence of Don José. For the rest it is obvious that the young tenor still has a lot to learn and even more to refine. But it is also obvious that he has a voice, as well as a personality and disposition able to transport his audience to heights of enthusiasm.

In the meantime, still in 1953, he made his debut in *Pagliacci*, another opera that Corelli would not sing frequently in his career.

Perhaps now is the time to point out that in spite of all those critics who would have liked to see his interpretations restricted to the verismo repertoire, it is a repertoire that Corelli—whether as a matter of choice, taste or disposition I can only guess—would sing on relatively few occasions. (*Chénier*, of course, was the most notable exception.) It doesn't seem unjustified to think that his innate musicality, his love for the beautiful melodic phrase, as well as the development of his vocalism toward a more demanding range, naturally led him to prefer the great pages of Verdi and Puccini.

With *Pagliacci* he came back to Spoleto to great acclaim in the summer of 1953. In the meantime the *Carmen*s multiplied and the *Norma*s started to appear more and more frequently. It was with *Norma* that he would open the season of the Teatro Verdi of Trieste, again with Maria Callas.

The year 1954 repeated and broadened the program of the previous year. Besides the already consolidated *Carmen* and *Norma* Corelli went from Allegra's *Romulus*, received with disapproval by critics, who spared only the singers,[10] to his first television experience with *Pagliacci*. (One wonders why such an opera was offered to him when it was the only one where, without a shadow of a doubt, he lacked the *physique du rôle*.)

But we also find, mysteriously, *Ifigenia in Aulide*, about which little can be said, since the recording is missing. In the spring he returned to the Maggio Musicale Fiorentino with an excellent *Agnese di Hohenstaufen*. In the summer he made his debut in *Tosca*. Finally in an almost incredible act of courage he gave four performances of *Don Carlo* at Rome.

With his voice in mind it is difficult to imagine how he did the *Don Carlo* of 1954, especially because it is an opera that Corelli will sing again quite differently as a mature artist only several years later.

On the other hand there are ample grounds to state that he was not received with disapproval by the critics, even by the critics who were hardest to please. For instance, we can read in *Opera*:

> *Franco Corelli lent his remarkable good looks, beefy vocal talent and ingenuous gestures to the tenor role.*[11]

On the whole, anyhow, it is undeniable that a simple reading of the chronology of those years produces a rather confused impression, an image of an artist who has not yet found his way, his style, in a word, his repertory.

Let it be said straight off that this repertory will continue to be anomalous in the years to follow, if in a very different way and because of definite choices. I refer to the way it ranges into fields traditionally considered incompatible, from Bizet to Bellini, from Mascagni to Donizetti, from Verdi to Puccini.

Without doubting the complexity, let's even say the completeness of this repertoire, it is possible from a certain moment to frame (and critics, of course, have not failed to do so) some points of reference which are very precise. Two threads at least are well-determined, two paths that, perhaps uniquely in his generation, as Giuseppe Pugliese observed,[12] Franco Corelli will continue throughout his career to pursue at the same time: the path of the heroic tenor and of the dramatic tenor.

To these two routes, which have been officially recognized, one must add a third which has been very neglected and underestimated, at least by Italian critics and public, though it is not for this reason one bit less important. Rather, precisely because it has been thus ignored it should receive particular attention as we read along: the raids, which are not even that rare, into the lyric repertoire, the trend that will start with *Tosca*, include *Bohème* and culminate in *Werther*.

"From a certain moment," I said. It is not difficult to establish precisely what moment, isolating it from the *Aida* debut. It will be necessary only to quote the judgment of Rodolfo Celletti, widely shared and also supported by the declarations of Corelli himself.[13]

After having mentioned that Caruso used *Aida*, at the beginning of his career, *as a passport to familiarize himself with the higher ranges of the romantic melodrama* Celletti goes on to say that, for Corelli, Radames was very likely *the first step of the progression that was destined to reach* Poliuto *and* The Huguenots.[14]

But before this debut, which will mark one of the key points in his career, Corelli faced another very important appointment: the first of six season-opening performances at La Scala. The 7th of December in 1954 La Scala opened sumptuously with an unusual opera, *La vestale* by Gaspare Spontini, with Maria Callas in the leading role and direction by Luchino Visconti.

Of the many malicious and irresponsible rumors that make the rounds of world opera theater, which I mention only because I must, some have hinted that the occasion demanded a tenor who looked good onstage and was unencumbered by great popularity, so that Franco Corelli appeared to have been custom-made for the part of Licinio.

Corelli himself will confess much later that he didn't really know to whom he owed the debut—to Maria Callas, a colleague to whom he was always linked by great esteem and gratitude, or to Visconti, or to Maestro Votto.[15]

I don't think I'm totally wrong to guess that all three of them of had some sort of influence, but that the deciding element was purely technical. If in fact Corelli did look custom-made for the part of Licinio, the inverse was also true. The role could have been written for him, at least during the phase of his career when his voice seemed to be bringing the age of "baritonal tenors" back to life.

When he debuted in *Vestale*, Corelli had already enjoyed success that year at the Maggio Musicale Fiorentino in another opera by Spontini, the *Agnese di Hohenstaufen*, giving the character of the young Enrico *noteworthy importance* with *beautiful declamation and expressive singing*.[16]

In its vocal aspect the role of Licinio is probably less rewarding for the tenor than that of Henry of Brunswick. Here also the range is tightly central, but the acting parts and the declaimed parts definitely prevail over the singing part. Except for the duets Licinio sings only a few lines, in fact, and he doesn't have available even one true aria in which his voice could expand and soar through the house with even, melodious phrases.

However, in spite of the objective difficulties of this role—and in spite of the emotion of his debut—Corelli still succeeded in giving his best and gained much warm applause for a *beautiful, warm and powerful voice, together with an athletic look, and intelligent acting.*[17]

Even such an attentive and severe critic as Eugenio Gara could not but note the debut artist's qualities:

> *We have heard a tenor who is new at La Scala, the young Franco Corelli, who if I am not mistaken very much looks like he wants to stay there for a long time. Corelli has all the right cards, the right numbers, that is, a warm, full and rich voice, and what is more important, the intimate conviction of what he is doing, the sure relationship between sound, gesture and word. Besides he is a beautiful, tall and athletic-looking fellow, and he holds the stage with true audacity, which is to say, not the stock tenor sort. People liked him right away.*[18]

Permit me the observation that even if it weren't true that an artist who wasn't encumbered by a big reputation was what people had been looking for to partner La Callas, it was at least true in the same way that the debuting tenor didn't let himself get carried away in reverential timidities. He sang a beautiful duet with Maria Callas in the second act, admirably holding his own, and concluded the opera with a flash of lightning on a high B-flat that stood out above the whole chorus and orchestra, and—philologists please forgive me—largely compensated for the score, which was limited to some rare A-naturals.

Perhaps already by the 7th of December in 1954 it is reasonable to suspect that the "baritonal tenor" phase really represents a period of orientation toward higher targets, higher even on the staff.

A month after the repeat performances of *Vestale*, on the 26th of January, 1955, we find another important debut in a totally different repertoire: *La fanciulla del West*, which marks at the same time Corelli's debut at the Teatro la Fenice of Venice. It was another happy event, according to Giuseppe Pugliese, even if it was tempered, as always, by correct and specific criticisms.

In the part of Johnson, Corelli has reconfirmed his extraordinary musical qualities, his fine appearance on the stage and his confidence. His magnificent phrasing and singing is all very accurate, succeeding in wringing a maximum of passion from the role. His voice is rich and wide, but not yet rigorously placed, which causes it to be uneven at times, but the sensitivity of the singer and the actor ends up imposing itself, as we have realized last night in the confident and intense interpretation of Johnson.[19]

In April of the same year another important but completely different sort of event took place: Corelli's first appearance on a "foreign" stage—a *Carmen* in Lisbon. And his international career had a totally positive beginning to judge from the comments of the local press:

This tenor, Franco Corelli, has the wherewithal to become famous very quickly.[20] *He is certainly one of the best Don Josés who has ever been on the stage of the São Carlos...*[21]

The review of the show also notes the applause he received and his repeated curtain calls at the end of the opera.

In July there was another important and eagerly awaited debut: at the Verona Arena with a triumphant *Carmen* which was received by critics with an unconditional approval that was no longer news, and by the audience with a most sensational acclamation,[22] so sensational that Corelli's Don José would compete at the last minute with Mario Del Monaco's Otello for the Arena Prize, begun by the Verona newspaper and based on audience opinion as expressed on a form distributed at each performance.

Then in August came the debut that was most hoped for

and most dreaded: *Aida*.

A small curiosity: this Arena performance constituted his offical debut, but in reality it had been preceded by another chance *Aida* two years before in Ravenna, improvised to save a situation that had become disastrous thanks to the last-minute unavailability of a tenor.

Corelli, in between performances of *Carmen*, had volunteered to cover the role of Radames, and was thus obliged, among other things, to sing for three consecutive nights.

A magazine published years afterward, and obviously aimed at naive female fans, gave currency to the legend that Corelli sang *Aida* on that occasion without knowing anything but the famous aria and the ending.[23] However, even if it is self-evident that a tenor cannot sing *Aida* without knowing it (he might get as far as *Macbeth*, staying silent in all the concertanti), it is obvious that this is not a debut that can be considered important even if we are left with unsatisfied curiosity as to how the emergency *Aida* sounded.

Anyhow, if the critical tribunal will accept indirect evidence, we can at least produce the testimony of one of the performers. Quite a negative testimony, at that, for the artist in question has no particular memory of the episode. From this we have deduced two things: Corelli's first performance in *Aida* did at least pass by without any damaging incident. Perhaps nothing he did led to enthusiasm, but neither did it lead to disapproval.[24]

Unfortunately, no recording exists so far as I know, and therefore to judge the event we must rely entirely on the critics of the time. The critics were in disagreement, as very often happens in that fraternity, although in a largely positive context. Two samples:

Franco Corelli's performance in the role of Radames was eagerly awaited, given the success he has enjoyed in Carmen. *Expectations were not disappointed at all, because from the character of Bizet to that of Verdi nothing has been lost in Corelli's beautiful singing. He has found the élan required by the part in the passionate emphasis he gives to the phrase and the fine emission of the high notes, and in the dramatic electricity, right up to the attenuation of the heartfelt "addio" in the last scene.*[25]

Corelli's range goes, therefore, from Bellini (Norma), to Bizet (Carmen) to Verdi (Aida). We have admired him in the first two, but in the last he didn't quite hit the mark. The important thing was that he tried. His preparation both from the vocal and the dramatic standpoint was still incomplete. Corelli's beautiful voice still needs to adapt completely to the range of Verdi. It is sure that he is on the right path.[26]

Corelli took on *Aida* again that same year, in Messina and in Catania, then the sudden indisposition of Mario Del Monaco resulted in his being urgently called to the Teatro San Carlo in Naples to substitute for him as Radames in the season premiere.

Finally we find ourselves in the ideal situation, at least from the point of view of the unlucky ones who were not there: we have available both some critical responses and a recording, and this allows us to judge the validity of the criticism, or at least to know what we are talking about if we share these opinions or reject them.

Excluding (by reason of their method) the more conventional and generic reviews, we believe it is fair to direct attention to two critics who were particularly qualified: the criticism of Cynthia Jolly for *Opera*, and that of Giuseppe Pugliese for the "Gazzettino" of Venice.

Franco Corelli is physically ideal for the part of Radames; and once he recovered from nervousness, which made "Celeste Aida" a tepid and disappointing affair, he went ahead with big bold notes that made the rafters ring, wrote Jolly.[27]

Franco Corelli's Radames was winning right from the start

thanks to the suitability of his imposing figure. He triumphs
almost always in the musical part, because of the intense,
intelligent beauty of his singing, and his sculpted phrasing.
His force and strength is becoming more and more reliable.
At last, with Corelli, we have a fourth act sung mezza voce,
wrote Pugliese in his review.[28]

Besides the identical remarks about his "aesthetic impact"
(which should be appended to our previous discussion of this
aspect), it is interesting to note how the reviewers refer to two
completely different parts of the opera. On the one hand we
have the "*Celeste Aida*," which in general and I think unfortunately gets the most attention. On the other hand we have the
last act, which is often rather neglected by critics. From listening to the recording I personally believe that there is a reasonable basis for both commentaries. The "*Celeste Aida*," perhaps
because of the emotion, as assumed by Jolly, perhaps because
of his as yet incomplete artistic maturity, is really rather disappointing. This, though, doesn't take away from the fact that
the remainder of the opera confirms the judgment of Pugliese,
and doubly confirms his reference to the fourth act.

The beautiful mezza voce with which Corelli sings the long,
repetitive, obsessive measures of the "*fatal pietra*" compen-
sates for any small uncertainty previously and will be succeeded
in the following years by performances that become more and
more smooth, more and more heartfelt. We can say the same
thing about the three B-flats in the finale which Corelli will
later deliver in an extraordinary way, and which provoked no
critical comment (limited to considering the smorzatura of the
same note that closes "*Celeste Aida*") However, already on
this first recording, these notes constitute a precise preview of
the technical perfection and emotive grandeur which he will
attain in the future.

In conclusion I can't help but record here, because it has
stayed in my heart and in my ear, the beautiful ending of an
Aida sung at the Metropolitan almost twenty years afterwards,
in 1973. Then the three B-flats had such a smoothness, and I

would say, if it didn't seem to me a little bit like an insult to the hard work of the interpreter, such an ease, that without the score in front of our eyes it would be difficult to believe that the *"raggio dell'eterno dì"* and the sky that opens up (*"si schiude"*) had climbed so high on the staff.

In the meantime, as I have indicated, the summer of 1954 saw another very important debut—in *Tosca*. And in 1955 we are lucky to have very early evidence of Corelli's interpretation of Cavaradossi, a part that he would sing with greater frequency as his career unfolded—gradually, naturally, giving him an ever greater vocal and psychological importance, as he did with all his other characters. The *Tosca* in question was recorded for television and broadcast in the autumn of that year.

No doubt the Cavaradossi we have here still has quite a way to go to reach the richness and nuance he will eventually acquire. Still, there are already moments of great lyricism and intensity, especially in the third act. Moreover, he now displays on the whole a noteworthy self-confidence on stage. There's nothing routine about a Cavaradossi who comes swinging down the scaffolding instead of walking down the stairs.

After the great, demanding debuts from 1953 to 1955, the two following years almost resemble a pause for concentration before the great leap of 1958, which, as we will see, will be a key year in Franco Corelli's career.

It is necessary to state clearly here that when I speak of a pause I do not mean to imply that there is a slowdown in his activity. On the contrary, these were some of the most intense years of his career in terms of the number and frequency of his commitments. At the same time, however, these were years of study and solidification, perhaps even of more hard work and sacrifice than ever before.

It is to these years and to those immediately following that Rodolfo Celletti refers when he states that *Franco Corelli accomplished a feat that usually only succeeds one time in a hundred, to learn how to sing while carrying on his career.*[29] And we can add, not only did he carry on with his career, but in one year, 1957, sang more than seventy performances. If we take away a month of well-deserved vacation, this amounts to an average of one performance every four to five days, without counting his travel for several commitments abroad, from Vienna to Lisbon to Bilbao to Enghien-les-Bains and to London.

And we mustn't forget to add to the account of those years a rather intense discographic activity, with the recording of many 45s, as well as his first complete opera (in 1956).

There was also in the same year (1956) his first (though according to many, it would certainly not be the last) experience with film: *Tosca*, in which Corelli's Cavaradossi is the only character who provides both voice and dramatic aspect.

I will here note in passing that during Corelli's whole career his participation in movies and musicals will be announced all the time, among them, supposedly, even a western with Giuliano Gemma! However, for one reason or another, none will ever come off. Only many years afterwards will *Andrea Chénier* be filmed, and even though it was a low-budget operation, it remains one of the very rare filmed documentations of his art. And there is also, in the same year, a *Carmen* for TV, which is now impossible to find, just as it is impossible to forget, especially for those like myself who did not have the good fortune to see others in the theater.

It cannot come as a surprise that within the framework of so much activity in those years we will see the debut of only two new operas: *Fedora* at La Scala in 1956, once again beside Maria Callas, and a *Chénier* at the San Carlo of Naples in March of 1957.

Giordano's two major operas will occupy very different places in Corelli's career. Unluckily, his Loris was not passed to future generations via recordings, but was received with favor, or better, with enthusiasm by his public, besides being appreciated by colleagues,[30] and above all by the maestro of that production.

Maestro Gavazzeni still remembers the Corelli-Callas duet as the grandest of any interpretation of *Fedora* he ever conducted—or attended as a spectator—both from a dramatic and a vocal standpoint. He says that *the duet of the second act was a piece of theater such as we will never again hear in that opera.*[31]

The opera perplexed the critics, maybe in part because, as the maestro remembers, *we were already living in times that disapproved of the so-called verismo, or at least the establishment critics did.*

Many judged Callas to be unfit for the vocal demands of *Fedora,* and Corelli to be insufficiently refined vocally and stylistically to be suitable for the role.

This was Eugenio Gara's opinion. Yet he was very positive about Corelli's performance:

On the whole the tenor Corelli has come through a difficult trial very well. His sincere outburst at the finale gives us the measure of a nature which is rich in promise. The critic remains convinced, as far as Corelli's voice is concerned, that it was *so warm, so resonant, that the management of the theater should see if they could not exploit it better in the heroic manner, maybe in the Wagner repertoire.*[32]

Anyway, as for a certain incompatibility between the Corelli voice and Loris, Maestro Gavazzeni decisively refutes its existence, even today. He remembers that

Corelli sang a beautiful "Amor ti vieta," then he performed the great narrative of the second act with great dramatic flair and extraordinary pathos.[33]

In any case it is our misfortune that Corelli would sing the part of Loris on only one other occasion in his career—at Oviedo in 1957.

Andrea Chénier, on the other hand, would become a glory of his repertoire, and would also be considered, almost unanimously, one of the more congenial roles for his voice and for his personality, even if sometimes it would create curious contradictions in his critics, who would define him from time to time, and without doubt according to personal taste, as too refined, too delicate, too loud.

The Chénier was extremely goodlooking and was led to dominate also by his wide-ranging and hugely powerful voice, the more delicate points in the vocal line. Compared to that of Del Monaco, Corelli's Chénier is without doubt more refined vocally—more sung, I would say, and less declaimed—but the accent is not as vibrant, nor is the timbre as warm, and then, in the phrasing, as in the dramatic comportment of the character, there is more the allure of the composed romantic hero than of the dynamic of a main character in a musical drama of the "young school." [34]

The tenor Franco Corelli, of course, steals the show, a singer that generally doesn't get my favor, as he is often led to the easy sob, to notes that aren't purely sung but taken from underneath and caressed. The phrasing is a little bit cold. But the Andrea Chénier *doesn't require good taste or finesse, it requires voice, and there's no doubt that Corelli has it.* [35]

I prefer to leave to the reader, and even more to those who would listen to extant recordings, any possible comment on the two sample criticisms I have quoted, which irresistibly bring to mind an ironic consideration of Rodolfo Celletti: to quote different opinions will *allow readers to have malicious and amusing thoughts on the fate of critics—namely, that they will rarely agree among themselves.* [36]

But I cannot help remembering, to illustrate my judgment, a short sentence of Pietro Caputo on the Chénier of Lauri-Volpi. *With Lauri-Volpi Chénier was once again the noble artist, the inspired poet, far away from any veristic temptation.* [37]

The above is, I believe, the best key to understanding Corelli's Chénier, which was no doubt inspired more by the age in which the poet lived than that in which the score was written. Chénier is a poet, an aristocrat, and a man of the eighteenth century. There is no "young school" that can transform him into poor Turiddu.

Anyhow, setting aside the two above-mentioned debuts, the most important characteristic of the years 1956 and 1957 is that they mark the launching of Corelli's international career.

After the first short visits to Lisbon, with the 1955 *Carmen* already mentioned and the revival of Zandonai's *Giulietta e Romeo* at his Roman debut, 1957 saw a grand European "tour"; again he visited Lisbon with *Chénier* and a *Simon Boccanegra* that would remain the only one in his career, and a surprising *Khovanshchina*; then came an *Aida* in Vienna and a *Norma* at Enghien.

Right after that was the London debut—together with his old friend and colleague from days in Florence, Gian Giacomo Guelfi—in an excellent *Tosca*.

Listening to the recordings gives us a precise idea of the reaction of his London audience, which, though very composed at the beginning, finally explodes after *"E lucevan le stelle"* into an ovation in which all the vaunted British self-control is shattered. In passing, that recording is, so far as I know, the first which documents the extremely delicate spinning out (*filatura*) of the "veli," destined to be after that, for years, the culminating point of a performance of the romanza which for intensity of emotion and beauty of phrasing I will say without hesitation could serve as a manual on the singer's art.

The debut was favorably judged also by British critics, who in general would never be very sympathetic to Corelli, and from whom would come the strongest attacks of his career, as we will have a chance to observe on other occasions. Here we will limit ourselves to noting the words of Rodolfo Celletti describing *the typical British intolerance for voices that are big and ringing,*[38] and those of the American critic Conrad Osborne who, speaking ironically of this tenacious British hostility toward Corelli, explained it by the fact that home-grown

British tenors all sound as if they are suffering from "advanced cases of pharyngitis."[39]

Joking aside, I believe it is basically a matter of taste, or if you like, of culture.

In general, the English critics loathe any manifestation of Mediterranean emotion, even on the stage, and in this regard it is rather logical to understand how a singer with a strongly dramatic nature can be defined as excessive, and in this particular case, as vulgar. It is not by chance that a similar hostility greeted the great singing actress Magda Olivero.

The period of vocal and technical evolution in Franco Corelli's career that I've singled out as including the passage from *Carmen* to *Aida*, followed by two years of intense activity, closed with a list of commitments which we can by this time define as routine: *Carmen, Tosca, La fanciulla del West, Andrea Chénier.*

But the years of intense study and passionate work to build his own technique, and learn how to dominate and bend to his will the extraordinary power of his voice, would bear fruit in the months that followed in the form of some of the most splendid debuts of his career, and—we can say it calmly today—some of the most exciting moments of opera in the last fifty years.

From the Pirate to the Huguenots

T HE YEAR 1958—a very important year in Corelli's career, as I have already indicated, for the many demanding debuts which were all important in different ways, but equally important—opened with an event destined to be described in all the chronicles of those days, and not for artistic or musical reasons: the opening of the season at the Teatro dell'Opera of Rome with *Norma*, once again beside Maria Callas.

The episode is too well-known for me to talk about it extensively: In front of an audience (or at least a part of the audience, as very often happens) that was hostile and determined to oppose her, Callas sang the first scene of the first act, and after the pause for the scene change refused to continue the performance, claiming she was indisposed. Since the theater had not provided an understudy for the role the performance had to be suspended even though the President of the Italian Republic, Giovanni Gronchi, was present in the theater.

The wrangling afterward was fierce and long. Corelli, naturally, was not involved except in a marginal way. True, there were suggestions that Callas's indisposition was at least aggravated because of the applause received by her colleague, stronger and more general than what she was accorded. There were also those who wanted to see the origin of Callas's "forfeit" in Pollione's power of voice, which could have covered hers.

This last hypothesis, which is still rather widespread these days, is objectively a mere fantasy for those who have a passing acquaintance with the opera. Still, I found in my hands a clipping from a newspaper of the time (dated January 2nd) from which the headline is missing, and fortunately for the author his byline also. Here we can literally read:

But when the tenor started the first notes, the worst took place. He had taken a C from the chest too vigorously, nearly drowning out the voice of the diva.

This was a matter of great importance, without doubt. The only problem was that the unfortunate commentator didn't seem to have noticed that when the performance was interrupted Norma and Pollione had not yet even sung one note together. What's more, they had not even met on the stage. Therefore the defection of La Callas could have been, if anything, a precaution, but in no case could it be considered an act of revenge.

Still, the existence of stories of rivalry between the two artists, or better, of Callas's hostility toward Corelli, are a reality. Seen from our time, all the "I heard"s and "I was told"s have not the slightest basis in fact, but they are still so widespread as to be included in Callas's biography.[1]

For example you can still nowadays meet someone who will insist on the fact that Corelli left La Scala because of such hostility. A simple checking of the dates will prove that Maria Callas stopped singing in the great Milanese theater much before he did, that is, except for the parenthesis of the *Poliuto* (1960), after the 1958 *Il pirata*.

The certain fact is that after the Rome episode Corelli and Callas sang together on several occasions. They starred together in the *Pirata* mentioned above only a few months after the mess in Rome, and the 1960 *Poliuto* brought them together on the Scala stage less than two years afterward.

Later, in 1964, the very same Callas was asking to have Corelli beside her for her Paris *Norma*. True, this time friction wasn't lacking. Reports had it that Corelli protested first of all because his name appeared in smaller letters than Callas's. What's more, for the first two performances their respective supporters would get very close to fistfights in the stalls and outside the theater.

But it is also true that we don't have any information about personal struggles between the two artists. On the contrary, after a certain number of calls on the evening of the first performance, Corelli disappeared behind the curtain and let his partner receive the applause alone. Three evenings afterwards, when the souls of their most violent partisans had calmed somewhat, the second performance would be, to say the least, a triumph (with fifteen curtain calls, if we can believe the newspapers). The following year Corelli and Callas came back to sing together for the last time at the Metropolitan in a handsome performance of *Tosca*.

Regarding these controversies it is perhaps time to say once and for all that, especially in the theater, hostility and rivalry are not at all synonymous.

Rivalry is a normal and physiological situation and doesn't imply at all, or necessarily imply, a tension in the personal relationship. In Corelli's career one of the clearest examples of rivalry (further on I will have the chance to produce several episodes) was the eternal battle of the high Cs with Birgit Nilsson, a battle that would also have its very hot moments, but would never prevent the two artists from having, up till now, a perfectly friendly relationship.

Anyhow, after the disaster of the evening of the 2nd of January, performances of the 1958 *Norma* went on in a regular way with a luxurious leading lady, Anita Cerquetti.

Right after this another event took place that was reported more for its gossip value than any musical reason—incidentally, both quite different—which fed the legend of a litigious, arrogant Corelli.

During the rehearsals of *Don Carlo* there developed between Corelli and Boris Christoff, who was playing Philip II, a controversy that degenerated, literally, into a duel, given that the two participants put their hands on their swords. Actually, to be specific, at the moment of the argument they already had swords in their hands because they were following their stage directions.

To put the events together is practically impossible, besides being useless. Each one of those present, not to mention the protagonists, has his own version of the episode. It is legitimate to suspect that at the time each version was influenced by the position the interested party wished to take or not to take in the quarrel, and now, after so many years, by a desire not to dig up bones of contention which would appear trifling or senseless by the light of day.

What we can say about the episode with some proximity to the truth is that in the confrontation with the king in defense of the Flemish deputies, Don Carlo moved a little too much downstage—upstaged King Philip, that is. But if this "too much" refers to the taste of Boris Christoff (as certain colleagues believed who found themselves in identical situations with him, though perhaps not as... bloodthirsty), or to the stage directions, remains to be established.

The fact is that the basso reproached the tenor, and the tenor had no intention of letting himself be reproached. A few curses passed between them and at some point there was even some swordplay. Christoff left the stage and Maestro Gabriele Santini terminated the rehearsal. Word of the doings then reached the newspapers.

There would be, thanks to the energies of the theater management, a public reconciliation, but Christoff still refused to sing and was replaced by Mario Petri.

These are the facts as much as it is possible to reconstruct them, but I think it important to stress something that in general the press has been inclined to overlook. Wide latitudes are usually given to the controversy, and nobody worries too much about following each development to its conclusion. The audience, the great public, might even have supposed that from that day on the two artists would never speak to each other.

However, the reality is quite different. The fight took place around the middle of January, and on the 15th of February the two were already singing together in Naples in *La forza del destino*, which marked, among other things, Corelli's debut in the role of Don Alvaro. I don't know, honestly, how friendly the meeting might have been, but it was certainly worthy of the professionalism of both singers.

So, early in a 1958 which was marked, as we have seen, by controversies, the first of that year's four debuts took place: as Don Alvaro in *La forza del destino* with Renata Tebaldi, with whom he had had his first professional meeting only a few days before, again in Naples, in *Tosca*.

One of the great Verdi characters, Don Alvaro was also one of those which Corelli would have in his repertoire for the length of his career without singing it very frequently. Preceding him as an example of this sort of role was Radames, which had an important number of performances in 1953 and 1973, and Don Carlo, which Corelli would interpret quite rarely over a period of eighteen years, 1954 to 1972.

Don Alvaro is widely recognized as one of the characters that was fully realized by Corelli.

I don't believe there is much to add to what Rodolfo Celletti wrote about the aria *"Oh, tu che in seno agli angeli"* several years after Corelli's debut acknowledging him as a great Verdi tenor.

In the case of Don Alvaro, the tessitura is often abnormal, now unbalanced toward the low notes, now stretched to make the tenor phrase on the high G and F, which forces the performer to take precautions of all kinds. Corelli, according to phonographic testimony of great value,* reaches in the recitative and the aria a variety of colors and inflections that are really rare. The first part of the recitative is placed

---

*Note that it can only be either the 45 RPM Cetra or the selections from the opera recorded together with Gian Giacomo Guelfi. These recordings are from 1956—that is they precede Corelli's supposed launching with *Pirata* by a couple of years. Thus it seems that Rodolfo Celletti is testifying against himself that Corelli was able to do something good, or a lot that was good, even before 1958.

intimisticamente *with a broad use of mezze voci, and just for this reason the phrase* "i miei parenti sognaro un trono" *sounds powerful and lacerating. The real aria is rich with superb vertical impulses, with this particularity, however: that not only are the B-flats of* "chiedo anelando ahi misero" *or of* "Leonora mia pietà" *thrown out with extraordinary force, but the entire phrase is started upwards as a bronze block of sounds.*[2]

The live recording of the performance of the debut, which is luckily still in existence, offers us much more of the aria of the third act. Sadly, according to the usual proceedings in Italy at that time, the second of the three duets with the baritone has been suppressed, but the two remaining are enough to confirm, even from that first performance, that Franco Corelli is a great Don Alvaro.

Certainly the character will become more and more refined vocally in the course of the years, and for instance, the two risky *smorzature* of the A-natural in the phrase "*vi stringo al cor mio*" require authentic bravery that is not yet present at the moment of the debut. Still, the pathos, the richness of the variety of colors and inflections his voice offers us in that recording, supported and reinforced magnificently with extraordinary velvet and exquisite nobility of accent of the authentic Verdi baritone, Ettore Bastianini, is already a singing lesson. A lesson too were the incisiveness of the recitatives and the effectiveness of certain phrases. Take for example the "*Signor di Calatrava!*" in the end of the first act, to which Verdi appends a pause which can become impressive, but only if the tenor is able to convey enough vehemence and noble authority with his voice to cow everyone present into a moment's silence.

The duet of the last act is also unforgettable for the dramatic interior conflict of Alvaro which is rendered with huge vocal richness and emotional effectiveness right up to the lacerating final resolution of "*Ah, segnasti la tua sorte!*" At that point the listener really *feels* that the character is being dragged to a tragic conclusion by his fate, by the "forza del destino."

The next step in Corelli's career came only two months afterward. *Il pirata* of Bellini is the fruit of an evolution that is already obvious, even if the role of Gualtiero presents an additional difficulty in the form of a very high tessitura. Of course Bellini had scored it for a *tenore contraltino*—and falsetto—such as Rubini.

Sadly only traces of that historic interpretation are left in the memories of the few who had the luck to hear it in the theater. The recording of Corelli's *Pirata*, as well as the *Traviata* with Magda Olivero, has become an Arabian phoenix for collectors. Sometimes someone will say there is one, but where it is nobody knows. Probably we have to accept the sad reality that it is impossible to find.

Anyhow, according to existing evidence, Corelli winningly confronted the difficulties of the Bellinian range in the same way that he triumphed at La Scala four years afterward as Raoul de Nangis, a part written for the falsetto singer, Nourrit.

Rodolfo Celletti commented as follows:

When, in 1958, I listened to Corelli in The Pirate, *the ease and the enormous power of the high notes stupefied me. Not only were these striking notes, but they would give a specific sense to the expression "a voice that fills up a theater," an expression that isn't applicable ninety-nine times out of a hundred. The Corelli who was confidently sustaining a range like Gualtiero's, and was delivering blazing high notes as well, frankly made me very enthusiastic. I would have been less struck with the extreme high notes if they had represented his only target and his only conquest. However, there were perceptible emissions here and there in mezza-voce and note filate. Sometimes his accomplishments didn't quite measure up to his intention, showing a certain lack of refinement, but it appeared clear that these attempts were not undertaken as sporadic, adventurous whims, but were part of a method.[3]*

I hope that I have made it clear by now that in 1958 Corelli's *filature* and *mezze voci* no longer represent "adventurous whims." If this doubt has truly been laid to rest, a largely positive judgment of Corelli's Gualtiero will emerge from these lines.

This judgment, nevertheless, is not shared unanimously, at least insofar as it concerns the correspondence between Corelli's vocal and interpretative strengths to those of the ideal Bellinian tenor.

Though he praises his performance for other aspects, the judgment of Eugenio Gara goes in this direction: *Corelli is most certainly not an authentic Bellinian tenor but he has a very beautiful voice, warm and thrilling, and noteworthy dramatic accentuation;*[4] while Massimo Mila expressed more or less the same thing as follows: *The pirate was Franco Corelli, a tenor with beautiful natural gifts who sings this repertoire of the 19th Century with an attitude which is little too robust and athletic;*[5] while Eugenio Montale judged him as *not angelic enough.*[6]

This criticism appears curious to me. How can we associate the adjective "angelico" with a character who enters the scene singing "*Nel* furor *delle tempeste, nelle* stragi *del pirata...*"; who, in what follows finds himself on the point of slaughtering an innocent child for the sole reason that he is the living evidence of a loved one's betrayal, and who, before his tragic surrender to his enemies to be beheaded, takes satisfaction in killing his rival in a duel.

Of course I realize that the judgment depends largely on the point of view the observer assigns himself. Without doubt in wanting to define the character as "angelic" Montale is thinking of the florid writing of his music, rich in vocal ornaments. Up to what point of perfection Corelli was able to execute the florid passages I cannot determine exactly, but surely he was able to make them very even for the most part, according to a practice which was widely observed in those years.

But if we take into consideration the aspect that we can

define as "theatrical," and opera is theater, inevitably we will attribute less importance to writing that—and let's not forget it—runs from one side to the taste of the times, but on the other is adapting itself to the characteristics of the singer who was called to create the role—which is also characteristic of the period.

From the point of the personality of the character I believe I can say that the Gualtiero, tormented and ferocious, passionate and bloody, the outlaw without love and without country, symbolically wrapped in his black coat, is an authentic proto-Romantic figure, perhaps the first representative of that Romantic myth of the beautiful, gloomy man that, as we have seen, Celletti saw embodied in Corelli's Ernani.

In this regard we must not forget that in 1827, the year of the first performance of *Il pirata*, Romanticism in literature was in full bloom. Victor Hugo's *Hernani*, for example, was published in 1830, and was therefore only three years younger than Gualtiero.

Placing the character in this historic perspective it becomes easier for someone who has never listened to him to imagine the *Pirata* as it was performed on the stage of La Scala in that spring of 1958.

And it is even easier to regret not being there.

Before trying himself in *Il pirata* Corelli had debuted in what would be for eighteen years one of the basic roles of his repertoire: the Unknown Prince in the *Turandot* of Puccini.

It was a rather low-key performance, a classic "provincial debut" with two performances in Pisa that didn't cause any outcry from the critics.

Corelli's Calaf would explode later that same year at the arena of Verona, and it would be a revelation.

With the prince of Puccini Franco Corelli has added another character to the gallery of his best interpretations. Gradually perfecting his vocal instrument so that he has conquered one by one the difficult notes in the upper reaches

*of his voice, he was able to offer the character of Calaf a
magnificent interpretation that he will be able, certainly, to
deepen further, making it one of his most important cre-
ations. The ever-increasing beauty of his phrasing, that romantic melancholy that is in the color of his voice, the severe
expressive composure, the upward impetus in his singing
allowed him to give excellent projection to a part that is
vocally beautiful but very ungrateful, very difficult, and to a
character who is not at all consistent,* wrote Giuseppe
Pugliese right after Corelli's debut in the Arena.[7]

As on other occasions, in this review, written while Corelli's
voice was still ringing in his ears, the Venetian critic is acutely
prescient. Corelli's Calaf—and here we have to say that the
judgment is almost unanimous—was bound to grow, become
refined and deepen until it was comparable to the Calaf of his
greatest predecessors, and until these days it has remained unsurpassed.

Un Calaf regale (a regal Calaf) is what Giuseppe Pugliese
will call him a number of years later, looking back over his
entire development. Of course it is difficult to refer to a model
because he received and synthesized in himself the characteristics of many great singers:

*Of course, Lauri-Volpi, the greatest, the legendary Calaf of
history; then, perhaps Del Monaco for the breadth of his
bronze phrasing. But this is still not enough. We will need
to remember, at least for the softness of certain sounds, and
some surprising* filature, *Fleta.*

But the reference to models is not enough either, because
we need to add:

*...the measure of the unique style and exceptional stature of
the interpreter. The more intense, vibrant, but severe and
noble expressivity, the perfect sharp diction and phrasing
that cannot fail in the very musical "Chopin-like" internal*

relationships, while the unlimited width of the fiati allows him a rhythmic consistency to which we owe, most of all, the impression of sumptuous beauty.

Finally, Franco Corelli's Calaf, Pugliese goes on to say, summing up and synthesizing his own remarks, was *vocally heroic, finely chiseled and extraordinarily virile.*[8]

It seems to me that these adjectives more accurately define the character of the singing if I compare them to the also very effective words—*impressive* and *titanic*—of Rodolfo Celletti[9] which, even if they reflect almost visually the huge power of the voice, do not highlight the nobility of the phrasing and the richness of the nuances.

The last debut of that very intense year is probably the most to be feared: *Il trovatore.*

Feared, perhaps, not so much for the intrinsic difficulties of the score, which are of some importance even so, but mainly because *Il trovatore* is an opera that the public judges from the *"pira,"* judging the *"pira"* in turn from one note. It is feared, therefore, with good reason by an artist who will state on various occasions that the tenor is more vulnerable than other singers because

he has those two or three famous notes at the top of the staff, and everything depends on them, or almost everything, in his relationship with the audience.[10]

Without a doubt it would be a beautiful experience and very clarifying to listen to the recording of that debut which took place in Bologna at the 1958-59 season premiere. Unfortunately, insofar as I could verify it, not only are there no recordings available, but the first bootleg tape is of a *Trovatore* interpreted at the Teatro Regio di Parma on the first of January 1961—which is to say, two years afterwards.

Though it seems paradoxical, since *Trovatore* is the opera, even today, most people typically think of as *his* ("The last great Manrico," declared Giorgio Gualerzi in a recent radio broadcast),[11] there are no phonograph records to document that triumphant debut (or many other performances that will take place in those years) and we must trust newspaper reports. Inevitably, from the mass of reviews (and opinions) it becomes hard to know what to believe, and even harder to give shape to a precise and personal idea.

There is no reason, though, to doubt the reliability of testimony about the debut in Bologna from an authoritative magazine.[12]

To begin an opera season is always a noteworthy commitment for any opera management. To begin it with Verdi's Trovatore *is a serious venture these days. If you then put in the middle of it a tenor, even a famous one, who is trying his wings for the first time in the title role, this is a risky business.*

(...) As fortune helps the bold, the experiment went very well as far as the first performance is concerned, where the tenor Franco Corelli, who has never sung this opera before, achieved a complete and well-deserved success.

[We need to add that Corelli, because of laryngitis, didn't sing the other two performances, nor was he able to sing *La fanciulla del West*, which was scheduled to have been performed right after. Ed.]

We have to agree that management has been fortunate in the choice of its cast. The main character, Franco Corelli, is one of the few living tenors who can make the opera a real success with his intelligence and also with the power of his expressive accents, with good looks and also with noteworthy stamina. His performance in the first act was brilliant, starting with the dangerous song from the coulisses, *and in the second it was a performance typical of someone who is wisely placing himself in a defensive posture, fully aware of what awaits him in the third. Here, in the famous "Di quella*

pira..." *his victory was complete and his success was transformed into enthusiasm, even excessive enthusiasm for a
theater which has always had a tradition of measured, reserved responses.*

Here we might deduce, reading between the lines, that he
brought down the house that night at the Comunale di Bologna.

The audience demanded and obtained an encore of the
"pira"—and how much that encore cost the main character,
without any doubt already troubled by the idea of singing it
once, may be very difficult for an outsider to imagine.

The commentator continues, judging as praiseworthy the
transposition of the aria a half-tone down. *(Anyhow, he adds,
given the raising of the diapason that has taken place, and
considering the constant tendency of orchestras to grow larger,
today's B is probably already higher than the C of Verdi's time.)*
He deprecated, however, ending on the tonic instead of the
dominant, or in lay terms he disparaged the famous and highly
anticipated high C (or, in the lowering of the aria a half-tone,
B-natural) of the *"Allarmi,"* which had been consecrated by
so much tradition, in favor of what was written in the score as
a mere G.

It was a rather curious observation for that time. The res-
toration was tried, as everybody knows, only more recently,
and was received with little enthusiasm. But it was surprising
to hear it demanded of a tenor, especially in 1958, right on the
day in which he was making his debut in the role of Manrico.
More than a philological operation it would be an attempted
suicide, at least in a professional sense.

There was only time enough to recover from his laryngitis,
or from the stress of the debut, or from both, before another
important moment came for Corelli, even though it was no-
where near as traumatic: another season-opening performance,
this time at the Teatro San Carlo in Naples with a beautiful
Chénier next to the passionate Madeleine of Antonietta Stella
and the suffering, extremely noble Gérard of Ettore Bastianini.

In December we find Corelli in Milan, where he was to sing at La Scala in a role that was very unusual for him: the part of Illo in the *Eracle* of Händel.

But, in the meantime, his fourth television commitment was waiting for him after *Pagliacci, Tosca* and *Carmen*: the recording of *Turandot*. And, unexpectedly for him, waiting also was an unforeseen debut, as close as anything one could imagine to a high-wire stunt without a net.

That year La Scala was opening its season with *Turandot*, and the protagonists were Giuseppe Di Stefano and the person who is considered as one of the greatest-ever interpreters of Puccini's princess, Birgit Nilsson, the greatest Wagner soprano of her time, the voice of "Swedish iron," at once blazing and overpowering.

At the repeat performance of the 17th of December a sudden forfeit of Di Stefano threw the theater into a crisis. Maestro Votto, who knew Corelli very well, and had believed in him from the time of his *Vestale*, had a solution ready. He called the tenor at the last minute and asked him to save the day—or evening.

Corelli abandoned the *Turandot* he was taping for television and ran to the theater. Arriving on time, at the raising of the curtain, he was onstage to sing what was the first of countless *Turandot*s next to (or perhaps it would be more correct to say "against") Birgit Nilsson.

There had been no time for introductions. The two artists met for the first time on the stage.

Surely it was traumatic for him to be facing such a *monstre sacré*. For La Nilsson, who did not know him and had hardly heard about him, it was a surprise—a happy surprise, she says today, remembering that fortunate meeting of long ago.[13] For both of them it was the beginning of an artistic partnership based on emulation, which led to clashes sometimes, as we will see, but it was also characterized by great esteem and reciprocal respect both on a professional and a personal level. This partnership would make of them, for longer than ten years, the signature Calaf-Turandot, a pairing which has been unsurpassed since.

After that unforgettable night Corelli regularly sang the four performances of *Eracle*.

The cast was very prestigious: Elisabeth Schwarzkopf, Fedora Barbieri, Ettore Bastianini, and Jerome Hines, who was making his La Scala debut in the title role.

It was precisely the presence of the American bass which created a funny little story which Hines remembers in a nice way in his book,[14] a typical example of those small stage rivalries which seem to be very serious at the time, especially to the people involved, but make everybody laugh soon after.

Corelli, whose stature varied according to the shoes he was wearing, a little bit above or below one meter, ninety centimeters, had become used to always being the tallest performer on the stage. The discovery that the Eracle was five centimeters taller started a mini-war of the heels between the two artists. Mrs. Hines, Lucia, secretly informed that Corelli had ordered supplementary heels for his boots, did the same for those of her husband. So, Hines remembers:

> At *the first costume rehearsal Franco stalked onstage a towering six foot seven, and found me waiting for him at six foot ten. He never quite got over it: years later, when we sang together at the Met, he always greeted me with, "No high heels, okay?" (Niente tacchi alti!)*

Many years afterward Corelli, too, would remember the episode. During the night in his honor which was organized in Ancona in 1981, showing the public a slide of that performance, the commentator observed in a joking matter, "Look, Franco is the shortest." And Corelli was quick to reply with the fine sense of humor that some people would deny him: "Yeah, and I was standing on tiptoes."

All kidding aside we must remember that the opera was a noteworthy success shared by all the characters, even though someone observed that Corelli didn't seem too much at ease in the Händel repertoire.

It was not, of course, an opera which was congenial to his nature. "I prefer melodrama," he would say that evening in Ancona, being subtly ironic about himself, but it would be wrong to underestimate the importance of these raids on the eighteenth-century repertoire. We can remember the *Giulio Cesare* of a few years before, and also the *Ifigenia* of Gluck in the beginning of his career when he was developing his voice.

He could succeed in this repertory also, because he wasn't doing things haphazardly, he was studying, states a great colleague who shared the Händel experience with him.[15]

This observation points up a key element in Franco Corelli's career. From here I don't believe it is going too far to state that the study of these operas contributed in no small way to refinements in technique which led to dominion over his vocal instrument. The result spoke for itself in the interpretation of *his* repertoire, which took him far away from every temptation of verismo, or at least of that decadent form of verismo which had come to mean an interpretive procedure that favored declamation over singing, theatricality over technique.

The year 1959 opened with an unforgettable performance of *Turandot* at the Teatro Regio of Parma. A few days afterwards it was repeated at the Teatro Massimo of Palermo. Right afterward, still in Palermo, there was an enthusiastic *Carmen* with the very young Mirella Freni in the part of Micaela. Then in February, at La Scala, there was a very important commitment which extended the great Verdi debuts of the previous year: *Ernani*. Many years afterwards Corelli would confess that he hadn't found the character particularly interesting from a vocal standpoint,[16] and had been forced to "move it along" with a certain number of *puntature* or interpolated high notes (much appreciated by the audience, and at that time not so reviled by the critics as they are in ours, the age of "philology").

Again because the recording can't be found it is impossible

for those who were not present in the theater to know something about the first *Ernani* which struck Rodolfo Celletti so favorably that he was moved to mention it in his profile of Corelli written for the Critical Biographical Dictionary, *Le Grandi Voci*. And to mention him not only for the impression he gave upon entering the stage, which we have already mentioned, but because

...vocally, Corelli displayed an amplitude and vigor of phrase that was very impressive. At the same time he shrewdly lightened his emission in the middle register and was able, therefore, to direct the flow of voice toward soft and modulated sounds as well as toward the upper register, where the notes were very secure, firm and full.

Celletti would later complain that Corelli's interpretation had only *grazed* the character—*even though he gave him great importance.* In fact Corelli would interpret Ernani in less than half a dozen productions, three of which were given at the Metropolitan with great success and one at Verona in one of his last appearances in the Arena.

Leaving aside this meaningful debut, however, I insist that 1959 is not the year of *Ernani*, or even the year of *Turandot* (which Corelli will sing on various occasions besides the two I have mentioned): it is the year of *Trovatore*.

After his debut in Bologna, Corelli's Manrico became much requested. In the first months of the year he took it from Lisbon to Genoa and in May he took it to La Scala. In the summer he would debut in front of the crowd of the Verona Arena, and then at the Terme of Caracalla. To mention the reviews would only be a long repetition of praise, interrupted here and there by some more or less marked dissent.

So it is that Giuseppe Pugliese could comment on the *Trovatore* at the Arena as follows:

...his vocal power continues to progress, the sculpted highlights of his phrasing, the pure Verdian spirit of his style,

*allowed him to beautifully graduate the realization of the
character with studied shrewdness, with beautiful musicality, with generous élan...*[17]

Yet we will also meet with opinions which were diametri-
cally opposed, though they were much less widely held:

*The beautiful qualities of his voice are known, the shimmer-
ing cover of the notes, the flashing of his squilli. From these
givens to also state that Corelli is a Verdi singer is a big leap.
Giving impetus to his voice and guessing right with some
accents isn't the same thing as phrasing, which is an ability
he has yet to develop, or good diction, which he has yet to
acquire completely, or precision, which isn't always depend-
able.*[18]

It was the same phenomenon in Genoa, where the *Trovatore*
had been staged a few months before. There was a chorus of
approval:

*Finally a real tenor! He has combined real power with thrust,
a variety of nuances with élan, the effectiveness of gesture
and portamento to the beautifully well-suited vocal gifts.
This was a beautiful formulation, a strong and careful interpretation (...) An admirable character for vocal power and
incision...*[19]

But there was also a critic who, years afterward, would
write[20]—and I stress the fact that all these critics are talking
about the same performance—that he had such a negative impression of the recitative that preceded the "*Ah si, ben mio,*"
that he had to leave the theater on the spot. (With how much
professional seriousness, I will let the reader be the judge.)

Here I don't believe that we need to comment further, except perhaps to note the age-old mystery of divergences among
critics who are too often more influenced by personal taste

than technical considerations.

It would not be useless to remember that such a great man of the theater as Rudolf Bing intended when he left the Metropolitan, and maybe not entirely as a joke, to force critics to obtain a license that would guarantee their professional seriousness.

"Anyone," he would say, "without knowledge or experience can set himself up as a critic of opera, with the freedom to say and print the most ridiculous things."[21]

After the undertakings in the big summer arenas there was a *Tosca* in Livorno that autumn with Renata Tebaldi. Then, still with La Tebaldi, Corelli's "official" debut as Maurice of Saxony was scheduled, to follow the actual debut in 1952 at the Rome Opera which had remained virtually unknown.

Adriana Lecouvreur would be the season opener for the Teatro San Carlo, and would represent his second consecutive season premiere at the Neapolitan theater.

On the 26th of November, at the general rehearsal, it appeared that everything was for the best, but the next day sudden laryngitis forced Tebaldi to cancel. The theater was forced to place an urgent call to Magda Olivero, who had just recovered, among other things, from a surgery that could hardly be called minor.

Without even a semblance of rehearsal, naturally, the opera was broadcast direct on television—though only from the second act on, sadly—and was a great success on the stage, notwithstanding the forced absence of a singer very much loved by the Neapolitan audience.

Fortified by a very steady professionalism, Maurizio and Adriana (flanked by the gravely sympathetic Michonnet of Bastianini and by the excellent Princess Bouillon of Simionato)[22] quickly found themselves and hit their stride. The leading lady of that evening's performance can't remember a single moment of difficulty or embarrassment, not even in the realm of stage business,[23] and the public decreed the performance an authentic triumph.

Even the judgment of the press was extremely favorable.

Franco Corelli, wrote Alfredo Parente in "Il Mattino," *returned to the stage of the San Carlo yesterday with increased breadth of sound and more beautiful vocal resources than ever, with generous volume and breath, without betraying the least effort, and lastly performed with intelligence and dignity as a singer and actor that is rare in his voice category. He has awakened real admiration in us—better, enthusiasm.*

Curiously, the only mishap took place in a moment shared by Maurizio and the Princess Bouillon.

The Princess looks suspiciously at the little bouquet of violets that the lover carries—or should carry—in his buttonhole and reproaches him for being late, perhaps because of a "perfumed commitment." He takes—or was supposed to take—the little bouquet of violets and give it to her, bending down. Unluckily when Maurizio put his hand to his buttonhole there were no violets. There was, understandably, a moment of panic. Giulietta Simionato saw the tenor go white under his makeup. Then, once again, professionalism took over. Maurizio mimed the gesture of giving her the violets and probably the audience didn't even note their absence.[24]

Around the end of 1959 or the beginning of 1960 Corelli had two engagements to sing *Andrea Chénier*, first in Bologna and afterward at La Scala.

It's worth the trouble to report an episode that passionate opera fans remember as a classic example of things that could only take place in the good old days. An indisposition forced Corelli to miss the premiere in January. But Mario Del Monaco volunteered to take his place. Still today the Milanese public sighs with nostalgia regretting the rich days in which there were great tenors that not only took turns singing various operas, but were even ready to substitute for each other.

In February Corelli was in the newspapers again for one of those episodes of "intemperance" which the press never fails to blow out of proportion.

This time, though, we have to admit that the tenor had made a big mistake. During a *Trovatore* in Naples, a spectator from a box loudly expressed his admiration for Fedora Barbieri, the Azucena. When the artists took their curtain calls at the end of the second act he insisted, it seems, that Barbieri should take a solo bow.

There is always tension during a performance, but this was one drop too much. The tenor was jolted into action, and without thinking twice about it he hurried along the aisles of the San Carlo with his coattails flying and with choristers and theater personnel in pursuit. He got into the box by putting his shoulder against it and confronted the incautious spectator sword in hand... Or at least this is the way the scene has been described many times, even if the sword is probably nothing but a note of color which has been added to the picture after the fact.

Then the manager of the theater arrived to quiet everyone down, and the incident was concluded in a peaceful way. A half an hour afterwards the production was able to resume.

The way the story goes, Corelli and the hapless spectator became friends afterward, though there remained for a certain time a degree of tension among the two singers. At the end even this episode became one more in the vast number of episodes under the heading "things that happen in the theater." Some years afterwards, telling of the incident in an interview, Corelli remembered most of all the comical side of it: the chorus, wigs flying in the wind, hunting the tenor along the aisles of the San Carlo.[25]

After this adventurous episode Corelli was hailed for his *Chénier* at Genoa with Gigliola Frazzoni, who had already been his partner a number of times in the opera, even in some performances at La Scala.

In March, then, he went back to the Milanese theater for *Turandot*, once again with Birgit Nilsson.

After the unscheduled debut a little more than a year before, this time it was Corelli, from the beginning, who was the main character. He was, according to the opinion of a critic who had judged him in the past, and sometimes quite severely

> *...an ideal Calaf... he has completely overcome the uncertainties of past years: his singing has grown more secure and the patina of his voice more gleaming. He is now an artist in a true state of grace.*[26]

Corelli's Calaf achieved other successes that year. First of all at the Fenice of Venice, and then on a particular occasion in Monte Carlo.

This time there was no question of a "great theater," whose productions were epochal, and the calm spectators were not easily moved to enthusiasm, but that afternoon unusual things took place.

> *The audience at Monte Carlo is not predominantly young and needs a certain amount of rousing; Corelli had them in a frenzy. After "Nessun dorma" the performance was quite literally held up. In vain Ping, Pang and Pong capered and Corelli shook his head and spread his hands despairingly. "Nessun dorma" had to be repeated.*[27]

In the summer the usual engagements were waiting for Corelli in Verona and at the Terme di Caracalla, preceded, in July, by some performances of *Tosca* in Enghien.

In Verona he was engaged for *Pagliacci* and *Fanciulla del West*. Indisposed, he had to cancel the first of the two operas. At the time there was concern that even the *Fanciulla* was in danger. Instead the opera went onstage without incident, and with an exceptional cast: Franco Corelli, Magda Olivero, and Gian Giacomo Guelfi. The result was an unforgettable success for all three main characters.

Fans, critics and colleagues were almost unanimous in recognizing that the character of Dick Johnson was exceptionally well-suited to Corelli in all its aspects. Declared Giuseppe Pugliese:

*We agree: in this musical-western things are made easier for
him in a very peculiar way from the so-called "physique du
rôle." I don't think anybody will remember a Johnson who
was more convincingly real except perhaps at the movies.*[28]

And his Minnies, as for that matter, his Toscas, and later
on his Juliets, found it very easy to get inside their characters,
making us believe they were really in love with him when he
went onstage asking boldly, "*Chi c'é per farmi i ricci?*"

But Corelli's Johnson is much more than a figure like John
Wayne and some beautiful "curls" (ricci). *Passionate and bitter, determined and brash he was a Dick of first order,* wrote
Carlo Bologna. *His aria of the third act one might define as
classic,* wrote Libera Danielis in *Opera.* And Eugenio Gara
defined him as *a Johnson who was admirable for his voice, for
his expressive accents and for his dramatic portrayal.*[29]

The trio Olivero-Corelli-Guelfi got together again a few
days afterwards at the Terme di Caracalla for *Tosca.* It is to be
much regretted that we have no recording to allow us to listen
to the Magda Olivero of those years portray Tosca alongside a
Cavaradossi who, writes Pietro Caputo, expressing an opinion that finds me in full agreement, *looked to be the best on
the contemporary scene.*[30]

Two more successful performances of *Fanciulla del West*
took place at Caracalla, then a couple of *Turandot*s in the fall.
Lastly the moment came for one of most important and meaningful commitments in Franco Corelli's career: *Poliuto.*

On the 7th of December he was called on to open the Scala
season for the second time and this would be the first of five
consecutive openings between 1960 and 1964, an absolute
record.

Once again there was an unusual opera on the program,
and once again the leading lady was Maria Callas, who, with
Paolina, was making what would be her last debut in a new
character.

Yet there was a substantial difference: at the time of *Vestale,* only six years ago, Corelli was engaged for his characteristic of "central tenor." The part of Poliuto, on the other hand, had a huge range and required a voice with marked extension as well as noteworthy facility in the high register. No further comment is needed: this was the measure of the transformation which Corelli had undergone in those six years to achieve his own sound and his own style.

Poliuto was an opera that, at the time (and, in passing, even in our time, in spite of some far from beautiful attempts) hasn't been performed for lack of a tenor able to sustain such a difficult role—a role that was one of Tamagno's warhorses and a great success for Lauri-Volpi. These are obviously mythic figures, and it's doubtful we'll see their like again. Even so Corelli came through gloriously and stood up to comparison with these immortals, *demonstrating, once again,* as Giuseppe Pugliese would have it

> *...how much progress can be accomplished with study and with a good school. How much maturity of style, of emission, of song, one can achieve by continuously perfecting one's art.* The critic goes on to say: *As regards the tessitura, the singing of* Poliuto *has been able to offer an excellent example of the typical 19th century style, with the chiseled beauty of the phrases, and also, and above all, for the intense, very musical expression typical of Donizetti. A strong character has been able to emerge complete.*[31]

His victorious scaling of the peaks of his range to master Donizetti's music closed the year 1960. But something had also taken place in 1960 that passed by the great audiences unobserved: Franco Corelli had taken a stand which would determine the rest of his career, and to a large extent his life, though very likely he himself could not foretell it.

Since March of 1960 the always very well-informed English magazine *Opera* announced that Corelli *had been engaged by the Metropolitan for the 1960-61 season.*

This was a difficult decision, postponed for a long time,

but in the end practically obligatory: inevitably, the itinerary of a great singer will reach that prestigious American theater, or run the risk of a great lacuna, and probably also "a measure of rest" in his or her international career.

Corelli faced the move to America without overwhelming enthusiasm—on the contrary, with a certain fear, because he confesses that he was afraid of the long plane trip. A new audience was waiting for him, curious to meet him and also difficult to conquer, as well as a way of living and working that was totally foreign to him, and an unknown language as well... Altogether enough to disturb the sleep of an artist even less emotional than he was.

Before his departure there was still the chance for a last dive into the warmth of a public embrace in one of his most beloved theaters: the first and third of January, 1961, Corelli was in Parma for two performances of *Trovatore*. To face the Parma audience in one of the most popular operas in the Verdi repertoire was no small matter; once again it was a winning undertaking.

Here too it would just be repetitious to quote the comments of the press, but one, though not a true review, is particularly meaningful.

The show was recorded by RAI, Italian state television, though today the recording is mysteriously impossible to find. When it was broadcast a few months later, on the first of May to be exact, Teodoro Celli told his audience that they were about to see the best Manrico it would be possible to find today, but gave them one warning:

> *Don't listen to him only in the "pira" in which he is an exceptional performer of the powerful high C; listen to him in the parts of immense nostalgia and tenderness in which you will be able to appreciate the art with which he is able to impart pathos to his voice without sacrificing virility.*[32]

This is an opinion which we can compare to another—the basic reaction of Gianandrea Gavazzeni, who would conduct

Corelli in the *Trovatore* at La Scala the following year:

I have heard the Trovatore *done by other great tenors, and in general I don't like to make comparisons; his was different for the sense of despair that he was able to give to Manrico; it was a Manrico who knew he was doomed to lose all his causes. Right from the beginning with his off-stage part, "Deserto sulla terra," he was a loser. He was unforgettable afterwards in the last scene, "Ha quell'infame l'amor venduto." There Corelli was truly able to find an accent of despair that has remained in my ear until today.*[33]

Again with *Trovatore* Corelli finally debuted at the Metropolitan on the 27th of January, 1961, on the occasion of the celebrations of the 60th anniversary of the death of Giuseppe Verdi. This was a debut whose result was not, in some aspects, one hundred percent satisfactory. Some of the critics put forward some reservations, even severe ones, but the very authoritative Harold Schonberg of "The New York Times" expressed a rather balanced judgment, though it was perhaps a bit cautious.

As for Mr. Corelli, in one respect he goes against the law of nature that decrees all tenors must be short. The Metropolitan includes, among his statistics, the fact that he is six feet two inches tall, and he weighs 180 pounds. He tops off this physical appearance with a handsome head—something of a cross between John Barrymore and Errol Flynn. Can he sing, too? Well, it is a large-sized voice, but not an especially suave instrument, and it tends to be produced explosively. It has something of an exciting animal drive about it, and when Mr. Corelli lets loose, he can dominate the ensemble. The nature of his upper register remains to be determined. He did take the D-flat in the Second Act [Note: probably it is the First Act, finale. Ed.], *but the ending of "Di quella pira" was transposed down, and he was unable to take the climactic note in one breath*[?]. *As a musician and an actor he did everything competently without ever being particularly imaginative about it. There is something about his work, however, that greatly excited the audience, pro and con. (...) The guess here is that Mr. Corelli could develop into an exceptional tenor, but his art does need some refining and polishing.*[34]

On top of everything, Corelli's debut at the Met took place at the same time as Leontyne Price's, an event very important for Americans because this was the first black singer to interpret the role of a soprano lead in America's most prestigious theater, and therefore the debut of the Italian became of secondary importance.

To compensate for this, as we have seen, the audience was immediately conquered, and although the review of the British critic Robert Sabin was a long pan (for example: *I am told that he is largely self-taught and I can only say that he should seek out a better teacher*), even he was forced to admit that *any tenor who knows how to provoke such ovations in a theater must certainly have something.*[35]

At the second performance, in spite of weather that covered New York with snow, the theater was very crowded.

During the performance a little accident took place. Behind the scenes Corelli stumbled and badly fell, ending up with a twisted or sprained ankle. The break between the first and second acts became longer and longer, and when the performance began again the Manrico was literally limping. By the second act he was returning from a battle in a very real sense.

Not all bad things do us harm, however. The event landed Corelli on the front page of "The New York Times," as the tenor himself would say, using his sense of humor during a long interview that took place a few days afterward and was published in March in *Opera News*, the magazine of the Metropolitan Opera Guild, the very night before the much awaited *Turandot*.

Puccini's opera had not been performed at the Metropolitan for almost forty years and its return was an exceptional event, prepared with a huge display of financial resources. As for the personnel taking part, the very best cast that could be found on the international scene was sought, and management went to the point of begging the aged Leopold Stokowski to lend his name to the production (who, in passing, would impose tempi on the performance that were exasperatingly slow). The part of Liù was taken by Anna Moffo and the Turandot could not be anybody but Birgit Nilsson.

The audience was literally assaulting the ticket counters, and this opera was a true triumph. With an Unknown Prince who was so sumptuous from both a musical and theatrical standpoint, Corelli had definitely begun his conquest of America.

And it began also in a material sense, because after his debut at the Metropolitan in *Don Carlo* he left for his first tour with *Turandot*.

As it did every spring the Metropolitan took all its productions to a series of American municipal theaters in an atmosphere which was suggestive of P. T. Barnum's "greatest show on earth." After necessary adjustments in proportion, it *was* truly a kind of circus that moved around with all its sets, costumes, orchestra members, choristers, and naturally, its soloists.

Turandot first landed in Philadelphia, the city which hurried to get its shows only a few days after their first performance in New York. Afterward it traveled to Cleveland, Atlanta, Chicago, Minneapolis, Detroit.

An incident during this tour became famous, and was later the basis of an anecdote illustrating the concealed rivalry among opera stars. The anecdote appeared in the memoirs of Rudolf Bing, and had different versions, very often incomplete.

I am here submitting a version that I hope will be definitive, because I am combining the versions of each of the two main characters.

First it must be made clear that the episode in question does not revolve around the high C of the riddle scene, as commonly believed, where the two characters sing in unison ("*Gli enigmi sono tre...*"), although this is famous by itself. Rather it refers to the finale of the second act, the moment in which the tenor sings the phrase "*No, no, principessa altera! Ti voglio ardente d'amor!*"

One night, in what has been called the "war of the high Cs," and might be more precisely defined as the war of the *fiati* (for in any case the culprit was not a C), La Nilsson "crowned" (held) for a long time, as she always did, by the way—the G of the concluding phrase: "*Mi vuoi nelle tue braccia a forza, riluttante, fremente?*" Being, as she says, "in particularly good shape" that night, she extended her G all the way to the tenor's entrance!

Corelli left the stage infuriated and Bing, very worried for the effect of possible repercussions on the performance, ran to the dressing room to try to calm him down. At this point he suggested to him a rather curious revenge: in the third act, when he was supposed to kiss Turandot, he could instead bite her.

Franco liked the idea, probably because it aroused his sense of humor, and this was enough to make him forget his anger, at least partially. Bing, anyhow, did not have the courage to stay and see how the dispute would end. He had to take off for New York before the end of the performance. *That is why,* states Birgit Nilsson, *he remained convinced that Franco had actually bitten me!*

In reality, the tenor didn't bite her or kiss her, but was very composed, very controlled. Yet he was cooking up a more subtle sort of revenge. When Turandot sang "*La mia gloria è finita*" he, taking advantage of the fact that most of the audience surely didn't know Italian, replied right away, "*Si, è finita!*"

This may sound like a declaration of war. Instead, Birgit Nilsson says today, the true friendship between these two artists dates from precisely that day... However, the "war of the high Cs" would continue throughout their careers.[36]

At the beginning of the summer Corelli returned to Italy and sang a shining *Chénier* at the Fenice and then was expected in Verona for *Carmen*. Here another episode, the details of which are contested, hit the papers, or at least certain papers, with headlines about the "tantrums" of the tenor.

In reality this story is very simple and, curiously enough, is told with great probability of verisimilitude by a magazine which came out with a piece entitled: *Corelli; his majesty the tenor*, and with, for good measure, the addition of a little explanatory window. *Franco Corelli has been throwing tantrums just like Callas.*

Anyone reading past the headline to the rest of the article would be rather surprised to know how things really went.

It was the evening of the 26th of July, the general rehearsal of *Carmen*.

Corelli, addressing Simionato, who was waiting for him to give her a flower while wrapping herself in a fur stole, started to sing. Verona, from the tables in the cafes on Piazza Bra, was all tense, listening: from outside you can hear everything perfectly, and you can perceive the smallest tic. Suddenly, still at the beginning, Corelli left a note unfinished. Crossly he pulled his hand from his pocket and waved it in the air. "I can't sing this way," he said. "I can't make it with this tempo!" Maestro Sevitzky lowered his baton. Verona was restive. Not a breath of music was still coming, a sign that something was very wrong, that someone was not feeling good or arguing. "I cannot make it," Corelli repeated. "This is an impossible tempo." The Russian maestro [in reality an American. Ed.] definitively put down his baton. "Please bear in mind," he replied, "that this is the tempo of Bizet." The tenor came back with, "I never sang it that way. The slow tempi you're imposing are breaking up the melody."

According to the writer of the article Sevitzky responded at this point with a little lecture that could be summed up as follows: "I am the conductor of the opera and it has to be done as I say." And he received the only possible answer: "Then go find yourself another tenor."[37]

The "whims," the great phenomenon of *divismo*—there you have it. It is more than obvious that in the game of "either he's out or I'm out" between a tenor of Corelli's class and a little-known conductor, the tenor would win. All the more since in preceding days Sevitzky had had disagreements with two other principals of the opera, Giulietta Simionato and Ettore Bastianini, who had been made unhappy by his lack of experience, and even the *comprimari*, starting with that singer of very high professionalism, Piero De Palma.[38] Nor was there any doubt that the audience crowding the arena had come to listen to Corelli and not Sevitzky interpret *Carmen*.

The conductor announced that he would give up the engagement and Maestro Molinari Pradelli, who knew all the principals very well for having conducted them countless times, agreed to fill in for his colleague.

The opera went onstage with a great success, and it makes me happy to report how, in spite of efforts of the press to dig up every possible scandalous angle, the more qualified critics took a very balanced stand.

This was not a matter of whims or absurd, groundless claims on the part of anyone, but only an incurable disagreement created by the maestro's obvious lack of experience, an experience of this particular melodrama and of the arena, wrote Giuseppe Pugliese in his newspaper.[39]

Later, and therefore with less emotional heat than someone on the spot, Giulio Confalonieri writing in *Epoca* was even more explicit:

According to totally reliable information, Maestro Sevitzky, who has been praised above, had supposedly never in his life directed an opera, but rather had been dedicated to his job as substitute and symphonic performer. Conducting an opera has nothing in common with the conducting symphonies or piano concerts.[40]

In the fall Corelli again donned Manrico's costume on two important occasions. The first was the unforgettable *Trovatore* in Berlin with the full resources of the Rome Opera. One of that night's principal performers, Fedora Barbieri, still remembers the enthusiastic scene. At the end, because the public refused to go away, Corelli, dressed in his street clothes, was forced to sing some tunes with Ettore Bastianini acting as a master of ceremonies—an uncommon case of supportive spirit in a world where competition between colleagues is often harsh.

A few days after, still with the *Trovatore*, Corelli opened the season at the Teatro Novo of Turin, and in December returned to open the season at La Scala in the year celebrating Italian unity, with Verdi's almost-forgotten *Battaglia di Legnano*.

The part of Arrigo, noble, unfortunate and heroic as any tenor could wish for a romantic character to be—though vocally very forbidding—joined a long list of his successes, of which it would be tiresome to speak.

Celletti wrote in his review of the live recording:

> *In the opening aria, "La pia materna mano," (Corelli) shows off a full, soft* cavata *with impassioned expression and beautiful high notes*, then concluded the third act *with irrepressible vehemence.*[41]

It is legitimate to add that he represented dying in the last scene with so much anguished conviction that he made some members of his audience helpless not to think of the nineteenth-century tenors, as Mario Morini recently led me to believe in a very interesting private conversation.

At the end of the following January, after a few performances of *Turandot* in Naples, Corelli returned to fulfill his American engagements, making the audience of the Metropolitan enthusiastic with his interpretation of Cavaradossi (*For a long time after "E lucevan le stelle" it was doubtful whether the performance could continue without an encore* wrote the commentator in "The New York Times")[42] and of Radames.

Then in March he debuted in an opera which he would sing a number of times in American theaters, though his Italian audiences would for the most part remain ignorant of his work in it: *La Gioconda*.

Though the part may be without great significance in the opera, the romantic and vehement character of Enzo Grimaldo admirably suited Corelli's voice, personality and presence. It goes without saying that, as with the others, even this character would undergo an evolution, and we are fortunate to possess a recorded documentation of it. A few years afterwards in a live recording of the aria Corelli would be able to give us a veritable singing lesson, both for the variety of tonal coloration and audacious, moving use of *smorzature*—though we must strain our ears to hear it because of the very poor technical quality of the recording.

In May Corelli returned to La Scala with *Turandot* and the event that was fated to mark the summit of his career, and of his development as a singer as well, was programmed for the end of that month. To close the season of the Milanese opera theater *Les Huguenots* of Giacomo Meyerbeer was going onstage on May 28th.

The last of the great Italian tenors that had dared to face *that sixth degree climb, which is what the tenor's tessitura in the Meyerbeer role represented,* had been Giacomo Lauri-Volpi, who had sung the part for the last time in 1955 on the RAI of Milan.[43]

The role of Raoul, as I have already mentioned, was written for Adolphe Nourrit, who, according to historical sources, from A-flat or A-natural on would emit all his high notes in a strong falsetto.

This system, rejected by modern taste, as Rodolfo Celletti notes in his introduction to the live record,

> *would very much alleviate the singer's work in taking high notes full voice, and in a range so high as Raoul's, would double it and triple it. In a strictly philological sense,* Celletti continues, *with the type of voice Corelli has he was not a perfect match for the extremely young, dreamy, naive characters (it was no accident that Meyerbeer associated the viola*

with the sound, in the recitative and aria "Bianca al par di neve alpina") and therefore is better suited to a clear silver timbre than to one of bronze.

Here I believe we are already slipping into a judgment based on personal taste. If it is true that the character of Raoul is very young, dreamy and naive, it is also perfectly true that the record demonstrates the sound of the viola, so rich and round, which perfectly matches the warm, dark voice of the tenor, and the other way around. There are actually moments in which the two voices reflect each other, so to speak. This correspondence of sound reminds one of the particularity of certain soprano voices mimicking the sound of a flute in the very famous cadenza of *Lucia di Lammermoor*.

On the other hand I confess that I don't attribute too much importance, as a general principle, to the type of voice for which a certain role has been written in its time. And this is for a very simple reason: while tenors, or in general singers, of the 19th century had at their disposal musicians who would write roles for them, up to a certain point *to measure* (Nourrit, it seems, sometimes even made personal contributions to the composition), contemporary singers don't have this good fortune—not even, as a consequence, the same obligations, therefore it is fair that they should be relatively free to interpret their roles according to their means and their sensibility.

Besides, as Sergio Segalini observed most acutely in his book on Meyerbeer, the composer,

as with all creative geniuses, wrote his operas for his interpreters, but was demanding from them, perhaps unconsciously, an evolution, a transformation that they could not realize.[44]

Thus, in the specific case of Raoul, it is really true that the role was written for Nourrit, but it is also true that in this role, the tenor was very soon replaced (not to say ousted) by his rival Duprez, who passed into history for, among other

things, inventing the high C taken from the chest, and therefore, presumably (it is always difficult and often dangerous
to hazard a guess about voices that none of us has ever heard)
possessed a very different voice quality.

Anyhow, behind these clarifications of a general character, we cannot but acknowledge that the La Scala version of
Les Huguenots found critics and audience practically unanimous in their appreciation of all the characters, and besides of
the beautiful mise-en-scène.

The real triumphs of the night, though, belonged to Corelli
and Simionato, both of whom had taken on very difficult roles.
Celletti again observed that Giulietta Simionato had offered a
performance that deserved to be ranked among the very best
of her career.

> *But the heaviest responsibility weighed on Corelli's shoul-
> ders because Raoul is one of those historical parts for a
> romantic tenor, and the singer's mastery of its complexity
> was almost enough by itself to give glory or disgrace. (...)
> Corelli creates a Raoul that is by turns ardent, chivalrous,
> heartbroken. He generates enthusiasm in the love duet of
> the fourth act (in spite of the omission of a passage that
> reaches a high D-flat) and overcomes the difficulties of the
> tessitura with a powerful voice which has exceptional range,
> but at the same time is flexible and emotional.*[45]

The audience of La Scala, traditionally rather cold, let itself be carried away with enthusiasm on this occasion. The
tenor part of the fourth act duet bristles with very difficult
attacks in mezza voce on G-flat, therefore right on the register
break (*"Dillo ancor!"*). There are numerous C-flats for both
voices (which is not quite the same thing for a singer as a B-
natural), abundantly crowned with *fermate*, and both artists
inserted a resplendent high C for good measure (optional for
the soprano and only written as A-flat for the tenor). The
members of the audience leapt to their feet and applauded for
several minutes (though people often say longer than twenty

minutes), and the singers in question, too engrossed in their music to worry about the audience, were shocked by the response or even dazed by it.[46]

With *Gli Ugonotti*, so long dreamed about and feared, and prepared so carefully, so tenaciously, or I would dare to say obsessively, Corelli's career clearly reached a key point, or better, a culmination.

It was a goal that only he among his contemporaries had wanted, and only he had been able to reach and surpass.

Today, a little bit egoistically, without taking into consideration the exorbitant price that the artist had to pay in terms of physical exhaustion and emotional strain, many fault him for not going on to greater things, to higher goals, just as arduous, just as demanding.

From another point of view these were legitimate expectations because Franco Corelli's vocalism had reached technical peaks that only a few critics at this point were ready to deny. His voice, at the beginning only an extremely powerful instrument, or very nearly that, had acquired after hours, days, nights, months, years of constant effort a flexibility that had made him unique among those who are commonly defined as *tenori di forza*.

How did he succeed? With sacrifices and continuous study, almost to the point of masochism, it has been said, with a piano tuned half a tone high,[47] taking out his frustration on his music stands, on closet doors and on himself (*I have seen him pulling his own hair, and not just metaphorically*, remembers Carlo Perucci)[48] over recalcitrant sounds, over a smorzatura that cracked, over a breath that ran out, studying, even during his vacations, in the basement of a hotel that had been crudely "soundproofed,"[49] confiding to the pitiless sincerity of the tape recorder all his efforts, and spending sleepless nights looking for defects in the recordings.

And, at the end of this steep trail, which Giuseppe Pugliese will call a Calvary (*And this is not too strong a word, not an exaggeration*)[50] he found not only the extreme high notes— *High notes that flash with heavenly light!* as Eugenio Gara put it[51]—not only the ability to diminuendo his top notes to the point that they are pure breath, but a comprehensive vocal organization that had its strongest point, as Rodolfo Celletti observed, right in what is traditionally considered the weakest point in the tenor's range, the so-called "zone of passage" [the *passaggio or ponticello*, the register break supposed to exist between middle and high registers, which singers try very hard to disguise—Ed.].

The zona mista [where the notes are mixed to disguise the register break, as above—Ed.], *from E-flat to G-flat, represents a rare but perfect welding of chest sounds characteristic of low and middle registers, and the "head" resonance of the high notes. (...) In Corelli the passaggio has the same volume, fullness, and vibration as notes at the center of his voice. Additionally it presents a certain typical phosphorescence from the high register, a phosphorescence that becomes accentuated as the voice ascends. But here we come upon a vocal phenomenon. Corelli's high notes, starting with G-flat, have the strength and fullness of a medium, baritone-like sound moved to a stratospheric zone with the addition of a sheen and spontaneity given by the head resonance.*[52]

It's a long speech, and perhaps too specialized for someone who is not directly involved with opera, but it explains technically what is a visual impression for some listeners: the voice arises like a column of sound, perfectly smooth, without being squeezed off or narrowed anywhere throughout its entire extension, higher and higher to the extreme high notes, which, though enveloped by shadow at first, become more and more refulgent.

A literary description exists that may be excessively baroque, and we shouldn't be amazed because it comes from the pen of Gabriele D'Annunzio. However, I feel that it is deeply relevant to Corelli's quality, especially in this decisive moment of his career, and in others to follow which, though less renowned, are also important: *purest metal wrapped in the soft-*

est velvet.[53]

After finishing five performances of *The Huguenots* Corelli was in Venice for *Carmen*. Right afterward he was expected in Enghien, but on the streets of Sempione, close to Sesto Calende, his car got involved in an accident while overtaking two trucks and ended up in a ditch. Luckily it was the vehicle that got the worst of it and the tenor only had minor wounds that didn't even require a hospitalization. The French engagement, though, had to be cancelled because of another event, and one of historic significance that has to be dealt with here. At the end of July the *Trovatore* was scheduled to be performed in Salzburg for the first time. Herbert Von Karajan, who was to conduct, had assembled an exceptional cast—without doubt the best of the moment. Besides Corelli there was Leontyne Price, Giulietta Simionato, and Ettore Bastianini.

The success was outlined starting with the general rehearsal, for which there was an audience of over 2,000 people. Of course the attendance was even greater for the first performance, which attracted not only what was usually called "the audience for great occasions," but also the main representatives of international critical opinion. For once these critics were in agreement, with minor reservations, in proclaiming the triumph of the performance.

A little later, and therefore more dispassionately, the comments remained extremely positive. Celletti himself, after repeating his well-known opinion that the character of Manrico was a perfect fit for Corelli, especially in the more lyric moments (and also stating, on I don't know what basis, that the *"pira"* had been lowered a tone, which is simply not true, as anyone could discover by listening to the recording), observed that

> ...*it was a variable interpretation, in which the exceptional fullness and density of his sound did not hinder his ability to soften his voice or employ* smorzatura *effects. In addition he gave lessons on how to sing, and at certain difficult*

moments ("Il presagio funesto, deh, sperdi o cara,") gave textbook examples of the passage between registers. (...) The duet with Azucena was exalted; and the curse, "Ha quest'infame l'amor venduto," sung this way explains why at one time, for some tenors, audiences required encores.[54]

The proof that it is impossible to make everyone happy comes once again from the British critics. Thus the reviewer for *Opera*, even if he can't help but note that the tenor has scored a fantastic success, finds reason for blame in the duration of the notes in his diminuendi which tended to drift below pitch.[55]

Here again the listener cannot but take cheer in the existence of the recording, which provides irrefutable testimony as to the precision of his delicate *smorzature* and his beautiful *mezze voci*.

Perhaps it would be appropriate to open a short parenthesis here to stress the fact that only a few critics note, now and then, imperfections in Franco Corelli's intonation. On the other hand (and taking for granted the fact that occasionally anyone can put out a wrong note in the theater as a result of a hundred unforeseen factors) practically all the musicians I have interviewed, conductors and singers, have expressly pointed to Corelli's musicality, precise intonation, and beauty of vocal line, as among his signature characteristics. Among the musicians who have responded to my request for an expert opinion I am once again lucky to have obtained the testimony of Gianandrea Gavazzeni, along with Maestro Ziino and Maestro Veltri—who, among other things, have known and conducted Corelli at both chronological extremes of his career—as well as, among his colleagues, Giulietta Simionato and Gian Giacomo Guelfi.[56]

In the last part of 1962 Corelli still had two engagements of extraordinary importance on his schedule: he was to be the first opera tenor to open the same season at both Milan's La Scala and New York's Metropolitan.

At the Metropolitan his *Andrea Chénier* was received as a historic event. To begin with the opera was performed entirely in the original key, which had happened for the last time 25 years before when the tenor was Beniamino Gigli. If we can believe the press, after the *"Improvviso"* twenty minutes of applause were recorded. And the following day the papers wrote that Corelli had brought down the house.

At La Scala no less than two months afterwards, the cast which had triumphally "re-exhumed" the previous season's *Battaglia di Legnano* got together again for *Trovatore*: Franco Corelli, Antonietta Stella, Ettore Bastianini—with the important addition of Fiorenza Cossotto in the role of Azucena.

The endless performances were extended, obviously with long breaks, until March. Right in one of the last performances an accident took place that was so unusual, not only is it reported on the back of the playbill preserved in the files of the theater, but is also mentioned by a note at the bottom of the page in the official chronology of La Scala.

The note says literally:

On the 2nd of March at the ninth performance, after the 2nd act, the tenor Corelli lost his voice. Gianni Jaia was prepared to substitute for him, but Corelli recovered, and after an hour break the performance was able to resume with the same cast.

This is the official version as far as it went. Someone hinted that loss of voice is a matter of nerves, or maybe a pure and simple matter of suggestion. Someone who didn't know (or admit) Corelli's professionalism also spoke of the tenor's "caprices." The explanation that appeared in the press had it that in the second act Corelli got too close to a brazier that was burning in the middle of the gypsy camp, getting a nagging irritation of the throat. It's a very plausible explanation because it corresponds to analogous, though definitely infrequent, experiences of other artists. Very well known is the case of Mario Del Monaco whose voice was "burned" in Verona from

Otello's "festive fires." I have personally heard recounted an identical misadventure at the Metropolitan, where Cornell MacNeil was the victim, again in *Otello*.[57]

Actually, in this performance at La Scala the break between the second and third acts was extended. (However, the third act brought the "*pira*" and, even more perilous, the "*Ah, si ben mio*," which was most certainly not a piece to face when conditions were less than perfect.) Between the third and the fourth acts the break was extended again, and Corelli's public and colleagues were notably ill at ease. "*I was supposed* to sing, '*D'amor sull'ali rosee,*' and I had to wait an hour," says Antonietta Stella, remembering the tension of that evening.[58]

At the end, anyhow, the substitute was not used, and the performance finally came to an end around two in the morning with the full complement of performers at their posts. The audience not only showed sympathy, but was also most eager to applaud the performers for having seen the opera through to the end amid so many difficulties.

In the meantime, in January, Corelli was back at the Metropolitan—first with a performance of *Aida* with Leontyne Price, then with a new production of *Adriana Lecouvreur*, of which Renata Tebaldi has particularly fond memories, and in which, according to Rudolf Bing, Corelli, beside her, was the ideal Maurizio.[59]

In March, after the last performance of *Trovatore* at La Scala, Corelli was once again Manrico at the Rome Opera. It was an important occasion, not only because he was going back, with one of his most successful roles, to the theater that had seen his first steps in the opera world. In the audience was a spectator that Corelli had expressly invited, whose judgment was particularly important to him: Giacomo Lauri-Volpi.

On the dates, regardless of their importance, of the artistic rapport with Lauri-Volpi, much has been said and written, and not always with due accuracy. Many are convinced that Corelli turned to his famous colleague to ask his advice for the preparation of those operas of which Lauri-Volpi had been one of few interpreters; that is, *Poliuto* and *Les Huguenots*.

In reality the true collaboration—let's say the friendship—between the two began later, between 1963 and 1964 to be precise. Before that there was an isolated meeting around the end of the fifties, and, on occasion, a few phone calls.

But Lauri-Volpi had often heard Corelli sing, and more than that, had followed him with attention from the beginning of his career, judging him very strictly. One of his pronouncements became famous: "If he continues this way we will find ourselves with one less tenor and one more baritone." As Corelli faced *Gli Ugonotti*, however, Lauri-Volpi didn't hesitate to acknowledge in him a worthy successor.[60]

It was during this period, then, that Corelli began a series of trips to Valencia, with longer and longer stays at Burjasot. The first year he stayed ten days, then twenty, then thirty... And every day there were three hours of study, one phrase after the other, one vocalise after the other, while people lingered under the windows to listen to those two extraordinary voices.*

Many still wonder, even today, what Corelli was looking for in Lauri-Volpi—since Corelli had already made his name, better, was already famous, and surely possessed an enviable technique. Maybe the answer is in this sentence from Corelli himself during an interview, a little bit after the death of the tenor from Lanuvio:

> *He didn't want to consider himself a master at all, he said it would have been act of presumption. He treated me as a colleague, who was coming there only to share his great experience, of which he was making me a gift with a great goodness of soul.*

It may well have been that beyond the technical advice,

---

*Franco Corelli himself tells of this in an interview inserted in a television program on Lauri-Volpi that was broadcast on March 24th, 1980. To be precise, Corelli said that Lauri-Volpi had an extraordinary voice, but I have taken the liberty of expressing my opinion that people were stopping to hear *both* voices.

which would still be very precious as such (and not so much, as is commonly thought, for the conquest of high notes as for the full control of the *mezze voci*: it was not by chance that the relationship with Lauri-Volpi would culminate in Corelli's debut in *Werther*), Corelli was seeking a colleague in the person of the old, indomitable tenor. In a certain, very particular sense, he was looking for his counterpart.

If it may seem paradoxical to use this word to define two personalities, two characters—and two voices—that were so different, we must not forget what the basically have in common: a deep respect, and an absolute, unconditional devotion to their art.

In the spring of 1963 Corelli again took part in the Metropolitan Opera tour, his second. This tour was as much expected in the cities of America as it was deplored by the general manager in his memoirs. In spite of all the efforts to organize it in the best way, wrote Rudolf Bing, the tour was still a scandal from an artistic point of view because the theaters weren't fit to host an opera performance. But, in spite of the technical and logistical difficulties, there was a series of other problems for the artists: frenetic transfers, almost daily cast changes, and the constant alternation in different roles, requiring the singers to make tiring and dangerous readjustments of their voices. It was enough to think that Corelli, in that tour of 1963, alternated between *Tosca* and *Pagliacci*, with the additional insertion of some performances of *Cavalleria rusticana*, the opera which he was preparing for his fourth season-opening performance at La Scala.

In September there was a second and more "official" debut in the role of Turiddu in Vienna. Then, while still in Vienna, there were two performances of *Don Carlo* about which, as one could read in the press, the tenor did not feel personally satisfied in spite of the public success. Finally, the reprise—even though with a different cast—of the *Trovatore* of the previous summer, that Von Karajan had adapted from a scenographic standpoint to the more intimate atmosphere of the Staatsoper, provided a worthy tribute to celebrate the 150th anniversary of Giuseppe Verdi's birth.

In December Corelli's debut in *Cavalleria* at La Scala was preceded by the episode of the famous "fight" with Maestro Gandolfi. The newspapers jumped on the scandal, and the accusation of "divism," and the requests for "humility" resurfaced, even though the chance cause and the authentic dynamic of the dispute were never completely clarified. There was talk of "old rust," but it wasn't clear if this was due to the fact that the curtain was lowered without any reason by Gandolfi, who was at the time the prompter at the Regio di Parma, or to a judgment expressed by the maestro himself in favor of another tenor (and the versions, of course, are conflicting).

Anyhow, the "case" quickly dwindled in significance and *Cavalleria* went onstage together with *L'amico Fritz* in a serene atmosphere and was a true success for the three main characters. Giulietta Simionato was the impassioned Santuzza, Gian Giacomo Guelfi was a strong and effective Alfio, and of course Franco Corelli gave an interpretation of Turiddu that was *manly and bold*, and about which critics were moved (if such a thing is possible) as never before to consider him *objectively closer to Caruso in his accentuations than, for example, to a Gigli or a Di Stefano.*[61]

After listening to the recording it's impossible for me to share the opinion that the sense of guilt that comes to the surface in the last-mentioned Turiddus cannot be perceived in Corelli. On the contrary, I share the opinion of Maestro Gavazzeni, who conducted the opera:

> *He is a different Turiddu, in which we can perceive the desperation of a man who is the prisoner of an irreversible contradiction, caught between two forces: the love for Santuzza, that is at this point less warm, and the moral obligation towards her, and the love for Lola.*[62]

In effect it seems to me very difficult to give a more heartfelt interpretation to "*Compare Alfio, lo so che il torto è mio*" without betraying the nature of the character.

During the first days of January another controversial event took place, and this, too, has never been clarified. On the contrary, the controversy was dropped and buried by the participants in it. I'm referring to the dispute-ridden *Fanciulla del West*, where in what turned out to be an intricate game the tenor and Antonietta Stella traded accusations of lack of professionalism. The soprano would end by walking out on the production, to be replaced by Gigliola Frazzoni, Corelli's partner in his first La Scala appearance as Dick Johnson.

Today it is more than understandable that Antonietta Stella has no wish to revive the controversy, and that she would attribute the cause of it to words that were twisted by envious colleagues. Sincerely I could see no reason to insist while facing an artist who was telling me, smiling, that the episode belonged to a past that is very far away by this time, and that more important to her were the beautiful memories of many other moments between them of shared anxieties and triumphs, of little gestures of solidarity, of breathless encouragements behind the scenes and on the stage.

To give an idea of the professional *rapports* between the two singers over the following years (the personal ones are still very good) I would like to quote an event that would seem to be especially meaningful.

Several years afterwards, in 1970, Corelli and La Stella sang a *Tosca* in Paris in an atmosphere of preordained conflict created by a certain segment of the public which was in principle against foreign singers.

Corelli, according to what Antonietta herself said, gave one of the most beautiful performances of his career that night. However, in the famous filatura of the sentence "*disciogliea dai veli*," his voice cracked almost imperceptibly, and this was enough to give the audience the chance to express their disapproval, which was way out of proportion. The tenor carried the performance to its conclusion and refused to return for the next. To show solidarity with her colleague, La Stella refused the offer to sing with another partner.[63]

Back in New York after performing the Scala *Fanciulla*, Corelli sang an important production of *Trovatore* under the direction of Thomas Schippers. Following this there were a couple of routine engagements—*Aida* and *Gioconda*.

There is another important date. In some ways, looking back, even a historical date in Franco Corelli's career: on February 29, 1964, he debuted at the Metropolitan in the role of Rodolfo in *Bohème*.

From Bohème to Bohème

I REALIZE THAT TO DEFINE Franco Corelli's debut in *Bohème* as a historic date obliges me to make a few explanations, because at that time the event passed almost unobserved. Or better, because it came to be considered, at least at the Metropolitan, a perfectly normal occurrence—so much so that the magazine *Opera News*, in its usual announcement of the Met's program for the week, didn't even mention it as an event of note.

The fact that Corelli sang *Bohème* didn't surprise anybody in the States, even if it would shock many in Italy. This is not because, as I sometimes hear, the audience of the Metropolitan is less competent or easier to satisfy than the audience of any great Italian theater. It is simply because it is in general less prejudiced, less bound by traditional preferences which almost obligatorily tie certain singers to certain operas.

Corelli's Rodolfo, in fact, was immediately a great success.

The February 29th La Bohème *is one of those performances that will be talked about for many years. Everything clicked and produced that special brand of magic and excitement that radiates from a superbly sung performance of a favorite like* Bohème. *Franco Corelli sang his first Rodolfo anywhere, and never at the Met has he seemed so at ease and so convincing. His was no wooden Indian portrait. He*

*looked the part and moved with ardor and spirit. Then too
it was wonderful to hear a lusty Radames-Manrico voice in
the part. Far from being overly heroic, Corelli's singing was
wonderfully virile, and the emotions of the final act combined the exact amount of sobbing and singing. For my
money there hasn't been such a Rodolfo since Björling.
Another first at the Met was Gabriella Tucci's Mimi. If Mr.
Corelli was all masculinity, Miss Tucci was the essence of
fragility. (...) Together they created a pair of lovers rare in*
Bohème *annals.*[1]

If his debut as Rodolfo was thought to be nothing unusual
on vocal grounds, his ever more frequent appearances in the
role began to seem quite natural. In fact, one of the greatest
American critics, Conrad Osborne, would expressly cite
Corelli's Rodolfo to show the distinctive characteristics of his
vocalism as compared to Del Monaco's (Del Monaco being
the only other tenor in his judgment commonly defined as "*di
forza*" who was worthy of comparison) which allowed Corelli
to take on the lyric repertory—which were, of course, his flexibility and his completely realized technical knowledge.[2]

Nonetheless it is undeniable that the debut in *Bohème*,
especially if considered after the fact, as I pointed out above,
if not a true turning point, was at least a portent of what
would become an opening in a new and unexpected direction.

Up to that moment, in fact, Corelli's career in general had
followed a series of perfectly logical stages, consecrated by
tradition and rendered foreseeable by his vocal development.
One by one he put in his repertoire the classic roles for tenor
voice, in particular Verdi and Puccini roles, with important
additions on the one hand of certain important 19th century
operas (Bellini and Donizetti) and on the other of certain true
verismo classics in the strictest sense (Leoncavallo, Mascagni,
Giordano).

He had arrived at a point where two paths had opened in
front of him, equally predictable—and equally within the reach
of his technical evolution. Wrote Giuseppe Pugliese:

Having reached the peak of his artistic itinerary—let us say after Poliuto *and* Huguenots—*Corelli could and should expand his repertory in two directions. That of the tenore belcantistico, with the difficult* tessiture *of* Puritani *and* William Tell, *and that of the tenor purely dramatic and heroic together, with* Otello. *In a few years, if we should be so lucky, perhaps we will have all three of these splendid archetypes of the operatic tenor's voice.*[3]

Instead, none of this took place. In 1964, within a few months of each other, Corelli debuted in two operas totally outside his traditional repertoire. Right after *Bohème* in fact, in April, he sang Gounod's *Roméo et Juliette* for the first time.

The debut in the role of Romeo did not take place at the Metropolitan, but in Philadelphia, with an isolated performance that was sufficient, however, to attract the attention of a critic with a very important name: Max de Schauensee, the correspondent for *Opera*, among other publications.

The season ended on April 14, when the Lyric gave Philadelphia its first performance of Gounod's Roméo et Juliette *in 18 years. Corelli, singing his first Romeo on any stage is the essence of visual romance and brought vibrancy and ardor to this new part. Some of his work was naturally tentative, but repeated performances in a role for which he is obviously suited should bring assurance to his French diction and to his stage deportment. Even so, he proved unusually effective.*[4]

Listening to the recording fully confirms the judgment quoted above. Sadly, we are left with the regret of not being able to verify the word "visual." Also, judging by the audio only, this is an outstanding Romeo in most respects, even if one could characterize it as somewhat unfinished in comparison to the role as he would present it three years later at the Metropolitan.

Perhaps it is no coincidence that the part was withheld for such a long time, as if the artist should let it ripen, understand it, take it into his being both vocally and psychologically and then wrench it from the depths and make of it one of the more meaningful successes of his career—though sadly one that is almost unknown to Italian audiences and is neglected by Italian critics.

But 1964 was not only the year of debuts in both *Bohème* and *Roméo*, it was also—without doubt coincidentally and not by choice—the year in which Corelli would sing his last performances of *Trovatore*.

There would be in the years to follow other plans to interpret the Verdi opera—in the 1969-1970 season at the Metropolitan, for example, when labor problems interfered—but for one reason or another none of them would ever bear fruit, and the performance in Chicago in October of 1964 would be the last of Corelli's career.

The fact is almost certainly accidental, but seen with hindsight, it acquires a particular meaning, almost that of a symbolic "passing of the baton." And in fact starting with the one *Bohème*, the successive, and very rare, Corelli debuts would all be part of his lyric repertoire. *Macbeth* would be the sole exception, but because of the tenor's limited role in it, that opera cannot be used as evidence of career tendencies.

Here I have touched upon another characteristic of Corelli's (almost exclusively) "American" years, between 1964 and 1971, during which we have no record of a single debut. The only enrichment of his repertoire is represented by Verdi's *Requiem Mass*, which was performed in Los Angeles in 1967 under the direction of Zubin Mehta.

When almost everyone was expecting a resurgence from him, a burst of new experiences, perhaps a trial that could equal or surpass his landmark performance of *Gli Ugonotti*, sadly Corelli stops and takes to the sidelines, renounces the job of building his repertoire further, and in one sense gives up on his career.

Still, the years between 1964 and 1971 were certainly seven

years of triumphs. They were also—as Italian audiences and critics would discover, often with surprise, during his rare returns to Italy—years of constant, uninterrupted technical refinement. Yet no matter how difficult it is to explain these years as an outside observer, it is an incontestably evident fact that they are seven years of routine, involving the repetition of no more than five or six fixed operas: *Turandot, Aida, Gioconda, Bohème, Tosca,* with rare performances, here and there, of *Chénier, Adriana, Ernani, Fanciulla del West,* and only one really important insertion: *Roméo et Juliette,* after the debut at the Metropolitan in 1967.

It was only natural that, especially in Italy, many asked themselves the reason for what had to be considered if not a *tacet* looming over his career, at least quite a few bars of unexpected rest.

The simplest explanation is also the most simplistic and insufficient by definition:

> *Corelli, after having given the best of himself artistically from 1958 to 1962, emigrated to America where the commercialization unexpectedly had the final result of arresting the beautiful historic arc of his development in a certain repertoire.*[5]

Frankly I don't completely understand the precise meaning of the word "commercialization" in the previous context, but in any case I think it is rather belittling in the way it brutishly seeks to measure artistic decisions in dollars and cents.

Surely I don't question the fact that the cachet of the Metropolitan had a weighty influence, but also it's impossible not to take into account the differences in the way American theaters were organized and managed, which enabled them to offer as well as impose—and this is the "bad side of the medal"—the safety of longterm engagements.

On the other side I'm convinced that these considerations of a practical kind are not enough by themselves to explain Franco Corelli's choices in those years.

Maybe the observer who got closest to the truth is once again Giuseppe Pugliese. According to this critic's writings Corelli's departure for the United States interrupted the plan which should have led to the development of the tenor's repertoire in the two directions mentioned above.

For years, Pugliese continues, *I believed that this was the only reason for his great renunciation. Today I'm not very sure about it. Why? I reflected a lot about this: only someone who has seen Corelli countless times, after every performance, dead tired, with his face altered by the ravages of fear and tension, and the weight of a huge, physical fatigue on the athletic body, and the weary look in his eye bespeaking total detachment or disgust, even after nights of triumph, can understand the incredible, inhuman price that Corelli had to pay to reach the goal that made him one of the most important stars in the opera world.*[6]

Even here the text requires a certain interpretive effort, but as far as I can judge, I believe the sense is as follows: you cannot ask a man to live eternally in the rarefied atmosphere of the alpinist, repeatedly climbing high peaks, or in other words, challenging himself and the world unceasingly, dizzy with exhilaration.

Since public acclaim was shaking the rafters of the theaters whenever he sang—reinforced by exposure on radio and television and the courtship of Hollywood producers and even some from Broadway, as well as White House invitations, and the fact that he was being spoiled by a smart general manager who stopped at nothing to guarantee appearances of the tenor the press was calling "Mister Sold-out" for whole seasons in advance—I don't think it unreasonable to suppose that Corelli was seeking a breathing space in the routine of the American theater, a harbor of relative tranquility. Moreover, after having paid such a high price to reach artistic primacy in technical and artistic terms, with ten years of hard work even before he was famous and beloved by his public, could it be unreasonable to suppose that, inevitably, projects that were never explicitly put aside slipped into the indefinite and always more misty future? And that thus, inevitably too, his appearances in European theaters became more and more rare?

In 1964 he had his keenly anticipated debut at the Paris Opera with *Tosca*. Right afterward Corelli sang the two performances of *Norma* with Callas which have already been described, and then finally *Don Carlo*.

The critical and public consensus about this debut was unanimous. The critic writing in "Le Figaro" called Corelli's a "sun-like voice."[7] The reviewer for "Le Monde" wrote that:

Corelli now owns the treasure that all the great singers dream about. He has found the ideal support for his breath that will allow him to pass from mezze voci *to high notes in full power, which makes the audience jump to their feet.*[8]

In the summer Corelli was supposed to be part of a La Scala tour to Moscow, but he had to cancel because of a vexatious exhaustion that would, however, not prevent unsparingly meanspirited people from hinting that he had been paid by the Metropolitan to stay at home (even mentioning the amount: fifty thousand American dollars!).

This was an inconvenience that ended up being providential because the vague organization of the tour invited so much spite and controversy that it was nicknamed "the Russian campaign."

In the fall Corelli opened the season at the Lyric Opera of Chicago with what, as I mentioned briefly above, would be his last *Trovatore*. Right afterward he also opened the Philadelphia season with a triumphant *Fanciulla del West* with Dorothy Kirsten and Anselmo Colzani.

The *Fanciulla* is an opera that doesn't go over too well in America. It is rather difficult to create a Western atmosphere that doesn't look like a parody to the audiences.

In Philadelphia it hadn't been mounted in over thirty years, but on this occasion the stage director and cast succeeded in making it credible, and the audience received it with great favor, in such a way that the Metropolitan decided immediately to add it to the playbill for the following season, with the same cast of singers.

As Max de Schauensee stresses, this is one opera that simply must be supported by a cast of great interpreters, and on this occasion

> *These three formed a team that was able to create a tremendous impact in the opera's big moments. (...) Corelli was in splendid voice and never has he seemed to be so sincerely within the frame of a performance. Handsome and stalwart, he had to take quite a bit of roughing up and violence during the evening. His last act aria was most beautifully and touchingly sung.*[9]

On the 7th of December, finally, Corelli participated in his sixth consecutive opening of the season at La Scala, an absolute record, but it would the last. It was a farewell, and everyone knew it. He had been contracted by the Metropolitan for four more years, and he would never come back to the Milanese theater, would never sing there again, even though in the following years in the press there would be some attempt to patch up the relationship, and the possibility of a comeback would be aired now and then.

Corelli left La Scala with *Turandot*. It was a choice that he didn't particularly enjoy, above all because it was an opera too well-known to the Milanese public. He would have preferred, if the declarations reported by the newspapers are correct, to open with a Verdi opera. There were hints regarding *La forza del destino*, that had never been sung at La Scala, or an opera less familiar to the public, such as a revival of *Gli Ugonotti* or *Poliuto*.

However, the disagreement about the choice of opera didn't prevent Corelli from singing on the 7th of December under the vibrant direction of Gianandrea Gavazzeni what was perhaps his greatest *Turandot*, of which the recording remains to us.

Eugenio Gara wrote:

With his even stream of sounds and accents he can be compared only to Lauri-Volpi.[10]

That night the tenor truly offered his audience a kaleidoscopic display of his artistic achievements. The luminous power of his *squillo*, the regal sumptuousness of his phrasing, the sensual richness of his timbre, the rainbow of *sfumature* with which he illumined and colored small moments throughout the score.

The "*Nessun dorma*" carried the audience to heights of enthusiasm which nearly caused Maestro Gavazzeni to stop the orchestra. But the splendid aria was only the crowning jewel of an unforgettable performance. For my part I remember with particular admiration a moment of singular beauty, though it may have escaped most, which was a clear sign of the most minute attention to the *sfumature* in the E-flat which concludes the sentence "*O divina bellezza, o meraviglia,*" which extends well beyond the entrance of the chorus, until there is almost no voice anymore, but pure sound resembling the note of a viola, dying away to nothing but still able to fill the theater with its extreme clarity.

In the two following years Franco Corelli would never put his foot in Europe professionally, except for a brief and not totally satisfying London appearance in *Turandot*, and in a few summer sessions recording complete operas, which was rare for him.

The American engagements absorbed him totally, and not only at the Metropolitan, but in the numerous cities that were within reach of the Metropolitan Opera tour: Philadelphia, Chicago, San Francisco, Los Angeles, San Diego, Miami and New Orleans.

From the simple reading of a chronology of that period one gets the impression of intense activity, of constant moving about, abrupt shifts in repertoire. Personally, and maybe wrongly, I also get the impression, as I have already indicated, of a frustrating routine.

By way of example I have outlined the calendar of a few months of activity from January to May 1965, and I believe its significance is plain without comment:

January:	7	Turandot (Scala)
	12	Turandot (Scala)
	17	Turandot (Scala)
	29	La forza del destino (Met)
February:	1	Turandot (Met)
	6	La forza del destino (Met)
	14	Turandot (Met)
	17	La forza del destino (Met)
March:	11	Ernani (Met)
	15	Ernani (Met)
	19	Tosca (Met)
	23	Ernani (Met)
	25	Concert (St. John's Univ., New York)
	28	Aida (Met)
	31	Gala performance (Met) (Bohème, Act I; Turandot, Act III)
April:	3	Tosca (Met)
	10	Ernani (Met)
	14	La forza del destino (Philadelphia)
	20	Turandot (Boston)
	23	Aida (Boston)
	26	Tosca (Cleveland)
	29	Turandot (Cleveland)
May:	1	Aida (Cleveland)
	6	Turandot (Atlanta)
	11	Tosca (Memphis)
	22	Aida (Minneapolis)
	25	Aida (Detroit)
	29	Tosca (Detroit)

It is possible on the other hand that this very heterogenous carousel of engagements has its positive, or even, according to the point of view, its amusing side. In the first place the Met shows were exported, so to speak, prepackaged, for in the tour there were no rehearsals, which were almost traditionally hated by singers and viewed as the most tiring part of the work. And then the caravan of the Met was received with banners and streets full of flags as testimony to an enthusiasm that would be difficult for a European operagoer to imagine. The biggest problem was for the singers to escape the parties that had been organized in their honor.

For an artist such as Franco Corelli, however, known as very shy and reluctant to attend parties and celebrations, the most important quality was the warmth of the audiences which, evening after evening, would crowd the theater, and for whom the arrival of the Metropolitan represented the *musical* event of the year.

This is without doubt a typical characteristic of the American experience: the opportunity to face and to conquer audiences of all kinds.

For example, one unforgettable night in March of 1965 Corelli gave one of his first concerts—also an experience that was almost totally new for him at the time—and not in a theater but on a covered basketball court at St. John's University before an audience that was composed primarily of students, most of whom had never seen an opera in their lives.

Still he poured out one song after another, one aria after another, and the audience was conquered. According to a commentator:

> *The end of the concert was greeted by endless ovations that might never have reached such a high intensity at the end of a basketball game in which St. John's came out ahead (...) And the audience didn't want to leave, not even after the end of the official program. Finally loud voices were raised for some encore or some song on the program. Finally Corelli sang "Core 'ngrato" and gave the* coup de grâce *to his public. (...) When we left the audience was still*

there clapping and getting out of control asking for encores. Maybe he was still singing when we were already back on the campus in the dark of night. Wouldn't the old ladies who frequent the Metropolitan be jealous?[11]

In the fall of the same year Corelli landed on the West Coast of the United States, stopping first in San Francisco, then on a brief tour in L. A. and San Diego, taking the *Fanciulla del West* into its natural environment, California, for the first time.

During the tour, in an *Andrea Chénier* in L.A., the last professional meeting took place with an artist with whom he had been tied forever by a great esteem, and with whom he had shared many exhausting experiences and many successes: Ettore Bastianini. It was also one of the last stage appearances on the stage of the baritone from Siena: Bastianini would die a little less than a year afterwards on the 25th of January in 1967.

In December the success of *Fanciulla del West*, rediscovered in Philadelphia in 1964, was repeated at the Metropolitan. The critics were almost unanimous, repeating the earlier reviews almost word by word. Harold C. Schonberg, writing in "The New York Times," said:

Corelli sang beautifully with strength and color. When he is in voice he is about the best, and he was in full voice last night.[12]

The year 1966 was historic for the Metropolitan. It was the year of the move to the new, huge and extremely modern buildings in Lincoln Center. The farewell to the old Met was given in April at the end of the season with a gala concert which saw the participation of 59 artists (with Franco Corelli among them, of course, who sang the second act duet from Puccini's *Manon Lescaut* with Renata Tebaldi) and twelve maestros.

The next season opened in the new building with two

premières: the first was the official grand opening of the new theater and was, understandably, an all-American night. The *Antony and Cleopatra* of Samuel Barber was given with Leontyne Price taking the female lead. The following evening the opening of the season took place with a scintillating new production of *Gioconda*, and to interpret it, Renata Tebaldi and Franco Corelli were called upon, and were thus the first Italian artists to walk on the stage as main characters for the new Metropolitan.

The other main event of the year can be defined as business as usual, if it is possible to speak of business as usual in referring to Corelli's activities, which were being crowned with success in those years.

The only black mark, as I have already hinted, was a *Turandot* in London. Certain critics found a way to disapprove of everything, from the opera itself, to the set design, to the costumes, to the interpretation of the tenor. Harold Rosenthal panned it in *Opera* with so much efficiency as to create a reaction among his readers, from whom the magazine would be forced to publish lively letters of protest. One indignant reader wrote:

> *If we should be fortunate enough to have Mr. Corelli for future performances it would be fairer if you could find someone on your staff who appreciates his style of singing. Certainly there were many in the theatre, particularly on the last night, who had the taste (no doubt bad) to do so...*

Another reader accused the editor of the review, without mincing words, of being "prejudiced."[13]

After the performances of *Turandot* Corelli stayed in London for the recording of *Faust* with Joan Sutherland—an artistic partnership whose single result was to be the regret that it was limited only to this opera. Though sources in the press would speak of a recording project for *I puritani*, it was never realized.

After the season opening at the new Metropolitan which has already been mentioned, 1966 closed with some trips from New York to Philadelphia for *Turandot, Aida, Gioconda* again and a rare *Don Carlo.*

Though it might seem meaningless to many, there was another small episode that year which deserves mention. It wasn't a matter of small consequence, nor would it be, I feel, for the artist to whom this work is dedicated.

In the April 1966 number of *Opera* the following review was published, referring to an *Aida* that was performed in February in Miami:

> *Under the stirring yet lyrical conducting of Emerson Buckley, the cast surpassed itself vocally and entered into the dramatic proceedings with vigour and enthusiasm. In the title role Mary Curtis Verna provided melting* pianis-simi *in the Nile and Tomb scenes, matched note for note by her Radames, Franco Corelli. The tenor seems determined to master completely the magnificent voice with which nature endowed him, and he showed new artistry by taking the high B-flat at the close of* Celeste Aida *softly, as the score demands.*[14]

This is the first review in my possession that bears witness to Corelli's *smorzatura* of the B-flat in "*Celeste Aida*" in a theater. Starting from the previous year, in the recording of the complete opera, Corelli left the proof of which Giuseppe Pugliese would write:

> *The B-flat* filatissimo *to the limit of silence reached with magical graduation, which Corelli performs in the* Celeste Aida *in the discographic edition is a prodigy of which no other tenor has been capable, Fleta included.*[15]

A witness that I consider as more than reliable told me in this regard that Corelli was unsatisfied for many years with his Radames because he was not able yet to diminuendo the

B-flat as Verdi indicated.[16]

When finally he was able to give the extraordinary performance of it that Pugliese remembers in the above quotation he would be deeply disappointed once the record was put on the market by certain malign hints that the note was not genuine but artificially created in the studio.

To face the risk and perform it countless times in the theater, evening after evening, performance after performance, would be his response.

In January of 1967 Corelli went back to sing in Italy after a two-year absence. He chose two cities to which he was united by ties of special affection: Florence, where in a certain sense his career had started (and in whose favor, after the flood of the previous autumn, he had also promoted a charitable concert in Philadelphia) and Parma, the city where he was a favorite. There are those who would see in this choice a veiled conflict with La Scala. Nobody knows, of course, how much of the hypothesis is based on fact, but it is certain that the people of Parma do not dislike the idea at all.

The return to Florence with *La forza del destino* was unfortunate. Even though he had a more than logical desire to present himself at the top of his form a sudden lowering of his voice constrained Corelli to save himself while singing, and therefore the success that everyone expected didn't quite come off.

Even so, observers who were more attentive to catch what might be the evolutionary status of Corelli's vocalism in the two years of absence from Italy did not forget to note his progress.

Giorgio Gualerzi wrote:

Not all bad things come to harm us. We were present at an enterprise that demonstrated the total and absolute control of his vocal instrument on Franco Corelli's part. Except for the romanza of the third act that resulted in a deserved ovation for him, and the following duet "on the stretcher," the

*tenor from Le Marche actually sang the whole part with
attenuated volume, but with full control of the sonority
and of the breath, which allowed him to frequently display*
mezze voci, legature *and* portamenti *that were excellent from
the standpoint of taste and style.*[17]

In spite of the comfort he took in these sympathetic ac-
knowledgments Corelli was, understandably, quite upset.
However, a few days later in Parma he would have a chance
to make abundant allowances for the partial disappointment
in Florence.

At the Teatro Regio two performances of *Tosca* were expected of him, an opera which had always been one of his
war-horses. The first one was a success, foreseen and foreseeable. If the most qualified critic—and we can even give his
name, which is that of Gustavo Marchesi—reproached him
slightly, he did so with great affection and great indulgence,
because he knew that Corelli had sung *Tosca* exactly as the
people of Parma had expected him to sing it.

*Corelli waited for "E lucevan le stelle" to subdue the audi-
ence. One began to see that his rushed pronunciation in the
beginning, his lack of devotion to the middle register, and
the aim that was exclusively on the high notes were already
a prelude, a calculation of the forces he would muster for
the finale. He evened the score with excruciating detachment: he calmed the strong desires of those who have been
waiting all season long for high notes as they are supposed
to be, better, a series of high notes. He whetted their appe-
tites for the soft passages. He has demonstrated conclu-
sively the resources of an authentic vibrato. And it pleased
him to surpass himself.*[18]

It was a memorable evening, then, to repeat the headline
in the local newspaper. Still, the best was yet to come. On the
21st of January *Tosca* was performed again. Some souls might
still have been warm with the memories of the first one. The

tenor was in particularly good form. Who can say what happens in such a case? What is sure is that we were present at one of those magic nights in which the alchemy of the emotions found the formula of an explosive mix. It was enough for a spark to get free among the artists and the audience to set the theater on fire.

The warmth of that night's performance is reflected also through its surrogate, the recording. I believe that everyone passionate about opera has had at least once the experience of such a night, in which you can feel materially the current which goes in both directions between the stage and the stalls, and that on one side stimulates the singer to give himself unconditionally, and on the other pushes the audience to support him almost physically in his performance. It is a reciprocal "charge" in which the technical value of the performance, regardless of how high it is, ends by losing importance in front of the love relationship establishing itself between the artist and his audience.

As the commentator in the "Gazzetta di Parma" would note, that evening would end with *an unsurpassable personal triumph, worthy of the heroic times of operatic art.*[19]

For a long time, and uselessly, the public clamored for an encore of the "*E lucevan le stelle.*" Someone, however, saw the tenor make a sign with his hand that meant "afterward." And "afterward," in fact, when the members of the audience refused to disperse, losing their voices in the rhythmic screaming of "*Bis, Franco,*" the manager had a piano carried to the stage and Corelli sang "*Core 'ngrato,*" gaining another endless ovation.

After one more engagement in Europe, in March, for an *Andrea Chénier* performed in Lisbon to celebrate the one hundredth anniversary of the birth of Umberto Giordano, Corelli went back to his American engagements.

In the fall the official debut in what will be one of his more successful roles, at least in America, was waiting for him: Romeo in Gounod's opera, which, as we have seen, had been tried out three years before in Philadelphia.

The Metropolitan gave this debut particular care, creating a new production, and the press and even television helped to create a climate of great expectation. *Time* magazine published a long interview with the future Romeo and television invited Corelli to present a documentary on Verona—complete of course with the balcony which couldn't be excluded, a target of many tourists—and to illustrate the history of Shakespeare's two unlucky lovers.

We can well say that Corelli's Romeo alongside Mirella Freni's sweet Juliet must have been exceptional if it gained Harold D. Rosenthal's approval. The critic who had so often deplored Corelli's presumed lack of style showed British fair play, writing a review that was decisively positive in its own way.

> *...With Corelli giving one of the best performances of his career—he even [!] sang several soft mezza-voce notes and fully involved himself in the action—and with Freni singing and acting with her usual simple charm, the great love scenes and final tomb scene had much to commend them.*[20]

Roméo et Juliette was immediately "exported" to Philadelphia, Seattle, Hartford. Then in December Corelli returned to Italy in order to keep a promise made to his fans in Parma: to inaugurate the opera season with *La forza del destino*, one of the best-loved operas of the Teatro Regio audience.

At the beginning the evening threatened to be a disappointment. Corelli appeared to be in rough shape, and was perhaps a little bit tired. He had arrived from America at the last minute and had participated only in the general rehearsal—without singing, however—and two acts passed by surrounded with a certain cold atmosphere, also because of the somewhat unexciting performance of the soprano Radmila Bakocevic, fresh from other performances that had been severely criticized.

The show started to take off starting with the romanza of Don Alvaro. The performance of the tenor in the duet "on the stretcher" was lengthily applauded, and even the less easily satisfied would admit that in the duet of the third act and in the *overwhelming big duet of the fourth act, sung with the usual vocal élan and noteworthy expressive fervor, we have found again the best Corelli, fairly singled out for approval by the spectators.*[21]

In January, the success of his Florence *Carmen* was irrefutable, even if some critics would come forward with an accusation of diminished professionalism because of the tenor's decision to sing the Flower Song in Italian while the opera was performed in the original language.

Right after that Corelli went back overseas where as usual a very intense program of activity was awaiting him, in which would figure, among others, an evening performance dedicated to American Italians with a program of popular songs which, predictably, gained an enthusiastic success with the public.

In the summer another totally new experience was waiting for him. The Metropolitan launched a program called "opera in the neighborhoods," a series of performances in the form of concerts in the New York parks, in which Corelli participated with *Carmen*.

But the most important appointment was in September: the grand opening of the Metropolitan season with *Adriana Lecouvreur*, beside Renata Tebaldi.

Critics continued to insist that the opera was musically inconsistent. The audience, however, received it with great favor, also, and above all, thanks to the performances of the main characters.

Looking at them singing *Adriana* one had the sensation of attending not an opera, but "great theater" according to the testimony of one American fan.[22]

Right afterward a new production of *Tosca* that had been prepared with particular attention was mounted. Even though Cavaradossi was by now nothing new at the Metropolitan, Corelli might also have scored a personal success because, as his leading lady, Birgit Nilsson, remembers, he committed himself in a particular way from the dramatic point of view, as always happened when he was in the hands of a great director.[23]

In the following year, 1969, there was practically no event worth recording besides an unexpected renunciation of the recording session of *Forza del destino* which had been scheduled for the summer.

On the other hand it must be remembered that the 1969 season was truncated because of a union dispute early on which turned into a protracted strike. *Andrea Chénier* and *Il trovatore* had to be cancelled and they were both operas in which Corelli had been scheduled to appear.

The season opened, finally, on the 29th of December, with a few shows "from the repertoire," as it is usually put. Great events were expected for January. This was a new production of *Cavalleria rusticana* under the baton of Leonard Bernstein, a guest conductor deluxe at the Metropolitan. The stage direction was in the capable hands of Franco Zefirelli. The Santuzza was Grace Bumbry, and Franco became Turiddu on the stage of Metropolitan, his first Turiddu anywhere in six years (he had sung two performances of *Cavalleria* in 1964).

Bernstein's reading of the score, even though valuable in many aspects, was deeply criticized for the exasperating slowness of the tempi he adopted. For as much as the maestro affirmed that these were the tempi indicated by the composer, which was somewhat questionable because if I'm not mistaken the Siciliana, for instance, gives no metronomic indication— and because of the *staccati* employed by Mascagni himself when he conducted a recorded performance. As one critic pointed out:

> *A lapse of taste was committed in the name of musicological exactness.*[24]

From the performers' point of view the problem was not only a matter of taste. The prolongation of the performance by ten minutes above the usual performance time not only served to reduce a great part of the tension of the score (the toast, in particular, acquired a slowness that was downright ridiculous) but to phrase meaningfully the singers were forced to employ abnormal and exhausting *fiati*.

Corelli, who took that evening's engagement very much to heart, perhaps in part because he was going back to the stage for the first time after a compulsory break of several months, was more worried than usual. It seemed at one point that he wanted to cancel, but then he decided to go onstage. Or better, offstage, where he sang a splendid Siciliana, but so slow that the next day a New York newspaper would publish a caricature of Franco Corelli passed out on the harp, destroyed by effort. And maybe this is not so far away from the truth...

To compensate for this, the critics were unanimous: Corelli had returned to the Met in great shape and had given an enthusiastic interpretation, vocally as well as dramatically.

This clamorous success marked the beginning of what can be defined without fear of contradiction as a year of grace for Franco Corelli. In some aspects, at least according to my personal judgment, it may have been the most illustrious year of his career.

And not so much because of extraordinary events that were taking place. We will have to wait another year for the debut in *Werther*, even though I consider this a necessary part, or better, a culmination of this splendid period, because it is the moment at which the three key elements of his art were combined—that is, vocal, artistic and (above all) technical maturity—to reach an ideal coexistence.

After a few years in which one could perceive now and then, at least through recordings, almost a sense of fatigue and even a certain "opacity" of the voice (but with important exceptions: for example I remember the splendid *Forza del destino* at the Metropolitan in 1968) in this period Corelli returned to the top of his form.

Italian audiences and critics soon realized this, when, in the summer, he made a triumphant reappearance: first in

Macerata with *Turandot*, then right afterward in the Verona Arena after nine years of absence.

When most people were waiting (or afraid, according to the point of view) for who knows what signs of the bad influences of the long American experience, or maybe for some warning sign of decline, Corelli sang for the first time in his native region. Happily, however, this authentic "prophet in his country," unlike the one in the adage, was received in a royal way.

A few days afterwards he was in the arena with the *Carmen* of his debut, and it was—to give the fullest idea of it as quickly as possibly—a *Carmen* that was described by Rodolfo Celletti one year later with a single but effective word: *blazing*.[25]

In that *Carmen*, which would have, among other things, a very troubled premiere, beset by rain and full of various incidents (including a horse that fell into the orchestra and a mad cat that ran between Don José's feet right at the moment that he was trying to settle his problems with Carmen) Italy rediscovered Franco Corelli.

It was a return which the tenor had feared as much or more than a debut because the public remembered, judged, compared and wasn't always (or better, was almost never) ready to be benevolent. But of benevolence there was no need at all. What prevailed was enthusiasm.

The critics, for once unanimous, used up their entire store of adjectives: "resounding," "in the best form ever," "extremely happy return," "in superb voice," "overwhelming intensity," "absolutely unforgettable" are only some of the responses hastily collected from the many.

The Corelli phenomenon explodes, after twenty years of career, was the title of Giorgio Gualerzi's commentary.[26]

Rodolfo Celletti would dedicate a very pointed criticism to this *Carmen*, yet one that was, in spite of some small note on the level of taste, extremely flattering:

I haven't heard Franco Corelli in person for a long time. He is in beautiful shape. The timbre has become more shiny. The sound is steadier. The singing is more smooth and clear. Corelli's Don José has received a clamorous success. It is a character that is extraordinary in many aspects, today more complete than yesterday in histrionic terms. He has the defect, in my opinion, of being, up until the Flower Song, too beautiful, too much of a cavalry officer. He doesn't have any mark of the man predestined to tragedy, nor any symptoms of ravenous and hallucinated passions. You would never expect anything from his love of Carmen but casual affairs, drunkenness, gambling debts, and to top it off, a hot check. Then the Flower Song, articulated in vivid tone colors and passionate sighs, takes us in medias res. *Corelli's* filatura *on the B-flat of the* "caro odor" *precisely captures the sense of sensual ecstasy. (...) He is still better at the finale of the third act. His* "Mia tu sei" *has, vocally and dramatically, a titanic vehemence. Things like that have never before been seen and heard.*[27]

After the eventful premiere the repeat performances carried on with regularity, but with the same success. During these, on the fourth to be precise, an episode took place revealing unprecedented kindness, according to the press. At the end of the second act a big bunch of flowers was given to Corelli who, among other things, had received an ovation after the romanza which was computed to have lasted seven minutes. While the audience kept applauding, the tenor spotted his partner of many great *Carmens*—Giulietta Simionato—in one of the first box seats. Impulsively he walked down from the stage (although it is probably not exact to state that he leapt over the orchestra pit, as it was reported in the newspaper. Even very fit athletes have their limits), and gave the flowers to his colleague.

The public applauded the gesture, but what escaped it, because it took place in the discreet, reserved way typical of Corelli, was an even kinder gesture. Fearing that his impulsive tribute had wounded the sensibilities of his partner in that evening's *Carmen*, Adriana Lazzarini, the tenor would later have a big bunch of roses delivered to her dressing room.[28]

On the wave of these successes Corelli's popularity in Italy saw a sudden revival. Articles in the tabloids, a long interview on the radio produced by Rodolfo Celletti and Giorgio Gualerzi, and a special on television (even though it was broadcast, as happens nowadays for music programs, late at night. There is nothing new under the TV sun.).

It was a happy resumption of contacts that had been lost or broken for a few years, and one that he would maintain until his career was over, coming back, even if not frequently, rather regularly, at least to Verona and Macerata.

The great return to Europe was another important and very happy occasion in October. There was a *Don Carlo* in Vienna with an absolutely exceptional cast: the extremely sweet and sad Elisabetta of Gundula Janowitz, the splendid Eboli of Shirley Verrett, who was making her Staatsoper debut a triumph, and the regal Philip II of Nicolai Ghiaurov (even though his Philip was diminished a little bit by the stage director's gimmick of making him sing his great aria in a nightgown), and of course Franco Corelli in the title role. In his long review in *Opera* Joseph Wechsberg wrote:

> For the first time in many years I felt that the opera was rightly called Don Carlos.[29]

Such a comment, it is worth noting, was meaningfully similar to what, thirty years afterward, would be said in the review of the live compact disc, published in 1990.

> In an opera in which it is often right that the tenor is missing, Corelli imposes himself as an authentic main character: a fascinating, romantic figure, wavering between heroism and desperate collapse. Corelli perfectly expresses this condition with his voice, which was robust, but at the

*same time capable of expressing what he felt within. Surely
his is a Don Carlo that has never been seen before (...) for
the features that have been sculpted with burning intensity
as well as for the overwhelming élan of the tenor.*[30]

Corelli finished his European tour with performances in
Belgrade in December. On the first of January he was back to
the Metropolitan with *Ernani*, and three days later, what could
have been a great event, but instead was only a bit of a mystery,
was his debut in the part of Edgardo in *Lucia di Lammermoor*.

Starting with the previous summer, during his stay in Italy,
Corelli had announced that he was about to debut in *Lucia*
and *Werther*, and the news was received favorably by at least
one faction among the critics.

*We will have, finally, an Edgardo which will return to the
tradition of Duprez and of Tamagno*, wrote Giorgio
Gualerzi, and about Werther he stated that it was a character with which *moving in the wake of his mentor Lauri-
Volpi and of Pertile, he is destined to offer an interpretation
clearly more dramatic than the version, weakened, ex-
hausted in its vocal affectation, that was Anselmi's, then
later through Macnez, Schipa and Tagliavini, has carried
over to Alva and Kraus in our day.*[31]

Some pages hence we will have occasion to consider
Werther at length. Here I only want to observe that it was a
real shame that after these interesting preliminary remarks,
not one Italian critic, as far as I can tell, made the effort to go
and listen to him in a live performance, and therefore to write
about his Werther, whether favorably or unfavorably, with
direct knowledge.

But let's return to *Lucia di Lammermoor*. Curiously this
Corelli debut came and went rather quietly, as *Bohème* had
done some time ago. This particular production of *Lucia* had
been mounted for the first time the preceding autumn with a
cast including Renata Scotto and Luciano Pavarotti, and had

already had numerous performances in October and November. When it was resumed in the beginning of 1971 Corelli simply took over the role of Edgardo in January and sang one performance. The next performance was scheduled for the 21st, and at the time the tenor was giving a regular performance of *Andrea Chénier* on the 14th and *Ernani* on the 16th.

On the evening of the 21st of January he sang the first act of *Lucia,* then went to conductor Carlo Franci's dressing room and told him that he didn't feel like continuing.[32] John Alexander sang the cover for the rest of the night, and he never interpreted the role of Edgardo again.

This was, in a few words, the history of Corelli's *Lucia di Lammermoor* from beginning to end. Few people know it, and Maestro Franci himself, when I questioned him, was not very sure that the tenor had sung at least one whole performance. Luckily we have the recording for verification. Even fewer people know that there was almost a sequel. Only "almost," however, since the Italian public missed the chance to enjoy Corelli's Edgardo.

The events can be pieced together as follows: Dr. Negri, general manager of the Teatro Regio of Parma, was in the audience for a performance of *Lucia* at the Arena Sferisterio in Macerata when the scheduled Edgardo had to forfeit the performance. Dr. Negri tried to get Corelli, who was also in the audience, to substitute for the ailing tenor. He was very close to accepting, but in the meantime the artistic directors had found a substitute, and the occasion vanished.[33]

The recording of the one performance doesn't help too much in explaining the enigma. True, some uncertainties might suggest the idea of insufficient preparation. This is Maestro Franci's opinion. But such a small thing only deepens the mystery, as we are here talking about a professional, Franco Corelli, who was known to be careful and methodical to a fault. Nonetheless, in my opinion, it is also certain that we had before us, a least potentially, a great Edgardo, an Edgardo who was *supremely manly and romantic*, as can be read in the only criticism that I have been able to find, a brief history of the interpretations of the opera signed by Giandonato Crico.[34]

Of course it is clearly almost impossible to judge Corelli's interpretation by only one performance. But if it is true that he *had a basic affinity with certain characters, marked by an intimate and irreparable melancholy,*[35] it is also sure that Edgardo, romantic hero par excellence, destined from the start to succomb to a contrary fate, among the ruins of his castles and the graves of his ancestors, was really "his" character.

It is an Edgardo who imposes the strength of his personality from the first lines. "*Sulla tomba che rinserra*" is incisive singing in the best Corelli manner, though perhaps a small tension is perceptible from the beginning of "*Veranno a te sull'aure*," but then, in the most dramatic moments of the opera, in the surge of "*Chi me frena in tal momento*," to the furor of "*Ah, vi sperda!*" and in the painful abandonment (and the exquisite phrasing) of "*Tombe degli avi miei*" and of "*Tu che a Dio spiegasti l'ali*," it's all a textbook of how to sing, besides being—as can be judged only from listening—an acting class as well.

Less than a month afterwards Corelli's debut in a new production of *Werther* was scheduled, to which *Opera News* dedicated ample space, as well as a beautiful cover. But not everyone was convinced by the following statement attributed to Rudolf Bing: "In Franco Corelli and Christa Ludwig we have finally found singers perfect for the revival of the Massenet opera."

At the premiere, word had it that there would be an actual demonstration of dissent organized by a group of faithful supporters of another tenor who "specialized in the role," and would have preferred that the opera had been given to their favorite.

Whether or not there was truth in the rumor it was made inconsequential when it was announced that Corelli, indisposed, would be replaced in that evening performance by the Italian-American Enrico Di Giuseppe.

On the 27th of February, the date of the second performance, everything proceeded in a regular way, and Franco

Corelli's Werther was a revelation.

Grace Bumbry, a spectator that evening, retained a most vivid memory of her emotion and of the enthusiasm of the audience.

> *People were carrying on, and they were screaming, and waving, and shouting like mad. I had never seen a demonstration like that before. I knew that Franco had an enormous following of fans, but to experience it was like being in another world. But they were right, because Franco was a great Werther.*[36]

And not only did the spectators allow themselves to be carried away with enthusiasm, even those in the know, professional critics dutifully attending the performance, were not far behind.

> *You were standing as if fascinated in front of a Werther who had Corelli's elegance and physical beauty. Of course this was theater that was dedicated to operatic sentiments, but this was fully realized opera theater, hinging as it did on the physical and vocal gifts of Corelli and Ludwig, and on their vibrant sensitivity,* wrote Antonino Fedele, describing the finale of the third act, *the most beautiful, passionate scene that has been lived on the stage of the Metropolitan. All the duets and all the soliloquies of the main character, in which he trusts himself with nature, with the beloved and with God,* the critic goes on to say, *have put in clear light Corelli's most natural and fascinating vocation. Seen with all the lines and accents of lyricism created in the heart of the enraptured artist, almost possessed with the drama, the love, the language, the deadly abandonment of the young Werther. Corelli was no doubt the "homo novus" in the circle of interpreters of the character of Goethe, recreated with a modern melodramatic profile. A certain tension that will disappear with time doesn't spoil the suggestive power of his characterization.*[37]

And if, by chance, some would like to accuse the Italian critic of a certain partisanship, to confirm his enthusiasm there is the perennially discontented British critic, as concise and detached as ever, and in this case unequivocal:

Corelli so handsomely looks the desperate romantic poet and sings with such sensual conviction that, for my part, I am almost ready to overlook his Italianate French and occasional stiffness as an actor.[38] So wrote Herbert Weinstock after having attended one of the last *Werther*s of the season.

As I have already pointed out, Italian critics, at least so far as I can find out, were largely absent from this debut. And the explanation, it seems to me, is to be found in a sentence of Rodolfo Celletti published in June, 1971—that is, when Corelli had already sung *Werther*, and his interpretation had become public property.

Even if he would come to give us an excellent Werther he would never make us able to forget what he has done in a few rediscoveries of historical importance and what he keeps doing in the realm of a certain gallant, romantico-veristic repertoire.[39]

I believe what Celletti has written here partakes of the sacrosanct, however discomforting, truth. This is a deep truth which reveals a widespread attitude, a mentality which encloses artists in a given repertoire and limits them to predetermined roles that a certain number of wise men insist are the only ones congenial to their voices and/or temperaments. When something else comes out of them, there are only two possible reactions: either the mandarins will scream "scandal" or they will totally refuse to acknowledge him.

This is not of course a matter of forgetting any part of what an artist has done, but rather one of welcoming and judging his choice of repertoire with a mind free of preconceptions.

Corelli didn't give us an "excellent" Werther; he gave us a *great* Werther, but in Italy nobody realized it except for the very few—and these were not critics, because in general the critics, especially the famous ones, rarely leave their comfortable armchairs—who heard him with their own ears. And I will mention, among Italian spectators who were enthusiastic about his Werther, or moved by it, thanks to his very felicitous combination of vocal mastery and virile passion: Renata Tebaldi, Michelangelo Veltri, Carlo Franci. I will also mention Anita Cerquetti, who heard only the romanza, and on the radio, at that, and remained astonished by it.[40]

Surely, Corelli's Werther imposes an effort that most people are rarely prepared to make, and that is to listen without preconditioned expectations.

The Italian tradition—that has grown up only because it was imposed by an artist as great as Tito Schipa—has consigned to us an absurdly dreamy Werther, which is to say, a Werther sexually neutered. And this is a key to the reading that contrasts profoundly both with the literary source of the character (the Werther of Goethe) and with both the text of the libretto and the musical writing of the opera. It is not by chance that in France (and not only in France) Werther has always been considered a part for a lirico-spinto tenor. [Albert Lance, for example. Ed.]

On the contrary, Werther is a character with an extraordinary range of nuances, whose complexity starts in the musical writing alone which, far from being "sweetened," underlines his states of soul and psychological nuances now with very delicate pianissimi in the strings and woodwinds, now with the overwhelming sound of the full orchestra (as, for example, in the finale of the first act, in the phrase "*Un autre, son époux*"). In this specific case Corelli's splendidly flexible voice follows it and accedes to it point by point and note by note.

Werther is a character whose basic characteristic is sensuality, or perhaps it would be more exact to say the conflict between his sensuality, meant in the larger sense of a compelling need to participate in life, as the opening invocation to nature suggests, and the abstract idealism of the poet.

Even without going back to Goethe the text of the original libretto* reveals unambiguous physicality, and I daresay even carnality in certain phrases: "*Je donnerais ma vie pour garder à jamais ses yeux, ce front charmant, cette bouche adorable,*" is Werther's first declaration of love; "*C'est moi, c'est moi qu'elle pouvait aimer! (...) tout mon corps en frissonne,*" he screams in his desperate jealousy after the wedding of Charlotte. "*Oui, je mentais!... je mentais!...*" he answers himself with anguish, after having asked himself if really his love for Charlotte was as chaste as he would like to believe, and to make others believe. "*Charlotte, tu fremiras!*" he cruelly writes to her in his letter; and the final, passionate finale of the third act certainly was not written to suggest the image of a dreaming Werther.

But this is not the only way in which Corelli's Werther is profoundly innovative, if not revolutionary.

Maybe for the first time we find here a character that is not, as traditionally believed, a "loser." The suicide of Werther is not a giving up, it is not a declaration of defeat. It is in the best tradition, as is obvious, of the literary romanticism of which Werther is the precursor and the prototype: a very clear act of self-affirmation, the deliberate choice of freeing himself from the dictates of passion to decide his own life—and his own death. And I hear echoes in the death of Werther, words of another character of Goethe which has been translated into music: the Faust of Gounod, who also reached the decision to

---

*The Italian text is often marred by an inappropriate translation (or perhaps one that has been intentionally expurgated). For instance, in the sentence, "*Je donnerais ma vie pour garder à jamais ces yeux, ce front charmant, cette bouche adorable, étonnée et ravie, sans que nul à son tour les contemple un moment!*" (I would give my life to keep these eyes forever, and this beautiful brow, this adorable mouth, surprised and carried away, so that no one after me would be able to contemplate it for a moment!) But in the Italian libretto the verb *custodire*, to keep, becomes *mirare*, to look at, totally changing the jealousy and possessiveness expressed in the sentence. And in "*tout mon corps en frissonne*" (my entire body thrills with it) the word "*essere*" (being) is substituted for the word "*corpo*" (body), which is absolutely not the same thing. And many more examples could be given.

kill himself before Mephistopheles offered him a second chance at youth and life. *"Je suis, avec ce breuvage, le seul maître de mon destin."* (With this potion I am the only master of my destiny.)

All this is in Corelli's Werther, and in no other among the versions that I know, and I nourish the hope that one of the recordings that are circulating only in the private and limited universe of the collector could be transferred to a commercial recording which would offer his Italian audience the chance to judge him directly.

For my part, to all people who would be curious to hear it, I would permit myself a small warning. Corelli's Werther can be liked or not liked, correspond or not correspond to the image everyone has of the character. You can accept it or refuse it, and this depends on individual taste and sensitivity. The true mistake would be to compare it to a previous one, to judge it on the basis of similarity or lack of similarity to one of the great Werthers of the past or present. This is not Schipa's delicate moonlit Werther, it's not Kraus's, vocally perfect and emotionally frigid: this is the burning Werther of Franco Corelli.

In the summer Corelli finally succeeded, thanks to his old friend and fellow student Carlo Perucci, artistic director in Macerata, in bringing to Italy what he would sometimes affirm to be the character dearest to him: Rodolfo. In the preparation of these performances of *Bohème* he committed himself with so much enthusiasm that his partner, Luisa Maragliano, believed for some time that it was his absolute debut in the opera.[41]

It was, instead, a challenge: to himself, to his public, to diffidence and prejudice, to the tenacious cliché, so commonplace, of an anemic and cold Rodolfo, who was maybe a little too sweet. To this Corelli really did prepare himself with the fastidiousness and humility of a debut artist. Raoul Grassilli, who was having his first experiences as an opera director, was rather worried at the idea of directing a *monstre sacré* who was likely to be convinced that he knew it all. Instead, to his great surprise, he found himself face to face with an artist who was not only anxious to collaborate, but to learn.[42]

With such a start to things obviously the show had a great success when it went to the stage. *A splendid* Bohème *with Corelli at the top of his form,* was the headline in a local paper. And the review offers a description from which can be discerned, besides admiration, perhaps a trace of stupefaction.

> *This was a magnificent Rodolfo, both on the vocal level (and who could doubt of it) and on the level of dramatic interpretation, as the character was led with intelligence and good taste from the easygoing beginning in the attic of dreams and youthful chimeras to the desperate finale. Throughout the whole performance there was a wise and measured control of vocal emissions: admirably contained in the moments of pure lyricism, generously offered in the pages where the poetry became drama.*[43]

On the fact that the tenor is in great shape from a vocal point of view the critics were unanimous. On his interpretation of Rodolfo, on the other hand, besides reviews that were more than merely positive (...*a Roldolfo that absolutely cannot be equaled, seductive onstage and capable of great vocal splendors,* wrote Mario Pasi, for example)[44], several reservations were put forth.

> *The tenor wasn't able to hide the uneasiness caused by the fact that his voice and stage presence didn't suit the petit bourgeois character created by Puccini. But class tells, and his was enough for him to turn in a third act of peculiar dramatic importance, with bursts of blinding vocal bravura,* wrote Giorgio Gualerzi in *Discoteca.*[45] And in his review as correspondent for *Opera* he would expressly cite the *magnificent smorzatura* of the phrase "alla stagion dei fior."[46]

Beyond these praises, though, remains the feeling that there was a certain incompatibility between the interpreter and the character, and this judgment requires clarification.

Corelli's *voice and stage presence* would be, as we have seen, absolutely unsuited to the creation of a *petit bourgeois character*.

Yet I believe that in these very words the reason for a mistake lies revealed. To qualify Rodolfo as a petit bourgeois character is a contradiction in terms. Loosely defined petit bourgeois indicates a figure in society who is petty, grasping, with a closed mind, clinging to the security of a modest, steady income, sheltered from the unforeseen; in a word, the exact opposite of a bohemian. In this sense there is only one petit bourgeois in Puccini's *Bohème*, and this is Benois, the landlord, who is not by chance teased and ridiculed by his tenants, who are always behind in the rent.

Besides, the condition of bohemian is not permanent in society. Either the bohemian dies of starvation or he goes back to the ranks of small-salaried workers, or he makes a career. Corelli's Rodolfo is clearly a bohemian of the last type, destined to have a career. Better yet, he is a bohemian who gives the clear impression that the statement *"ho un zio milionario"* is not braggadocio at all but the pure truth.

I have heard his Rodolfo castigated for not being brazen enough or devil-may-care. Maybe so, but just because of this, Corelli's interpretation gives me the clear impression at times of a bohemian life looked at with detachment. I can almost perceive the flavor of a story that is not being lived in the present, of a memory of far-off days of youth, days that are being revisited with mixed feelings of tenderness and regret by a bohemian who has become in reality what he has always been in his soul: a *gran signore*, a lord.

I recognize that this is a very personal point of view, but I'm comforted by the thought that a few people who do know Franco Corelli very well haven't rejected it at all. On the contrary one of these persons made the following observation, more or less: "I have always thought that Franco's Rodolfo was too much of a lord, but now that I look at him from this point of view I understand why."

In the fall after a concert tour in Germany Corelli left for his first tour in the Far East, a tour where the word "triumph" can be used without the slightest risk of overstatement. The five concerts in Tokyo, in various theaters that were always packed, represented an unforgettable event for the Japanese public. It was also broadcast on television.

Interest was even livelier in Seoul, where fans rarely had the opportunity to hear a great Western tenor. A Korean critic even went to Japan to listen to Corelli in advance and pass the news to his countrymen. I have the good luck to possess this article thanks to the patient love of the person who preserved it with many others over the years, and kindly passed it to me. It is extremely interesting.

The author begins the review describing the impatience of the public awaiting Corelli. Then a tall, beautiful, wide-shouldered man with straight long legs came in, moving with elegance. As explained to me by the very kind Korean soprano who translated the article, this feature of Corelli's physique received particular attention in the Orient, especially by Oriental women, who usually have rather short legs.

But in the article there is much more than this first sketch of innocent admiration. It is obvious that the person writing was a person of great competence and also great sensitivity.

In the first aria the voice sounded somewhat cold, still, with a long note in the middle register coming across as uncertain, and even the attitude was a little bit shy. The tenor warmed up after the second piece. It is a voice with a beautiful timbre and great volume which fascinated the public. He has an incredible, surprising legato, and I was shocked by the fiati.[47]

It seems appropriate to point out one more interesting fact: in another of these Korean articles, written by a singer who had studied in Italy, and had heard Corelli several times at La Scala, one can find, besides the rather exact stress given to his flexibility, to his capacity for *smorzature* and phrasing, also one of the most concise and useful definitions of his voice: *a lirico-spinto tenor voice, with, however, a way of singing— the style, we would say—of a dramatic tenor.*[48]

In December Corelli returned to Europe, to Belgrade. There was a general agreement with the Teatro Regio of Parma that he would eventually insert, between one engagement and another, a performance in the city where he was always welcomed with great affection. The occasion presented itself after the premiere of *Norma* which opened the season in Parma. The cast that night were all more or less sick, and the tenor Pier Miranda Ferraro, was even replaced during the performance.

At this point Dr. Negri decided to play his card. He called Milan, where Corelli had just come back from Yugoslavia. He explained the problem to him. With some surprise on the part of the superintendent the tenor offered immediately to go to Parma.

Of course the result was taken for granted, even though the performance was preceded only by some rushed rehearsals with piano. Some attacks were not exactly correct, but it was not enough to dampen the audience's enthusiasm, for whom Corelli's presence had the value of a Christmas gift. Indeed, a weekly magazine carried the title *Gesù bambino ha portato un tenore!*[49] [Baby Jesus has brought us a tenor! (In Italy Baby Jesus brings the gifts.) Tr.]

This episode, even more than a success, should probably be defined as a celebration in the sense that for the people of Parma Corelli's presence was more important than his actual performance. If so, it was a real pity, for I believe that this, the last Pollione of Corelli's career, was a Pollione of the greatest importance.

In comparison with the previous recordings (from way back in 1958) this one clearly displays, as perhaps on only a handful of other occasions, the full measure of the extraordinary vocal and artistic evolution of the tenor, without losing the strength and virility the character has acquired in vocal and psychological refinement. It was a Pollione that had been filtered and enriched by his lyric repertoire, a Pollione that had gone through Rodolfo and Werther, and for these reasons was more than unique.

The festive evening in Parma closed an intense year, and as we have seen, a very important one.

The following year, 1972, would not see events that were so exciting in the same way. The most relevant from the point of view of the Italian public would be Corelli's return to Verona once again to open the summer season with the first preparation of *Ernani* in the history of the Arena.

This was a version that was abbreviated because of a sudden storm in the middle of the final trio. Critical comments were mixed.The set design and stage direction were appreciated by some, criticized by others, as always happens when there is a judgment of taste to be made.

Even among the company of singers the criticism was divided, though the positive evaluations, above all of Corelli's performance, clearly prevailed.

Franco Corelli once again offers us the "beautiful gloomy man" of Victor Hugo. Twelve years after the incredible debut at La Scala, he has kept himself as high in public esteem as he ever was, above all with a fourth act of extremely high vocal and expressive accomplishment, wrote Giorgio Gualerzi.[50]

And Mario Messinis concluded a discourse begun in a negative key *("He has abused all the nineteenth century poses (...) multiplying the breaks and sighs with every bar, his fermate, his held notes, extending to the limits of the credible")* with an explicit enough recognition, even if only regarding the vocal aspect:

Certainly the tenor has refined his vocal material, and suc-

ceeded in resolving on a technical level the "enigma" of performing Ernani, *having recourse to a type of vocalism and emission of proto-Romantic origin, with the result that he is offering us a heroic character, but at the same time, not forgetting the whole bel canto tradition, so that the sound is never violently attacked.*[51]

These favorable comments were shared also by Lorenzo Arruga:

The leading man was Franco Corelli, that is to say, the most intense tenor voice that one could hope to hear, where the fullness of the timbre and magisterial behavior together express force and romantic pathos...[52]

but they were totally contradicted by the following harsh criticism, which I report only because impartiality is my duty:

A curious performance for a Verdi tenor; with vulgar, open, irritating emissions.[53]

This last response reopens the problem of the different "readings" of critics, already mentioned many times, and not worth the trouble of further discussion.

For my part, after listening to the recording of three of the performances I believe I can express the opinion that one heard in that *Ernani* a Corelli who had his ups and downs, and was not at the top of his form. The voice, especially in the cabaletta at the beginning, always seemed a little forced, often opaque, and the diction was unusually approximate. But the situation improved clearly with each succeeding opera.

In the meantime let it be said in advance that I haven't heard him multiplying his "breaks" nor his "sighs." In the duet of the second act (*"Ah, morir potessi adesso con te Elvira sul mio petto"*) the *mezze voci* and exquisite *filature* (perhaps these are the "nineteenth-century affectations" deprecated by Mario Messinis—that I am obstinate in appreciating so much) hark back to Corelli at his best, as does the invective "*Oro, quant'oro ogni avido*," and of course the always great last act, about which I fully share the opinion of Giorgio Gualerzi which has already been cited.

In the same season Corelli also sang two high-voltage performances of *Aida* at the Verona Arena, where he scored his usual success with the public. (I refer to the one on Ferragosto day, as August 15th is called in Italy, and one immediately afterward.)

Back in America, after a few performances of *Aida* and *Roméo et Juliette* at the Metropolitan, a long tour of concerts with Renata Tebaldi was scheduled for a great number of American cities.

They were welcomed in an enthusiastic way, even on a social level. Local luminaries and, above all, their wives, were in competition to organize beautiful parties and receptions. The Tebaldi-Corelli duo was a winning formula that would be exported in the following years to Europe and the Far East, always with great success.

Meanwhile between 1972 and 1973 Corelli made the film of *Andrea Chénier* for RAI which we mentioned earlier.

Uncertain at first about the validity of this kind of operation, the tenor ended up convincing himself that television was a valid way to bring opera to the public, and a much bigger public than the one which regularly attended performances in opera theaters.

From the theatrical point of view it was deplorable that for lack of production facilities the stage which supposed to have been "outside" was instead rudely enclosed in a few square meters of studio space. But the most important aspect of the operation was the way Corelli was offered to the great Italian audience. The opera was broadcast in May of 1973, and many were very surprised by it—not only by the unchanged physical aspect of the tenor almost twenty years after his first appearances on TV, but most of all by the technical metamorphosis of his vocalism which only the few who had followed his rare appearances in Italy up to that moment could appreciate.[54]

During the winter and the spring Corelli fully resumed the operatic activity which had been suspended the previous fall in order to make room for the concert tour mentioned above. In April and in May he participated, as usual, in the Metropolitan Opera tour, and on that occasion made his last debut, as Macduff in *Macbeth*.

It was a choice that really appeared to be haphazard, since Macduff is most certainly not the leading role. *I couldn't believe that he would sing Macduff*—so spoke the American fan whose testimony has already been quoted in these pages, who had been following him closely throughout his career. *Even so, he sang it, and with a magnificent result. Macduff, naturally, has only one great scene and aria and Franco got the most out of it.*[55]

This was practically the same opinion expressed, even in the same words, by the professional critic.

Franco Corelli has to be commended for his willingness to accept the ungrateful role of Macduff, which qualifies him as a real trooper, for it offered him only one aria of any consequence. He made the most of that, however, and elsewhere he provided fine presence and solid contribution to ensembles.

So wrote a commentator from Minneapolis, where Corelli sang the third and last performance of Macbeth.[56]

The leading lady of those performances remembers Corelli's presence with a feeling that comes very close to gratitude.

I am so glad he sang Macduff, because Macbeth *really needs an important tenor like that. I know the role is beneath him, because he is too important a tenor, but it gave such an injection to the performance to hear that voice! His aria is the only right moment, the only positive moment in the whole opera. Maybe the Banco aria, too, but it is not the same kind of positiveness. Everything else is gloomy in the whole opera, it is murder and remorse, and then finally you hear this moment of hope, this moment of beauty, this moment of sunlight. I think the importance of Franco's voice was needed, and he is the only important singer I know who had the nerve to sing that part onstage. I think it was a plus for Franco, to his glory.*[57]

After concluding a very intense opera season in June, Corelli resumed his concert activity with Renata Tebaldi, first of all in the United States, and then after a short break, in Europe, in London. In October he left for a second and longer tour of the Far East, still with Tebaldi.

The two artists would perform in Manila where Imelda Marcos would arrange a royal welcome for them, then in various Japanese cities, and lastly in Seoul and Hong Kong, presenting with constant and repeated success an extensive program of songs, arias and duets.

The following year the most noteworthy event, at least in the beginning, was the return to *Turandot*, which had been missing from Corelli's repertory from the time of his debut four years ago in Macerata. And that summer the tenor would also take another of the key operas in his repertoire to Macerata: *Carmen*.

It would be a rather strange *Carmen*—bilingual. It was performed in Italian, but the title character, Grace Bumbry, was much more at ease with the French words.

The public success of *Carmen* was equal to expectations. The critics put forth some reservations, judging that Corelli had lost his concentration somewhat, especially in the first part of the opera. But in the more dramatic moments they rediscovered the tenor they knew:

Then, bless him, with suggestive phrasing and strength of accent he proceeded with a display of fiati and sonorous pathos to underline the dramatic crescendo of Don José.[58]

Corelli returned to the Metropolitan in September with a long series of *Turandot*s, punctuated by some performances of *Roméo et Juliette*.

Still with *Roméo*, in the following January, he was at Miami, and in the spring he took *Roméo* together with *Bohème* on the Metropolitan tour. In the beginning of the summer he sang three performances of the Puccini opera in a Met tour of Japan.

In July he was expected once again in Verona in the Arena, and certainly at the moment no one could imagine that this would be his last return, his last great "season opener."

Corelli went back to the Arena with *Carmen*, an opera that had always given him, all over the world, and maybe in a very special way in Verona's amphitheater, many satisfactions and many triumphs. On this occasion as well an audience of more than twenty thousand people welcomed him evening after evening with the usual warmth.

> *After the Flower Song, where he spun out the notes* (filando), *the audience exploded. There was a long ovation, endless, which resounded from the orchestra up the terraced seats* ... These were the words of Ettore Mo in the "Corriere della sera" right after the premiere.[59]

Listening to the various extant recordings (we are by now in the period of miniaturization, and the fans go to the theater loaded with devices that are getting easier and easier to hide) we find evidence not only of a magisterial performance of the aria, but also the usual, vibrant, involving generosity in the dramatic crescendo of the two last acts.

The conclusion of the season at the Arena for Corelli was partially troubled by an accident, as trivial as it was annoying. During the last performance of *Carmen*, in the scene full of action that concludes the first act, the tenor received a strong blow to the ribs because of the excessive enthusiasm of a chorister which left him with a painful thoracic contusion.

In spite of it Corelli decided to still honor his engagement to sing two performances of *Turandot* (the first of which on the Ferragosto evening) *in order not to disappoint the great*

audience of the Arena which was expecting him, as was officially announced over the loudspeakers before the show.

Anyone who knows what is physically required of an opera singer (or who simply knows how difficult it is only speaking or moving with rib pain) will be surprised after hearing
the recordings of that night to find that, despite his compro-
mised physical condition, Corelli was vocally committed as
ever. He allowed himself no "discounts." He didn't even give
up the famous optional high C in the phrase "*Ti voglio ardente
d'amor*" which, after Lauri-Volpi, he had been the first to re-
discover.

Physically improved he would then sing one performance
the following week, incidentally without getting paid, joining
a venture launched by a few colleagues to call attention to the
increased costs the Enti Lirici had to sustain.

All in all Corelli's Arena season, in spite of the little accident, was not only a popular success, but a critical one as well.

His interpretation of Don José in particular was reviewed
very favorably. Paolo Isotta spoke of the *generous, intrepid
virility of the singing* and of *a refulgent tenor squillo that was
fascinating*,[60] and Luigi Rossi found that the flower aria had
been *miniaturized and refined*, and remembered the *high interpretive temperatures of the last acts*,[61] and similar appre-
ciations were expressed by Rodolfo Celletti and Lorenzo
Arruga.[62]

Meanwhile, during Corelli's stay in Italy the possibility
was also aired of his much-awaited return to La Scala the
following spring, regarding which some press sources claimed
he had already signed a contract.

In the fall Corelli went back to the Metropolitan where a
very important commitment was awaiting him in one of his
most acclaimed and representative roles: Pollione in *Norma*,
perhaps the only great interpretation of his repertoire (excluding, of course, the so-called "re-exhumations") that he had
never taken to the stage of American theaters.

Here the regret of "not being there" may be greater than for other occasions because we don't have available even the consolation of a recording, and the only thing you can do is envy those who were present and who refer to a scintillating general rehearsal.

It was at this point, on this happy note, vocally speaking, that something happened which, judged superficially, seems impossible to explain. After the general rehearsal Corelli canceled the show, and not only that, but canceled a series of ensuing engagements.

Here only Corelli himself is capable of clarifying what happened, and I will quote his comments later on. Still, the phenomenon could be defined, though imprecisely, as a sudden, unexpected nervous breakdown. Such a thing was certainly not a unique occurrence in our stressful world, especially in the upper reaches of the opera world where the stars came and went.

History knows of many important examples of such behavior (one commonly quoted is that of Rosa Ponselle), and for the rest I have personally heard famous artists who ended their careers far too much in advance, relate the cause of their leaving the stage to a certain moment when they were overtaken by an inability to sustain the emotions and tensions of performance, making it difficult sometimes merely to stand upon a stage.

It is not therefore incomprehensible that such a thing would befall an artist who had faced so many engagements and met so many challenges as Franco Corelli. "It's not the voice that I'm missing," he himself would declare later in an interview. "It is that I don't have any more of that peace, tranquility, and strength that is necessary to sustain the emotions of the show."[63]

Today, analyzing the memories of that period he deepened his explanation still more. "Maybe I had taken my career too seriously, I had given too much."

The conquest of the high register, the choice of repertoire that was so diverse in its demands—and sometimes almost "unexplored"—the obstinacy, finally, to challenge himself continuously, studying as already mentioned on a piano that was tuned a half-note high (when Maestro Gavazzeni went once to put his hands to it he was horrified at the risk) had ended by having an influence on the nervous force of the artist.

At the moment he felt the need to give himself a break, and the need above all to get back to some of the simple aspects of life that his professionalism had forced him to give up.

To stop his theatrical activity for some time meant that he would have the chance to recover what he had largely lost in the moment that he had chosen a career that required so much commitment: his freedom.

It was almost a discovery: to live like anybody else, without a schedule. To go out even in bad weather. To see the sun instead of always working at night. It seemed almost too beautiful to be true.

Thus, little by little, the period of three months of rest which had been scheduled at the beginning was extended, and the decision to go back to the theater was put off.

Corelli would reappear in Italy in June, but not to sing, rather to participate in a night in honor of Giacomo Lauri-Volpi in Busseto, within the framework of a celebration to mark the seventy-fifth anniversary of the death of Verdi.

The resumption of theatrical activity was scheduled for the summer with two performances of *Bohème* at Torre del Lago. But it isn't easy for any artist to resume contact with an audience after a long break. As Grace Bumbry relates:

I even called him to urge him not to extend his absence. I knew from personal experience that the longer you stay away from the theater, the more returning becomes a source of tension. To me it still happens when I go on vacation. After two months I almost don't have any courage left to take the stage![64]

In fact, upon his arrival in Torre del Lago, where he was expected by so many admirers who were passionately awaiting the rare occasion of hearing him again in Italy, Corelli declared that he didn't feel like singing.

To renounce or not to renounce a performance is a difficult decision. Probably the urging and advice that was coming to him on all sides didn't help him to make it. The hour of the beginning of the opera had passed for a long time when finally Corelli, in order not to create embarrassment for the organizers of the show, decided to go on.

Another, perhaps, would have tried to survive, to conclude the evening with the least fatigue and the least risk possible. Franco didn't. The recording is ample proof that he wasn't capable of stealing from the audience what they had the right to expect. He was there to sing, and as usual, he committed himself to give the maximum that he could, to attend to the least nuances of a phrase, particularly in matters of interpretation.

I have in my ear, for instance, Rodolfo's phrase in the second act. In Corelli's interpretation this becomes a full visual picture of the character: strong, bold, perhaps a little cocky at the beginning (*"perché son io il poeta"*), then bringing in tender nuances with the delicate mezza voce of the conclusion (*"essa la poesia"*).

In the first bars the artist is rather stiff, and one can perceive it. He starts to loosen up when the real singing starts. At the expense of being accused of heresy I here affirm that the *"Che gelida manina"* heard that night, from the standpoint of phrasing, was one of the most beautiful ever heard, with a rainbow of color, a lesson on how to interpret with deep sensitivity, with an intimate coherence between text and music, instead of merely singing the notes, as so many singers are content to do with that page of music. And my judgment is not modified by the fact that a certain tension appears here and there, shortening some *fiati* and slightly compromising in a few spots the usual, extremely musical fluidity of the singing.

With the obstacle of the aria overcome the tenor became more and more self-confident. The audience was warmly applauding the passionate phrases of the duet with Marcello, first, and then the one with Mimi in the third act, and, of course, in the finale, which the artist infused with an intense, painful involvement which would genuinely touch the hearts of those who heard him.

The present difficulty appeared, therefore, to have been overcome. Three evenings later he would sing a second great performance. In September, after the usual period of rest that he allowed himself in Cortina, he would continue to study and vocalize as always.

Still, freedom—and the peace he had tasted in the previous months—was a very strong temptation. Again he postponed the start of artistic activity.

Months passed by, almost without his knowing. Gradually, in spite of the passionate expectations of his fans and his own purposes, his silence was prolonged.

Sparks in the Night

FOUR LONG YEARS OF SILENCE.
In spite of great pressure Franco Corelli did not go back to singing in public. He almost didn't appear in public, as if he wanted his contacts with the theatrical world to be interrupted for good.

In 1979, the year following the death of Lauri-Volpi, he was seen again in Italy, at Reggio Emilia, where he was, rightfully, the first recipient of the prize dedicated to the memory of the deceased tenor.

But not even on this occasion did Corelli sing. The audience had to be satisfied to applaud the many beautiful recordings that turned the meeting into a concert. Then, all of a sudden, in the long dark parenthesis of silence, there was a spark. In June 1980, thanks to the insistence of Lucia Hines, wife of the American basso, organizer of the yearly ball of the New Jersey State Opera, Corelli consented to sing two songs during the traditional celebration organized to sustain the theater financially.

As Jerome Hines described it

The result was a joyous pandemonium when the audience heard the Franco Corelli of many years ago, with all the beauty and power of his voice unchanged. Hines continued: *The evening after the ball I reached the tour of the Met*

in Boston. The news spread very fast and the manager wel-
comed me with a fervent prayer: "How can we have him
back?"[1]

Apparently the supplication fell into the void. But the idea
had been broached and the intention of making a return had
begun to define itself. During the summer, while he was staying in Italy, Corelli gave a few interviews that appeared in the
newspaper under promising headlines. For example: *Franco
Corelli: The fear is gone, I will go back to singing*, appeared
above a four-column article in the "Corriere d'informazione."[2]

In another interview he declared that he had held a concert in Berlin in the last few days, and had scheduled another
one in America for a specific date, the 14th of November,
besides a tour on the West Coast.[3]

In reality, at least for as much as we have been able to
verify (it's possible, naturally, that some concert escaped our
research) almost another year would pass before Corelli would
reappear in public. In compensation, however, this time it
appeared that he was making an authentic comeback.

His great colleague Carlo Bergonzi may have provided
crucial encouragement at this stage when he expressed the
opinion that Corelli was in exceptionally good voice. In any
case, as he had announced in Italy, Corelli agreed to take part
in some concerts.

The 25th of April in 1981 he was expected in Newark, a
few steps from Manhattan, on the opposite side of the Hudson
River, to participate in a concert in honor of Licia Albanese
and Jerome Hines, for the support given by the two artists to
financing the theater. On the stage, one after another, appeared
Klara Barlow, Ferruccio Tagliavini, Virginia Zeani, Nicola
Rossi Lemeni, besides one of the persons being feted, Jerome
Hines. But it was the second part of the concert which created
the biggest expectations, even if few dared to hope that it would
really take place.

Robert Connolly described what took place for *Opera*
magazine:

The orchestra was reshuffled, a piano rolled out onto the stage, and Corelli finally came out, still handsome, slimmer than before, and nervous as a cat. Scheduled to sing three Italian songs with orchestral accompaniment, he began with "Pecché" by Pennino and the audience held its breath. He began tentatively and, if there was somewhat less velvet on the cords than 20 years ago, sounded infinitely more secure than the Corelli of ten years ago. This was followed by "L'ultima canzone" and "O marenariello." By this time his confidence was coming back, the clarion tones were pouring out easily, and the largely Italian audience was going mad. The transformation was amazing—a bit like watching one of those stop-camera films in which we see a flower unfold in fifteen seconds. He then proceeded to give five encores, each one freer and more exciting than the last, accompanied sympathetically at the piano by Alfredo Silipigni. It can hardly be said that he caressed the songs, or that he delved deeply into their essence. No—this was a time for testing his high notes, which is what Corelli has always felt his fans expect from him. He went up only to high B-flats, but they were big, secure, sustained and thrilling. Running out of encores, he ended the evening by repeating "L'ultima canzone," singing it better than before. All in all, then, whatever one's reservations, Corelli still produces the biggest, most vibrant and most exciting tenor sound today.[4]

After this unforgettable night, in which it is difficult to say which was the bigger emotion—the public's for having found intact a voice it had given up hope of hearing again, or the artist's for having succeeded in breaking the ice and getting back in contact with the warmth and love of his audience—the intention of coming back probably became even more concrete.

In July of that year, still in Newark, the concert that would mark Corelli's official, definitive comeback was put together.

The extremely demanding program seems to confirm this

impression. Some opera arias had been added to the usual Neapolitan songs and concert arias, and the night's crowning glory was nothing less than the death of Otello, "*Niun mi tema.*"

Corelli started with élan, full of energy, with "*Ch'ella mi creda*" from *Fanciulla del West* and carried on with the beautiful aria from Massenet's *Le Cid*: "*Ô souverain, ô juge, ô père.*" It was a very delicate piece that required above all an intimate sweetness. There we found once again, unchanged, the great Corelli, with *smorzature* and *mezze voci*, which were comparable in every respect to those of fifteen years before.

But, as I said, the focal point of the evening was the death of Otello. It was a choice that could not but give the impression of a challenge, but perhaps challenge is not the right word. It was a moment of self-affirmation, a demonstration more for himself than for his public. To us it was a brief glimpse, a brief blazing glimpse, of the Otello we could have had, but alas, did not.

As always happened in his career, the artist "grew" perceptibly through the course of the evening. Some of his *fiati* were slightly shorter than those which we had become used to hearing but were compensated in a grand way by incredible *smorzature*. There were phrases, for example in the song "*Occhi di fata,*" where the immutable perfection forced us, literally, to hold our breath.

Toward the end of the concert there were also some small concessions to all those among the audience, as would be observed by the correspondent for *Opera* in the review quoted above, who were waiting mostly for the high notes. This time, too, Corelli went no higher than the B-flat, but in "*Mamma mia che vo' sa'é*" and in "*Core 'ngrato,*" that beautifully rounded out the evening. These were two notes so powerful and refulgent that the audience was driven to a frenzy.

At this point it seemed like a *fait accompli*. It was obvious to everybody that the tenor's voice would allow him to return to the stage without difficulty, at least on a concert level, and of course, there was not a theater that wasn't ready to open its doors to him.

Instead the silence would descend again—forever.

Do we have to regret what happened to him?

I've heard many admirers protest that the two concerts in Newark had only been two meteors, two sparks in the night. I've heard them say that singing as he had sung on those occasions Corelli could have given us so much more, for years.

It's true, without doubt. Listening to recordings of those concerts, hearing a voice so beautiful and powerful, so surprisingly intact, one cannot avoid sharing these regrets.

Still, I'm not in complete agreement with such a view.

There is a sentence of Enrico Caruso's that I once heard from Corelli, too, in almost the same words, and I am convinced that it is not by chance that two artists of their stature felt the same kind of self-respect and the same respect for the public:

A great artist ought to have the dignity to say farewell to his public when still in full possession of his powers, and never let the world apprise him of his falling off.[5]

I believe that those who admire Franco Corelli should be grateful to him to have left us the way he did. To have saved himself, and us, a few months or years later, the humiliation of applauding out of sympathy, the sad shake of the head, the sighing as we would remember better times.

Instead he left us, once again, enchanted by his voice. He left us—please allow me to steal the beautiful words of a great writer—*emptied and changed and sad as every great emotion can leave us.*[6]

And of this, as for all the wealth of joys and emotions that his art has given me, I am profoundly grateful to him.

One Page Before the End

PARMA, 24TH OF DECEMBER, 1988. In the newspaper on the page devoted to local news an article appeared almost hidden between the photograph of a meeting, an announcement for a show of paintings, an advertisement for home accessories and a note about the parking plan established by the city hall.

The importance given to the news is modest, but the headline is sensational: *Corelli sings in the church of the Cappuccini* (Capuchins).

The text is brief, but it is enough to awaken the incredulous enthusiasm of the fans.

> *Franco Corelli, the great tenor who said farewell to the stage fifteen years ago* [in reality only twelve. Ed.] *comes back to sing tonight in the church of the Capuchin friars in the piazzale Rondani. The singer has complied with the invitation of a few friends who wished him to sing the Ave Maria of Schubert at the midnight mass with the accompaniment of a violin quintet and of the "Ildebrando Pizzetti" chorus, directed by Maestro Adolfo Tanzi.*[1]

The report that Corelli had consented to sing at the midnight mass was correct. Probably, though, it was not destined for the press but should have stayed within a small circle of friends. Once it had appeared in the paper, reinforced by a picture and interview, the news spread very quickly, even in surrounding towns. As a result, on Christmas night the little church was crowded in an incredible way. There were people coming all the way from Mantua, defying ice and fog, lining up as they would for an opera house, and crowding the aisles of the convent and even the choir stalls behind the altar to such an extent that at one point the celebrant, with a thin "Capuchinesque" spirit that reminds me of Manzoni, expressed the hope that the crowd intended to hear the religious service as well.

The expectations would not be fulfilled. Corelli participated in the mass but he did not sing. The audience was forced to go away disappointed, having missed the chance of participating in what any fan would not have hesitated to call a "historical event."

In referring to the episode a few days afterwards the "Gazzetta di Parma" also quoted a statement from the tenor.[2] "A slight indisposition deprived me of my confidence, so that it somehow didn't seem right for me to sing. I am really sorry. I hope there will be another chance."

So did all those who still rallied around him after twelve years of retirement from the stage and seventeen years of absence from Parma (at least in a professional sense, since Corelli felt at home in Parma as in no other Italian city)—in fact they were exalted by the prospect of being able to hear his voice again.

Would there be another occasion? That would depend entirely on him. The audience would not lose hope so easily.

Which explains why this is only the last page but one of his career—why I want to finish with an opening to the future. Though only a few lines above I wrote of my gratitude for the timing of his retirement, I would be grateful to him in the same way for the inestimable joy of hearing him again.

I hope that, as in the line from Dante, "The long study and the great love" will be enough to gain me the reader's understanding and forgiveness for this inconsistency.

Lost Chances

THERE IS A GHOST WHICH SURROUNDS the career of Franco Corelli, a ghost which will keep appearing for many years in a punctual, periodic rhythm, in the pages of the newspapers, that still materializes nowadays almost every time people talk about him with critics, colleagues, or fans: the ghost of Otello.

The first consistent rumors about *Otello* appeared in the press exactly at the moment that it was most logical to expect them, which was in the first place right after the historic revival of *Gli Ugonotti* and in the second, after the tenor's definitive Middle-European consecration in the historic first-ever performance of Verdi's *Trovatore* in the land of Mozart.

When, after the success in Salzburg in 1962, Corelli sang *Trovatore* for the second time in the following year with Von Karajan, and recorded with him a state-of-the-art edition of *Carmen* in Vienna, word began to make the rounds in Vienna that the great conductor would have declared himself very happy to direct him in *Otello* if he would decide to take on the title role.

In its caution this formulation almost looks like a signal, a message slipped to Corelli in a diplomatic way to check his intentions.

Anyway, if it was a signal, for the moment it fell on deaf ears. Almost three more years would pass before a small article of two lines would appear in *Opera* announcing that Franco Corelli was studying the part of Otello, to debut at the end of 1966.[1]

And in truth, *Otello* was spoken of quite frequently in 1966, and the tenor may have come closest to a decision about it then. Newspapers reported that he had asked advice of Gino Cervi, and had even gone to Laurence Olivier in London when articles and public discussion about Olivier's film portrayal of Othello coincided with Corelli's month-long stay there to sing *Turandot* and record *Faust*. Word had it the renowned English actor was available to take charge of the stage direction of Verdi's opera—if he could have Corelli as a main character.

Instead time went by and the decision kept on being postponed. Two years later, in 1968, it was announced almost officially that Franco Corelli and Mirella Freni would be the principals of an *Otello* in Salzburg under Von Karajan

The Salzburg *Otello* would actually come to pass, and Mirella Freni would be the leading lady, but Jon Vickers took the title role.

Still, expectations were undimmed. If anything they were mounting.

At the Metropolitan Rudolf Bing was particularly insistent that the tenor give him *Otello* as a gift before he left his position as general manager, but he would retire in 1972 without being able to show off that very desirable flower in the buttonhole. (Could there have been a more fitting send-off, a better way to cap the career of a brilliant man of the theater like Rudolf Bing than a Corelli *Otello*?) Bing would only have, almost as a consolation prize, the duet from the first act which Corelli would sing with Teresa Zylis-Gara at the farewell concert in his honor.

In Italy the expectation was no less alive. The symptoms could be discerned when the magazine *Discoteca* began the feature called: "You make the interview," which offered the public the opportunity to pose questions of their favorite artists. Of the eight readers whose questions were chosen for the Franco Corelli interview, all of six made reference to *Otello*.[2]

Without doubt, since the seventies began quite happpily for him, as we have seen, that would have been the perfect time to take his career to what everybody seemed to feel would be its culminating glory.

Both from a vocal and an artistic point of view it was obvious, at least from the sidelines, that the tenor was more than ready for the great commitment and high dramatic content offered by the role of the Moor. This is proved, even if in an entirely different repertoire by the extraordinary account he gave of Werther—also from a dramatic point of view—which has already been amply documented for us by those who witnessed it.

Renata Tebaldi has no hesitation in comparing the intensity of his Werther interpretation with what Corelli had made his audiences expect of him in the last act of *Carmen*.[3] Nor is it entirely fortuitous, as we see it, though it might appear a fleeting comparison at first sight, that a critic (perhaps someone without a very great name, but not for this reason any less acute) compares *the imploring and lost and bloody plea of Don José* in the fourth act of *Carmen* to the *despairing, incisive and dire last music of Otello*. A few lines further on he defines Bizet's character as Corelli's *most complete, most congenial, most mature and in a word, his greatest interpretation*.[4]

Don José, Werther, Otello. The roles are vocally demanding in very different ways, but are perhaps of equal psychological and dramatic intensity. The first was completely realized and interiorized down to the smallest nuance over the course of his whole career. The second was tackled for only a year, with less than twenty-five performances in all, but it was created in the artist's full maturity, sketched in all its facets, then constantly refined from the first to the last performance. As for the third, he studied it, courted it, feared it and maybe never totally understood it, but he made it his own in an intimate way... and therefore never took it to the stage.

For that matter, Franco Corelli wasn't the only great tenor

who lost the opportunity to sing *Otello*. Two great artists keep him good company in that regard, Enrico Caruso and Beniamino Gigli. Perhaps, at least in part, this was so for the same reason. They were too great. Too great to gamble a whole career by playing one wrong card in the attempt to perform it.

Perhaps it isn't too risky to formulate the hypothesis that in facing *Otello* Corelli had in mind the experience of Giacomo Lauri-Volpi. His was a different Otello, anti-conformist, in many noteworthy aspects, such as his refusal to perpetuate the cliché of the cruel savage who was not understood or appreciated.

Still, the excessive expectation that surrounded Corelli's hypothetical *Otello* with the passing years may have become the main reason that the performance was never realized. Because, at that point, the risk *was* too high, the Corelli's Otello could not have found a tepid welcome or mixed reviews. It had "to be" a historic Otello or "not to be" at all, to borrow from another problematical Shakespearian character.

Today everybody, or almost everybody, is of one mind in believing that, had it come to pass, this would have been a historic Otello. Curiously, however, or perhaps not too curiously, all or nearly all of those I have asked about it imagine the character in a very similar way and describe him with nearly the same words: an Otello with extraordinary vocal power, but more lyric, more introspective, more interior, with more profound psychological delineation. The "more" in the above comparison obviously has to refer to the last great Otello of our times, Mario Del Monaco.

There are those who say that Corelli was afraid of this comparison. Even if this is true, to say today that he had nothing to fear is much too easy. Who could say such a thing with full knowledge of the competition he faced twenty or twenty-five years ago?

Anyhow, doubtless Corelli's scruples were excessive, and the hard-to-satisfy professionalism was at the bottom of the "great refusal." For years he kept the score on his piano, and for years he repeated, even in response to offers only to commercially record the opera, his feeling that he wasn't "ready." "Otello is the ultimate achievement in a tenor's career. You must do it well or not do it at all," he declared in an interview in 1973.⁵ He would continue to repeat this statement until it was too late.

Meanwhile, as I indicated above, at the crucial moment of his artistic maturity Werther appeared unexpectedly. It appeared to take the place of Otello, one might say, as the ghost of Banquo occupies the throne of Macbeth.

Why did he take on the role? More important, was he taking something that didn't belong to him?

After having thought really quite a lot about the problem, and taken into consideration all the countless elements that make a judgment extremely complex, I believe that I can answer this last question: no. And for the simple reason that I have found an answer for the question "Why Werther and not Otello?" This answer will probably appear excessively simple to many, or to others insufficiently documented. I am putting it forward therefore as a hypothesis, and even more as a feeling: because Corelli, man and artist, *is* much more Werther than Otello.

Otello is not, in any case, the only character missing from the repertory of Franco Corelli. On the contrary, I can say that each person I have asked about the matter has some personal regrets: it might even be possible to make a sort of "hit parade" of his lost opportunities.

A few are operatic characters that Franco Corelli did take into consideration in reality, in various ways at various times in his career. Of those where a press announcement was made of these roles as coming attractions it is possible to cite *I puritani*, which was said to be coming soon, after *Faust*, a record that was made with Joan Sutherland; a *Rigoletto* that was even supposed to become a movie; then *William Tell*, which was offered to him, it seems, by La Scala; then *I vespri siciliani*, with which the tenor was invited to open the new

Teatro Regio di Torino in 1973 (though he would refuse).

Above all in the list of regrets, second only to Otello, was the Des Grieux of Puccini, which by the way Corelli himself would define as one of the most beautiful roles for a tenor, regretting never having had the chance to sing it.[6] (But there are even those who regret the Des Grieux of Massenet. "Think of the seduction scene in the third act!" I was told, for example, by Jeannette Pilou, who made of Massenet's Manon one of her most completely realized characterizations.) And there are those who speak of Lohengrin and even of Tannhäuser (among them Birgit Nilsson, of course), and those who, doubtless according to personal taste, or the way they have of "feeling" Corelli's voice, think of the Riccardo of *Un ballo in maschera*, of Samson, of Mercadante's *Bravo*, or of the Meyerbeer roles of Vasco da Gama in *L'africaine* and Robert le Diable.

It is a long list in which admiration, affection, memories and imagination all play their role in putting together a perfect picture of the ideal character, the more perfect and the more ideal, the more impossible to realize.

My personal regret, perhaps a small one in light of some of the other figures on the list, is Paolo, in Zandonai's *Francesca da Rimini*. Corelli has left us a recording of a splendid duet with Renata Tebaldi that is more than sufficient proof that Paolo deserves to be added to the select company who should have been called and brought to life but live on only in our dreams.

PART THREE

Emotions

*"There is no other tenor of modern times whose voice
sounds as vibrant.
Every single note carries with it a
white-hot emotion."*

ALAN RICH

To Perform While Singing

All of us, including old Adriano Belli, who was then the president of the Centro Sperimentale di Spoleto, when we saw him appearing in the last act, and in the final scene of that great masterpiece that is Carmen, *said to each other: "This is not only a great singer, but a great actor. Which, especially in the category of tenor, is saying a lot. And he has always kept these characteristics."*

THESE ARE THE WORDS of Giuseppe Pugliese, pronounced in one of his critical summations of the career and of the art of Franco Corelli, during the already mentioned televised transmission of the series *I grandi della lirica*, which was dedicated to the tenor in 1983. Moreover, these words, far from being new or unheard of, are a summary of everything the Venetian critic has had to say over many years on this particular aspect of Corelli's art: his interpretation, not only with his voice, but by dramatic means.

It's an evaluation, however, that isn't universally shared, even though it is by no means isolated. On the contrary, the topic of interpretation is one of the most controversial on a critical level. Giuseppe Pugliese sees in Corelli from the first moment an instinctive, surprising ability to act. Others are of a very different, and sometimes opposite, opinion. The gamut runs from those who define him as *"monocorde"* ("Johnny-one-note") and static, to those who find him too agitated, too much of a show-off, or even vulgar, to those who note a gap between the expressiveness of his voice and a certain scenic coldness, to those who see in him simply a serious professional who, without being an extraordinary actor, moves onstage with competence and precision.

Someone who is accustomed to reading such reviews quickly stops being surprised by all these differences of opinion. Even less will such a person be surprised, then, when the review concerns an aspect in which individual taste plays a predominant part.

It is easy to affirm that such and such an artist is or is not a certain character depending on the fact that his interpretation or the timbre of his voice corresponds—or does not correspond—to our mental image of the character himself. Professional critics certainly do not escape this weakness. What is less acceptable, let it be said very clearly, is that the professional very often indulges in the practice of presenting his personal taste as an Aristotelian truth... even at the cost, sometimes, of risking a fall into ridicule.

Thus it is possible while discussing Franco Corelli's voice to arrive at the judgment—and to the tell the truth I am citing an extreme case, and as far as I can tell, one that is unique in its absurdity—that *the fundamental quality of the sound is far away from glowing or possessing luminous* squillo.[1]

And it was once again, without doubt, a judgment of taste that induced Rodolfo Celletti to state on several occasions that Corelli's voice lacked sensuality, that his tone was too cold for love songs.

True, this has been an opinion shared only by a few, according to what I have been able to discover (and I would like to stress that accepting or rejecting it does not depend on the listener's sex), but it is as respectable as any other, because the judgment of sensuality—in the same way and more as that of what constitutes beauty—is entirely linked not only to the taste and sensitivity of each one of us, but to a complex of reactions that are quite subtle and difficult to define, to a deep affinity that either exists or doesn't exist, that one cannot impose on himself or others in any sense whatsoever.

With these preliminary remarks it should not be too surprising if we find ourselves trying to reconcile opinions that are not only different but clearly opposite. I have already had occasion to mention some of them in another chapter of this book. Here I will quote only four more by way of illustration. If I had to mention all that I gathered there would be an encyclopedia to compile.

I chose on purpose two pairs of critics, one Italian and the other American, to prove, among other things, a small corollary that follows an old saying, which is no less true for being old, that "all the world is a village."

Here, therefore, are two reviews of the *Tosca* performed at the Metropolitan in January of 1962. The newspapers are respectively "The New York Times" and the "New York Journal-American," and both carry the date of January 29th.

Mr. Corelli returned with what seemed like more girth, but no lessening of beauty and power in his voice. There are probably no finer tenor voices around today. In his two big arias and the "Vittoria!" scene he held on to notes long enough to displease the musical purists and to kindle the voice buffs. For a long time after "E lucevan le stelle" it was doubtful whether the performance could continue without an encore, the audience response was so vehement. But Kurt Adler, who conducted, was able to go on eventually without violating tradition. Mr. Corelli deserves credit for singing the rest of the part straight enough and responding actively to what was going on around him. His shudder just before he fell dead was a nice little touch.[2]

The lack of artistry demonstrated in the third act suggested that Mr. Corelli is too much a law unto himself. Interpretation of text can mean little to him (...) His present manner of singing becomes most distressing, wonderful though the voice is.[3]

The two reviews that follow refer instead to the *Trovatore* which was performed at the Rome Opera in March of 1963.

Franco Corelli has reached today what should be the target of every singing artist: to bring his voice into harmony with musical spirits, to bend the physical vibration to the expressive animation.[4]

Franco Corelli (we say this for the use of all those who love this kind of interpretation) appeared to be in beautiful shape. It's a pity that in the sfumati *he is equal to absolutely zero, and onstage he overacts in a comic way that fifty years ago would have been judged antiquated.*[5]

Here an elementary, basic truth becomes obvious without further comment: there are critics (as there are, for that matter, spectators) who like Corelli and others who do not. But it is rather curious to note that there are also more complicated cases of preconceived hostilities, sometimes even quite venomous, even though they too are not without internal contradictions, that in my opinion deserve to be read from the psychoanalytic point of view, so evident is the contrast between the charm exerted by the artist and the refusal to submit to it.

Thus is it innocently written in a review of *Andrea Chénier* that

One feels ashamed to confess to falling for all those scoops and sobs, and all that heart-throb passion...[6]

While another reviewer seems really to want to exorcise a perverse attraction:

And now let's come to Franco Corelli, that perpetual, fasci-

nating enigma, that volcano of talent used badly, in an absurd way, magnetic, exasperating, a creation of pure, insolent imagination. From the throat of Corelli things came out the other night that are simply out of the reach of any other living tenor. There was in his stage presence a vibrant ease, animal-like, that could sometimes almost be exchanged for acting.

At this point the review is practically a long pan (in order to explain the talent that was badly used) with particular insistence on a series of vocal defects that can be defined only as deplorable, foremost among them "disgusting diction."[7] The last comment, particularly, upon which the critic often insists, leaves me a little bit perplexed, to tell the truth, having to do as it does with the judgment of an American critic of an Italian artist's diction when he is singing in his own language.

On the other hand, this case is no different than the one quoted from the memoir of Rudolf Bing as an example of preconceived hostility against an artist:

Take Franco Corelli, one of the outstanding talents of our time. Of course, he has some faults, but I for one think his Werther was an outstanding theatrical performance. He is the incarnation of opera—this fantastic-looking fellow who sings like that, a special timbre, a soft sound, without apparent effort. From the moment he stepped on the stage, he was the Romantic poet. One critic tore him to pieces time after time, complaining particularly about his French diction—when I know that the man doesn't speak a word of French himself.[8]

Leaving these extreme cases aside, however instructive they might be, we are still faced with the problem of arriving at a sufficiently precise judgment of Franco Corelli's art when it comes to interpretation and the dramatic and pictorial creation of a character. If at the beginning of my research I had thought that having never seen him onstage would be an insurmountable handicap I am now not so sure about it. Of course a direct experience would allow me to express a personal opinion, but it would be an opinion, obviously, of no more value than anyone else's—and I have seen and heard so many contrasting opinions that mine wouldn't make much of a difference one way or the other.

I have therefore held as valid another more analytic method of judgment. I consulted as many written reviews as possible, I asked colleagues, orchestra conductors, simple spectators, and I watched the little that exists on video, and only as a last resource I searched my memory for impressions that were really personal: the memory that was very clear and indestructible, even after 34 years, of the televised *Carmen*, and the other, more blurred, of the *Trovatore* broadcast a few years after. In all honesty I believe that I have reached a balanced conclusion, still in the realm of what constitutes my own taste, of course.

The turning point, the thread which led to my conclusion, is to be found in a sentence Corelli himself offered during an interview which was broadcast by local radio during his American concert tour with Renata Tebaldi in December, 1972.

The interviewer asked the two artists, among others, a question that was totally foreseeable, maybe even obvious: which roles did they prefer to sing?

Renata Tebaldi answered first, mentioning Adriana, Tosca, Violetta, Desdemona. Corelli's answer was not nearly so straightforward:

I don't know, he began. *It depends on how I feel on a given night. You don't have to think that I sing every night with my heart. I don't always sing with my heart, sometimes I only sing for the voice. If one night I don't feel very well I only take care of the voice, the vocal emission. But on the evenings when I feel well I sing with my heart, and maybe on that night I would like to sing an opera in which there is a beautiful phrase, beautiful as a sentiment, not only vocally.*

The interviewer insisted that Corelli give her a name, a title, and Corelli for his part insisted on refusing to give her one.

I don't know, because all operas are full of beautiful moments. You see, one opera gives you success because of some beautiful high notes that literally tear the applause from the audience, and another because there are some beautiful arias that an audience loves. I don't know because I don't have a favorite opera.

The journalist at this point started to suggest—and, parenthetically, I believe her suggestion very indicative of preferences of the American public regarding Corelli's repertoire at that time—Werther, Romeo...

"I don't know," Corelli repeated. "It depends on how I feel that night."

"But you can't go and say to the impresario that night that you feel romantic and you want to sing *Werther* instead of *Aida*," Tebaldi put in, in a practical spirit. And Corelli interrupted her: "That's my problem."

Thus the interview concluded and the question, in appearance so simple, did not receive an answer.

I feel this short exchange is deeply revealing when compared to the many opinions that I have gathered, and my conclusion is as follows: it is not possible to arrive at an absolute, unequivocal definition of Franco Corelli as an actor. Without doubt his main worry—and his main expressive means—was the voice. His dramatic expression was in second place, and more subject to variation from evening to evening and role to role, though it was always on a high professional level.

Dramatic commitment, of course, is bound to vary in quality and quantity from one portrayal to the next. The accusation of being static onstage would have been—was, because it was made often enough—ridiculous when referring to characters like Calaf or Pollione, who by their nature required hieratic, statuesque presence. Of course such a presence would have become absurd in an interpretation of Don José, for example, or Rodolfo.

Corelli's high professionalism came through in this area the way it did in all other aspects of his work, as we are able to affirm from the unanimous opinions of his colleagues: above all others, Magda Olivero, a superb actress as we all know, who must have been demanding, and who remembers always to have found Corelli, punctually, "where he had to be," even in the famous *Adriana Lecouvreur* in Naples that went to the stage before the two artists had ever sung it together, even in rehearsal.[9]

If there is a problem it concerns when and in what measure Corelli can be defined, dramatically, as the "great actor" that the audience of Spoleto saw in him at the time of his debut. And this, as he says himself in the interview that I have reported above, depends: it depends first of all if, on a particular night, he is more or less worried about the condition of his voice. It depends on various other factors that are, to start with, accurate stage directions and an adequate number of rehearsals; then, a soul-felt affinity with the psychology of a given character; his concentration; the atmosphere of the theater; the response of the public.

To be a great singing actor means that at a certain point an artist's emotional involvement has to be sufficient to conquer worries about the voice which are always present. Then the greatest Don José is born—the greatest Dick Johnson, Cavaradossi, Loris, Werther, Romeo: transcendent interpretations that are never forgotten.

But the achievement of this ideal contact between voice and character is not always easy, or even possible. It depends on many very subtle nuances that influence an artist's performance—and are particularly important with a hypersensitive artist like Corelli.

On the other hand, can one be a great artist without being hypersensitive? I don't believe so. At the most you can acquire an unexceptionable technique and become a mechanical nightingale. It is a species which is not rare in the opera world, but it is not the species to which Franco Corelli belongs.

He belongs to quite another species—and school—different in every way.

Some years before the end of his career Corelli stated in an interview:

> *Rossini said the most important quality for an opera singer was "voice, voice, voice," like a machine. But what made Caruso's voice special is that heart that nobody else ever had. His heart was bigger than his voice, full of the sun of Naples, but filled with* tristesse, *too.*[9]

I do not intend to make an annoying and sterile comparison in these pages that would anyhow necessarily be superficial. But I want to stress that Franco Corelli had no reason at all to envy his great predecessor the fullness of sentiment that appears from the color, the timbre, the very essence of his voice.

It is something that many—very many (and I have already remembered what Maestro Gavazzeni told me regarding Corelli's Manrico and his Turiddu) have recognized and still recognize in him.

I will mention here only a few:[11]

> *In the singing of Corelli you can perceive (and it is very beautiful) something faintly fearful that makes his expression very human and warm.*

> *What makes Don José his greatest interpretation is that sense of very deep, almost tragic melancholy, that completeness of expression in the rage, in the crying, in the imploring, that in the last two acts reaches unsurpassable heights.*

> *It is not easy to explain what is so strange and pleasing about his voice. Certainly it is not only a sound effect, for as much as it is enjoyable and exceptional it is all, and most of all, something that is united to the powerful tone and noteworthy range, and the palpitation of warm, felt, and*

suffered interiority.

The ideal royal couple of Birgit Nilsson and Franco Corelli has been reconstituted: always rivals for power and splendor, they are now equal even in interpretive strength, and globally in the characters they have created, and in certain moments of revelatory enchantment: the arcane melancholy and the depth of his phrases, opening fully then closing far away: "All'alba morirò..." Or the violence, bright and hard as a diamond, that fades into breathless emotion in her phrase, "So il tuo nome."

A voice that is still beautiful, full of harmonies and mysterious in its unmistakable old-time color and a sense of loss that captures your soul.

The typical melancholy color of his voice, now more flexible, has drawn a tonal picture, more primal than the purely theatrical one, that is absolutely unforgettable.

Nothing that I could add could give a more precise image of the art of Franco Corelli than these comments which, more than critical remarks, appear to be—and are, and simply have to be—palpitations of emotion.

There is much more in his art. There is the foundation of a rare technique, there is the control of the volume of the emission in every note in his entire vocal range, there is the extraordinary homogeneity of the timbre in all the registers; there is the blazing squillo and the smorzatura to the edge of silence. But, beyond the technique—*through* the technique but in an emotional dimension that transcends it—there is the *heart*. The violence, the rage, the pride, the sweetness, the jealousy, the passion. There are all the characters, all true, all different, all intensely lived.

And there are, for those who listen to him, so many unforgettable moments, so many different and equally intense emotions.

PART FOUR

Within the Tenor

*"His daily nourishment consisted of
the uncertainties, the painful, everlasting questions,
the obsession with the sounds,
the perennially suffered dissatisfaction,
the severity and the cruel sincerity with which
he judged himself."*

GIUSEPPE PUGLIESE

Humility

In this way I ensured that the nineteenth-century school did not die. I left it as a legacy to someone who keeps practising it with humility and perseverance.

THIS SENTENCE (which by now has almost become "historic") was written by Giacomo Lauri-Volpi concerning Franco Corelli at the end of a letter to Rome music critic Pietro Caputo, dated April 14, 1965. In that same letter, as Caputo himself remembers, "he talked at length about Corelli and his magnificent vocal organ, which, thanks to the great Roman tenor's coaching, was capable of unique technical and expressive accomplishments."[1]

Ever since reading this statement I have wondered what Lauri-Volpi meant exactly when referring to Franco Corelli's "humility." All the more since it is no secret that "humility" was not Lauri-Volpi's own most outstanding virtue.

Doubtless Lauri-Volpi was referring to the "humility before art," meaning that art with a capital A of which he thought himself, and readily proclaimed himself, to be both devotee and prophet. It is a kind of humility that Franco Corelli certainly possessed, even though it wasn't always easy to recognize, and has variously been called "professionalism," "scruples," "self-criticism," "perfectionism," "exactness"...and in its extreme manifestations, "anguish" and "fear."

All in all, perhaps it was an aspect of this "humility" which prompted Corelli, at certain points in his career, to seek the veteran's help and advice.

According to what Lauri-Volpi stated in an article he wrote some years later,[2] Corelli turned to him the moment he had what the teacher defined as a "crisis of artistic conscience."

Even allowing for the consideration that Lauri-Volpi sometimes writes over-imaginatively (almost in D'Annunzio's style) there is no doubt that Corelli asked him for advice in times that were, if not exactly "crises," at least moments of self-examination, for example, when preparing new repertory choices.

Let us check the first of these times: it is 1963, late summer. Corelli has reached a peak in his career. He has triumphed at La Scala singing *Gli Ugonotti* (*Les Huguenots*, 1962), he has already conquered the Metropolitan Opera (with *Trovatore*, *Turandot*, *Ernani* in 1961-62), he has brought *Il trovatore* to the birthplace of Mozart (Salzburg, 1962), and in the interval of a few months he has opened the opera seasons at two of the greatest theaters in the world (La Scala, the Met). He is almost unanimously considered the greatest living tenor... and yet he is looking for something that still eludes him.

Why? What is he looking for? What does he want?

He is looking for the most hidden secrets of "the technique," of course. He is searching "with the same spirit of a devout going to the sanctuary"[3] for that impossible miracle— the mythic, unreachable certainty of an absolute control over his vocal instrument. But, perhaps, he is also looking for the assurance that he made the right life choice.

Corelli asks of Lauri-Volpi (and probably obtains) the reassurance that his sacrifices are not in vain, that he must not regret having had "a normal youth interrupted by sudden success"[4]—reassurance that the ascetic life, the agonies, the labors, the sleepless nights, all the sacrifices *are* worthwhile.

In much the same vein there is a Corelli statement about Lauri-Volpi which I think very revealing: "He was a man conscious of his destiny."[5]

This is a sentence he could just as well have used to define himself: because the voice is a gift of destiny, a gift as great and terrible as a sacred vocation, and the possessor of it has the duty to give it to the world. It is a gift one must guard, invest in and be responsible for like the parable of the talents. (St. Matthew 25:14-30.) But unlike that parable, this is a gift which offers less in satisfaction than it asks in sacrifice. That is why the greatest reward is neither success nor money, but— when one achieves it—the knowledge of using well what destiny has given, of having a fixed aim, or rather a limit to oneself, and of having surpassed it.

Then the theater, the audience, the applause fades, losing any of its meaning. Only a man remains: a man whose life is a perpetual challenge to himself. A man who sometimes allows himself this secret, invaluable reward: to be able to admit to himself that he has won.

One must not only submit to this way of living, one must also love it.

"He taught me how to love the theater..." This is another of Corelli's tell-tale statements about his teacher, or rather, his mentor.[6]

Lauri-Volpi always thought that singing, and *his* singing in particular, was a mission in an almost religious sense, a spiritual elevation. It is no wonder, then, that he conveyed to his pupil the "humility" to accept (or, if you like, suffer) this mission with the same spirit that a mystic accepts and suffers his vocation (a sort of "fiat mihi secundum verbum tuum"— in English, "let it happen to me according to thy word." Luke 1:38).

But many people talk about Franco Corelli's "humility" in a different sense, to which other words would probably be more suitable. Maybe more than a word is needed to describe this facet of his personality, because no one by itself is sufficient to give an exact idea. Or maybe we could choose a negative definition: Franco Corelli is not a "divo," but quite the opposite.

This is something one realizes at once, after just a few minutes of conversation with him. An earnestness, a kindness, a humanity, a way of "giving himself"—in spite of an initial reluctance, which seems (and maybe is) diffidence, but after all is just shyness. Characteristics so ingenuous that they are completely at odds with any "anti-divo" pose.

Fellow artists, friends, fans have told me about so many moments, so many examples of this "modesty," as it is sometimes called, but which I prefer to call his inner, tenacious pursuit of "normality."

There is one episode, a very simple one at that. I like it most because I think it is really "like him," truly revealing—so emblematic, in fact, that it is almost a photograph.

It is part of the American fan's personal journal from which I have already quoted. I give it to my readers as I received it, without comment, which would be utterly superfluous.

I will only point out the situation. It is the evening of May 18, 1973. Bill has gone to see *Macbeth* in Dallas. After the performance he joins Corelli in his dressing room. The tenor chooses not to attend the party given for the cast, and Bill volunteers to drive him to his hotel.

"I went to get the car and when I returned he was ready; but first he signed many autographs outside with great patience.

"We talked during our ride to the Stoneleigh Hotel and he particularly commented on the beauty of the 'Sleepwalking aria' music. When I suggested that Bumbry should not have sung the top note, he said that performances were too often judged on one note. He was particularly interested in how the Milnes voice sounded in the theater as to size, tone, etc.

"I thought what a charming and humble person Corelli is. When I commented that I would much rather have seen him in *Tosca* than in *Macbeth*, he said perhaps Macduff was better since he had contracted a virus in Atlanta and was taking large doses of penicillin.

"We arrived at the hotel, and while I went in to see if the dining room was still serving, he stayed outside and walked the dog. The dining room was closed so we decided to drive to Lucas B & B, meeting the on-tour conductor of *Tosca* on the way (Carlo Felice Cillario) who was also looking for some food, and he came with us.

"The conductor went inside to order the sandwiches (corned beef and 7-up for Franco) while Corelli and I walked in the parking lot discussing the new duet album with Tebaldi they had just recorded. Parts of it were good, he thought. When I could not think what the duet from *Adriana* was, he sang part of it for me, not full voice of course, as well as 'snatches' from other things.

"We drove back to the hotel and he decided to take his sandwich up to the room. He then bid me a good-night profuse with thanks."

Courage and Fear

They say that to sing Manrico a tenor needs a throat as steady as a sword and steel lungs. For someone who has the venturesome spirit to sing Manrico in the Arena, one must add: much courage.

THIS SENTENCE CAN BE FOUND in the famous Italian critic Giuseppe Pugliese's admiring review of the *Trovatore* Franco Corelli sang in 1959 at Verona.[1] It is something one can't help but ponder. A rather strange sentence, referring to a singer whose best-known, most talked-about, and I hasten to add least-understood distinctive trait is fear.

About the famous Franco Corelli "fear" many things (perhaps too many) have been said and written. In my case his "fear" was the very first piece of information I acquired about his personality, and I remember being intrigued and curious about it. So much so that I can say it was somehow the first incentive to my research: the curiosity—or rather the need—to understand the human, day-to-day, off-stage personality of a man who was capable, with his artistry, of giving me so much emotion, and yet under Manrico's armor, below Calaf's shining jacket, beneath Radames's golden breastplate, a man who trembled at the idea of going onstage as a little school-boy before an exam.

Many people, over-simplifying, speak of "fear of the public," or "stage fright"—the French theater slang is often heard: "*avoir le trac*"—but I have never found this a satisfactory explanation for this simple reason: any artist can (more or less) feel anxiety, or even panic when he or she is on the point of stepping on a stage. If Franco Corelli's "fear" was so well known, so characteristic, and if everyone spoke so much about it, this necessarily had to be different, partially at least, from the one we can define as "normal"—the physiological kind that many of us might face, for whatever reason, when presenting ourselves in front of an audience.

The first conclusion I reached was that Corelli's fear had little to do with the audience, or at least, nothing beyond what I would have defined as "normal." On the contrary, and this may sound like a contradiction (but it isn't) the audience actually was an incentive for Corelli. It acted almost as a spur. In fact it was the presence of an audience which helped him to find the courage he needed to face the performance.

I drew this conclusion from the different comments of many fellow artists, critics, fans and friends concerning the excitement and energy at fever pitch that Corelli could induce on stage during his performances.

In particular I was helped by a very subtle comment from one of Corelli's colleagues, tenor Piero De Palma. As a singer who performed with him countless times in every major Italian theater, and since he sang secondary roles (not having to be as totally involved as the principals), he could observe Corelli from an extremely favorable point of view.

"Franco did not like to rehearse," he told me. "But not because he considered himself a 'divo,' or out of any laziness. Simply, if he was not out in front of an audience, he did not feel involved enough, he was not spurred on to give the best of himself."[2]

As I already mentioned some pages back, in talking about Franco Corelli's "humility"—it may be that feature which is actually one of the elements to his "fear." Or rather, its mirror image, the other side of the coin.

His professional ethic, his belief that he will never be entirely "ready," the constant fear of the unpredictable, of the choking drop of saliva or the irrepressible coughing that can ruin a whole evening, the anxiety of needing to be always at his best, because the audience always expects the best every evening, in any circumstances, explain very well the anguish which seizes the artist at any given performance, all the more so when the performances is much anticipated and of great importance.

Then even the simple action of stepping outdoors to go to the theater can become an unbearable effort. This, and not any divisive attitude, is why Corelli always arrived at the very last moment to sing: to have only the time strictly necessary to get dressed (and even in this, his professionalism prompted him to prepare with the greatest of care in the smallest of details with his makeup, wig, costume, etc.) to cut off any "dead time," that is, time spent waiting.

"If I had to wait in the wings for five minutes, I would die," he would confess to his fellow singers, giving them his ice-cold hands to hold. He would seek a bit of relief by telling some sympathetic ear the mysterious, but nevertheless very real, sickness which was squeezing his stomach and cutting off his breath at the moment he had to go on... And sometimes while he was already onstage, as well.

Corelli now confesses that sometimes, in his "being sick" there is also a bit of superstition, the irrational fear that after having assuredly said, "I am well," some real "illness" would show up out of the blue.

But doubtless, the tension did exist, whatever its components. The nightmare was always there, whether real or imagined.

"Madam, I can't," was a statement several leading ladies heard from him (and I can mention Giulietta Simionato and Magda Olivero) in the very middle of a performance.

Actually—and this is the main point—Corelli *could*, every time. The professional scruples which tormented him in the form of fear, were the same ones which prompted him to overcome it!

His forfeits in a twenty-five year career can be counted on one's fingers, and none of them, as far as I know, were due to "fear."

On the contrary, in Franco Corelli's career, there are so many acts of courage—and here I am back to Giuseppe Pugliese's comment which was the starting point in my elaboration. You need courage to sing *Il trovatore* in the Verona Arena. But you need even more courage to sing your *first Aida* there, as Franco Corelli did also. You need courage to present yourself to a La Scala audience to sing an opera which weighs disproportionately on the tenor's shoulders, like *Poliuto*, but even more courage to sing on an evening whose main feature is the fashionable event of Maria Callas's great return (which couldn't help but make the doings of the opera's true protagonist of secondary importance). You need courage to make *Chénier*, *Ernani*, and *Turandot* sensational by means of your unique contributions, but even more courage to unearth the long-forgotten *Huguenots*.

Finally it takes courage, when you've been labeled a "heroic" and "dramatic" tenor, to sing *Roméo* and *above all Werther*—and sing the last-named as Corelli did: *his* interpretation of Werther, without models, without imitation, without any reverential awe.

And all of this was possible because neither "humility" nor "fear" prevented Franco Corelli from fulfilling his destiny.

I hope that nobody thinks that this is an exaggerated or over-dramatic word: but if there is (and *there is*) in him a bit of fatalism, it is more than justified by the events in his life and his career.

From his debut onwards, his life and his career became one and the same thing: the story of a man who was not made happy by success; a man both prisoner and guardian of a gift that was perhaps too great. A man for whom singing ceased to be a joy, often became an agony, and sometimes a psychological nightmare.

This was a man in whom two different and often opposing components of his nature would clash. On the one hand there was the exhibitionism, the need for top billing, the narcissism, without which (I think) he could not have become one of the greatest artists of his time. On the other hand there was a basic restraint, a shyness, a reserve, so that the inevitable combat between these opposing characteristics was transformed into an exhaustive need to perfect his artistry, almost as if justifying the irrepressible impulse to exhibit it, even aggressively at times, out of exasperation.

He is a man spurred on by a "*possanza arcana*" which compels him to follow a path conflicting in so many ways with the strongest part of his nature. (Andrea Chénier: "*Credi al destino? Io credo. Credo a una possanza arcana...*"; in English, "Do you believe in destiny? I do. I believe in a mysterious force.") He is basically a quiet, private man, who even now finds himself (and, I think, in spite of himself) turned into a sex symbol. A man who can only find true peace with himself on a stage (conquering the "fear") where at last the clashes cease and he is able to find unity and coherence in becoming his operatic character, identifying with another personality, forgetting his own contradictions.

"Life is a dream. Life is not the one we live, but the one we dream," Franco Corelli said in an interview.[3]

If so, singing became a way to express himself, to fulfill his persona, a way *to be himself* that was more true than the ordinary ways in daily life.

For a man who was never fully reconciled with his own reality, it became a way to live in a dream and to make a dream live.

PART FIVE

Corelli and the Record

*"It is a very strange, incomprehensible thing,
this divorce between
Corelli and the recording process."*

MARIO MORINI

Starting Points for a Discussion

A PRELIMINARY REMARK: I certainly don't intend—and it wouldn't be possible in any case—to venture in this space an analysis of the discography of Franco Corelli.

This would undoubtedly be an attractive pursuit—or perhaps fascinating is the more exact word—but it would demand (or will demand? Why use the conditional? It's a dream and it's a project that I would really love to realize...) the entire space of a book, of course.

Here I would like to limit myself to considerations of a general character and a few hints for reflection.

Yet even the most general analysis of Corelli's discography imposes an examination also, and above all, of Corelli's live recordings, which are the only ones which enable us to acquire a comprehensive idea of his art and technique throughout his repertoire and over the complete span of his career. It is our good fortune that such recordings started to appear in recent years with increasing frequency, filling up, even for the great audiences which are kept outside the close circle of collectors, the gaps left by the poor little group of official recordings.

And here I have finally reached an explanation for the reason I have quoted Mario Morini's words at the head of this part of the book, almost as an epigraph. Like all simple things which appear obvious after someone said them or wrote them,

I was struck forcibly by his words during a private conversation: the first evidence that jumps to the eye when we examine Corelli's official discography is the scant number of recordings.

This poverty is to be found not only in the comparison with contemporary singers who now record everything over and over, as on an assembly line (even in pieces and fragments, among another hundred commitments: perhaps even with the help of sophisticated technical devices that allow them to put together duets recorded separately, and perform other well-known tricks that are even more open to question), but even with *his* contemporaries.

Considering that only eleven operas (of which two, *Carmen* and *Aida*, were recorded in two different productions) constitute Corelli's entire discographic production—we are speaking only of complete operas, obviously—one cannot help being surprised or perplexed by this seeming divorce.

And the phenomenon is even more surprising because Corelli began making records quite early in his career. The first of several 45 records (and before, of some 78s) go back to the middle of the fifties, that is to say, less than four years after his debut at Spoleto, and with all probability were linked to the success, on the one hand, of his debut at La Scala, and on the other to his first television experiences.

The first recording of a complete opera, *Aida*, is dated 1956, and therefore almost immediately follows Corelli's debut as Radames. This edition remains a treasure not only for its uniqueness, but because it remains a precious document of the tenor's interpretive accomplishments in those years. The successive versions that appeared on the market (nowadays quite difficult to find) were in fact "live" recordings from 1961. [There is now a "live" recording of a 1955 *Aida* on CD, however. Ed.]

The 1956 edition is—and I mention it in passing to be faithful to my commitment not to analyze the merits of the individual recordings—one that could be recommended for those who are today hanging on to the legend of a Corelli who was eternally *"vociferante"* (shouting). This is so true that Rodolfo Celletti himself—who still maintains, elsewhere, his distinction between the Corelli before and after 1958, and his thumbs down on the pre-1958 Corelli—doesn't hesitate in recognizing him as *powerful and soft together*, and to define what he has heard as a *good performance, which becomes optimal in the last act, where we can hear phrases that are particularly eloquent, for instance:* "Morir sì pura e bella," *and suggestive* smorzature.[1]

Still, in spite of this promising beginning, four years will pass before in 1960 the recording of second complete opera is realized: *Norma*, immediately followed by *Pagliacci*. Two years afterwards there is a recording of *Cavalleria rusticana* which, moreover, Corelli at that time had not sung in a theater. The discographic activity intensifies—even if it is improper to use this term for a rhythm of one or two recordings per year—in the following period: *Carmen* and *Chénier* in 1963, *Il trovatore* in 1964, *Turandot* in 1965, *Faust* and *Tosca* in 1966. Continuing from there we have a recording of *Roméo et Juliette* in 1968 on the heels of the success the opera received the previous year at the Metropolitan, and lastly, his second *Carmen* in 1970.

It is convenient to say right now, though it is probably unnecessary to be so specific, that these recordings correspond much less to artistic requirements than to commercial speculation by the recording companies. We find ourselves, therefore, facing choices at the time that are far from pleasant (why, for instance, should we wait till 1960 to have a recording of the *Norma* of Maria Callas beside a Pollione who is truly her equal?), and casts that are not well balanced, as in the case of the pale Santuzza of Victoria de los Angeles, or of a Robert Merrill who was not particularly brilliant in the role of Escamillo in the splendid *Carmen* directed by Von Karajan, and even worse as the Count di Luna in *Trovatore*, or in the case of the inopportune insertion of the Scarpia of Dietrich Fischer-Diskau between two extra-powerful voices like Corelli's and Nilsson's. Not to mention the *Carmen* that was built around Anna Moffo in which one gets the impression that Corelli was called to legitimize with his name and his presence an operation that was absurd and unsustainable by itself. As a result an interpretation that I consider noteworthy ends by passing unobserved, dragged down into the mud of an insignificant recording.

In the already reduced number of complete operas that Corelli has left us, therefore, the recordings that I would deem really historical, that create an authentic image of the interpreter which can be passed to future generations, are even less. I would list among these at least the *Norma*, of which it can only be regretted that we don't have the Callas of a few years before, and the Von Karajan *Carmen*, as well as those of *Chénier*, *Trovatore* and *Aida*. Already more of a minor effort—even though, and let's be very clear about this, on a very high level—are *Tosca* and *Turandot*, and in certain aspects (the impression is that it came at a somewhat unhappy time for Corelli vocally) there is *Roméo et Juliette*.

I am convinced that it is to these recordings Sergio Segalini is referring when he observes that *Corelli has recorded little for official discographic houses, and not always under the best conditions,* adding that the tenor *takes his revenge thanks to the parallel recordings,* that is to the live recordings.[2]

It is good to specify, in fact, that when I am calling one of Corelli's recordings "a minor effort" I am referring as a basis of comparison to live evidence of his interpretation of the opera in question. Most admirers of Franco Corelli would agree that the black market or bootleg tapes of performances of *Tosca* or *Turandot* (but also *Carmen*, *Aida*, *Chénier*) are more exciting than the performances that were consecrated as official recordings.

Here we are broaching a rather delicate and complex subject, though in one sense it bears on the description of Corelli as being divorced from recordings. Not only is the number of official recordings limited, but in the judgment of many Franco

Corelli's voice—and above all his art—are not phonogenically rendered by the record in their wholeness and intensity.

As far as the voice is concerned it is nothing new to affirm that other voices exist which are more suitable for mechanical reproduction. Many great singers from Giacomo Lauri-Volpi to Gina Cigna have often complained of the infidelity of the record to the real quality and fascination of their voices. The vibrancy and the richness of harmonics that expand in a theater are lost in a recording studio.

Corelli himself, in one of his very first American interviews, raised the subject.[3]

Each voice, he stated, has its own characteristic in terms of how it records. Some small voices can be exalted by records while a few great voices tend to be "reduced to nothing." This is one of his problems. Invariably the exceptional power of his voice induces the technical people to turn down the volume controls. For this reason he kept experimenting with different kinds of microphones without ever being totally satisfied with the quality of his voice as it was reproduced on records. (*After all*, he observed in the above interview, *I hear that Frank Sinatra carries his own with him. Why should I not be as particular about my microphones?*)

Records today, he will declare in another interview many years afterward,[4] *don't reflect voices for what they are. Many times I hear the voice of a colleague in the theater and when I hear it on a record, I don't recognize it. It is not the same, it is a machine voice. The engineer can make a voice larger or smaller, although he cannot give you sweetness.* His own records, he says, never sound the same because the voice changes with the studio, the recording equipment, the engineer. *A singer can tell the difference between a Decca record and those of RCA or Angel, because each has a different sound. If you really want to know your voice*, he adds, *you must use a tape recorder which conceals nothing.*

This is certainly a statement that the better part of his admirers are ready to understand, as I have personally verified when, not having, unluckily, ever heard Franco Corelli's voice in a theater I began to ask around, humbly, if the fullness of his art had been and would be forever denied to me. The lucky ones who had followed his career for years had comforted me. The black market tapes, they told me, or at least many of them, did preserve a great part of the fascination of his voice and could give me an almost perfect idea of it.

Of course, the sound or quality of the voice is one thing and quite another is the dramatic interpretation, and here we get to the second aspect of the much-discussed relationship between the official recordings and the live recordings.

Sergio Segalini, quoted by Rodolfo Celletti, affirms without mincing words that *Corelli was the shadow of himself in a recording studio.*[5]

It is perhaps an excessively drastic statement, but it is doubtless that the outstanding majority of people who had seen and heard him in the theater, colleagues included, were ready in some measure to share it.

Obviously even the supporters of the official recordings, as well as those of the live recordings, can muster valid points to support their preferences.

First of all are the quality and clarity of sound which are often rather unstable in live recordings.

It is undeniable, besides, that in the studio recordings the singer is subject to minor tensions which can be calmed by the possibility of repeating the piece until he is totally satisfied with it (even though, Corelli complained in an interview, ever the perfectionist, *if you stay there two days to record a piece, they won't allow you to do it!*),[6] and can follow the score's markings with more precision, and also venture performances that he would judge too risky in a theater. We can quote as an example the famous high C in the *"pira"* which Corelli, as far as I know, has never performed in a theater, which even so remains as historical testimony in the discographic edition of *Trovatore.*

It remains to establish—and this depends on a strictly subjective judgment—if this high C is more or less or equally important as many of his other high Cs or B-flats (for instance *Turandot, Ugonotti, Roméo, Don Carlo, La battaglia di Legnano, Trovatore* again in the finale of the first act), beautifully performed in the theater and luckily preserved for history as well in the live recordings.

So this doesn't take away from the fact that Corelli allowed himself (and allowed us) the luxury of extraordinary *filature* in the huge amphitheater of the Verona Arena and that twenty thousand people listened to him in religious silence, covering him right afterward with applause, as a sign that even the heterogenous public of the Arena knew how to recognize and appreciate technical refinements when they heard them.

There is also another and very valid subject of discussion in favor of the official recordings, an argument that involves the much more widespread, and widely discussed problem of faithfulness to the score, the observing of the written markings, a faithfulness or fidelity that doesn't always enjoy the same luck, and that in the course of the history of melodrama has been at some moments excessively neglected, and in other periods perhaps excessively exalted.

It goes without saying that this is a problem I do not expect to resolve, or even to deal with in this work, but it is necessary to mention it because in the relationship between theatrical performance and recording studio performance we often tend to make a distinction. Freedoms that are allowed or at least tolerated in the theater are not acceptable at all on the record, which has to authenticate the ability of the interpreter (singer or conductor) to follow the composer's indications most precisely.

Now, as everybody knows, following the composer's indications is not Corelli's favorite way of interpreting a role, but it is necessary to make yet another distinction. It is one thing to have the technical ability to respect the written sign, and the performer must absolutely show that he is capable of this respect, and is obliged to show it on records as well as in the theater, and in this aspect Franco Corelli has always been strongly committed as have few others. Interpretation is quite another thing, however. Here a little flexibility must be given to the artist, if one would wish that he be an interpreter and not a mere source of mechanical repetitions.

This is more than ever obvious in the romantic and veristic repertoire. Vocal technique is, much more than in the previous periods, at the service of the dramatic elements of the work. I heard a computer warble the Queen of the Night's aria from *The Magic Flute* with ice-cold perfection but I will never hear a computer singing (not performing) "*E lucevan le stelle*," or "*Come un bel dì di Maggio*," or "*Ah, si ben mio*." And I also doubt that Puccini or Giordano or Verdi would be pleased by such metronomic observance of their scores.

Sometimes I do not agree with the composer, Franco Corelli stated. *I feel another expression is more appropriate. I think eighty percent of the time we must oblige the composer by remaining faithful to the score, but we cannot become enslaved by tradition. Times change. What was beautiful fifty years ago may not be considered beautiful now.*[7]

Personally I don't believe it is possible to sustain that a vocal photocopy of every note and expressive marking can be called an interpretation. To interpret means to infuse life into what was before the artist's intervention nothing but a page covered with small black marks, symbols of an intention often difficult to reconstruct with any accuracy when the hand and the brain that drew them have been gone for fifty or a hundred years.

Perhaps this limit or obligation of not "getting out of line" that the fans perceive in his recordings—Corelli definitely imposed it on himself much more on records than he did in the theater—has a certain coldness of emotional involvement, of the artist first and of the listener after.

"What you give in the theater you cannot give on a record."[8] Corelli himself made this statement which, in a certain sense, closes the discussion. Actually, listeners cannot receive what a record cannot give: the emotion of the story that develops from the beginning to the end; the suggestion of the set design and costumes; the presence of the audience itself, which is part of the artistic process in the way it reacts; the experimentation of the artist with different nuances in certain passages (incidentally, quite typical of Corelli); finally there is the charm of risk which is renewed every evening, always slightly different because of changes in mood, changes in the physical and psychological disposition of everyone who is participating in the show on the stage and in the theater.

All of this can be offered fully only by direct attendance, physical presence. And its best substitution certainly cannot be the cold, over-elaborated, perfect, impeccable official recording. This will be able to give us other emotions, different, of a rational, technical nature, but will never get closer, especially in the case of an artist capable of such great dramatic intensity as Franco Corelli, to the emotional involvement of a performance that takes place in a certain way at a certain moment in front of an audience. Live recordings, however, can transmit something of this.

At this point I really do need to repeat that I do not mean to lessen the historical and technical value of what Corelli has left us on his records, but merely to underline the fact that if we didn't have available any other documentation, we would have a totally insufficient and somewhat distorted idea of his artistry, besides having a very limited knowledge of his repertoire.

It is enough to want to ask ourselves what we could say of Corelli's art if we had never listed to his Poliuto, his Raoul of the *Ugonotti*, his Arrigo in the *Battaglia di Legnano*, his Don Alvaro, his Don Carlo, his Dick Johnson, his Rodolfo, his Werther, all characters that the official records have not passed down to us.

But we wouldn't know too much either if we couldn't listen to so many of his splendid interpretations of *Tosca* (the famous one of Parma could stand for all of them), to his blazing *Turandot*s (and let's remember the last season-opener for La Scala), to his furious, bloody, desperate *Carmen*s; pages where the artist projected himself beyond the score, where his art was not submitted simply, but added to that of the composer to create a higher opera, more perfect, greater because real, alive, in the here and now of the performance, made flesh and blood, warm with passion and emotion.

I can't finish the discussion I intended to make on Corelli and his recordings (from which I have digressed a bit without regret) without examining two recordings that in my opinion deserve, for different reasons, a particular recommendation.

First is the recording of Gounod's *Faust*, and I believe I must at least mention it since it is an opera that Corelli never sang in the theater and therefore I never had a chance to comment on it in the biographical part of my book.

The Faust interpretation even more than many others has created contrasting critical responses, which is understandable because Faust, like Rodolfo, like Werther, and in certain respects like Romeo, too, is a character around whom something similar to a vocal cliché has been created, and one that is very precise: Faust must at all costs be considered a "lyric" tenor.

So, even if it is true that you can find a critic who can recognize in Corelli "*a portrait of a Latin and Gounodian Faust in the best sense of the word: warm, vigorous, sometimes heroic, sometimes languid, always rich and refulgent, without excessive mawkishness, and to our good fortune, without that drained and stylized* badinerie *that has made Faust, let's say it, so completely antipathetic and sexless for us, a Faust of strictly French interpretive origin.*"[9] In other cases the misunderstanding is such that even Giorgio Gualerzi defines Faust as a "*student looking for facile, sentimental adventures.*"[10]

Of course, if we interpret the character of Faust in this key (on my side I don't see how one can include in such a definition either the Faust of Goethe or that of Gounod, even though he is quite different. Are we by any chance talking about Siebel?), we cannot but conclude that Corelli *is not Faust*.

The Faust of Gounod is an old scholar who has been disappointed by philosophy and by faith, who turns to Satan to obtain from him a second chance to enjoy the pleasures of life, and sells him his soul in exchange for the ephemeral possession and purely physical enjoyment (because he doesn't have the least intention of marrying Marguérite) of an innocent girl. Faust is a character full of sensuality, and not a fresh, natural, spontaneous sensuality, such as Werther's. Rather it is a perverse and senile sensuality by which he himself is dragged to damnation and anyone associated with him is ruined. *This* is Franco Corelli's Faust, made younger in the body but immeasurably older in spirit, full of contradictions and regrets, dramatic, passionate. And, let's not forget that the part is very rich in nuances, and Faust is a main character, not only in the memorable first act and in a soaring romanza but in the great love duet during the splendid meeting with the voice and technique of Joan Sutherland.

To conclude, I would finally like to cite one more record that is not too well known, and probably also not very much appreciated in those days, though it's one which I believe (and I'm not alone) is a key accomplishment, perhaps in some ways the summit of Franco Corelli's artistry. It is the record of religious songs (*Canti Religiosi*)* recorded around the end of 1963, and issued the following year—and unfortunately impossible to find today.

This was a record Corelli worked on for months with even greater than usual care and commitment, starting with long

---

*For the most part what I have written about the record of the *Canti Religiosi* I owe to Mario Morini, with whom I have spoken at length about this particular artistic experience. I recognize my debt all the more because we found ourselves during those two conversations to be in perfect harmony in the matter of taste and judgment. What I have written represents, therefore, my opinion as well as his (that I have correctly reported) or better, the agreement of both.

research with collectors and with careful, passionate listening to the records his greatest predecessors had left.

The result was a record that must be heard in a particular spirit because it has been desired, conceived and performed in a particular spirit: to make of his singing, before all else, not an example of something purely hedonistic, but rather a vehicle of dedication.

This represents a way of elevating himself and his listeners by the intense giving of himself which is restrained by a constant commitment to emotional, vocal and technical control. He makes of it an authentic singing class, a sample of *everything you can find in a vocal handbook*, as Mario Morini writes in his jacket notes.

It is, above all, a document of a more secret, more intimate meeting with music, shorn of the slightest vestige of theatricality that is linked to the traditional image of the tenor. Corelli's artistic endowment is rich in such theatricality, but here he knows how to overcome it and enter into a totally interior spiritual dimension.

Maybe it is just for these characteristics that the record didn't turn into a glamorous commercial success. The record company which produced it has never hinted that it would be reissued. [EMI recently reissued the *Canti Religiosi* on CD. Ed.]

Still, it would be really desirable that someone would give a thought to reissuing it because it is a unique and irreplaceable document of an important aspect of Franco Corelli's art and personality. The great public might find it very helpful in better understanding his will and his ability to communicate joy, suffering, faith, hope, and passion through his singing.

Will and ability here are joined by means of the total identification of the artist's spirituality in the privileged tool of expression that he received as a gift: a vibrant and living image of *a man* and of *a voice*.

Almost a Conclusion

DURING MY RESEARCH on the career of Franco Corelli so many people asked me in return questions about him, about how and what he was doing, and where he lived.

And I was there to answer with the very little I knew that was exact. That he lived in New York right on the corner of Central Park, a stone's throw from the Metropolitan, but that he didn't go to the theater. That he was the director of a state school for the perfection of singers, but that often he was unsatisfied with teaching because young people no longer had all the passion and the spirit of sacrifice that young singers had formerly. Now and then he would turn up in Italy, one stop in Milan, one visit with his friends in Parma, one quick hop over to Ancona, a vacation in Cortina... And, finally, that he has a secret dream, but not too secret: to come back and live in Italy, to open a singing academy for advanced students in Milan.

"And...does he sing?" is regularly the question that follows.

The answer is: "Yes, he sings."

In those who have admired him so much, and those who have had so much from his art, the hope of hearing him once again, one more time, is renewed.

He sings. But only a few can listen to him outside the walls of his house—that have been made completely soundproof by means of acoustical engineering.

Most of all, the students of his master class can listen to him, young people to whom he listens and gives advice, to whom he gives, with the captivating goodness that is typical of him, treasures of experience that were accumulated over so many years of deep study: problems of technique, of breathing, of emission, of control of the voice. I have been told that one of his young students happened to be at the Scala at an audition and was talking with enthusiasm of the beauty of his high register and of the unfailing precision with which he illustrated his own teaching by placing every note.

And then, to everyone who asks me, "How is he?" I leave this image, the image that I have of him. A kindly lord, tall and straight, with a forty-year-old's body, the face a little haggard, the eyes unchanged, beautiful eyes, the usual smile, composed, that vibrates for a moment below the eyes and at the corners of the mouth, before expanding to make the entire face shine.

And he sings, studies, vocalizes in order to preserve his voice in a fresh, ready condition, so that the emission is as spontaneous as ever, and can be offered as an example to his pupils.

Franco Corelli, who once used to feel a prisoner of his voice (stating that while everybody sang when they were happy he had become the slave of the requirements and responsibilities of his profession) has won a beautiful freedom. Now he sings to transmit to young people his own technique and art, and he sings, finally, if only for himself, only for the joy of singing.

1. Corelli as a baby. Born Ancona, April 8, 1921.

2. Corelli at age 5.

3. Corelli at age 11.

4. Early publicity photo of Corelli. [1953]

5. Early publicity photo.

4

5

6. Corelli as Don José in *Carmen* with Giulietta Simionato. [Verona, 1955]

7. In *Carmen* at Messina [Sicily] in August 1954 with Miriam Pirazzini.

8. In *Carmen*. [Verona, 1957]

9. Corelli as Don José in *Carmen*. [1960]

7

8

9

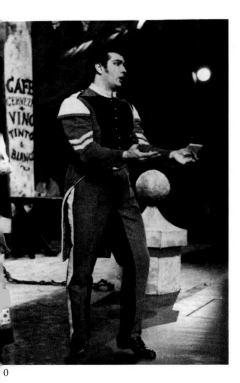

0

10. Corelli as Don José at La Scala. [1960]

11. In *Carmen*. [Verona, 1961]

12. In *Carmen* at the Arena di Verona. [July, 1970]

11

2

13. With Grace Bumbry in the Macerata production of *Carmen*. [July, 1974]

14. As Maurizio in *Adriana Lecouvreur*, with Magda Olivero and Giulietta Simionato. [Naples, 1958]

15. As Maurizio di Sassonia in *Adriana Lecouvreur*. [Naples. November, 1959]

16. Taking a bow after *Adriana Lecouvreur* with Magda Olivero, Giulietta Simionato, Ettore Bastianini. [Teatro di San Carlo, Naples. November, 1959]

18

17. Corelli as Pollione in an early *Norma*.

18. As Pollione in *Norma* at the Verona Arena. [July, 1958]

19

20

19. Taking curtain calls after *Norma*.

20. After *Norma*, being kissed by leading lady Cristina Deutekom and Renata Tebaldi (who was in the audience). [Parma, December, 1971]

21. As Pollione, taking curtain calls with Cristina Deutekom (Norma). [December, 1971]

21

22. As Canio in *Pagliacci*.

23. As Canio in *Pagliacci* at La Scala [January, 1957]

22

23

24. As Radames in *Aida* at the Teatro Verdi di Trieste. [November, 1956]

25

25. As Radames in *Aida* at La Scala.
[December, 1956]

26. As Radames in *Aida* at La Scala.

26

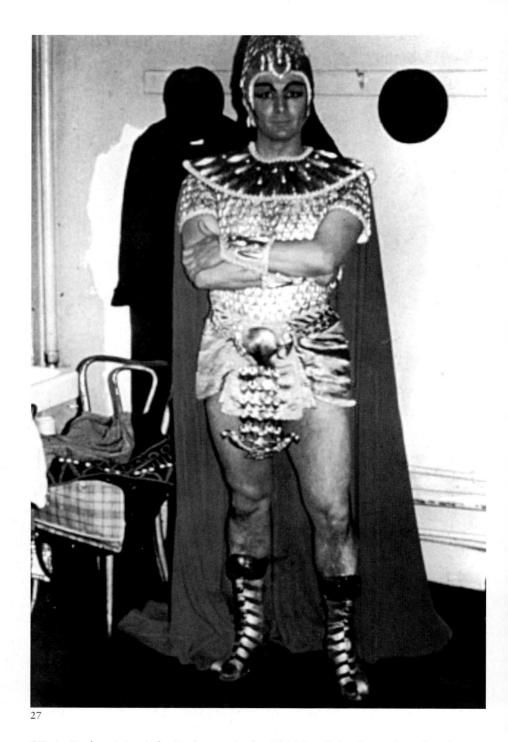

27

27. As Radames in *Aida*. Backstage at the Old Met. [Met Opera Broadcast]
28. As Don Carlo in *Don Carlo* at the Teatro dell'Opera di Roma. [March, 1954]

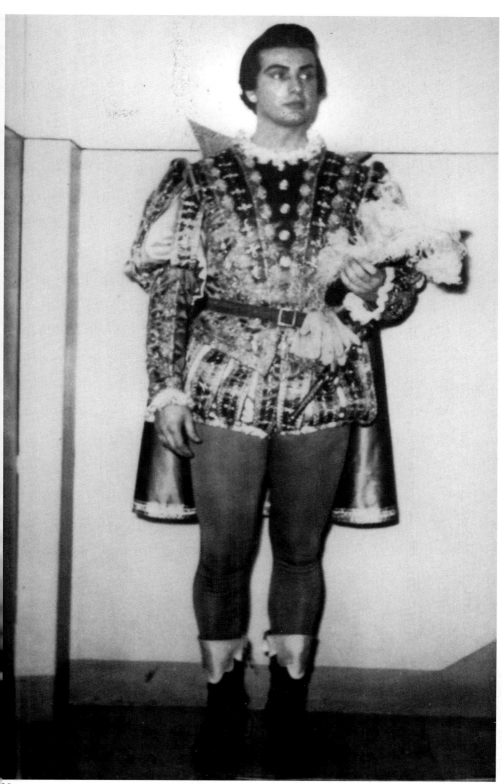

29. As Don Carlo at the Vienna State Opera. [September, 1963]

30. With Montserrat Caballé during curtain calls after *Don Carlo* at the Metropolitan Opera. [April 12, 1972]

31. As Cavaradossi in the filmed version of *Tosca*. [1956]

32. With Frances Duval in film version of *Tosca*. [1956]

33, 34. (next page) With Frances Duval in film version of *Tosca*. [1956]
35. (next page, opposite) With Maria Callas in *Tosca* at the Metropolitan Opera. [1965]

33

34

36. As Cavaradossi in *Tosca* at the Metropolitan Opera.

37. As Licinio in *La vestale* at La Scala. [December, 1954]

38. As Dick Johnson in *La fanciulla del West* at La Scala. [April, 1956]

39. As Dick Johnson in *La fanciulla del West*. [1960]

40

40. As Dick Johnson in *La fanciulla del West*, Teatro alla Scala di Milano. [January, 1964]

42

41

41, 42. As Dick Johnson in *La fanciulla del West* at La Scala.

43. In *Giulio Cesare*.

44. As Loris in *Fedora*.

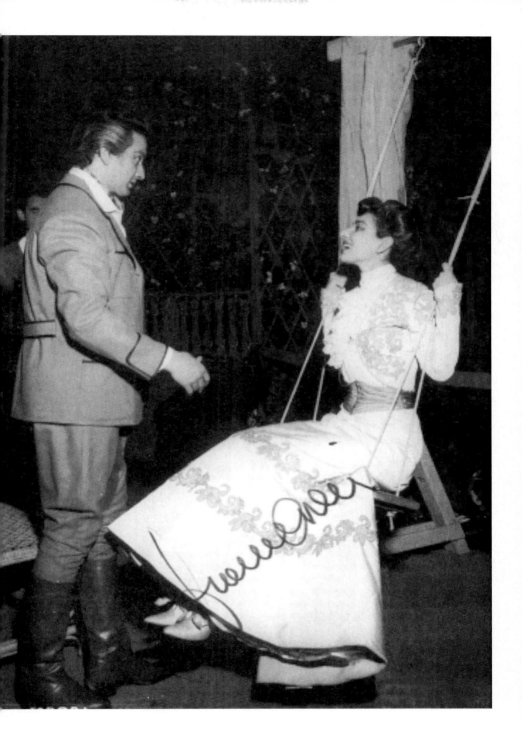

5. With Maria Callas in *Fedora* at La Scala. [May, 1956]

46. In the title role of *Andrea Chénier*.

47. Act III of Giordano's *Andrea Chénier* with Anselmo Colzani as Gérard.

46

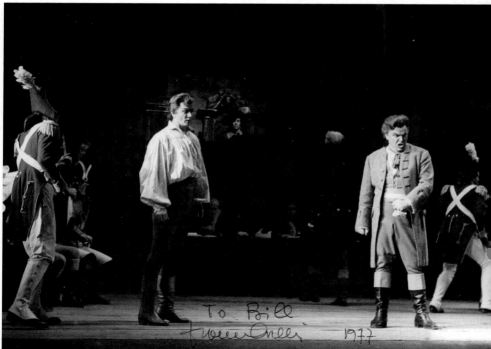

47

48

48. With Renata Tebaldi in *Andrea Chénier* at La Scala.

49. In *Andrea Chénier* at La Scala.

49

51

50. As Andrea Chénier. [March, 1957]

51. As Andrea Chénier at La Scala. [January, 1960]

52. As Don Alvaro in *La forza del destino* at the Teatro di San Carlo di Napoli. [March, 1958]

53. As Don Alvaro in *La forza del destino* at the Vienna State Opera.
[1963]

54. As Don Alvaro in *La forza del destino* at Parma. [December, 1967]

55. With Bastianini in *La forza del destino* at the Metropolitan Opera. [January, 1965]

54

55

56. As Calaf in *Turandot* at the Metropolitan Opera. [1961]

57. As Calaf in *Turandot* at the Metropolitan Opera. [1961]

58. In *Turandot* at the Metropolitan Opera. [June, 1970]

57

58

59

59. As Calaf the Unknown Prince in *Turandot* at La Scala. [May, 1962]

60. As Calaf in *Turandot* at La Scala. [May, 1962]

61. As Calaf in *Turandot*.

60

61

62, 63. In *Il pirata* at La Scala. [May, 1958]

62

63

64. Manrico in *Il trovatore* at La Scala. [May, 1959]

65. Manrico in *Il trovatore* at La Scala. [May, 1959]

66. As Manrico in *Il
trovatore* at the Verona
Arena. [July, 1959]

67. In *Il trovatore* with
Giulietta Simionato at the
Salzburg Festival. [July, 1962]

66

68. As Manrico in *Il trovatore* at La Scala. [December, 1962]

69. As Manrico in *Il trovatore*. [1962]

70. With Leontyne Price in *Trovatore* at the Salzburg Festival. [July, 1962]

69

70

71. With Leontyne Price in *Il trovatore* at the Metropolitan Opera. [February, 1964]

72. In *Hercules (Eracle)* at La Scala. [December, 1958]

73. In the title role of *Ernani* at La Scala. [February, 1959]

74. In *Ernani* with Margherita Roberti at La Scala. [February, 1959]

75

75, 76. In *Ernani* at La Scala.
[February, 1959]

76

. In the title role of *Poliuto* with Maria Callas at La Scala. [December, 1960]

78. In *Poliuto* at La Scala. [December, 1960]

79. In *Poliuto* with Ettore Bastianini at La Scala. [December, 1960]

80. In *Poliuto* with Maria Callas at La Scala. [December, 1960]

79

81

82

83

81, 82, 83. In *Poliuto* at La Scala.
[December, 1960]

84, 85. As Arrigo in *La battaglia di Legnano* at La Scala. [December, 1961]

84

85

86, 87. As Arrigo in *La battaglia di Legnano* at La Scala. [December, 1961]

86

87

88. As Enzo in *La Gioconda* with Renata Tebaldi in the title role. [1967]

89. As Enzo in *La Gioconda* at the Metropolitan Opera. [1967]

90. As Raoul in *Gli Ugonotti*. Milan, La Scala. [May, 1962]

91, 92. As Raoul in *Gli Ugonotti*. Milan, La Scala. [May, 1962]

93. As Raoul in *Gli Ugonotti*, taking a bow with Giulietta Simionato at La Scala. [May, 1962]

91

92

93

94. As Turiddu in *Cavalleria rusticana* with Giulietta Simionato at La Scala on December 7, 1963.

95, 96. As Turiddu in *Cavalleria rusticana*. Met/La Scala.

95

96

97. As Turiddu in *Cavalleria rusticana*. Met/La Scala.

98. As Rodolfo in *La bohème* at the Chicago Lyric Opera on October 22, 1965 with Mirella Freni, Sesto Bruscantini, Raffaele Arie and Renato Cesari.

99. As Rodolfo in *La bohème* at the Metropolitan Opera. [February, 1964]

100. As Roméo in *Roméo et Juliette*. Metropolitan Opera. [September, 1967]

101. With Mirella Freni {Juliette) in *Roméo et Juliette*. [September, 1967]

102. Backstage after *Roméo et Juliette*. [October, 1968]

101

102

103. In *Roméo et Juliette* with Colette Boky. [March, 1970]

104

105

104, 105. As Werther with Christa Ludwig in *Werther* at the Metropolitan Opera.
[February, 1971]

106. In *Werther* at the Metropolitan Opera. [1971]

107. Studying score. [1958]

108. Publicity photo from Angel Records.

109. With his automobile. [1962]

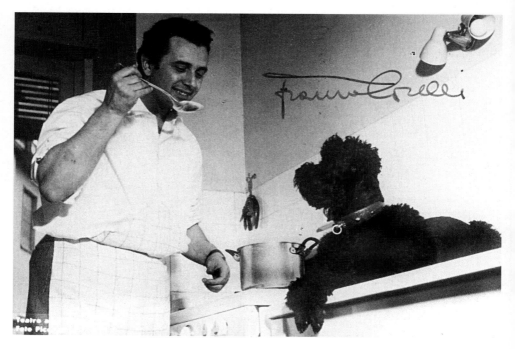

110. Cooking soup with his dog.

111. Looking at the La Scala stage from the house.

112. With Ettore Bastianini.

113. Sightseeing in Verona between performances of *Carmen*. [1970]

114. Eating with Lauri-Volpi in Valencia (Spain). [1969]

115. With Valentino and Mirella Bertinotti, wife Loretta, and Renata Tebaldi at the Grand Hotel, Rimini, ca. 1970.

116. With Teresa Zylis-Gara at the Metropolitan Opera Gala in honor of Rudolf Bing. [April, 1972]

117. Welcoming the alpine morning with a high note from his balcony in Cortina, Switzerland. [early 1970s]

118. Backstage after *Tosca* in Boston with fan Stefani Santini on April 24, 1973.

117

118

119. With Renata Tebaldi at a student opera concert in Milan.

120. Eating cake with author Marina Boagno at book signing in Parma.
[November 28, 1992]

Seen from the Outside

I think Franco is by nature a very shy and timid gentleman.

GRACE BUMBRY

I BELIEVE I OWE THE READER an explanation (besides a translation).

There is a precise reason for the words I have chosen to summarize this brief, heterogenous anthology of memories or impressions of Franco Corelli reported in their original language. The reason is this: when I have tried to translate them I found out that it was impossible. It was impossible first of all to translate the nuances of a word such as "gentleman," so loaded with Anglo-Saxon cultural implications, then also the meaning of the words "shy" and "timid," which, even if they are synonyms cover the entire spectrum that goes from *"timido"* to *"schivo,"* to *"riservato,"* to *"ombroso,"* to *"scontroso,"* and finally to *"timoroso."* (Shy, bashful, reserved, touchy, peevish, antisocial or fearful.) To choose two of the adjectives would mean to intervene and somehow to force the original sense, and to understand how much the original sense is important you need to listen to the decisive "diction," the parsed phrases of Grace Bumbry, as she underlines her accurate, thoughtful word choices. It was obvious that she was trying to find synthetic definitions that would be exhaustive of Franco Corelli's personality, and I believe that, with those three words, she succeeded.

A short warning again on the order in which the tributes or testimonies here gathered are reported (unless otherwise indicated, all come from my interviews). The way of gathering them together has been a very difficult choice, and sometimes it may appear arbitrary, because the criteria used have of course been subjective, though respectful, whenever possible, to the need for affinity to our subject.

Anyhow, I believe that this is not a relevant problem. They all contain a small fragment of Franco Corelli's portrait, and I leave to my readers the duty and the pleasure of putting together the pieces of the mosaic according to their own logic.

Fragments of a Portrait

AROUND 1952 THE NEWS HAD COME to us that there was a young singer at the Rome Opera who was surprising everybody, and this singer was Corelli. So we called him for an audition.

He came and did the audition, and he was nervous, very nervous, because he has always been a very tense person. He sang the first aria, and now I don't remember which one, which was rather good. At a certain point, because we were planning another *Adriana*, we asked him (we from the orchestra seats to him on the stage), if he knew *Adriana Lecouvreur*. He answered, "Yes, something, but I haven't really studied it. But, if you want, I will sing it."

The fact is, nervous as he was, at a certain point it seemed that the audition of *Adriana* wasn't going too well. He lost his temper, quit singing and walked out on us. Leaving the stage he met the impresario who had been present at the audition, who really did not encourage him too much right then.

The fact is that this boy, who was invited then the following year and then two years after and then three didn't want anything more to do with us, while for us he came to be an element of great interest. Finally, we called him for an opening with the director Luchino Visconti and with Maria Callas, and this flattered him. So, even though somewhat reserved, he ended by saying: "Very well, I'll do *La vestale* if you guarantee me you'll do it with Callas and Visconti."

LUIGI OLDANI

Sometimes it is part of a General Manager's job to nurse along high-strung major artists who cannot face the idea of a public performance on any day when they don't feel *simpatico* with the world—keeping Franco Corelli cheerful, for example, long seemed to me one of the things for which I was paid (in this instance, grossly underpaid). (*5,000 Nights at the Opera*)

RUDOLF BING

Corelli who seemed the most dangerous in the end was always the one who gave me the least problems. It is true that he would keep us on tenterhooks until the last minute. Sometimes he would arrive at the last minute, and therefore we felt bad, because, knowing his personality we would exaggerate our fears, and we would think that he would not come or that he would give up the performance, because, until the last, he was always more in favor of not singing than singing. Then when he would come onstage, he was the boss.

GIUSEPPE NEGRI

In Parma they said that there was "a cooperative society of tenors" because listening to him was like hearing I don't know how many tenors rolled into one. Someone insisted that he would overact because he had abilities that others didn't have. He had the ability to hold a note *filata*, for instance in *Tosca*. It wasn't overacting, it was just that others weren't able to do it.

He was such a powerful, strong tenor; still, he had this taste for the *mezze voci* and *filature*. Therefore, if he was someone who could make his voice light at will in such a way, why should he not have sung the *Werther* if he wanted? Or even the *Elisir d'amore*, if he felt like it?

GIUSEPPE NEGRI

Many stories circulated about his temperament and, I am sure, with a good share of exaggeration. But to deny he has a highly emotional makeup would be a downright falsehood, and indeed it probably contributes much to the excitement he creates onstage, an animal excitement, as some describe it. All singers become nervous before important performances, and Franco is no exception, but he always seems to transform his nerves into dynamic energy on the stage, resulting in an electrifying performance.

JEROME HINES

I remember once, in *Tosca*, at the "*Vittoria! Vittoria!*" that Maestro Votto, in the orchestra, looked at his watch, because it never finished. But it brought down the house!

GIGLIOLA FRAZZONI

Corelli has always had the reputation of being capricious, of being a "divo." I deny this in the most absolute way because I knew him too well. It was just a matter of worrying about his vocal technique, because he was more exacting than just about anybody. His "indispositions" might have looked like whims or caprices, but in fact they were authentic. Just before going to the theater, or even in the theater itself, he felt that he wasn't a hundred per cent. Then his scruples could become excessive: even when he was in condition to give 99% of what his nature and his equipment were able to give, he wanted to give 100. Even when the audience was going crazy, he would come into his dressing room between acts to ask. "How did I do? Tell me the truth!"

This happened from the beginning of his career. If he didn't feel that his performance was up to the 100 percent he would start to avoid everything and everybody and become impossible to approach, and nervous in an incredible way, and for these reasons it seemed that Corelli was crazy or showing off. It was nothing like this, though: he was honest. Also, when it would happen, there was big trouble: for the managers of the theater, for the colleagues, for everybody, his dog included.

But it was not his fault. He was the first victim of his perfectionism.

Still, in spite of his fears, he was the one who, on the stage, would wink his eyes while you were singing an aria, or make you a gesture maybe even in a duet, turning his shoulder to the audience to say, "You are doing well. Bravo, carry on this way!"

ANSELMO COLZANI

Corelli has always been Corelli, from the beginning, since the times when we sang our first Carmen together. He had voice to spare, and he used to sing the Flower Song of *Carmen* so well, *"E lucevan le stelle"*... I've never heard anyone sing the *"Ah, si, ben mio"* the way he could, it was exceptional. And the *"Improvviso"* of *Chénier*! In *Turandot*, then, he was something enormous. Of course we have never sung it together, but I used to go to listen to him. It was a pleasure to go and listen to him. I was in the theater when he sang the *Cavalleria rusticana* with Bernstein. Only someone with Corelli's *fiati* would have been able to sing it. It was something impossible. For me, Mascagni was turning over in his grave.

Still, you could see that he was suffering, that already before starting the opera he was thinking, "This note, I will put it here, this one I will do this way..." We had sung together for longer than ten years and he always arrived in his dressing room ten minutes before the show. He used to pass in front of my door and I would greet him as usual, "Hi, Franco. How are you." Never once did he answer, "I'm fine."

He was even afraid of giving encores. When we used to sing *La fanciulla del West* together and he was singing *"Ch'ella mi creda libero e lontano,"* I was standing right behind his shoulder and it was a pleasure to hear him. Then the audience would ask for the encore and he didn't want to know anything about it. I would tell him, "Come on Franco, give them this encore and then we'll go and get something to eat," and he would keep on saying no. And I would continue, "Come on, Franco, what do you think it is, it's only two B-flats! C'mon, Franco, otherwise we're not going to eat here!"

GIAN GIACOMO GUELFI

He used to have, besides his voice, this charm, this charisma about his person. Always onstage he would appear in an unreal dimension. Maybe his suffering could be seen, the audience would perceive it, and I think that this was good for him. Of course he didn't do that consciously, but when he would go before the public he would do so as if saying, "Here I am! I am going to give you my all, even if maybe I'm wrong..." This would be just what happened, and where the public was concerned, it was transformed into affection.

CARLO FRANCI

All his career has been studying, studying and more study and sacrifice. There are maybe not more than two or three examples in the history of singing of a singer who felt the weight of responsibility the way he did, even excessively. He was a perfectionist, always challenging himself. Even his choices of repertoire, in so many different directions, are a challenge—proving something, first of all to himself.

CARLO PERUCCI

I don't believe that he worried about his colleagues, that he was afraid of the competition. As I saw it, his greatest antagonist was himself. He gave me the impression of a person who was suffering a lot, depressed, worried. I had the feeling that this was because he wanted to give the maximum every time, surpassing his previous performance.

JEANNETTE PILOU

An honest appraisal of his sensational career discloses that below the surface of that high-voltage nature lies a keen, determined mind, consumed with a passionate desire to know more and more about the voice. Franco had sung with me during my vocal slump, which had begun in the late 60s, and my recovery after 1972 fascinated him. He often questioned me, trying to fathom how I had engineered such a recovery. This developed into a series of discussions, sometime highlighted with a look at Franco's vocal cords, or a turn at the piano sharing the challenge of some difficult vocal exercises. One time in 1978 I showed him a type of fast-moving scale that he simply could not begin to do. It was then that I got an in-depth view of the driving spirit in Corelli that had impelled him to stardom. I didn't realize how much it upset and challenged him to find he couldn't master that type of scale, until I saw him several days later and discovered he had spent most of his waking hours attacking the problem with a bulldog tenacity, almost with a fury. Not only did he conquer it in the next two weeks, but he put it in his throat all the way up to a high C-sharp. (*Great Singers on Great Singing*)

JEROME HINES

I think that ordinary people, not the best sorts, are the ones who create problems for maestri, colleagues, conductors. This was not the case with Franco, whom I believe to be a very sensitive man and a precious artist. Truly for me it has been a joy to conduct him for his great dramatic, artistic and vocal qualities. There was, and is, an extreme sensitivity there. He is a person of great sweetness and correctness. An exquisite person, truly.

I believe that he belongs to that category of great artists, the greatest artists, and it won't be easy for us to find his like again. I say this out of respect for the man, for the person that I knew and still know. He had a great virility in his voice, a passion, a sound... I'm not even able, in cases where he might have had them, to criticize his defects, because he would compensate in such a way with all the rest that it wasn't possible to stay there looking for some tiny thing that went wrong.

MICHELANGELO VELTRI

When we recorded *Aida* together, something happened and he was very nice to me about it.

In the triumphal scene I had a high C, and he wanted to sing it as well together with me. When we heard the first recording, his high C couldn't be heard and we had to record that part of the piece a second time. Evidently the technicians had opened Franco's microphone a little too much, and in the second run-through, we couldn't hear *my* high C any more. The triumph scene was the best part for my voice, and after all, the high C was written for me, not for him! This made me so angry that I went to the technical people and told them, "You don't need me here. You already have an Aida to sing my high C, and I'm going home." The technician was horrified by the idea of saying this to Franco and asked me to stay and to record the scene again, but I insisted: "No, he's perfectly able to sing my entire part!"

I was really leaving, too, when Franco, averted by the technician, caught up with me. "Birgit, I wasn't even thinking," he told me. "I'm not going to sing the high C. Forgive me, forgive me."

BIRGIT NILSSON

We were recording " 'O sole mio" for the LP of Neapolitan songs. Franco was almost finished when he gave me a look and a thumbs-up sign, signalling me that he had decided to go up and insert a passage that hadn't been programmed. In fact he shot out a high C-natural so brilliant that the cool professionals in the orchestra exploded in applause, irremediably spoiling the recording.

The technicians were furious. But Franco should have been

the maddest of all. Instead, no, he didn't take it badly, not for a moment. He just limited himself to performing a series of high C-naturals, none of which, however, satisfied him completely. Anyhow, we ended up picking one. The technicians of EMI "sewed up" the rest of the recording with an ability that could challenge any ear, but we were left with the regret of that C-natural that had been so perfect, the more perfect, perhaps, because we had lost it.

FRANCO FERRARIS

He has always been, besides the greatest of artists, a scrupulous professional, respecting himself, his public and the people who were paying him.

I remember, at the Arena of Verona, at the end of an *Aida* rehearsal, I went for a short stroll with Luisa [meaning, naturally, Luisa Maragliano, and the year was 1972. Ed.] on Liston and in the Piazza Bra, and there I ran into Corelli who was passing by, doing *solfège* exercises to himself the whole time, going over his part.

TRISTANO ILLERSBERG

I remember a Metropolitan tour that we did together. He was always overdressed with hat and scarf, even in Dallas where it was so hot. But a few times we succeeded in going out with him and then you could see his humanity, his desire to be normal and live as a normal person, going around wearing only a shirt, going to see something instead of staying locked up in his hotel.

CARLO FRANCI

One year we did *Don Carlo* [the year was 1961. Ed.]. The soprano was without voice, you couldn't hear her, and we had to make an announcement asking the audience to be tolerant.

Corelli was in the theater, so I said, "Let's have him do the announcement!"

We forced him, pushed him outside, and he didn't want to... In the end he spoke so softly that from the loges they screamed to him, "*Voce! Voce!*" Can you imagine, from the Parma gallery they are screaming "Voice!" to Corelli? It's something that certainly never happened when he was singing.

GIUSEPPE NEGRI

When we did *Aida* together, the first year of his career, some of us, behind the curtains, maybe after the first act, when Franco had sung the romanza, would give him compliments and say to him, "Bravo, Franco, bravo!" And he would shrug his shoulders. "What bravo? Come on, what bravo?" He was never pleased with himself, never.

ANITA CERQUETTI

We were doing *Aida* at the Metropolitan in the 70s and one time, while we were on the way from the stage to our dressing rooms, I told him, "You know, Franco, you have the most beautiful voice I've ever heard as Radames. You're simply perfect." He was so shy to hear it, so embarrassed! But he couldn't hold me back. There are moments when you absolutely have to say something.

GRACE BUMBRY

An opera usually known as *Aida* has concluded the 1971 visit of the Met to Dallas. Saturday evening, anyway, it was called *Radames*, and the person responsible for this change is the tenor Franco Corelli, who appeared in the role of the Egyptian warrior. (Review of *Aida* on May 15, 1971 in Dallas).

JOHN ARDOIN

I have a beautiful memory of our *Bohème* in Chicago, where I was making my debut. Franco was a force of nature in the third act. I have never heard a power like that. In Rodolfo's moments of desperation he was beautiful, but he also knew how to be gentle and sweet in the delicate moments. True, when he would open his throat he would scare you. I was younger then, with a lyric voice... But it would enchant me to listen to him. Our voices would blend well and sounded good together, even when we had done so many performances of *Roméo et Juliette*. There had been hints that it would be done at La Scala and Franco phoned to ask me if I would be available, because it would have made him happy to do it with me. I would have been very happy about it. And also to do the *Otello* people were talking about, though he never did it, I don't know why.

His voice, with that beauty and security singing the high notes has always had a tremendous effect on me, both when I was listening to him as a spectator and when I was on the stage. Even when you are involved in the action, if a voice gives you emotion, if you tremble while you are there waiting for your lines, for your replies, you cannot be isolated. While he was singing *"Non piangere Liù"* I really didn't have anything to do and then I was able to listen to him, and it was a joy. And also in *Roméo et Juliette* when he was singing *"Ah, lève-toi soleil,"* and I was ready to go out on the stage for the duet... The aria ends with a B-flat, and he would take it, and hold it evenly and then diminuendo on it... It was such a marvelous thing. And in order to do it, a tenor with a voice like this, so big and powerful, it means that, besides having great qualities, has worked very hard. Therefore I have the greatest respect for him.

MIRELLA FRENI

Franco's voice was different from the voice of any other tenor. I don't know if it was more beautiful or less beautiful, but it was different. It had inside a sensuality, a beautiful pathos.

His Chénier, for instance, was more complete than any other. Not only in the vocal aspect but in the stage presence and deportment, and most of all in the passion he would put into the voice, because inside the sentences, inside the lines that he was saying, there was the passion, the pain, everything. In the first act he turned towards me after having embellished the romanza and he would say those lines: "*Udite, non conoscete amore?*" he would say them in a way that would give me gooseflesh, and I would be transformed. He would drug me. I was hypnotized by his way of handling the sentence and by his hands... I was a passionate person by nature, but he would charge me, he would give me more.

GIGLIOLA FRAZZONI

No other colleague inspired me as much. In *Carmen*, when he sang the Flower Song, I felt something in me, I felt a real sorrow for Don José growing in me, because I had to be in love with Escamillo. And it only happened that way with him. Then in the scene in which I danced... I was supposed to be seductive, and with Franco that was possible, because he gave me something, he helped me, in the way he gave me his hands, trying to reassure me. He helped me a lot in all the little things: not only at the big moments, but with the little nuances that came to him, and to no one else. I believe that he was very undervalued as an actor.

Also in *Cavalleria rusticana* I believe that there was never a Turiddu as dramatic as Franco. At the Metropolitan, Zeffirelli's stage direction required that, while he was singing the "*Siciliana*" I would enter and make a great show of dramatizing the music of the overture. I heard his voice and his voice inspired me so much that I felt all the nuances, all the dynamic signs, all the motifs in the orchestra. He was fantastic, because in every note that he sang one heard passion and suffering, which are the same thing, because passion is full of suffering.

GRACE BUMBRY

I had never seen or heard Franco Corelli. There was only one rehearsal with solo singers and chorus, and after having sung my lines I had stayed on the apron of the stage trying to concentrate on what I had to do, and trying to memorize the scene and evaluate how I would give my voice. All of a sudden I heard behind my shoulder a voice of such power and beauty, with such an incredible B-flat that I was paralyzed, unable to sing the next line. Turning I recognized Franco Corelli standing at the back of the stage. I froze where I stood. I've never seen a tenor more gifted by nature, beautiful, tall, with long legs and a voice that was coming out so strong, so powerful, and with such extraordinary beauty. (*Galina, a Russian Story*)

GALINA VISHNEVSKAYA

They used to say that women would fall in love with him. On the contrary, Corelli used to make me mad! When I saw him going onstage in *Chénier* with that costume, I thought: "This guy has already achieved half the performance. How much more will I have to sing to make the audience notice me!"

In *Bohème*, humbly dressed, he was easier to take, but when he was wearing tights he was too much!

Still I always had the impression that he was suffering a lot, because he wanted to give a lot and he felt the weight of what the public was expecting from him.

And then he studied. It would happen that I would hear him going over a phrase... "*O dolci mani*," with that mezza voce... He would never have the presumption to say, "I'm Corelli, and I'm going to make it."

LUISA MARAGLIANO

There's this wonderful *Poliuto* in 1960 that confirms his artistic maturity, his *Battaglia* in 1961, his *Trovatore* and his

Huguenots of 1962, his *Cavalleria* of 1963 and his *Turandot* of 1964 (his last opening of the La Scala season). Mastering perfectly a voice with exceptional possibilities, in those years he could allow himself everything. Singing legato and *sul fiato*, the science of the "pianissimi" opened the doors of romanticism for him, the power and the authority of the accent, the fervor of the emission would make him a Verdi tenor. The beauty and sensuality of the timbre made him ideal for the verismo repertoire. His Raoul is miraculous, he has no heir as Manrico, and his Calaf was stupefying. (Review of the album, "Biography in Music" in *Opera International*, July/August 1989)

Sergio Segalini

An opera that Franco felt a lot was *Carmen*, particularly in the third and fourth acts. He would enter the stage literally distraught, and the same would happen in *Werther*, in the duet of the third act with Carlotta and in the death scene. There, truly, something different would come out in comparison with the other times. Usually he was worried about his voice. You could see that he was waiting for the moment of being able to construct a certain phrase just in order to hear the audience burst into applause. Instead in these two operas you could feel that it was a thing that he had in his soul, that he was digging out from inside, and really, it was a very impressive thing. I know that it is not easy to accept Corelli in the role of Werther. In Italy everybody is surprised when I talk about it because we are used to listen to Werthers that aren't very manly, with small voices. But it was stupendous to see Franco's figure when he entered in the first act, and then in all the rest of the opera. It added up to a passionate Werther.

Another part that he often insisted on taking was Romeo, and this was also a stupendous part for him. He centered the character fully, he was truly Romeo. Mister Bing put him on a stage that was right for him, which he succeeded in doing again afterward with the *Werther*. I believe that Franco would have been happy, satisfied, to sing those three characters, Rodolfo, Romeo and Werther, that he *felt* so deeply.

RENATA TEBALDI

He was an unforgettable Werther. He used to sing Werther in the way that I believe is the right one, because those who would have Werther a "*tenore di grazia*" are sacrificing his virility. Instead Franco would give Werther a great charge of virility. I'll say it again, it was unforgettable. It is maybe the most beautiful thing I ever heard him sing. I went many times to listen to him just because I was fascinated by his interpretation. It was very believable from a dramatic point of view.

CARLO FRANCI

I wish you could have seen Corelli just once on the stage. When they say class, that was class. When they say voice, that was a voice.

GRACE BUMBRY

Notes

The author would like to thank Dantina Chiesi and Seo Yumi, respectively, for their translations of German and Korean reviews.

PART ONE – UNDER HIS PILLOW

Spoleto

1 This, as with the citation of Maestro Ziino's memories to follow, was taken from an interview of Feb. 15, 1990.
2 *Il Teatro Lirico Sperimentale di Spoleto nel suo primo ventennio*, Rome, 1966.
3 *Il Messaggero*, Rome, Aug. 28 and 31, 1951. Unsigned.
4 "Vice" — *Il Tempo*, Rome, Aug. 27, 1951.
5 Giuseppe Pugliese — *Franco Corelli* in *Lirica*, installment n. 23, Fabbri, 1988.
6 Giuseppe Pugliese — *Il Gazzettino*, Venice, Sep. 6, 1951.
7 Giuseppe Pugliese — *Franco Corelli*, cit.
8 Giuseppe Pugliese — Television broadcast. *I Grandi della Lirica — Franco Corelli* by Guido Guarnera, RAI, Nov. 14, 1983.

A River of Voice

1 Rodolfo Celletti — *Un uomo chiamato tenore*, in *Discoteca*, June 1971.
2 Giorgio Gualerzi — *Bilancio canoro di vent'anni*, in *L'Opera* n. 1, 1965.
3 Giuseppe Pugliese — *Franco Corelli*, cit.
4 Giorgio Gualerzi — *Bilancio canoro di vent'anni*, cit.
5 The citation is taken from the accompanying copy, unsigned, of the compact disc *Franco Corelli* of EMI. Apart from its unmistakable style, Rodolfo Celletti has personally confirmed its authorship.
6 Rodolfo Celletti — *Un uomo chiamato tenore*, cit.
7 Jerome Hines — *Great Singers on Great Singing*, Doubleday & Co., Garden City N.Y., 1982.

8 Giuseppe Pugliese — *Franco Corelli*, cit.
9 Giuseppe Pugliese — *Franco Corelli*, cit.
10 Valeria Pedemonte — *Fate voi l'intervista*, in *Discoteca*, Mar. 1973.
11 Angelo Sguerzi — *Le stirpi canore*, Bongiovanni, Bologna, 1978.
12 Rodolfo Celletti — Copy accompanying CD EMI *Franco Corelli*, cit.
13 Radio Broadcast: *Franco Corelli* in *I Vip dell'Opera*, moderated by Rodolfo Celletti and Giorgio Gualerzi, RAI, Jan. 24, 1971.

Looking the Part

1 Shirley Fleming — *High Fidelity*, June 1962.
2 Guido Guarnera — Television broadcast already cited.
3 Pier Maria Paoletti — *Di cosa hai paura splendido Pollione?*, in *Quella sera alla Scala*, Rusconi, Milan, 1983.
4 To set the record straight this was a very loose version of *Andrea Chénier* (with Marcella Pobbe in the role Maddalena), and of *Denise*, a nineteenth-century *feuilleton* taken from a romance by Dumas fils.
5 Precisely because the citations have been chosen at random, I feel that it isn't worth the trouble to cite the sources. One could have found a dozen in the reviews of the period.
6 Richard Crowther — *Opera*, Sep. 1957.
7 Elliott Stein — *Opera*, Nov. 1958.
8 Giuseppe Pugliese — *Franco Corelli*, cit.
9 Robert Connolly — *Opera*, Oct. 1981.
10 Rodolfo Celletti — *Voce di tenore*, Idealibri, Milan, 1989.
11 Claudio Sartori — *Opera*, Aug. 1958.
12 Harold Rosenthal — *Great Singers of Today*, Calder and Boyers, London, 1966.
13 Harold Schonberg — *The New York Times*, Sep. 20, 1967.
14 Joseph Wechsberg — *Opera*, Jan. 1971.

15 Rodolfo Celletti — *Franco Corelli*, in *Le Grandi Voci*, Istituto per la Collaborazione Culturale, Rome, 1964.
16 Pier Maria Paoletti — *Quella sera alla Scala*, cit.
17 Rodolfo Celletti — *Franco Corelli*, in *Le Grandi Voci*, cit.
18 Magda Olivero — interview of Oct. 3, 1989.
19 Rudolf Bing — *5000 Nights at the Opera*, Doubleday & Co., Garden City, N.Y., 1972.
20 Anselmo Colzani — interview of July 28, 1989.

PART TWO – DAY AFTER DAY, NIGHT AFTER NIGHT

From Carmen to Aida
1 Maestro Ottavio Ziino — interview already cited.
2 Evening in honor of Franco Corelli, Ancona, Teatro Sperimentale, Oct. 25, 1981.
3 Giulietta Simionato — interview of Mar. 1, 1990; Maestro Gianandrea Gavazzeni — interview of May 8, 1990.
4 Evening in honor of Franco Corelli, cit.
5 Maestro Tristano Illersberg — interview of Oct. 21, 1989.
6 See for example Angelo Sguerzi — *Le stirpi canore*, cit.
7 Pier Maria Paoletti — *Quella sera alla Scala*, cit.
8 Cynthia Jolly — *Opera*, June 1953.
9 Giancarlo Landini — *Musica*, Mar. 1987.
10 *Se l'opera non è caduta, molto lo si deve alla bravura dei cantanti* — *La Scala*, Mar. 1954 (unsigned).
11 Cynthia Jolly — *Opera*, June 1954.
12 Television broadcast: *I Grandi della Lirica* — *Franco Corelli*.
13 Television broadcast: *I Grandi della Lirica* — *Franco Corelli*.
14 Rodolfo Celletti — *Un uomo chiamato tenore*, cit.
15 Evening in honor of Franco Corelli, cit.
16 Giuseppe Pugliese — *Il Gazzettino*, Venice, May 7, 1954.
17 Claudio Sartori — *Opera*, Mar. 1955.
18 Bardolfo (Eugenio Gara) — *Candido*, Dec. 19, 1954.
19 Giuseppe Pugliese — *Il Gazzettino*, Venice, Jan. 27, 1955.
20 *Diario de Noticias*, Lisbon, Apr. 30, 1955 (unsigned).
21 *O seculo*, Lisbon, Apr. 30, 1955 (unsigned).

22 *Il Gazzettino*, Venice, *Verona chronicles*, July 31, 1955, article unsigned.
23 Mila Contini — *Timido ma bello il fusto della lirica*, in *Amica*, n. 19, July 27, 1962.
24 Elena Nicolai — interview of Dec. 28, 1989.
25 *Il Gazzettino*, Venice, Verona chronicles, Aug. 11, 1955, article unsigned.
26 *L'Arena*, Aug. 11, 1955, article unsigned.
27 Cynthia Jolly — *Opera*, Feb. 1956.
28 Giuseppe Pugliese — *Il Gazzettino*, Venice, Nov. 25, 1955.
29 Rodolfo Celletti — *Un uomo chiamato tenore*, cit.
30 Anselmo Colzani — interview already cited.
21 Maestro Gianandrea Gavazzeni — interview already cited.
32 Bardolfo (Eugenio Gara) — *Candido*, May 27, 1956.
33 Maestro Gianandrea Gavazzeni — interview already cited.
34 Rodolfo Celletti — in *Umberto Giordano*, edited by Mario Morini, Sonzogno, Milan, 1968.
35 Review of the complete opera (EMI 1964). Signed W.W., and, judging from the style and the content, we have reason to suppose we are dealing with William Weaver. (Heading and date missing.)
36 Rodolfo Celletti - Preface to edition I and II of *Il Teatro d'Opera in Disco*. Third Edition, Rizzoli, Milan, 1988.
37 Pietro Caputo - *Cotogni, Lauri-Volpi e...*, Bongiovanni, Bologna, 1980.
38 Rodolfo Celletti - *Il Teatro d'Opera in Disco*, cit.
39 Conrad L. Osborne - *Franco Corelli in and out of Costume*, in *High Fidelity*, Sep. 1967.

From the Pirate to the Huguenots
1 See for example Mario Pasi - *Maria Callas, la donna, la voce, la diva*, International Music of Italy, 1981.
2 Rodolfo Celletti - *Un uomo chiamato tenore*, cit.
3 Rodolfo Celletti - *Un uomo chiamato tenore*, cit.
4 Eugenio Gara - *Musica d'oggi*, N. 7, July 1958.
5 Massimo Mila - *L'Espresso*, June 1, 1958.
6 Eugenio Montale - *Prime alla Scala*, Mondadori, Milan, 1981
7 Giuseppe Pugliese - *Il Gazzettino*, Venice, July 25, 1958.
8 Giuseppe Pugliese - All the citations are taken from *Franco Corelli*, cit.

9 Rodolfo Celletti - *Pavarotti - 25 anni per la musica*, Ruggeri, 1986.

10 The text of the phrase can be found in Rodolfo Celletti - *Un uomo chiamato tenore*, cit.

11 I have not found the exact date, but this is part of the history of the Teatro Regio of Turin, by Giorgio and Valeria Gualerzi, which was disseminated as part of the broadcast *Foyer*, (RAI-RADIOTRE) in Mar. 1989.

12 Adone Zecchi - *La Scala*, Dec. 1958.

13 Birgit Nilsson - interview of Jan. 29, 1990.

14 Jerome Hines - *Great Singers on Great Singing*, cit.

15 Fedora Barbieri - interview of Feb. 21, 1990.

16 Valeria Pedemonte - *Fate voi l'intervista*, cit.

17 Giuseppe Pugliese - *Il Gazzettino*, Venice, July 28, 1959.

18 Carlo Bologna - *L'Arena*, Verona, July 1959 (the exact date is missing).

19 Respectively: ABC in *La gazzetta del lunedì* (Genoa); E.S. in *Il lavoro nuovo* (Genoa); unsigned, in *Il Corriere mercantile* (Genoa); unsigned, in *Il corriere del pomeriggio* (Genoa). Dated Mar. 29 and 30, 1959.

20 Guido Tartoni, in *La lirica e i suoi protagonisti - Il divo*, in *Radiocorriere*, n. 2L May 19/25, 1974.

21 Interview of Herbert Weinstock - in *Opera*, Oct. 1966.

22 I stole the adjectives from Mario Morini in his introductory copy for the Cetra "live" record.

23 Magda Olivero - interview already cited.

24 Giulietta Simionato - interview already cited.

25 Joan Downs - *Franco Corelli*, in *The Tenors*, edited by Herbert H. Breslin, Macmillan Publishing Co. Inc., New York, 1973.

26 Claudio Sartori - *Opera*, June 1960.

27 Patrick Turnbull - *Opera*, May 1960.

28 Giuseppe Pugliese - *Il Gazzettino*, Venice, Aug. 1, 1960.

29 Respectively in: *L'Arena*, Verona, Aug. 2, 1960; *Opera*, Summer Festivals 1960; *L'Europeo*, Aug. 14, 1960.

30 Heading and exact date are missing.

31 Giuseppe Pugliese - *Il Gazzettino*, Venice, Dec. 8, 1960.

32 Teodoro Celli - Heading is missing.

33 Maestro Gianandrea Gavazzeni - interview already cited.

34 Harold Schonberg - *The New York Times*, Jan. 28, 1961.

35 Robert Sabin - Heading is missing.

36 Birgit Nilsson - interview already cited.

37 Edgarda Ferri - Heading and exact date are missing.

38 Piero De Palma - interview of Mar. 9, 1990.

39 Giuseppe Pugliese - *Il Gazzettino*, Venice, July 28, 1961.

40 Giulio Confalonieri - *Epoca*, Sep. 3, 1961.

41 Rodolfo Celletti - *Il Teatro d'Opera in Disco*, cit.

42 Raymond Ericson - *The New York Times*, Jan. 29, 1962.

43 Mario Morini - *Raoul da Lauri-Volpi a Corelli*, in *Il Corriere del Teatro*, n. 9, 1962.

44 Sergio Segalini - *Meyerbeer. Diable ou prophète?*, Beba, Paris, 1985.

45 Rodolfo Celletti - Introductory copy for Cetra "live" disc.

46 Giulietta Simionato - interview already cited.

47 Mario Morini - *Raoul da Lauri-Volpi a Corelli*, cit.

48 Carlo Perucci - interview of Feb. 27, 1990.

49 Giuseppe Negri - interview of Feb. 19, 1990.

50 Television broadcast: *I grandi della lirica - Franco Corelli*, cit.

51 Eugenio Gara - *L'Europeo*, June 10, 1962.

52 Rodolfo Celletti - *Un uomo chiamato tenore*, cit.

53 Gabriele D'Annunzio - *Il Fuoco*, Mondadori, Milan.

54 Rodolfo Celletti - *Il Teatro d'Opera in Disco*, cit.

55 André Tubeuf - *Opera*, Summer Festivals 1962.

56 Interviews, respectively, of May 8, 1990, Feb. 15, 1990, Dec. 5, 1989 and Mar. 1, 1990.

57 Anselmo Colzani - interview already cited.

58 Antonietta Stella - interview of Jan. 29, 1990.

59 Rudolf Bing - *5000 Nights at the Opera*, cit.

60 Mario Morini - *Raoul da Lauri-Volpi a Corelli*, cit.

61 C.F. — Introductory copy for the Cetra "live" disc.

62 Maestro Gianandrea Gavazzeni - interview already cited.

63 Antonietta Stella - interview already cited.

From Bohème to Bohème

1 J.A. (almost certainly John Ardoin) - *Musical America*, Apr. 1964.

2 Conrad L. Osborne - *Franco Corelli in and out of Costume*, cit.
3 Giuseppe Pugliese - *Franco Corelli*, cit.
4 Max de Schauensee - *Opera*, Aug. 1964.
5 Giorgio Gualerzi - *Voci e vocalità del nostro tempo*, in *Musica e Dossier* N. 26, Feb. 1989.
6 Giuseppe Pugliese - *Franco Corelli*, cit.
7 *Le Figaro*, Paris, June 5, 1964 (unsigned).
8 Olivier Merlin - *Le Monde*, Paris, June 5, 1964.
9 Max de Schauensee - *The Evening Bulletin*, Philadelphia, Nov. 11, 1964.
10 Eugenio Gara - *L'Europeo*, Dec. 1964.
11 A. Fedele - *Il progresso italo-americano*, New York, Mar. 29, 1965.
12 Harold C. Schonberg, *The New York Times*, 2 Dec. 1965. 13 *Opera*, respectively July, Sep. and Nov. 1966.
14 Gerald Fitzgerald - *Opera*, Apr. 1966.
15 Giuseppe Pugliese - *Franco Corelli*, cit.
16 Carlo Perucci - interview already cited.
17 Giorgio Gualerzi - *Discoteca*, Feb./Mar. 1967.
18 Gustavo Marchesi - *La Gazzetta di Parma*, Jan. 20, 1967.
19 Gustavo Marchesi - *La Gazzetta di Parma*, Jan. 22, 1967.
20 Harold Rosenthal - *Opera*, Dec. 1967.
21 Giorgio Gualerzi - *La Stampa*, Turin, Dec. 27, 1967.
22 Bill Park, Dallas (Texas).
23 Birgit Nilsson - interview already cited.
24 Herbert Weinstock - Opera, Apr. 1970.
25 Rodolfo Celletti - *Memorie di un ascoltatore*, Il Saggiatore, Milan, 1985.
26 Giorgio Gualerzi - *Stampa Sera*, Turin, Aug. 1970 (the exact date is missing).
27 Rodolfo Celletti - *Da Verona con gelo e fervore*, in *Discoteca*, Oct. 1970.
28 The episode referenced by press sources was personally confirmed to me by Adriana Lazzarini (interview of Sep. 27, 1990).
29 Joseph Wechsberg - *Opera*, Jan. 1971.
30 D.A. (Davide Annachini) - *L'Opera*, May 1990.
31 Giorgio Gualerzi - *Radiocorriere*, n. 32, Aug. 9/15, 1970.
32 Maestro Carlo Franci - interview of Mar. 28, 1990.
33 Giuseppe Negri - interview already cited.
34 Giandonato Crico - *Lucia di Lammermoor*, Gremese, Milan.
35 Rodolfo Celletti - *Un uomo chiamato tenore*, cit.
36 Grace Bumbry - interview of July 27, 1990.
37 A. Fedele - *Il progresso italo-americano*, New York, Mar. 3, 1971.
38 *Opera*, June 1971.
39 Rodolfo Celletti, *Un uomo chiamato tenore*, cit.
40 Interviews already cited. Anita Cerquetti - interview of Feb. 15, 1990.
41 Luisa Maragliano - interview of Oct. 21, 1989.
42 Raoul Grassilli - interview of Feb. 19, 1990.
43 Paolo Accattatis - *Corriere Adriatico*, Ancona, July 5, 1971.
44 In *Corriere della sera*, Milan, July 5, 1971.
45 Giorgio Gualerzi - *Discoteca*, Sep. 1971.
46 Giorgio Gualerzi - *Opera*, Summer Festivals, 1971.
47 I Yu Son. Note that I have summarized the article, citing the most important phrases.
48 Chong Byung Sun.
49 Alfredo Mandelli - *Oggi*, Jan. 1972.
50 Giorgio Gualerzi - *Stampa Sera*, Turin, July 18, 1972.
51 Mario Messinis - *Il Gazzettino*, Venice, July 17, 1972.
52 Lorenzo Arruga - *Il Giorno*, Milan, July 18, 1972.
53 Roberto Zanetti - *L'Avanti*, Rome, July 18, 1972.
54 For example, a great colleague has particularly insisted on this point—Elena Nicolai, who did not have the chance to hear Corelli after their professional encounters in the 1950s (interview already cited).
55 Bill Park.
56 John H. Harvey - *St. Paul Dispatch*, Minneapolis, May 1973.
57 Grace Bumbry - interview already cited.
58 Giorgio Gualerzi - *Discoteca*, Oct. 1974.
59 Ettore Mo, *Il Corriere della Sera*, Milan, July 15, 1975.
60 Paolo Isotta, *Il Giornale*, Milan, July 15, 1975.
61 Luigi Rossi, *La Notte*, Milan, July 14, 1975.
62 Respectively in *Discoteca*, Oct. 1975, *Il Giorno*, Milan, July 15, 1975.
63 Quoted from Adriano Bassi, "...*la vita è un sogno...*" in *Opera*, July/Aug. 1987.
64 Grace Bumbry, interview already cited.

Sparks in the Night
1 Jerome Hines - *Great Singers on Great Singing*, cit.
2 *Il Corriere d'Informazione*, Milan, Aug. 25, 1980 (unsigned).
3 Carlo Brusati - Aug. 1980 (heading is missing).
4 Robert Connolly, *Opera*, Oct. 1981.

5 Enrico Caruso - *The Art of Singing*, The Metropolitan Opera Company Publishers, New York 1909.
6 Ernest Hemingway - *Death in the Afternoon*, translated by Fernanda Pivano, Mondadori, Milan.

One Page Before the End
1 *La Gazzetta di Parma*, Dec. 24, 1988 (article unsigned).
2 *La Gazzetta di Parma*, Dec. 27, 1988 (article unsigned).

Lost Chances
1 *Opera*, Feb. 1966.
2 Valeria Pedemonte - *Fate voi l'intervista*, cit.
3 Interview already cited.
4 Giulio Cardi - *L'Adige*, Trento, Aug. 1961 (the exact date is missing).
5 Valeria Pedemonte - *Fate voi l'intervista*, cit.
6 Valeria Pedemonte - *Fate voi l'intervista*, cit.

PART THREE – EMOTIONS

To Perform While Singing
1 Angelo Sguerzi - *Le stirpi canore*, cit.
2 Raymond Ericson - *The New York Times*, Jan. 29, 1962.
3 *The New York Journal-American*, Jan. 29, 1962 (unsigned).
4 Guido Pannain - *Il Tempo*, Rome, Mar. 26, 1963.
5 Gianfranco Zaccaro - *Mondo lirico*, 1963 (the exact date is missing).
6 Richard Crowther - *Opera*, June 1967.
7 Alan Rich - *The New York Herald Tribune*, Dec. 2, 1965.
8 Rudolf Bing - *5000 Nights at the Opera*, cit.
9 Joan Downs - *The Tenors*, cit.
10 The quotations are taken from the following, respectively: Alfredo Parente, *Il Mattino*, Naples, Nov. 29, 1959; Giuseppe Pugliese, *Il Gazzettino*, Venice, July 28, 1961; Luigi Ceolari, *La Notte*, Milan, July

1961 (the exact date is missing); Lorenzo Arruga, *Il Giorno*, Milan, July 8, 1970; Lorenzo Arruga, *Il Giorno*, Milan, July 13, 1970; Luigi Rossi, *La Notte*, Milan, July 21, 1970.

PART FOUR – WITHIN THE TENOR

Humility
1 Pietro Caputo - *Cotogni, Lauri-Volpi e...*, cit.
2 Giacomo Lauri-Volpi - *A lezione dal veterano*, in *Musica e dischi*, Jan. 1968.
3 Giuseppe Pugliese - *Franco Corelli*, cit.
4 Giuliano Ranieri — *Le tre paure di Franco Corelli*, in *Epoca*, July 27, 1970.
5 Television broadcast: *Il protagonista - Giacomo Lauri-Volpi*, RAIDUE, Mar. 24, 1980.
6 See the preceding note.

Courage and Fear
1 Giuseppe Pugliese - *Il Gazzettino*, Venice, July 28, 1959.
2 Piero De Palma, interview already cited.
3 Quoted from Adriano Bassi - *"...la vita è un sogno,"* cit.

PART FIVE – CORELLI AND THE RECORD

Starting Points for a Discussion
1 Rodolfo Celletti - *Il teatro d'opera in disco*, cit.
2 Sergio Segalini - *Opera International*, Sep. 1989.
3 Shirley Fleming - *High Fidelity*, cit.
4 Joan Downs - *The Tenors*, cit.
5 Rodolfo Celletti - *Il teatro d'opera in disco*, cit.
6 Valeria Pedemonte - *Fate voi l'intervista*, cit.
7 Joan Downs - *The Tenors*, cit.
8 Valeria Pedemonte - *Fate voi l'intervista*, cit.
9 Aldo Nicastro - *Disclub* (date is missing).
10 Giorgio Gualerzi - *Discoteca* (date is missing).

Repertory

Allegra, Salvatore   ROMULUS (Remo)

Bellini, Vincenzo   NORMA (Pollione)
IL PIRATA (Gualtiero di Montalto)

Bizet, Georges   CARMEN (Don José)
In Italian and in French

Cilea, Francesco   ADRIANA LECOUVREUR (Maurizio di Sassonia/
Maurice of Saxony)
In Italian

Donizetti, Gaetano   LUCIA DI LAMMERMOOR (Edgardo [di] Ravenswood)
POLIUTO (Poliuto)

Giordano, Umberto   ANDREA CHÉNIER (Andrea Chénier)
FEDORA (Loris Ipanov)

Gluck, Christoph Willibald   IFIGENIA IN AULIDE [IPHIGENIA IN AULIS]
(Achille)

Gounod, Charles   FAUST (Faust)
In French
ROMÉO ET JULIETTE (Romeo)
In French

Guerrini, Guido   ENEA [AENEAS] (Turno and Orfeo)

Händel, Georg Friedrich   GIULIO CESARE (Sesto)
ERACLE [HERCULES] (Illo)

Leoncavallo, Ruggero   PAGLIACCI (Canio)

Mascagni, Pietro	CAVALLERIA RUSTICANA (Turiddu)
Massenet, Jules	WERTHER (Werther) *In French*
Meyerbeer, Giacomo	LES HUGUENOTS [GLI UGONOTTI](Raoul de Nangis) *In Italian*
Mussorgsky, Modest	BORIS GODUNOV (Grigori) *In Italian* KHOVANSHCHINA (Andrey Khovansky) *In Italian*
Ponchielli, Amilcare	LA GIOCONDA (Enzo Grimaldo)
Prokofiev, Sergei	GUERRA E PACE [WAR AND PEACE] (Piero Besukov)
Puccini, Giacomo	LA BOHÈME (Rodolfo) LA FANCIULLA DEL WEST (Dick Johnson) TOSCA (Mario Cavaradossi) TURANDOT (Calaf)
Spontini, Gaspare	AGNESE DI HOHENSTAUFEN (Enrico di Braunshwig/Henry of Brunswick) LA VESTALE (Licinio)
Verdi, Giuseppe	AIDA (Radames) LA BATTAGLIA DI LEGNANO (Arrigo) DON CARLO (Don Carlo) ERNANI (Ernani) LA FORZA DEL DESTINO (Don Alvaro) MACBETH (Macduff) MESSA DI REQUIEM [REQUIEM MASS] SIMON BOCCANEGRA (Gabriele Adorno) IL TROVATORE (Manrico)
Zandonai, Riccardo	GIULIETTA E ROMEO (Romeo)

Chronology of Debuts

edited by Gilberto Starone

1951

SPOLETO — TEATRO NUOVO
Aug 26   Carmen

1952

ROME — TEATRO DELL'OPERA
Jan 31   Giulietta e Romeo
May 8   Adriana Lecouvreur
Dec 14   Boris Godunov

1953

ROME — TEATRO DELL'OPERA
Mar 11   Enea (world premiere)
Apr 9   Norma

FLORENCE — TEATRO COMUNALE
May 26   Guerra e pace (first performance in Italian)

ROME — TERME DI CARACALLA
July 2   Pagliacci

RAVENNA — OPEN-AIR THEATER
Sep 12   Aida

1954

ROME — TEATRO DELL'OPERA
Jan 28   Romulus
Mar 4   Don Carlo
Apr 17   Ifigenia in Aulide

FLORENCE — TEATRO COMUNALE
May 6   Agnese di Hohenstaufen (first performance in Italy)

SAN REMO (IM) — TEATRO DELLE PALME
July   Tosca

MILAN — TEATRO ALLA SCALA
Dec 7   La vestale

1955

VENICE — TEATRO LA FENICE
Jan 26   La fanciulla del West

ROME — TEATRO DELL'OPERA
Dec 26   Giulio Cesare

1956

MILAN — TEATRO ALLA SCALA
May 21   Fedora

1957

NAPLES — TEATRO DI SAN CARLO
Mar 3   Andrea Chénier

LISBON — TEATRO DE SÃO CARLOS
May 3   Khovanshchina
May 25   Simon Boccanegra

1958

NAPLES — TEATRO DI SAN CARLO
Mar 15   La forza del destino

PISA — TEATRO VERDI
Apr 12   Turandot

MILAN — TEATRO ALLA SCALA
May 19   Il pirata

BOLOGNA — TEATRO COMUNALE
Nov 6   Il trovatore

MILAN — TEATRO ALLA SCALA
Dec 29   Eracle (first performance in Italy)

1959

MILAN — TEATRO ALLA SCALA
Feb 25   Ernani

1960

MILAN — TEATRO ALLA SCALA
Dec 7   Poliuto

1961

MILAN — TEATRO ALLA SCALA
Dec 7   La battaglia di Legnano

1962

NEW YORK — METROPOLITAN OPERA HOUSE
Mar 9   La Gioconda

MILAN — TEATRO ALLA SCALA
May 28   Les Huguenots (Gli Ugonotti)

1963

MINNEAPOLIS — NORTHROP AUDITORIUM
May 17   Cavalleria rusticana

1964

NEW YORK — METROPOLITAN OPERA HOUSE
Feb 29   La bohème

PHILADELPHIA — ACADEMY OF MUSIC
Apr 14   Roméo et Juliette

1967

LOS ANGELES — PHILHARMONIC AUDITORIUM
Nov 14   Requiem Mass

1971

NEW YORK — METROPOLITAN OPERA HOUSE
Jan 11   Lucia di Lammermoor
Feb 27   Werther

1973

MEMPHIS — MUNICIPAL AUDITORIUM
May 15   Macbeth

Chronology of Operas and Concerts

edited by Gilberto Starone

1951

SPOLETO (PG) — TEATRO NUOVO
Aug 26   *Carmen* (4 perf.)
[repeated Aug 30,
Sep 7, 12]

L. Danieli, O. Di Marco, M. Spatafora,
O. Ziino cond.
[Experimental Debut Theater]

1952

ROME — TEATRO DELL'OPERA
Jan 31   *Giulietta e Romeo* (3)
[Feb 3, 9]

M. Fortunati, M. Micheluzzi, A. Poli,
G. Conti, O. Ziino cond.

May 8   *Adriana Lecouvreur* (1)

M. Caniglia, M. Benedetti, T. Gobbi,
V. Bellezza cond.

ROME — TERME DI CARACALLA
July 12   *Carmen* (4)
[July 15, 20, 24]

P. Tassinari, F.C. Forti/A. Leonelli/
L. Carol, R. De Falchi, A. Questa cond.

CIVITAVECCHIA (RM), TERRACINA (LT), CAGLIARI — OPEN-AIR THEATERS
July-Aug   *Carmen*

M. Pirazzini, A. Pini, G.G. Guelfi,
F. Patanè cond.

TRIESTE — CASTELLO DI SAN GIUSTO
July 31   *Carmen* (3)
[Aug 2, 5]

G. Simionato, S. Zanolli, M. Stefanoni,
V. Susca, B. Ronchini, P. Cappuccilli
(Morales), G. Bamboschek cond.

SAN REMO (IM) — TEATRO DELLE PALME
Aug 11   *Carmen* (1)

P. Tassinari, C. Broggini, M. Stefanoni,
E. Tieri cond.

TURIN — TEATRO NUOVO
Oct 18   *Carmen* (3)
[Oct 21, 26]

G. Simionato, E. Tegani, A. Mongelli,
G. Antonicelli cond.

ROME — TEATRO DELL'OPERA
Dec 14   *Boris Godunov* (4)
[Dec 16, 20, 28]

B. Christoff, M. Pirazzini, A. Pini,
V. De Taranto, P. Munteanu,
A. Zerbini, V. Gui cond.

1953

PALERMO — TEATRO MASSIMO
Feb 20   *Carmen* (4)

P. Tassinari, R. Noli, A. Colzani,
O. De Fabritiis cond.

ROME — TEATRO DELL'OPERA
Mar 11   *Enea* (2) World Premiere
[Mar 15]

A. Stella, O. Moscucci, M. Pirazzini,
B. Christoff, A. Zerbini, E. Tieri cond.

Apr 9   *Norma* (4)
[Apr 12, 15, 18]

M. Callas, F. Barbieri, G. Neri,
G. Santini cond.

Apr 23   *Carmen* (6)
[Apr 26, 28,
May 2, 9, 27]

P. Tassinari/G. Pederzini, M. Pintus/
M. Minazzi/B. Fabrini, P. Silveri/
G.G. Guelfi, V. Bellezza cond.

FLORENCE — TEATRO COMUNALE
May 26   *Guerra e pace* (4)
[May 29, 31,   Premiere in Italian
June 2]

R. Carteri, F. Barbieri, C. Broggini,
M. Picchi, E. Bastianini, A. Colzani,
R. Capecchi, I. Tajo, F. Corena,
A. Rodzinski cond.

ROME — TERME DI CARACALLA
July 2   *Pagliacci* (2)
[July 6]

C. Petrella, A. Protti, M. Borriello,
A. Zagonara, G. Morelli cond.

BOLZANO — OPEN-AIR THEATER
July 9   *Carmen* (2)

G. Simionato, L. Carol, A. Colzani,
O. Ziino cond.

ENNA — CASTELLO DI LOMBARDIA
Aug 1   *Carmen* (2)

G. Pederzini, B. Fabrini, G.G. Guelfi,
F. Capuana cond.

NAPLES — ARENA FLEGREA
Aug 21   *Carmen* (4)
[Aug 23, 27, 28]

G. Simionato, E. Rizzieri/L. Perlotti,
A. Protti, P. De Palma, F. Reiner cond.

SPOLETO (PG) — TEATRO NUOVO
Sep 6   *Pagliacci*

L. Pinnarò, U. Borghi, R. Scorsoni,
A. Paoletti cond.

RAVENNA — TEATRO ALIGHIERI
Sep 11   *Carmen* (2)
[Sep 13]

M. Pirazzini, M. Pintus, L. Di Lelio,
A. Manca Serra, A. Questa cond.

RAVENNA — OPEN-AIR THEATER
Sep 12   *Aida* (1)

C. Mancini, E. Nicolai, A. Protti, G. Neri,
P. Clabassi, L. Di Lelio, A. Questa cond.

TRIESTE — TEATRO VERDI
Nov 19   *Norma* (4)
[Nov 22, 24, 29]

M. Callas, E. Nicolai, B. Christoff,
A. Votto cond.

NAPLES — TEATRO DI SAN CARLO
Dec 19   Carmen (6)   G. Simionato/P. Tassinari, S. Jurinac,
                                              U. Savarese/G. Taddei, A. Rodzinski cond.
                                              [Also with Howard Vandenburg]

1954

PIACENZA (CARNEVALE 1953/1954) — TEATRO MUNICIPALE
Jan   Carmen   P. Tassinari, E. Camellini, A. Mongelli,
                                              F. Molinari Pradelli cond.

MODENA — TEATRO COMUNALE
Jan 4   Norma   L. Kelston Ferraris, D. Minarchi,
                                              S. Catania, O. De Fabritiis cond.

PARMA — TEATRO REGIO
Jan 9   Norma (2)   C. Mancini, E. Nicolai, G. Ferrara,
[Jan 13]   O. Ziino cond.

PAVIA — TEATRO FRASCHINI
Jan 16   Carmen (2)   P. Tassinari, M. Pintus, A. Mongelli,
                                              A. Brainovich cond.

ROME — TEATRO DELL'OPERA
Jan 28   Romulus (3)   E. Barbato, M. Benedetti, G.G. Guelfi,
[Jan 13, Feb 3]   A. Romani, O. De Fabritiis cond.

Mar 4   Don Carlo (4)   C. Mancini, E. Nicolai, T. Gobbi,
[Mar 7, 10, 13]   B. Christoff, G. Neri, G. Santini cond.

Apr 17   Ifigenia in Aulide (4)   M. Pobbe, E. Nicolai, B. Christoff,
[Apr 19, 22, 26]   A. Colella, S. Maionica, G. Santini cond.

FLORENCE — TEATRO COMUNALE
May 6   Agnese di Hohenstaufen (3)   L. Udovich, D. Dow, G.G. Guelfi,
[May 9, 11]   Italian Premiere   F. Albanese, E. Mascherini, A. Colzani,
                                              V. Gui cond.

SAN REMO (IM) — TEATRO DELLE PALME
July   Tosca (1)   E. Barbato, E. Mascherini, M. Luise,
                                              O. De Fabritiis cond.

ROME — TERME DI CARACALLA
Aug 3   Carmen (3)   G. Simionato/P. Tassinari, O. Di Marco/E.
[Aug 7, 9]   Tegani/E. Farroni, R. De Falchi/E. Viaro,
                                              V. Bellezza cond.

FERMO (AP) — TEATRO DELL'AQUILA
Aug 10   Tosca (2)   M. Caniglia, A. Dadò, A. Gambelli,
[Aug 11]   A. Paoletti cond.

MESSINA — OPEN-AIR THEATER
Aug 22   Carmen (2)   M. Pirazzini, M. Pintus, A. Colzani,
                                              L. Di Lelio, R. Huder, E. Sivieri cond.

BOLOGNA — TEATRO DUSE
Sep   *Tosca*   G. Frazzoni, P. Campolonghi,
O. Marini cond.

MILAN — RAI [Televised performance]
Sep 26   *Pagliacci*   M. Micheluzzi, T. Gobbi, M. Carlin,
L. Puglisi, A. Simonetto cond.

BOLOGNA — TEATRO DUSE
Sep 27   *Carmen*   M. Pirazzini, S. Croci, A. Mongelli,
O. Marini cond.

ROVIGO — TEATRO SOCIALE
Oct 24   *Carmen* (2)   F. Sacchi, O. Di Marco, A. Colzani,
[Oct 27]   O. Ziino cond.

MILAN — TEATRO ALLA SCALA
Dec 7   *La vestale* (5)   M. Callas, E. Stignani, E. Sordello,
[Dec 9, 12,   N. Rossi Lemeni, A. Votto cond.
16, 18]

PIACENZA — TEATRO MUNICIPALE
Dec 29   *Norma* (2)   C. Mancini, D. Minarchi, M. Stefanoni,
O. De Fabritiis cond.

1955

VENICE — TEATRO LA FENICE
Jan 26   *La fanciulla del West* (4)   E. Barbato, G.G. Guelfi, M. Caruso,
I. Vinco, G. Vanelli, O. De Fabritiis cond.

REGGIO EMILIA — TEATRO MUNICIPALE
Feb 3   *Norma* (2)   C. Mancini, M. Pirazzini, G. Algorta,
[Feb 6]   A. Narducci cond.

PIACENZA — TEATRO MUNICIPALE
Feb 10   *Pagliacci*   A. Beltrami, R. Roma, O. Ziino cond.

REGGIO EMILIA — TEATRO MUNICIPALE
Feb 15   *Carmen* (2)   P. Tassinari, M. De Osma, P. Guelfi,
[Feb 17]   F. Patanè cond.

RAI
Mar 15   Concert   M. Rossi cond.
            Werther: Ah! Non mi ridestar

CATANIA — TEATRO MASSIMO BELLINI
Mar 19   *Tosca* (3)   A. Guerrini, G. Taddei/U. Savarese,
A. Erede cond.

LISBON — TEATRO SÃO CARLOS
Apr 29   *Carmen* (2)   G. Simionato, M. Pobbe, E. Campi,
A. Colzani, P. De Palma, V. Susca,
O. De Fabritiis cond.

RAVENNA — TEATRO ALIGHIERI
May 26   Norma (2)   C. Mancini, E. Stignani, E. Ticozzi,
[May 29]   U. Novelli, M. Parenti cond.

FLORENCE — GIARDINO DI BOBOLI
June 26   Norma (7)   A. Cerquetti/L. Kelston Ferraris, F. Barbieri/
[June 28, 29, 30,   M. Pirazzini, G. Neri, G. Santini/
July 1, 2, 3]   A. Quadri cond. [Also with Mario Ortica]

ROME — TERME DI CARACALLA
July 7   Norma (4)   L. Udovich, F. Barbieri, G. Neri,
[July 10, 14, 16]   G. Santini cond.

THIENE (VI) — OPEN-AIR THEATER
July   Pagliacci (1)   L. Di Lelio, C. Tagliabue, V. Zanetti,
                                             C. Flemi, G. Peguri cond.

VERONA — ARENA
July 24   Carmen (3)   G. Simionato, R. Ferrari/B. Fabrini/
[July 30, Aug 3]   M. Pobbe, A. Colzani/A. Protti,
                                             A. Votto cond.

Aug 10   Aida (3)   A. Stella, A. Lazzarini/F. Barbieri, A. Protti,
[Aug 13, 15]   G. Neri, F. Molinari Pradelli cond.

MESSINA — OPEN-AIR THEATER
Aug 18   Aida (2)   A. Cerquetti, M. Pirazzini, E. Viaro,
                                             G. Tozzi, A. Questa cond.

BOLOGNA — TEATRO DUSE
Sep   Tosca   G. Frazzoni, P. Campolonghi, A. Baracchi.
                                             O. Marini cond.

MILAN — RAI [Televised performance]
Sep 24   Tosca   R. Heredia Capnist, C. Tagliabue,
                                             V. De Taranto, A. Votto cond.

TURIN — TEATRO CARIGNANO
Oct 29   Tosca (3)   M. Caniglia, G.G. Guelfi, P.L. Latinucci,
[Nov 3, 6]   F. Molinari Pradelli cond.

CATANIA — TEATRO MASSIMO BELLINI
Nov 12   Aida (3)   C. Mancini, F. Barbieri/L. Danieli,
                                             A. Protti, S. Maionica, N. Verchi cond.

NAPLES — TEATRO DI SAN CARLO
Nov 24   Aida (4)   A. Stella, F. Barbieri, A. Colzani,
                                             P. De Palma, G. Modesti, M. Petri,
                                             V. Gui cond. [Also with Mario Filippeschi]

TRIESTE — TEATRO VERDI
Nov 30   La fanciulla del West (4)   G. Frazzoni, G.G. Guelfi, A. Zagonara,
[Dec 3, 7, 11]   E. Sordello (Sonora), F. Capuana cond.

ROME — TEATRO DELL'OPERA
Dec 26   Giulio Cesare (4)   O. Fineschi, F. Barbieri, B. Christoff,
                                             M. Petri, A. Cassinelli, F. Mazzoli,
                                             G. Gavazzeni cond.

1956

MILAN — RAI
Jan 17   Martini & Rossi Concert   R. Carteri, O. De Fabritiis cond.
                 Adriana Lecouvreur: La dolcissima effige
                 Carmen: Il fior che avevi a me tu dato

MILAN — RAI
Jan   Concert
                 Andrea Chénier: Improvviso
                 L'africana: O paradiso

VENICE — TEATRO LA FENICE
Feb 2   *Carmen* (4)   G. Simionato, R. Scotto, G.G. Guelfi,
[Feb 5, 8, 12]   L. Di Lelio, O. De Fabritiis cond.

Feb 29   *Aida* (4)   A. Cerquetti, A. Lazzarini, G.G. Guelfi/A.
[Mar 3, 7, 11]   Protti, G. Algorta, L. Di Lelio,
                                               A. Questa cond.

MILAN — TEATRO ALLA SCALA
Apr 4   *La fanciulla del West* (4)   G. Frazzoni, T. Gobbi, F. Ricciardi,
[Apr 7, 11, 15]   N. Zaccaria, E. Sordello (Sonora),
                                               A. Votto cond.

ROVIGO — TEATRO SOCIALE
Apr 18   *Aida* (1)   S. Dall'Argine, G. Consolandi, M. Zanasi,
                                               A. Colella, F. Molinari Pradelli cond.

LISBON — TEATRO DE SÃO CARLOS
Apr 27   *Giulietta e Romeo* (2)   M. Curtis Verna, R. Azzolini,
                                               O. De Fabritiis cond.

COIMBRA (PORTUGAL) — TEATRO AVENIDA
May 1   *Tosca* (1)   M. Curtis Verna, R. Azzolini, P. De Palma,
                                               G. Giorgetti, L. Di Lelio, I. Savini cond.

MILAN — TEATRO ALLA SCALA
May 21   *Fedora* (6)   M. Callas, S. Zanolli, A. Colzani,
[May 23, 27, 30,   P. Montarsolo, G. Gavazzeni cond.
June 1, 3]

BERGAMO — TEATRO DONIZETTI
June 9   *Carmen*   M. Mas, M. Adani, R. Capecchi, A.
                                               Cattelani, L. Di Lelio, C. F. Cillario cond.

MILAN — RAI [Televised performance]
June 13   *Carmen*   B. Amparan, E. Ribetti, A. Colzani,
                                               N. Sanzogno cond.

ROME — FILMED OPERA
                 Tosca   M. Caniglia, G.G. Guelfi, V. De Taranto,
                                               A. Relli, O. De Fabritiis cond. (Orchestra
                                               and Chorus from Rome's Teatro dell'Opera)

VERONA — ARENA
Aug 9   *Tosca* (4)   G. Frazzoni, T. Gobbi, M. Luise,
[Aug 12, 14, 16]   A. Votto cond.

ADRIA (RO) — TEATRO COMUNALE
Sep   *Tosca*   S. Dall'Argine, A. Dadò, N. Santi cond.

BERGAMO — TEATRO DONIZETTI
Oct 9   *Carmen* (3)   M. Rose/M. Mas, M. Adani, R. Capecchi,
[Oct 11, 13]   L. Di Lelio, C.F. Cillario cond.

TRIESTE — TEATRO VERDI
Nov 14   *Aida* (4)   A.M. Rovere, D. Minarchi, G.G. Guelfi,
[Nov 18, 20, 23]   G. Neri, A. Massaria, A. Votto cond.

MILAN — TEATRO ALLA SCALA
Dec 10   *Giulio Cesare* (4)   V. Zeani, G. Simionato, N. Rossi Lemeni,
[Dec 13, 16, 19]   M. Petri, A. Cassinelli, G. Gavazzeni cond.

Dec 23   *Aida* (3)   A. Stella, G. Simionato, D. Dondi/
[Dec 26, 30]   G.G. Guelfi, N. Zaccaria, S. Maionica,
     A. Votto cond.

TURIN — RAI [Recording session]
     Aida   M. Curtis Verna, M. Pirazzini, G.G. Guelfi,
     G. Neri, A. Questa cond. (Orchestra and
     Chorus from Turin's RAI)

1957

MILAN — TEATRO ALLA SCALA
Jan 10   *Pagliacci* (4)   E. Ratti/G. Frazzoni/C. Broggini,
     R. Roma/A. Protti, L. Alva,
     E. Sordello/N. Sanzogno cond.
     [The Jan 17 performance was suspended to mourn
     Arturo Toscanini's death]

ROME — TEATRO DELL'OPERA
Jan 26   *Aida* (4)   A. Cerquetti, G. Simionato, G.G. Guelfi,
[Jan 30, Feb 3, 6]   G. Neri, G. Santini cond.

NAPLES — TEATRO DI SAN CARLO
Feb 9   *La fanciulla del West* (4)   M. Caniglia, G.G. Guelfi, P. De Palma,
[Feb 13, 17, 23]   O. De Fabritiis cond.

Mar 3   *Andrea Chénier* (3)   A.M. Rovere/M. Coleva, G.G. Guelfi,
     P. De Palma, N. Monte, A. Erede/P. De
     Angelis cond. [also with Antonio Gallié]

PALERMO — TEATRO MASSIMO
Mar 14   *Andrea Chénier* (4)   A. De Cavalieri, G.G. Guelfi, G. Borrelli,
     F. Mazzoli, P. Ferrara, L. Di Lelio,
     F. Molinari Pradelli cond.

LISBON — TEATRO DE SÃO CARLOS
Mar 17   *Andrea Chénier* (2)   G. Frazzoni, T. Gobbi, P. De Palma.
     P. De Freitas Branco cond.

PALERMO — TEATRO MASSIMO
Apr 2   *Don Carlo* (4)   A. Cerquetti, A. Lazzarini/M. Pirazzini,
                                                         E. Mascherini, B. Ladysz, E. Campi,
                                                         L. Di Lelio, M. Rossi cond.

LISBON — TEATRO DE SÃO CARLOS
May 3   *Khovanshchina* (2)   M. Pobbe, B. Christoff, R. Arié,
                                                         V. Gui cond.

May   Concert   M. Pobbe, A. Pini, J. Valtriani,
  Carmen: Il fior che avevi a me tu dato   G. Dal Ferro, P. De Palma, G. Malaspina,
  Turandot: Nessun dorma; Non piangere Liù   R. Arié (piano: M. Pellegrini, C. Pasquali)
  Tosca: E lucevan le stelle

MADRID — TEATRO LA ZARZUELA
May 6   *Tosca*   A. De Cavalieri, G. Taddei,
                                                         A. Quadri cond.

VIENNA — STAATSOPER
May 15   *Aida* (4)   A. Stella, G. Simionato, A. Protti,
[May 18, 21, 24]   N. Zaccaria, A. Votto cond. (Orchestra and
                                                         Chorus from Milan's Teatro alla Scala)

LISBON — TEATRO DE SÃO CARLOS
May 25   *Simon Boccanegra* (2)   M. Pobbe, T. Gobbi, B. Christoff,
                                                         G. Malaspina, V. Gui cond.

RAVENNA — TEATRO ALIGHIERI
May 30   *Andrea Chénier* (2)   A. De Cavalieri, A. Cattelani, A. Protti,
[June 2]   G. Calò, L. Di Lelio, M. Parenti cond.

ENGHIEN-LES-BAINS (FRANCE) — THÉÂTRE DU CASINO
June   *Norma*   F. Cavalli, A. Lazzarini, A. Ferrin.
                                                         Mario Parenti cond. (Orchestra and chorus
                                                         of the Teatro Comunale of Reggio Emilia)

LONDON — ROYAL OPERA HOUSE (COVENT GARDEN)
June 27   *Tosca* (3)   Z. Milanov, G.G. Guelfi, F. Robinson,
[July 1, 3]   A. Gibson cond.

VERONA — ARENA
July 18   *Norma* (2)   A. Cerquetti, G. Simionato, G. Neri,
[July 21]   F. Molinari Pradelli cond.

PESARO — PALAZZO DELLO SPORT
July 21/28   *Carmen* (2)   M. Pirazzini, A. Meletti, A. Colzani,
                                                         N. Annovazzi cond.

VERONA — ARENA
Aug 1   *Carmen* (5)   F. Barbieri, C. Broggini, E. Bastianini,
[Aug 4, 10, 15, 18]   F. Molinari Pradelli cond.

ROME — TERME DI CARACALLA
Aug 22   *Carmen* (1)   F. Barbieri, O. Di Marco, G. Malaspina,
                                                         E. Tieri cond.

Aug 25   *Andrea Chénier* (3)   M. Caniglia, G.G. Guelfi, A. Erede cond.
[Aug 29, Sep 1]

Aug 27	*Tosca* (1)	G. Frazzoni, G.G. Guelfi, A. Paoletti cond.
Sep 9	*Aida* (1)	A. Cerquetti, F. Barbieri, T. Gobbi, G. Neri G. Santini cond.

BILBAO (SPAIN) — TEATRO COLISEO ALBIA

Sep 16	*Pagliacci* (1)	A. Beltrami, E. Bastianini, V. Pandano, R. Cesari, N. Rescigno cond.
Sep 18	*Carmen* (1)	B. Amparan, A. Beltrami, E. Bastianini, A. Quadri cond.
Sep 21	*Tosca* (1)	M. Roberti, G. Taddei, A. Quadri cond.

OVIEDO (SPAIN) — TEATRO CAMPOAMOR

Sep 24	*Carmen* (1)	B. Amparan, J. Valtriani, A. Colzani, L. Di Lelio, N. Santi cond.
Sep 27	*Fedora* (1)	N. De Rosa, L. Di Lelio, E. Sordello, N. Santi cond.

LIVORNO — TEATRO GOLDONI

Oct 10	*La fanciulla del West* (2)	G. Frazzoni, P. Guelfi, A. Mercuriali, U. Novelli, G. Belloni. A. Quadri cond.

BERGAMO — TEATRO DONIZETTI

Oct 19 [Oct 23, 29]	*Andrea Chénier* (3)	G. Frazzoni/R. Heredia Capnist, U. Savarese, L. Di Lelio, O. De Fabritiis cond.

1958

ROME — TEATRO DELL'OPERA

Jan 2	*Norma* (1)	M. Callas, M. Pirazzini, G. Neri, G. Santini cond. [The performance was suspended after the first scene of the first act]
Jan 4 [Jan 8, 11]	*Norma* (3)	A. Cerquetti, M. Pirazzini/F. Barbieri, G. Neri, G. Santini cond.

PARMA — TEATRO REGIO

Jan 14 [Jan 16]	*Carmen* (2)	F. Barbieri, P. Lorengar, E. Bastianini, L. Di Lelio, F. Ghione cond.

ROME — TEATRO DELL'OPERA

Jan 23 [Jan 26, 28, Feb 1]	*Don Carlo* (4)	A. Stella/M. Coleva, C. Mancini, T. Gobbi, M. Petri, G. Neri, G. Santini cond.

PALERMO — TEATRO MASSIMO

Feb 6	*La fanciulla del West* (4)	M. Olivero, G.G. Guelfi, A. Ferrin, G. Mazzini, M. Caruso, E. Campi, F. Ghione cond.
Feb 21	*Norma* (4)	A. Cerquetti, G. Simionato, G. Modesti, L. Di Lelio, T. Serafin cond.

NAPLES — TEATRO DI SAN CARLO
Mar 6   *Tosca* (5)   R. Tebaldi/M. Coleva, T. Gobbi/
                                               E. Bastianini/P. Guelfi, L. Pudis,
                                               U. Rapalo cond. [also with
                                               Giuseppe Gismondo]

Mar 15   *La forza del destino* (3)   R. Tebaldi, O. Dominguez, E. Bastianini,
[Mar 18, 20]   B. Christoff, R. Capecchi,
                                               F. Molinari Pradelli cond.

NICE — THÉÂTRE DE L'OPÉRA
Mar   *Tosca*

PISA — TEATRO VERDI
Apr 12   *Turandot* (2)   A. Corridori, L. Coppola, F. Lidonni,
[Apr 14]   S. Catania, M. Cordone cond.

MILAN — TEATRO ALLA SCALA
May 19   *Il pirata* (5)   M. Callas, E. Bastianini, P. Clabassi,
[May 22, 25,   A. Votto cond.
28, 31]

WIESBADEN — GROSSES HOUSE
June 3   *Tosca* (1)   G. Tucci, A. Colzani, M. Luise, P. De
                                               Palma, F. Capuana cond. (Orchestra and
                                               Chorus from Rome's Teatro dell'Opera)

STUTTGART — STAATSOPER
June 10   *Tosca* (1)   G. Tucci, A. Colzani, M. Luise, P. De
                                               Palma, F. Capuana cond. (Orchestra and
                                               Chorus from Rome's Teatro dell'Opera)

MUNICH — PRI' IZREGENTENTHEATER
June 17   *Tosca* (1)   G. Tucci, A. Colzani, M. Luise, P. De
                                               Palma, F. Capuana cond. (Orchestra and
                                               Chorus from Rome's Teatro dell'Opera)

ENGHIEN-LES-BAINS (FRANCE) — THÉÂTRE DU CASINO
June 26   *Andrea Chénier* (2)   A. De Cavalieri, A. Colzani, L. Di Lelio,
[June 28]   A. Bonato, P. Castagnoli, F. Patanè cond.
                                               (Orchestra and Chorus of the Teatro di San
                                               Carlo of Naples)

ROME — TERME DI CARACALLA
July 6   *Pagliacci* (2)   V. Montanari, A. Protti, A. Zagonara,
[July 11]   F. Lidonni, O. Ziino cond.

July 13   *Aida* (5)   A. Stella/S. Dall'Argine, M. Pirazzini/
[July 17, 21,   D. Minarchi/A. Lazzarini, T. Gobbi/
26, 31]   G.G. Guelfi, F. Ghione/A. Paoletti cond.

VERONA — ARENA
July 24   *Turandot* (6)   F. Yeend/A. Corridori, R. Carteri/
                                               M. Cucchio, I. Vinco, R. Capecchi,
                                               A. Votto cond.

Aug 2   *Aida* (3)   L. Price/A. Stella, F. Barbieri, G.G. Guelfi,
[Aug 6, 9]   T. Serafin cond.

ROME — TERME DI CARACALLA
Aug 17   *Turandot* (1)   L. Udovich, P. Malgarini, P. Clabassi, S. Meletti, V. Bellezza cond.

Aug 23   *Tosca* (2)   L. Bertolli, G.G. Guelfi, A. Questa/
[Aug 28]   A. Paoletti cond.

BERGAMO — TEATRO DONIZETTI
Oct 4   *Tosca* (2)   G. Frazzoni, G.G. Guelfi, V. Carbonari, A. Camozzo cond.

BOLOGNA — TEATRO COMUNALE
Nov 6   *Il trovatore* (1)   M.L. Nache, A. Lazzarini, D. Dondi, A. Zerbini, L. Di Lelio, F. Capuana cond.

NAPLES — TEATRO DI SAN CARLO
Nov 29   *Andrea Chénier* (4)   A. Stella, E. Bastianini, M. Pirazzini, L. Di Lelio, A. Pirino, A. Cassinelli, F. Capuana cond.

MILAN — TEATRO ALLA SCALA
Dec 17   *Turandot* (1)   B. Nilsson, R. Carteri, G. Modesti, M. Ferrara, R. Capecchi, P. De Palma, A. Votto cond.

MILAN — RAI [Televised performance]
Dec 23   *Turandot*   L. Udovich, R. Mattioli, P. Clabassi, M. Borriello, F. Previtali cond.

MILAN — TEATRO ALLA SCALA
Dec 29   *Eracle* (4)   E. Schwarzkopf, F. Barbieri, E. Bastianini,
[Jan 1959- 1, 5, 7]   J. Hines, L. Von Matacic cond.

1959

PARMA — TEATRO REGIO
Jan 4   *Turandot* (1)   A. Corridori, R. Terzi, R. Cesari, A. Marchica, M. Carlin, V. Belezza cond.

PALERMO — TEATRO MASSIMO
Jan 17   *Turandot* (5)   L. Udovich, M. Olivero/I. Ligabue/ E. Fusco, I. Vinco, G. Mazzini, R. Ercolani, F. Ricciardi, O. Ziino cond.

Feb 3   *Carmen* (4)   G. Simionato, M. Freni/G. Tavolaccini, G.G. Guelfi, L. Di Lelio, P. Dervaux cond.

MILAN — TEATRO ALLA SCALA
Feb 25   *Ernani* (6)   M. Roberti, E. Bastianini/D. Dondi/
[Feb 28, Mar 3, 5,   C. MacNeil, N. Rossi Lemeni/N. Zaccaria,
8, Apr 12]   P. De Palma, G. Gavazzeni cond.

LISBON — TEATRO DE SÃO CARLOS
Mar 12   *Turandot* (2)   I. Borkh, N. Panni, A. Votto cond.

Mar 23   *Il trovatore* (1)   R. Crespin, L. Danieli, E. Bastianini, L. Di Lelio, S. Maionica, A. Votto cond.

GENOA — [RIADATTAMENTO DEL] TEATRO CARLO FELICE

Mar 28	*Il trovatore* (3)	L. Gencer, F. Barbieri, A. Colzani, A. Ferrin, L. Di Lelio, O. De Fabritiis cond.

MILAN — TEATRO ALLA SCALA

Apr 9 [Apr 15, 18, 20, 23, 26]	*Carmen* (6)	G. Simionato, A. Beltrami/R. Scotto, G.G. Guelfi, N. Sanzogno cond.
May 11 [May 14, 17, 19, 23, 26, 31, June 2]	*Il trovatore* (8)	M. Roberti/M.L. Nache, G. Simionato/ F. Barbieri/E. Nicolai, E. Bastianini, N. Zaccaria/I. Vinco, A. Votto cond.
June 26	Gala evening	[In honor of Presidents De Gaulle and Gronchi and their wives]
	Ernani [Act III, with scenery and costumes]	G. Tucci, E. Bastianini, N. Rossi Lemeni, G. Gavazzeni cond.

VERONA — ARENA

July 26 [July 30, Aug 1, 5, 12, 15]	*Il trovatore* (6)	G. Tucci/L. Price, G. Simionato/ A. Lazzarini, E. Bastianini/A. Protti, A. Mongelli, O. De Fabritiis cond.

ROME — TERME DI CARACALLA

Aug 20 [Aug 23, 26, 29]	*Il trovatore* (4)	M. Roberti, L. Danieli, A. Protti, A. Cassinelli, O. De Fabritiis cond.

BILBAO (SPAIN) — TEATRO COLISEO ALBIA

Sep 3	*Il trovatore* (1)	M. Roberti, F. Barbieri, E. Bastianini, G. Modesti, E. Wolf Ferrari cond.
Sep 7	*Aida* (1)	M. Roberti, F. Barbieri, E. Bastianini, G. Modesti, M. Stefanoni, E. Wolf Ferrari cond.
Sep 12	*Turandot* (1)	G. Grob-Prandl, G. Tucci, G. Modesti, M. Ausensi, V. Pandano, B. Bardaji, E. Wolf Ferrari cond.

OVIEDO — TEATRO CAMPOAMOR

Sep 17	*Il trovatore* (1)	M.L. Nache, G. Consolandi, A. Protti, G. Modesti. E. Wolf Ferrari cond.
Sep 22	*Tosca* (1)	M.L. Nache, A. Protti, R. Claverol. F. Patanè cond.

LIVORNO — TEATRO LA GRAN GUARDIA

Oct 21 [Oct 24]	*Tosca* (2)	R. Tebaldi, A. Colzani, P.L. Latinucci, M. Parenti cond.

BOLOGNA — TEATRO COMUNALE

Nov 6	*Turandot* (4)	L. Udovich/R. Heredia Capnist, E. Vincenzi/A.M. Vallin, I. Vinco, V. Pandano, F. Ricciardi, C. Masini Sperti, O. De Fabritiis cond.

NAPLES — TEATRO DI SAN CARLO
Nov 28   *Adriana Lecouvreur* (4)   M. Olivero/G. Frazzoni, G. Simionato,
[Dec 1, 6, 9]   E. Bastianini, M. Caruso, A. Cassinelli,
                                                   M. Rossi cond.

[Nov 29   General Rehearsal with R. Tebaldi]

BOLOGNA — TEATRO COMUNALE
Dec 22   *Andrea Chénier* (2)   G. Frazzoni, G.G. Guelfi, P. Mantovani,
[Dec 26]   S. Maionica, A. Questa cond.

1960

MILAN — TEATRO ALLA SCALA
Jan 11   *Andrea Chénier* (7)   R. Tebaldi/G. Frazzoni, E. Bastianini/
[Jan 15, 17, 20,   U. Savarese, F. Cossotto, E. Vincenzi,
24, 28, 31]   P. De Palma, G. Gavazzeni cond.

BRESCIA — TEATRO GRANDE
Feb 4   *La forza del destino* (2)   M. Roberti, M. Pirazzini, E. Mascherini,
[Feb 7]   L. Gaetani, R. Cesari, N. Annovazzi cond.

NAPLES — TEATRO DI SAN CARLO
Feb 13   *Il trovatore* (6)   M. Parutto/A.M. Rovere, F. Barbieri/A.
                                                Lazzarini/L. Danieli, G.G. Guelfi/
                                                M. Zanasi/W. Alberti, G. Modesti/
                                                S. Catania/I. Riccò, G. Santini cond. [Also
                                                with Achille Braschi]

MONTE-CARLO — THÉÂTRE DE L'OPÉRA
Feb 28   *Turandot* (2)   A. Lund Christiansen, G. Mazzoleni,
                                                G. Foiani, R. Cesare, W. Artioli,
                                                C. Masini Sperti, A. Simonetto cond.

GENOA — [RIADATTAMENTO DEL] TEATRO CARLO FELICE
Mar 8   *Andrea Chénier* (3)   G. Frazzoni, G. Carturan, U. Savarese,
                                                A. Maddalena, F. Molinari Pradelli cond.

MILAN — TEATRO ALLA SCALA
Mar 21   *Turandot* (6)   B. Nilsson/M. Casals Mantovani, C.
[Mar 24, 27,   Petrella/I. Tosini, G. Modesti, E. Sordello/
31, Apr 3, 6]   C. Meliciani, M. Ferrara, P. De Palma,
                                                A. Mercuriala, A. Votto cond.

Apr 9   *Carmen* (5)   G. Lane, G. Tucci, D. Dondi/A. Protti,
[Apr 12, 16,   N. Sanzogno cond.
20, 23]

VENICE — TEATRO LA FENICE
May 14   *La forza del destino* (3)   M. Roberti, L. Didier Gambardella,
[May 17, 22]   U. Savarese, R. Capecchi, N. Rossi Lemeni,
                                                E. Gracis cond.

May 30   *Turandot* (4)   L. Udovich, N. Panni, P. Clabassi,
[June 1, 5, 7, 12]   G. Mazzini, A. Zagonara, C. Masini
                                                Sperti, F. Previtali cond.

VIENNA — STAATSOPER
June 26   *Andrea Chénier* (2)   R. Tebaldi, E. Bastianini, R. Ercolani,
[June 29]   K. Paskalis (Fleville), L. Von Matacic cond.

ENGHIEN-LES-BAINS (FRANCE) — THÉÂTRE DU CASINO
     Tosca
     Andrea Chénier

VERONA — ARENA
July 31   *La fanciulla del West* (5)   M. Olivero, G.G. Guelfi, P. De Palma,
[Aug 3, 7, 10, 13]   R. Capecchi, W. Ganzarolli,
     O. De Fabritiis cond.

ROME — TERME DI CARACALLA
Aug 20   *Tosca* (4)   M. Olivero, G.G. Guelfi,
[Aug 23, 27, Sep 3]   A. La Rosa Parodi cond.

Sep 1   *La fanciulla del West* (1)   G. Frazzoni, G.G. Guelfi,
     O. De Fabritiis cond.

MILAN — TEATRO ALLA SCALA
Sep 5, 12   *Norma*   M. Callas, C. Ludwig, N. Zaccaria, P. De
     Palma, T. Serafin cond. (Orchestra and
     Chorus from Milan's Teatro alla Scala)

Sep   *Pagliacci*   L. Amara, T. Gobbi, M. Zanasi, M. Spina,
     L. Von Matacic cond. (Orchestra and
     Chorus from Milan's Teatro alla Scala)

LIVORNO — TEATRO LA GRAN GUARDIA
Oct 4   *Turandot*   M.L. Nache, M. Micheluzzi, A. Cassinelli,
     M. Parenti cond.

LAUSANNE (SWITZERLAND) — THÉÂTRE DE BEAULIEU
Oct 10   *Turandot* (2)   R. Heredia Capnist, M. Micheluzzi,
     A. Zerbini, O. De Fabritiis cond.
     (Orchestra and Chorus from Bologna's
     Teatro Comunale)

VIENNA — STAATSOPER
Oct 19   *Tosca* (1)   H. Zadek, E. Bastianini. N. Santi cond.

Oct 23   *La forza del destino* (2)   G. Schyrer, B. Cvejic, W. Kreppel,
     K. Donch, B. Klobucar cond.

Oct 29   *Tosca* (3)   H. Zadek/C. Martinis, E. Kunz, E. Lorenzi.
[Nov 1, 13]   A. Erede/B. Klobucar cond.

MILAN — TEATRO ALLA SCALA
Dec 7   *Poliuto* (8)   M. Callas/L. Gencer, E. Bastianini,
[Dec 10, 14, 18,   P. De Palma, N. Zaccaria, A. Ferrin,
21, 26, 29,   A. Votto/A. Tonini cond.
Jan 15, 1961]

BOLOGNA — TEATRO COMUNALE
Dec 20   *Tosca* (4)   G. Frazzoni, G.G. Guelfi, C. Badioli,
     G. Foiani, O. De Fabritiis cond. [Also with
     Daniele Barioni]

1961

PARMA — TEATRO REGIO
Jan 1   *Il trovatore* (2)   I. Ligabue, A. Lazzarini, M. Zanasi,
[Jan 3]   S. Catania, A. Basile cond.

NEW YORK — METROPOLITAN OPERA HOUSE
Jan 27   *Il trovatore* (6)   L. Price/L. Amara, I. Dalis/N. Rankin/
[Feb 4, 8, 18,   J. Madeira/M. Dunn, R. Merrill/M. Sereni,
Mar 6, 18]   W. Wildermann, F. Cleva
                                               [Commemoration of the 60th anniversary of
                                               Giuseppe Verdi's death]

Feb 24   *Turandot* (8)   B. Nilsson, A. Moffo/T. Stratas/L. Amara/
[Mar 4, 9, 13, 24,   L. Albanese, B. Giaiotti, W. Wildermann,
 29, Apr 8, 11]   F. Guarrera, R. Nagy, C. Anthony,
                                               L. Stokowski cond.

WASHINGTON (D.C.)
Mar 16   Concert   R. Tebaldi
                                               [Centenary of Italian Unity]

PHILADELPHIA — ACADEMY OF MUSIC
Mar 21   *Turandot* (1)   B. Nilsson, L. Price, B. Giaiotti,
                                               L. Stokowski cond.

NEW YORK — METROPOLITAN OPERA HOUSE
Apr 3   *Don Carlo* (2)   M. Curtis Verna, N. Rankin/I. Dalis,
[Apr 15]   M. Sereni, G. Tozzi/J. Hines, H. Uhde,
                                               N. Verchi cond.

CLEVELAND — PUBLIC AUDITORIUM (MET SPRING TOUR)
Apr 26   *Turandot* (1)   B. Nilsson, L. Amara, B. Giaiotti,
                                               F. Guarrera, R. Nagy, C. Anthony,
                                               K. Adler cond.

ATLANTA — CIVIC AUDITORIUM (MET SPRING TOUR)
May 1   *Turandot* (1)   B. Nilsson, L. Amara, B. Giaiotti,
                                               F. Guarrera, R. Nagy, C. Anthony,
                                               K. Adler cond.

ST. LOUIS — KIEL AUDITORIUM (MET SPRING TOUR)
May 10   *Aida* (1)   B. Nilsson, I. Dalis, R. Merrill, B. Giaiotti,
                                               R. Nagy, C. Ordassy, N. Verchi cond.

CHICAGO — McCORMICK EXPOSITION CENTER (MET SPRING TOUR)
May 13   *Turandot* (1)   B. Nilsson, L. Amara, B. Giaiotti,
                                               F. Guarrera, R. Nagy, C. Anthony,
                                               K. Adler cond.

MINNEAPOLIS — NORTHROP AUDITORIUM (MET SPRING TOUR)
May 17   *Turandot* (1)   B. Nilsson, L. Amara, B. Giaiotti,
                                               F. Guarrera, R. Nagy, C. Anthony,
                                               K. Adler cond.

DETROIT — MASONIC TEMPLE AUDITORIUM (MET SPRING TOUR)
May 22   *Turandot* (1)   B. Nilsson, L. Amara, B. Giaiotti,
                                               F. Guarrera, R. Nagy, C. Anthony,
                                               K. Adler cond.

May 26   *Aida* (1)   B. Nilsson, M. Dunn, F. Guarrera,
E. Flagello, N. Scott, N. Verchi cond.

TORONTO — O'KEEFE CENTER (MET SPRING TOUR)
May 30   *Turandot* (1)   B. Nilsson, T. Stratas, B. Giaiotti,
F. Guarrera, R. Nagy, C. Anthony,
K. Adler cond.

VENICE — TEATRO LA FENICE
June 19   *Andrea Chénier* (3)   A. Stella, C. Betner, M. Puppo,
[June 21, 15]   E. Bastianini, A. Cassinelli, V. Pandano,
O. De Fabritiis cond.

VERONA — ARENA
July 27   *Carmen* (7)   G. Simionato, R. Scotto, E. Bastianini,
[July 30, Aug 2, 5,   F. Molinari Pradelli cond.
9, 12, 15]

BERLIN — THEATER DER WESTENS
Oct 1   *Il trovatore* (2)   M. Parutto, F. Barbieri, E. Bastianini,
[Oct 3]   A. Ferrin, O. De Fabritiis cond. (Orchestra
and Chorus from Rome's Teatro dell'Opera)

TURIN — TEATRO NUOVO
Oct 19   *Il trovatore* (3)   M. Roberti, F. Barbieri, D. Dondi,
[Oct 24, 29]   A. Cassinelli, M. Rossi cond.

BARCELONA — GRAN TEATRO LICEU
Nov 4   *Tosca*   L. Maragliano, P. Cappuccilli,
E. Wolf Ferrari cond.

MILAN — TEATRO ALLA SCALA
Dec 7   *La battaglia di Legnano* (8)   A. Stella, E. Bastianini/D. Dondi,
[Dec 10, 13, 16,   M. Stefanoni, G. Gavazzeni cond.
19, 23, 26, 30]   [Celebrating the centenary of Italian unity]

1962

NICE (FRANCE) — THÉÂTRE DE L'OPÉRA
Jan   *Tosca* (1)   C. Castelli, J. Faggianelli

NAPLES — TEATRO DI SAN CARLO
Jan 13   *Turandot* (5)   L. Udovich, L. Gencer/R. Noli/P. Malgarini,
R. Cesari/M. Borriello, J. Hecht/G. Foiani/
G. Rigiri, O. De Fabritiis/P. De Angelis
cond. [Also with Giuseppe Gismondo]

NEW YORK — METROPOLITAN OPERA HOUSE
Jan 27   *Tosca* (5)   M. Roberti/B. Nilsson/Z. Milanov/L.
[Jan 31, Feb 6,   Albanese/L. Price, A. Colzani/M. Meredith/
Mar 22, Apr 7]   W. Cassell/C. MacNeil, S. Baccaloni/G.
Pechner/E. Flagello, K. Adler cond.

PHILADELPHIA — ACADEMY OF MUSIC
Feb 4   *Tosca* (1)   M. Roberti, A. Colzani, G. Pechner,
A. Guadagno cond.

NEW YORK — METROPOLITAN OPERA HOUSE

Feb 16 [Feb 28, Mar 3, 20]	*Aida* (4)	L. Rysanek/G. Tucci, I. Dalis/N. Rankin, A. Colzani/C. MacNeil/C. Bardelli, E. Flagello/G. Tozzi, G. Schick cond.
Feb 24 [Mar 12, 28]	*Turandot* (3)	B. Nilsson/M. Curtis Verna, L. Albanese, E. Flagello/W. Wildermann, F. Guarrera/ C. Marsh, R. Nagy, C. Anthony, K. Adler cond.

NEW YORK — THE ED SULLIVAN SHOW

Feb 28	Televised performance: "Tu ca nun chiagne" (De Curtis)

Mar 9 [Mar 24, 31]	*La Gioconda* (3)	Z. Milanov/E. Farrell, N. Rankin, M. Dunn, R. Merrill, G. Tozzi, L. Chookasian, F. Cleva cond.

NEW YORK —THE BELL TELEPHONE HOUR

Mar 16	Televised performance: "E lucevan le stelle" and "Amaro sol per te" (*Tosca*) with Lisa Della Casa

ENGLEWOOD (NJ) — ACADEMIC HALL, DWIGHT MORROW HIGH SCHOOL

Mar 18	Concert	piano: Alberta Masiello

Carmen: Il fior che avevi a me tu dato
Silenzio cantatore (Lama)
I te vurria vasà (Di Capua)
Pescatore 'e Pusilleco (Tagliaferri)
O sole mio (Di Capua)
Tu ca nun chiagne (De Curtis)
Fedora: Amor ti vieta
'A vucchella (Tosti)
Tosca: Recondita armonia
La fanciulla del West: Ch'ella mi creda

PHILADELPHIA — ACADEMY OF MUSIC

Apr 3	*Carmen* (1)	M. Horne, A. Colzani, A. Saunders, A. Guadagno cond.

CHICAGO — LYRIC OPERA

Apr	*Tosca*

NEWARK (NJ) — SYMPHONY HALL

Apr	Concert

Tosca: Recondita armonia
La fanciulla del West: Ch'ella mi creda
Il fior che avevi a me tu dato (*Carmen*)
Rigoletto: La donna è mobile
Fedora: Amor ti vieta
'A vucchella (Tosti)
Silenzio cantatore (Lama)
I te vurria vasà (Di Capua)
Pescatore 'e Pusilleco (Tagliaferri)
O sole mio (Di Capua)
Tu ca nun chiagne (De Curtis)

MILAN — TEATRO ALLA SCALA

May 3 [May 6]	*Turandot* (5)	B. Nilsson/A. Shuard, M. Freni/R. Carteri, G. Modesti, R. Capecchi, A. Votto cond.

May 28   *Gli Ugonotti* (5)   J. Sutherland, G. Simionato, N. Ghiaurov/
[May 31, June 2,   I. Vinco, F. Cossotto, G. Tozzi,
5, 7]   W. Ganzarolli, G. Gavazzeni cond.

VENICE — TEATRO LA FENICE
June 17   *Carmen* (4)   F. Cossotto, E. Vincenzi, M. Sereni,
[June 20, 22, 24]   A. Cassinelli, O. De Fabritiis cond.

SALZBURG — NEUES FESTSPIELHAUS
July 31   *Il trovatore* (6)   L. Price, G. Simionato, E. Bastianini,
[Aug 4, 11, 20,   N. Zaccaria, H. Von Karajan cond.
25, 30]   [Vienna Philharmonic Orchestra]

VIENNA — STAATSOPER
Sep 1   *Turandot* (3)   A. Shuard, H. Gueden/L. Price,
                                            A. Erede cond.

Sep   *Tosca* (6)   L. Price/A. Stella, E. Bastianini,
                                            H. Von Karajan/A. Erede cond.

PESARO — SPORTS PALACE
Sep   *Il trovatore*   G. Nerozzi, V. Calma, C. Scaravelli,
                                            G. Sisti. N. Verchi cond.

LUGANO (SWITZERLAND) — KURSAAL
Sep 29   *Tosca*   M.L. Nache, O. Gualtieri,
                                            F. Del Cupolo cond.

NEW YORK — METROPOLITAN OPERA HOUSE
Oct 15   *Andrea Chénier* (4)   E. Farrell/Z. Milanov, M. Dunn,
[Oct 19, 25,   J. Madeira/L. Chookasian, R. Elias,
Nov 17]   R. Merrill/A. Colzani, A. Velis,
                                            F. Cleva cond.

PHILADELPHIA — ACADEMY OF MUSIC
Oct 31   *Il trovatore*   L. Udovich, S. Warfield, L. Quilico,
                                            N. Scott, F. Patanè cond.

                 Tosca   L. Price, C. Bardelli

NEW YORK — METROPOLITAN OPERA HOUSE
Nov 10   *Ernani* (5)   L. Price, C. MacNeil/M. Sereni, J. Hines/
[Nov 14, 22, Jan 8,   G. Tozzi, T. Schippers cond.
24, 1963]

Nov 20   *Aida* (1)   L. Amara, G. Simionato, V. Ruzdak,
                                          G. Tozzi, L. Sgarro, N. Santi cond.

MILAN — TEATRO ALLA SCALA
Dec 7   *Il trovatore* (10)   A. Stella/M. De Osma, F. Cossotto,
[Dec 10, 13 16, 20,   E. Bastianini/A. Protti, I. Vinco,
23, 30, Feb 27, 1963   G. Gavazzeni cond.
Mar 2, 17, 1963]

ROME — TEATRO DELL'OPERA [Recording session]
                 Cavalleria rusticana   V. De Los Angeles, A. Lazzarini, M. Sereni,
                                           C. Vozza, G. Santini cond. (Orchestra and
                                           Chorus from Rome's Teatro dell'Opera)

1963

NEW YORK — METROPOLITAN OPERA HOUSE
Jan 4   *Aida* (1)   L. Price, R. Gorr, M. Sereni, J. Hines,
                 N. Santi cond.

PHILADELPHIA — ACADEMY OF MUSIC
Jan   Concert

NEW YORK — METROPOLITAN OPERA HOUSE
Jan 21   *Adriana Lecouvreur* (6) R. Tebaldi, I. Dalis/B. Cvejic/M. Dunn,
[Jan 28, Feb 1,   A. Colzani, W. Wildermann/L. Alvary,
5, 9, 13]   P. Franke, S. Varviso cond.

NEW YORK — THE ED SULLIVAN SHOW
Feb 3   Televised performance: "I te vurria vasà" (Di Capua)

NEW YORK — METROPOLITAN OPERA HOUSE
Feb 17   *Turandot* (1)   B. Nilsson, L. Albanese, B. Giaiotti,
                                           F. Guarrera, R. Nagy, C. Anthony,
                                           K. Adler cond.

ROME — TEATRO DELL'OPERA
Mar 25   *Il trovatore* (4)   L. Udovich, L. Danieli, C. MacNeil,
[Mar 28, 31,   A. Colella, T. Serafin cond.
Apr 2]

MONTE-CARLO — THÉÂTRE DE L'OPÉRA
Apr 6   *Il trovatore* (2)   L. Maragliano, A. Lazzarini, E. Sordello,
[Apr 9]   A. Cassinelli, A. Quadri cond.

NEW YORK — METROPOLITAN OPERA HOUSE
Apr 13   *Adriana Lecouvreur* (1) M. Curtis Verna, I. Dalis, A. Colzani,
                                           W. Wildermann, P. Franke, S. Varviso cond.

BOSTON — JOHN B. HYNES CIVIC AUDITORIUM (MET SPRING TOUR)
Apr 16   *Tosca* (1)   G. Tucci, A. Colzani, G. Pechner,
                                           S. Varviso cond.

Apr 18   *Pagliacci* (1)   T. Stratas, M. Sereni, N. Mittelmann,
                                           G. Shirley, F. Cleva cond.

CLEVELAND — PUBLIC AUDITORIUM (MET SPRING TOUR)
Apr 23   *Tosca* (1)   M. Curtis Verna, A. Colzani, G. Pechner,
                                           S. Varviso cond.

ATLANTA — CIVIC AUDITORIUM (MET SPRING TOUR)
May 4   *Pagliacci* (1)   T. Stratas, M. Sereni, C. Marsh,
                                           C. Anthony, F. Cleva cond.

DALLAS — STATE FAIR MUSIC HALL (MET SPRING TOUR)
May 11   *Pagliacci* (1)   T. Stratas, A. Colzani, C. Marsh,
                                           G. Shirley, F. Cleva cond.

MINNEAPOLIS — NORTHROP AUDITORIUM (MET SPRING TOUR)
May 17   *Cavalleria rusticana* (1) E. Farrell, H. Vanni, M. Meredith,
                                           F. Cleva cond.

DETROIT — MASONIC TEMPLE AUDITORIUM (MET SPRING TOUR)
May 23   *Tosca* (1)   M. Curtis Verna, A. Colzani, G. Pechner,
                                               S. Varviso cond.

May 25   *Cavalleria rusticana* (1)   E. Farrell, R. Elias, W. Cassell,
                                               K. Adler cond.

NEW YORK — VOICE OF FIRESTONE [Video Artists International]
Jun 6   Televised performance: "Viva il vino spumeggiante," "Addio all madre"
                (*Cavalleria rusticana*); "I te vurria vasà" (Di Capua); "Non
                piangere Liù" (*Turandot*); "O paese d'o sole" (D'Annibale).
                With Firestone Orchestra and Chorus, W. Handle cond.

ROME — TEATRO DELL'OPERA [Recording Session]
July   *Andrea Chénier* (1)   A. Stella, M. Sereni, P. Montarsolo,
                                               P. De Palma, G. Santini cond. (Orchestra
                                               and Chorus from Rome's Teatro dell'Opera)

VIENNA — STAATSOPER
Sep 26   *Cavalleria rusticana* (1)   G. Simionato, L. Rysanek, K. Paskalis,
                                               O. De Fabritiis cond.

Oct 8   *Don Carlo* (2)   S. Jurinac/H. Zadek, F. Cossotto,
                                               E. Bastianini/E. Waechter, C. Cava,
                                               L. Welter/I. Vinco, N. Santi cond.

Oct 24   *Il trovatore* (6)   I. Ligabue, F. Cossotto/M. Lilova,
                                               E. Waechter/E. Bastianini, N. Zaccaria/
                                               I. Vinco, H. Von Karajan/A. Erede cond.
                                               [Celebration of the 150th Anniversary of the birth of
                                               Giuseppe Verdi]

VIENNA [Recording session]
Nov   *Carmen* (in French)   L. Price, M. Freni, R. Merrill,
                                               H. Von Karajan cond. (Vienna
                                               Philharmonic Orchestra and chorus from
                                               the Vienna Staatsoper)

MILAN — TEATRO ALLA SCALA
Dec 7   *Cavalleria rusticana* (3)   G. Simionato, G.G. Guelfi, G. Carturan,
[Dec 10, 17]   G. Gavazzeni cond.

1964

MILAN — TEATRO ALLA SCALA (Continued)
Jan 7   *La fanciulla del West* (5)   G. Frazzoni, G.G. Guelfi, A. Ferrin/
[Jan 11, 15,   G. Modesti, P. De Palma,
19, 22, 25]   G. Gavazzeni cond.
                                               [The performance of January 15 was suspended to
                                               mourn the death of Prof. Cassinis, Sindaco di Milano
                                               and Presidente dell'Ente Autonomo Teatro alla Scala]

NEW YORK — METROPOLITAN OPERA HOUSE
Feb 1   *Il trovatore* (3)   L. Price/G. Tucci, B. Cvejic/N. Rankin,
[Feb 21, 24]   M. Sereni/C. March, J. Macurdy/
                                               W. Wildermann, T. Stratas (Ines),
                                               T. Schippers cond.

Feb 7 [Feb 13]	*Aida* (2)	L. Amara, N. Rankin, M. Sereni, J. Hines/ J. Macurdy, K. Adler cond.

PHILADELPHIA — ACADEMY OF MUSIC

Feb 18	*La Gioconda* (1)	M. Curtis Verna, M. Dunn, G. Kriese, B. Giaiotti, C. Bardelli, A. Guadagno cond.

NEW YORK — METROPOLITAN OPERA HOUSE

Feb 29	*La bohème* (1)	G. Tucci, E. Söderström, F. Guarrera, B. Giaiotti, F. Corena, F. Cleva cond.
Mar 7	*Don Carlo* (1)	L. Rysanek, I. Dalis, N. Herlea, G. Tozzi, H. Uhde, J. Diaz [un frate], K. Adler cond.
Mar 11 [Mar 20, Apr 11, May 5]	*Pagliacci* (4)	L. Amara, N. Herlea/A. Colzani, C. Marsh, F. Ghitti, N. Santi cond.
Mar 22 [Mar 30, Apr 8]	*Tosca* (3)	R. Tebaldi/M. Curtis Verna, T. Gobbi/ C. MacNeil, F. Corena, J. Diaz/N. Scott (Angelotti), F. Cleva cond.

NEW YORK — THE BELL TELEPHONE HOUR

Mar 25   Televised performance: "Teco io sto" (*Un ballo in maschera*)
[duet from Act II] with Régine Crespin

NEW YORK — METROPOLITAN OPERA HOUSE

Mar 28 [Apr 2]	*Cavalleria rusticana* (2)	I. Dalis/M. Curtis Verna, C. Bardelli, M. Dunn/J. Martin, N. Santi cond.

NEW YORK — THE ED SULLIVAN SHOW

Apr 4   Televised performance: "Addio alla madre" (*Cavalleria rusticana*)

— — —

	Concert *Turandot*: Non piangere Liù	D. Vorhees cond.

PHILADELPHIA — ACADEMY OF MUSIC

Apr 14	*Roméo et Juliette* (1)	G. D'Angelo, M. Lampi, A. Ferrin, P. Gottlieb, S. Sgarro, A. Guadagno cond.

BOSTON — JOHN B. HYNES CIVIC AUDITORIUM (MET SPRING TOUR)

Apr 18	*Tosca* (1)	B. Nilsson, G. London, F. Corena, F. Cleva cond.

CLEVELAND — PUBLIC AUDITORIUM (MET SPRING TOUR)

Apr 20	*Il trovatore* (1)	G. Tucci, I. Dalis, M. Sereni, J. Macurdy, T. Schippers cond.
Apr 21	*Aida* (1)	B. Nilsson, R. Gorr, C. MacNeil, J. Diaz, C. Siepi, S. Varviso cond.
Apr 25	*La bohème* (1)	R. Tebaldi, J. Fenn, C. Marsh, E. Flagello, G. Schick cond.

NEW YORK — METROPOLITAN OPERA HOUSE

May 1	*Aida* (1)	B. Nilsson, I. Dalis, C. MacNeil, E. Flagello, S. Varviso cond.

May 8   *Il trovatore* (1)   G. Tucci, R. Resnik, R. Merrill,
W. Wildermann, T. Schippers cond.

ATLANTA — CIVIC AUDITORIUM (MET SPRING TOUR)
May 12   *La bohème* (1)   R. Tebaldi, J. Fenn, C. Marsh, J. Hines,
C. Harvuot, F. Cleva cond.

PARIS — THÉÂTRE DE L'OPÉRA
June 3   *Tosca* (2)   C. Castelli/R. Crespin, G. Bacquier,
[June 22]   J. Thirache, C. Rouquetty, J. Mars,
G. Prêtre cond.

June 6   *Norma* (2)   M. Callas, F. Cossotto, M.L. Bellary,
[June 10]   I. Vinco, C. Cales, G. Prêtre cond.

June 15   *Don Carlo* (3)   S. Sarroca, R. Gorr, L. Quilico,
[June 20, 26]   N. Ghiaurov, H. Santana, J. Mars,
Pierre Dervaux cond.

ROME — TEATRO DELL'OPERA [Recording session]
July/Aug   *Il trovatore*   G. Tucci, G. Simionato, R. Merrill,
F. Mazzoli, T. Schippers cond. (Orchestra
and Chorus from Rome's Teatro dell'Opera)

CHICAGO — LYRIC OPERA
Oct 9   *Il trovatore* (4)   I. Ligabue, G. Bumbry, M. Zanasi, I. Vinco,
[Oct 14, 17, 19]   B. Bartoletti cond.

Oct 23   *Carmen* (5) (in French)   G. Bumbry, N. Panni/I. Gonzales,
[Oct 26, 29, 31,   R. Massard, R. Cesare (Il Dancairo),
Nov 4]   P. Dervaux cond.

PHILADELPHIA — ACADEMY OF MUSIC
Nov 10   *La fanciulla del West* (1)   D. Kirsten, A. Colzani, A. Dobiansky,
A. Guadagno cond.

MILAN — TEATRO ALLA SCALA
Dec 7   *Turandot* (10)   B. Nilsson/A. Shuard, G. Vishnevskaya/
[Dec 10, 12, 15,   M. Freni/M. Bonifacio, N. Zaccaria,
19, 27, 30, Jan 7,   R. Capecchi, P. de Palma,
12, 17, 1965]   G. Gavazzeni cond.

1965

NEW YORK — METROPOLITAN OPERA HOUSE
Jan 29   *La forza del destino* (2)   G. Tucci, E. Bastianini, G. Tozzi, J. Grillo,
[Feb 6]   E. Esparza. N. Santi cond.

Feb 1   *Turandot* (2)   M. Curtis Verna/B. Nilsson, L. Albanese,
[Feb 14]   B. Giaiotti, F. Guarrera, R. Nagy,
C. Anthony, F. Cleva cond.

Feb 17   *La forza del destino* (1)   G. Tucci, K. Paskalis, C. Siepi, J. Grillo,
E. Esparza, M. Rich cond.

Mar 11   *Ernani* (4)   L. Price, C. MacNeil/M. Sereni, J. Hines,
[Mar 15, 23,   C. Siepi, T. Schippers cond.
Apr 10]

Mar 19   *Tosca* (2)   M. Callas/R. Crespin, T. Gobbi/G. London,
[Apr 3]   L. Davidson, G. Pechner, F. Cleva cond.

NEW YORK — ST. JOHN'S UNIVERSITY
Mar 25   Concert   Anton Guadagno cond.
                Jota (De Falla)
                'A vucchella (Tosti)
                Tosca: Recondita armonia
                La fanciulla del West: Ch'ella mi creda
                Il trovatore: Di quella pira
                Le Cid: Ô souverain (Massenet)
                O sole mio (Di Capua)
                The World Is Mine Tonight (Posford)
                Tu ca non chiagne (De Curtis)
                Panis Angelicus (Franck) (with choir)
                O Holy Night (Adam) (with choir)
                Core 'ngrato (Cardillo)

NEW YORK — METROPOLITAN OPERA HOUSE
Mar 28   *Aida* (1)   B. Nilsson, R. Elias, M. Sereni, C. Siepi,
                                               W. Steinberg cond.

Mar 31   Gala performance (with other artists)
                La bohème, Act I   R. Tebaldi, C. Marsh, C. Harvuot, C. Siepi,
                                               G. Schick cond.

                Turandot, Act III   A. Valkki, L. Albanese, B. Giaiotti,
                                               C. Marsh, R. Nagy, C. Anthony,
                                               K. Adler cond.

PHILADELPHIA — ACADEMY OF MUSIC (MET SPRING TOUR)
Apr 14   *La forza del destino* (1)   E. Farrell, J. Grillo, A. Colzani, E. Flagello,
                                               G. Pechner, A. Guadagno cond.

BOSTON — JOHN B. HYNES CIVIC AUDITORIUM (MET SPRING TOUR)
Apr 20   *Turandot* (1)   G. Kuchta, T. Stratas, E. Flagello,
                                               F. Guarrera, R. Nagy, C. Anthony,
                                               F. Cleva cond.

Apr 23   *Aida* (1)   M. Curtis Verna, G. Simionato,
                                               N. Mittelman, J. Macurdy, L. Sgarro,
                                               K. Adler cond.

CLEVELAND — PUBLIC AUDITORIUM (MET SPRING TOUR)
Apr 26   *Tosca* (1)   R. Tebaldi, R. Merrill, L. Alvary,
                                               J. Rosenstock cond.

Apr 29   *Turandot* (1)   G. Kuchta, L. Amara, B. Giaiotti,
                                               C. Marsh, R. Nagy, C. Anthony,
                                               F. Cleva cond.

May 1   *Aida* (1)   M. Curtis Verna, G. Simionato,
                                               F. Guarrera, J. Macurdy, K. Adler cond.

ATLANTA — CIVIC AUDITORIUM (MET SPRING TOUR)
May 6   *Turandot* (1)   G. Kuchta, L. Amara, B. Giaiotti,
                                               F. Guarrera, R. Nagy, C. Anthony,
                                               F. Cleva cond.

MEMPHIS — CIVIC AUDITORIUM (MET SPRING TOUR)
May 11   *Tosca* (1)   R. Tebaldi, A. Colzani, G. Pechner,
                                               J. Rosenstock cond.

ST. LOUIS (MET SPRING TOUR)
May 17   *Turandot* (1)   G. Kuchta, T. Stratas, J. Macurdy,
                                               F. Cleva cond.

MINNEAPOLIS — NORTHROP AUDITORIUM (MET SPRING TOUR)
May 22   *Aida* (1)   L. Amara, G. Simionato, N. Mittelmann,
                                               E. Flagello, K. Adler cond.

DETROIT — MASONIC TEMPLE AUDITORIUM (MET SPRING TOUR)
May 25   *Aida* (1)   M. Curtis Verna, G. Simionato, C. Bardelli,
                                               E. Flagello, K. Adler cond.

May 29   *Tosca* (1)   R. Tebaldi, A. Colzani, E. Flagello,
                                               J. Rosenstock cond.

ROME — TEATRO DELL'OPERA [Recording session]
June/July   *Turandot*   B. Nilsson, R. Scotto, B. Giaiotti,
                                               F. Molinari Pradelli cond. (Orchestra and
                                               Chorus from Rome's Teatro Dell'Opera)

July   *Aida*   B. Nilsson, G. Bumbry, M. Sereni,
                                               B. Giaiotti, Z. Mehta cond. (Orchestra and
                                               Chorus from Rome's Teatro Dell'Opera)

PHILADELPHIA — ACADEMY OF MUSIC
Oct 11   *Turandot* (1)   B. Nilsson, M. Reale, E. Flagello, R. Torigi,
                                               A. Graham, G. Bullard, A. Guadagno cond.

CHICAGO — LYRIC OPERA
Oct 22   *La bohème* (4)   M. Freni, S. Bruscantini, E. Martelli,
[Oct 25, 27, 30]   R. Arié, R. Cesari, G. Tadeo,
                                               C. F. Cillario cond.

SAN FRANCISCO — WAR MEMORIAL OPERA HOUSE
Nov 2   *Tosca* (1)   D. Kirsten, R. Vinay, A. Foldi, J. Hecht,
                                               P. Bellugi cond.

LOS ANGELES — SHRINE AUDITORIUM (SAN FRANCISCO OPERA TOUR)
Nov 7   *Tosca* (1)   D. Kirsten, R. Vinay, A. Foldi, J. Hecht,
                                               P. Bellugi cond.

SAN DIEGO — RUSS AUDITORIUM (SAN FRANCISCO OPERA TOUR)
Nov 10   *La fanciulla del West* (1)   M. Collier, C. Ludgin,
                                               F. Molinari Pradelli cond.

LOS ANGELES — SHRINE AUDITORIUM (SAN FRANCISCO OPERA TOUR)
Nov 13   *La fanciulla del West* (1)   M. Collier, C. Ludgin,
                                               F. Molinari Pradelli cond.

LOS ANGELES — MUSIC CENTER PAVILION (SAN FRANCISCO OPERA TOUR)
Nov 16   *Andrea Chénier* (1)   R. Tebaldi, C. Turner, E. Bastianini,
                                               H. Fried, J. Hecht,
                                               F. Molinari Pradelli cond.

NEW YORK — METROPOLITAN OPERA HOUSE
Dec 1   *La fanciulla del West* (5)   D. Kirsten, A. Colzani, E. Flagello/
[Dec 7, 17, 23,   B. Giaiotti/J. Macurdy, F. Cleva/
Jan 8, 1966]   J. Behr cond.

NEW YORK — PHILHARMONIC HALL
Dec 12   Concert   D. Kirsten, A. Antonini cond.
                                               (New York Philharmonic Orchestra)
               Macbeth: Ah, la paterna mano
               Tosca: Recondita armonia
               Tosca: [duet from Act III]
               La fanciulla del West: Ch'ella mi creda
               La bohème: Che gelida manina
               La bohème: O soave fanciulla [duet from Act I]

NEW YORK — METROPOLITAN OPERA HOUSE
Dec 14   *La bohème* (1)   R. Tebaldi, A. Rothenberger, F. Guarrera,
                                               J. Hines, C. Harvuot, F. Corena,
                                               F. Cleva cond.

Dec 29   *Aida* (3)   G. Tucci/M. Arroyo, R. Gorr/I. Dalis,
[Jan 3, 22, 1966]   A. Colzani/S. Milnes, N. Ghiuselev/
                                               J. Macurdy, Z. Mehta cond.

1966

NEW YORK — METROPOLITAN OPERA HOUSE (Continued)
Jan 11   *La bohème* (1)   R. Tebaldi, H. Krall, T. Uppman,
                                               R. Goodloe, N. Ghiuselev, R. Michalski,
                                               G. Schick cond.

Jan 17   *La fanciulla del West*   E. Steber, A. Colzani, J. Macurdy,
                                               P. Franke, J. Behr cond.
                                               [Only sang Act I, then replaced by Gaetano Bardini]

Jan 25   *Tosca* (3)   B. Nilsson/R. Crespin, A. Colzani/
[Mar 30, Apr 11]   W. Cassel, L. Alvary/F. Corena,
                                               G. Schick cond.

Jan 30   *Andrea Chénier* (2)   R. Tebaldi, M. Dunn, A. Colzani, A. Velis,
[Feb 5]   N. Casei, L. Gardelli cond.

MIAMI — DADE COUNTY AUDITORIUM
Feb 14   *Aida* (2)   M. Curtis Verna, J. Grillo, A. Colzani,
[Feb 19]   E. Flagello, E. Buckley cond.

MIAMI — MIAMI BEACH THEATER
Feb 16   *Aida* (1)   M. Curtis Verna, J. Grillo, A. Colzani,
                                               E. Flagello, E. Buckley cond.

NEW ORLEANS — MUNICIPAL AUDITORIUM
Mar 3   *Andrea Chénier* (2)   M. Caballé, C. Ludgin, R. Frankenburger,
[Mar 5]   K. Andersson cond.

HARTFORD — BUSHNELL MEMORIAL AUDITORIUM
Mar 11   *Aida* (1)   E. Ross, G. Hofmann/G. Kuchta, C. Ludgin

NEW YORK — METROPOLITAN OPERA HOUSE
Mar 13   *Aida* (1)   L. Price, E. Cernei, S. Milnes, J. Hines, Z. Mehta cond.

CLEVELAND — PUBLIC AUDITORIUM
Mar 17   Concert   (Orchestra and Piano)
              Arianna: Lasciatemi morire
              Allegro s'apre e vive in libertà
              Una lacrima (Donizetti)
              I Lombardi alla Prima Crociata: La mia letizia infondere (Verdi)
              L'ultima canzone (Tosti)
              O Holy Night (Adam)
              Panis Angelicus (Franck)
              A la Barcillunisa (Favara)
              Tu, ca nun chiagne (De Curtis)
              Core 'ngrato (Cardillo)
              I te vurria vasà (Di Capua)
              'A vucchella (Tosti)
              O sole mio (Di Capua)

NEW YORK — METROPOLITAN OPERA HOUSE
Mar 18   *La fanciulla del West* (1)   D. Kirsten, A. Colzani, J. Diaz, J. Behr cond.

Mar 22   *Andrea Chénier* (1)   E. Farrell, R. Merrill, R. Pospinov, A. Velis, F. Molinari Pradelli cond.

PHILADELPHIA — ACADEMY OF MUSIC
Apr 5   *Andrea Chénier* (1)   M. Caballé, D. Dondi, A. Guadagno cond.
Apr   Concert   L. Stokowski cond.

NEW YORK — METROPOLITAN OPERA HOUSE
Apr 16   Gala farewell concert   (with other artists) F. Cleva cond.
              Manon Lescaut: Tu, tu amore [duet from Act II] with Renata Tebaldi

NEW YORK — THE ED SULLIVAN SHOW
Apr 17   Televised performance: *La bohème*: O soave fanciulla
              with Dorothy Kirsten

BOSTON — JOHN B. HYNES CIVIC AUDITORIUM (MET SPRING TOUR)
Apr 19   *Andrea Chénier* (1)   R. Tebaldi, M. Sereni, G. Schick cond.

LONDON — PALLADIUM
May   Concert
              Recondita armonia (*Tosca*)
              'A vucchella (Tosti)

LONDON — ROYAL OPERA HOUSE (COVENT GARDEN)
May 20   *Turandot* (3)   A. Shuard, E. Vaughan, J. Bonhomme,
[May 24, 28]   J. Dobson, R. Lewis, C. Mackerras cond.

LONDON [Recording session]
May/June   *Faust* (original language)   J. Sutherland, N. Ghiaurov, M. Sinclair, R. Massard, R. Bonynge cond.
              (The London Symphony Orchestra — The Ambrosian Opera Chorus and the Choir of Highgate School)

ROME [Recording session]
July   *Tosca*   B. Nilsson, D. Fischer-Dieskau,
                                                   A. Mariotti, L. Maazel cond. (Orchestra
                                                   and Chorus from the National Academy of
                                                   Santa Cecilia)

NEW YORK — THE ED SULLIVAN SHOW
Sep 18   Televised performance: "Vicino a te" (*Andrea Chénier*)
                        [duet from Act IV] with Renata Tebaldi

NEW YORK — METROPOLITAN OPERA HOUSE
Sep 22   *La Gioconda* (9)   R. Tebaldi, B. Cvejic/M. Dunn, M. Dunn/
[Oct 10, 22, 29,   B. Amparan/R. Baldani, C. MacNeil/
Nov 3, 10, 14,   A. Colzani, C. Siepi/B. Giaiotti/G. Tozzi,
23, 29]   F. Cleva cond.

Sep 26   *Turandot* (8)   B. Nilsson, A. Walkki, T. Stratas/M. Freni/
[Oct 3, 7, 15,   A. Moffo, B. Giaiotti/E. Flagello,
Nov 26,   T. Uppman, F. Guarrera, R. Nagy,
Dec 3,6, 17]   C. Anthony, Z. Mehta cond.

PHILADELPHIA — ACADEMY OF MUSIC
Oct 18   *La Gioconda* (1)   R. Tebaldi, M. Dunn, A. Colzani, J. Hecht,
                                                   L. Chookasian, A. Guadagno cond.

Oct 25   *Don Carlo* (1)   R. Kabaivanska, O. Dominguez, L. Quilico,
                                                   N. Ghiaurov, N. Ghiuselev,
                                                   A. Guadagno cond.

NEW YORK — THE ED SULLIVAN SHOW
Nov 20   Televised performance: "Tu ca nun chiagne" (De Curtis); "O surdato
                        'nnammurato" (Cannio); "Torna a Surriento" (De Curtis)

NEW YORK — METROPOLITAN OPERA HOUSE
Dec 10   *Aida* (3)   G. Tucci, E. Cernei, A. Colzani/F. Guarrera,
[Dec 14, 20]   J. Diaz, T. Schippers cond.

PHILADELPHIA — ACADEMY OF MUSIC
Dec 15   Concert   R. Tebaldi, L. Albanese, F. Labò,
                        Core 'ngrato (Cardillo)   B. Giaiotti, A. Guadagno cond.
                        O sole mio (Di Capua)   [For the flood victims of Florence]
                        Granada (Lara)

1967

FLORENCE — TEATRO COMUNALE
Jan 7   *La forza del destino* (4) I. Ligabue, B. Casoni, P. Cappuccilli,
[Jan 10, 12, 15]   P. Washington, G. Giorgetti,
                                                   O. De Fabritiis cond.

PARMA — TEATRO REGIO
Jan 19   *Tosca* (2)   V. Gordoni, A. D'Orazi, V. Carbonari,
[Jan 21]   G. Morelli cond.

LISBON — TEATRO DE SÃO CARLOS
Mar 2   *Andrea Chénier* (2)   L. Maragliano, D. Dondi,
                                              O. De Fabritiis cond.
                                              [Centennial celebration of Umberto Giordano's birth]

NEW YORK — METROPOLITAN OPERA HOUSE
Mar 22   *La bohème* (1)   R. Tebaldi, M. Collier, M. Sereni,
                                              R. Goodloe, B. Giaiotti, F. Corena,
                                              F. Cleva cond.

Mar 27   *La Gioconda* (1)   R. Tebaldi, R. Elias, R. Pospinov,
                                              C. MacNeil, B. Giaiotti, F. Cleva cond.

NEW ORLEANS
Apr 2   Concert   A. Guadagno cond. (New Orleans
                                              Symphony Orchestra)

BOSTON — WAR MEMORIAL AUDITORIUM (MET SPRING TOUR)
Apr 21   *Aida*   L. Price, N. Rankin, C. MacNeil,
                                              J. Macurdy, T. Schippers cond.
                                              [Only in Act I, then replaced by William Olvis]

CLEVELAND — PUBLIC AUDITORIUM (MET SPRING TOUR)
Apr 24   *La Gioconda* (1)   R. Tebaldi, R. Elias, B. Amparan,
                                              C. MacNeil, J. Diaz, F. Cleva cond.

Apr 28   *Aida* (1)   L. Price, N. Rankin, C. MacNeil,
                                              J. Macurdy, T. Schippers cond.

ATLANTA — FOX THEATER (MET SPRING TOUR)
May 1   *La Gioconda* (1)   R. Tebaldi, R. Elias, B. Amparan,
                                              C. MacNeil, B. Giaiotti, F. Cleva cond.

MEMPHIS — ELLIS AUDITORIUM (MET SPRING TOUR)
May 8   *La Gioconda* (1)   R. Tebaldi, R. Elias, B. Amparan,
                                              C. MacNeil, B. Giaiotti, F. Cleva cond.

DALLAS — FAIR PARK AUDITORIUM (MET SPRING TOUR)
May 12   *La Gioconda* (1)   R. Tebaldi, R. Elias, B. Amparan,
                                              C. MacNeil, B. Giaiotti, F. Cleva cond.

MINNEAPOLIS — NORTHROP AUDITORIUM (MET SPRING TOUR)
May 17   *La Gioconda* (1)   R. Tebaldi, N. Rankin, B. Amparan,
                                              C. MacNeil, B. Giaiotti, F. Cleva cond.

DETROIT — MASONIC TEMPLE AUDITORIUM (MET SPRING TOUR)
May 23   *Turandot* (1)   B. Nilsson, A. Moffo, B. Giaiotti,
                                              F. Guarrera, R. Nagy, C. Anthony,
                                              Z. Mehta cond.

May 26   *La Gioconda* (1)   R. Tebaldi, R. Elias, R. Pospinov,
                                              C. MacNeil, B. Giaiotti, F. Cleva cond.

PHILADELPHIA — CIVIC CENTER (MET SPRING TOUR)
May 29   *Turandot* (1)   B. Nilsson, B. Tucci, B. Giaiotti,
                                              F. Guarrera, R. Nagy, C. Anthony,
                                              Z. Mehta cond.

June 3   *La Gioconda* (1)   R. Tebaldi, R. Elias, R. Pospinov,
                                              C. MacNeil, B. Giaiotti, F. Cleva cond.

NEW YORK — METROPOLITAN OPERA HOUSE
Sep 19   *Roméo et Juliette* (8)   M. Freni/J. Pilou, J. Reardon, C. Anthony,
[Sep 22, 27, Oct 2,   J. Macurdy/J. Diaz,
 7, 10, 16, 26]   F. Molinari Pradelli cond.

PHILADELPHIA — ACADEMY OF MUSIC
Oct 20   *Roméo et Juliette* (2)   G. D'Angelo/J. Pilou, K. Creedn, N. Tyl,
[Oct 24]   C. Marsh, A. Guadagno cond.

SEATTLE — SEATTLE OPERA HOUSE
Oct 31   *Roméo et Juliette* (8)   G. D'Angelo/C. Todd, R. Mazzarella,
[Nov 1, 2, 4, 8,   J. Forst, N. Moscona/L. Lishner,
 9, 10, 11]   E. Buckley cond. [Also with Mauro Lampi]

LOS ANGELES — PHILHARMONIC AUDITORIUM
Nov 14   Requiem Mass (1)   G. Jones, G. Bumbry, E. Flagello,
                                              Z. Mehta cond.

NEW YORK — METROPOLITAN OPERA HOUSE
Nov 18   *La Gioconda* (3)   R. Tebaldi, M. Stojanovic, N. Rankin/R.
[Nov 22, Dec 2]   Elias, J. Grillo/L. Chookasian, A. Colzani,
                                              J. Hines/J. Macurdy, F. Cleva cond.

Nov 25   *Roméo et Juliette* (1)   J. Pilou, C. Anthony, J. Reardon,
                                              J. Macurdy

CLEVELAND — PUBLIC AUDITORIUM
Dec 10   Concert   Anton Guadagno, cond.
                Arianna: Lasciatemi morire (Monteverdi)
                Elisir d'amore: Una furtiva lagrima (Donizetti)
                Tosca: Recondita armonia
                Canzonetta (Rotani)
                L'Arlesiana: 'E la solita storia del pastore (Cilea)
                I Lombardi alla Prima Crociata: La mia letizia infondere (Verdi)
                O Holy Night (Adam)
                Panis Angelicus (Franck)
                Cavalleria rusticana: Addio alla madre
                Il paese del sorriso: Tu che m'hai preso il cor (Lehar)
                A la Barcillunisa (Favara)
                I te vurria vasà (Di Capua)

HARTFORD — BUSHNELL MEMORIAL AUDITORIUM
Dec 15   *Roméo et Juliette*   A. Moffo, L. Sgarro, A. Guadagno cond.

PARMA — TEATRO REGIO
Dec 26   *La forza del destino* (2)   R. Bakocevic, B. M. Casoni, R. Bruson,
[Dec 29]   A. Ferrin/N. Ghiuselev, C. Giombi,
                                              F. Vernizzi cond.

1968

FLORENCE — TEATRO COMUNALE
Jan 11   *Carmen* (4)   S. Verrett, A. Cannarile Berdini,
[Jan 14, 18, 21]   W. Ganzarolli/P. Cappuccilli/G.G. Guelfi,
                                                          F. Molinari Pradelli cond.

NEW YORK — METROPOLITAN OPERA HOUSE
Feb 5   *Tosca* (3)   R. Crespin/L. Rysanek, G. Bacquier/
[Feb 7, 13]   C. MacNeil, S. Pezzetti, P. Plishka,
                                                          Z. Mehta/G. Schick cond.

PHILADELPHIA — ACADEMY OF MUSIC
Feb 20   *Aida* (1)   M. Arroyo, M. Dunn, M. Ausensi,
                                                          B. Giaiotti, A. Guadagno cond.

NEW YORK — METROPOLITAN OPERA HOUSE
Feb 23   *La forza del destino* (2)   L. Amara/L. Price, M. Sereni, J. Hines,
[Mar 9]   L. Pearl, F. Corena, M. Rich/
                                                          F. Molinari Pradelli cond.

PASADENA — CIVIC AUDITORIUM
Feb 28   *Tosca* (2)   P. Curtin, B. Rayson, C. Gonzales,
[Mar 2]   A. Jensen cond.

NEW YORK — THE ED SULLIVAN SHOW
Mar 3   Televised performance: "Tu lo sai" (Berrefato)

NEW YORK — METROPOLITAN OPERA HOUSE
Mar 12   *La Gioconda* (1)   M. Stojanovic, M. Dunn, C. MacNeil,
                                                          J. Macurdy, L. Chookasian, F. Cleva cond.

Mar 16   Gala performance   [with other artists]
                          Core 'ngrato (Cardillo)   F. Molinari Pradelli cond.
                          I te vurria (Di Capua)

NEW YORK — CARNEGIE HALL
Mar 20   Concert   A. Guadagno cond.
                          La biondina in gondoleta (Lago/Mayer)
                          La Montanara (Ostelli/Pigarelli)
                          Firenze sogna (Cesarini)
                          La campana di San Giusto (Aronna/Drovetti)
                          Venezia no! (Tortorella)
                          Arrivederci Roma (Rascel)
                          'Na gita a li castelli (Silvestri)
                          A la Barcillunisa (Favara)
                          Mattinata Fiorentina (Danzi/Galdieri)
                          Pescatore 'e Pusilleco (Murolo/Tagliaferri)
                          O surdato 'nnamurato (Califano/Cannio)
                          Tu, ca nun chiagne (De Curtis)
                          'A vucchella (Tosti)

NEW YORK — METROPOLITAN OPERA HOUSE
Mar 28   *Roméo et Juliette*   J. Pilou, C. Anthony, J. Reardon,
                                                          J. Macurdy, F. Molinari Pradelli cond.
                                                          [Only in the first two acts, then replaced by
                                                          George Shirley]

NEW YORK — PHILHARMONIC HALL
Apr 7   Concert   M. Caballé, B. Giaiotti, A. Silipigni cond.
                                          [In memory of Dr. Martin Luther King, Jr.]
               Macbeth: Ah, la paterna mano
               Le Cid: Ô souverain (Massenet)
               L'africana: O paradiso
               Andrea Chénier: Vicino a te [duet from Act IV]
               'A vucchella (Tosti)

NEW YORK — METROPOLITAN OPERA HOUSE
Apr 13   Tosca (2)   R. Tebaldi, A. Colzani, F. Corena/L. Alvary,
[Apr 18]   P. Plishka, Z. Mehta/G. Schick cond.

BOSTON — WAR MEMORIAL AUDITORIUM (MET SPRING TOUR)
Apr 23   La forza del destino (1)   L. Amara, R. Merrill, B. Giaiotti, L. Pearl,
                                          F. Corena, F. Molinari Pradelli cond.

CLEVELAND — PUBLIC AUDITORIUM (MET SPRING TOUR)
Apr 30   La forza del destino (1)   G. Tucci, R. Merrill, B. Giaiotti, L. Pearl,
                                          F. Corena, F. Molinari Pradelli cond.

May 3   Roméo et Juliette (1)   M. Freni, C. Anthony, J. Macurdy,
                                          J. Reardon, F. Molinari Pradelli cond.

ATLANTA — FOX THEATER (MET SPRING TOUR)
May 11   Roméo et Juliette (1)   M. Freni, C. Anthony, J. Macurdy,
                                          J. Reardon, F. Molinari Pradelli cond.

MINNEAPOLIS — NORTHROP AUDITORIUM (MET SPRING TOUR)
May 15   Roméo et Juliette (1)   M. Freni, C. Anthony, J. Macurdy,
                                          J. Reardon, F. Molinari Pradelli cond.

May 18   La forza del destino (1)   L. Amara, R. Merrill, G. Tozzi, L. Pearl,
                                          F. Corena, F. Molinari Pradelli cond.

DETROIT — MASONIC TEMPLE AUDITORIUM (MET SPRING TOUR)
May 22   La forza del destino (1)   G. Tucci, R. Merrill, E. Flagello,
                                          N. Williams, F. Corena,
                                          F. Molinari Pradelli cond.

May 25   Roméo et Juliette (1)   M. Freni, C. Anthony, J. Macurdy,
                                          J. Reardon, F. Molinari Pradelli cond.

PHILADELPHIA — CIVIC CENTER (MET SPRING TOUR)
May 29   Roméo et Juliette (1)   M. Freni, C. Anthony, J. Macurdy,
                                          J. Reardon, F. Molinari Pradelli cond.

June 1   La forza del destino (1)   L. Amara, R. Merrill, J. Hines,
                                          N. Williams, F. Corena,
                                          F. Molinari Pradelli cond.

MEMPHIS — ELLIS AUDITORIUM (MET SPRING TOUR)
June 5   Roméo et Juliette (1)   M. Freni, C. Anthony, J. Macurdy,
                                          J. Reardon, F. Molinari Pradelli cond.

DALLAS — FAIR PARK AUDITORIUM (MET SPRING TOUR)
June 8   Roméo et Juliette (1)   M. Freni, C. Anthony, J. Macurdy,
                                          J. Reardon, F. Molinari Pradelli cond.

NEW YORK — METROPOLITAN OPERA IN CROCHERON PARK, QUEENS
June 11   *Carmen* (1)   R. Elias, J. Fenn, R. Merrill,
                                                 A. Lombard cond. [Concert version]

NEW YORK — METROPOLITAN OPERA IN BOTANICAL GARDENS, BRONX
June 14   *Carmen* (1)   R. Elias, J. Fenn, R. Merrill,
                                                 A. Lombard cond.

PARIS [Recording session]
July/Aug   *Roméo et Juliette*   M. Freni, R. Cardona, H. Gui, X. Deprez,
                 (in the original language)   E. Lublin, A. Lombard cond. (Orchestra
                                                 and Chorus from Paris's National Opera
                                                 Theater)

NEW YORK — METROPOLITAN OPERA HOUSE
Sep 16   *Adriana Lecouvreur* (4)   R. Tebaldi, I. Dalis/E. Cernei, A. Colzani,
[Sep 21, Oct 29,   M. Meredith, P. Franke, F. Cleva cond.
Nov 4]

Oct 4   *Tosca* (6)   B. Nilsson, G. Bacquier, F. Corena,
[Oct 12, 15, 18,   F. Molinari Pradelli cond.
21, 24]

SEATTLE — SEATTLE OPERA HOUSE
Nov 13   *Andrea Chénier* (4)   M. Pobbe, M. Manuguerra, N. De Lazzari,
[Nov 16, 20, 23]   R. Best, A. Guadagno cond.

NEW YORK — METROPOLITAN OPERA HOUSE
Nov 27   *Tosca* (1)   D. Kirsten, W. Dooley, F. Corena,
                                                 F. Molinari Pradelli cond.

Nov 30   *Roméo et Juliette* (2)   M. Freni, C. Anthony, J. Macurdy,
[Dec 7]   J. Reardon/W. Walker,
                                                 F. Molinari Pradelli cond.

HARTFORD — BUSHNELL MEMORIAL AUDITORIUM
Dec 10   *Andrea Chénier* (1)   E. Renzi, R. De Carlo, C. Meliciani,
                                                 L. Sgarro, C. Moresco cond.

NEWARK (NJ) — STANLEY THEATER
Dec 18   Concert   M. Freni, P. Latorre. A. Boyajian piano.
                 Rigoletto: La donna è mobile
                 Andrea Chénier: Un dì, all'assurro spazio
                 Sogno (Tosti)
                 L'ultima canzone (Tosti)
                 La bohème: O soave fanciulla

NICE — THÉÂTRE DE L'OPÉRA
Dec 27   *Tosca* (2)   S. Sarroca, J. Haas, G. Borrot,
                                                 P. Jamin cond.

1969

NEW YORK — METROPOLITAN OPERA HOUSE
Apr 4	*La bohème* (3)	R. Bakocevic/R. Tebaldi, C. Carson,
[Apr 12, 16]		F. Guarrera/M. Sereni, B. Giaiotti,
		P. Plishka, G. Boucher,
		F. Molinari Pradelli/K. Adler cond.

Apr 19	*Adriana Lecouvreur* (1)	R. Tebaldi, I. Dalis, A. Colzani,
		M. Meredith, P. Franke, F. Cleva cond.

BOSTON — WAR MEMORIAL AUDITORIUM (MET SPRING TOUR)
Apr 25	*Adriana Lecouvreur* (1)	R. Tebaldi, R. Resnik, A. Colzani,
		P. Franke, L. Alvary, J. Behr cond.

CLEVELAND — PUBLIC AUDITORIUM (MET SPRING TOUR)
Apr 29	*La bohème* (1)	L. Amara, C. Carson, F. Guarrera,
		J. Macurdy, G. Boucher, F. Corena,
		C. Franci cond.

May 2	*Adriana Lecouvreur* (1)	R. Tebaldi, I. Dalis, A. Colzani, P. Franke,
		L. Alvary, P. Plishka (Quinault),
		J. Behr cond.

ATLANTA — CIVIC CENTER (MET SPRING TOUR)
May 8	*Adriana Lecouvreur* (1)	R. Tebaldi, N. Rankin, A. Colzani,
		P. Franke, M. Meredith, J. Behr cond.

DALLAS — STATE FAIR MUSIC HALL (MET SPRING TOUR)
May 15	*Adriana Lecouvreur* (1)	R. Tebaldi, I. Dalis, A. Colzani, P. Franke,
		M. Meredith, J. Behr cond.

MINNEAPOLIS — NORTHROP AUDITORIUM (MET SPRING TOUR)
May 19	*La bohème* (1)	L. Amara, C. Carson, F. Guarrera,
		B. Giaiotti, R. Christopher, F. Corena,
		C. Franci cond.

May 23	*Adriana Lecouvreur* (1)	R. Tebaldi, N. Rankin, A. Colzani,
		P. Franke, L. Alvary, J. Behr cond.

DETROIT — MASONIC TEMPLE AUDITORIUM (MET SPRING TOUR)
May 27	*Adriana Lecouvreur* (1)	R. Tebaldi, N. Rankin, A. Colzani,
		P. Franke, L. Alvary, J. Behr cond.

NEW YORK — METROPOLITAN OPERA HOUSE (JUNE FESTIVAL)
June 2	*Tosca* (1)	R. Tebaldi, A. Colcani, F. Corena,
		P. Plishka (Jailer), G. Schick cond.

June 7	*La bohème* (1)	R. Tebaldi, C. Carson, W. Walker,
		B. Giaiotti, R. Christopher, F. Corena,
		C. Franci cond.

VIENNA — STAATSOPER
Nov 15	*Tosca*	S. Jurinac, G. Bacquier

PHILADELPHIA — ACADEMY OF MUSIC
Dec 2	*La bohème* (1)	R. Tebaldi, C. Carson, J. Darrenkamp,
		A. Guadagno cond.

1970

NEW YORK — METROPOLITAN OPERA HOUSE

Jan 8	*Cavalleria rusticana* (5)	G. Bumbry, F. Guarrera/W. Cassel,
[Jan 12, 20, 30,		N. Casei/J. Forst, L. Bernstein cond.
Feb 7]		

Jan 17	*Aida* (3)	L. Amara/G. Tucci, I. Dalis, S. Milnes/
[Jan 24, 27]		W. Dooley, E. Flagello,
		F. Molinari Pradelli cond.

Feb 10	*Don Carlo* (2)	R. Kabaivanska, G. Bumbry, R. Merrill,
[Feb 14]		G. Tozzi, J. Macurdy/R. Michalski,
		K. Adler cond.

PARIS — THÉÂTRE DE L'OPÉRA

| Mar 4 | *Tosca* (1) | A. Stella, G. Bacquier, J.C. Benoit, |
| | | J.P. Hourtau, A. Daumas, A. Erede cond. |

NEW YORK — METROPOLITAN OPERA HOUSE

Mar 16	*Roméo et Juliette* (7)	J. Pilou/C. Boky, J. Reardon, C. Anthony,
[Mar 24, 28,		J. Macurdy/R. Michalski/J. Diaz,
Apr 2, 10, 13, 18]		F. Von Stade (Stephano),
		A. Lombard/M. Rich cond.

MIAMI — DADE COUNTY AUDITORIUM

| Mar 19 | Concert | R. Tebaldi, A. Lombard cond. |
| | | [The Greater Miami Philharmonic Society] |

NEW YORK — METROPOLITAN OPERA HOUSE (JUNE FESTIVAL)

| June 2 | *Cavalleria rusticana* (1) | M. Arroyo, M. Meredith, J. Forst, |
| | | K. Adler cond. |

June 6	*Turandot* (2)	E. Ross/B. Nilsson, P. Lorengar/L. Amara,
[June 10]		R. Michalski, T. Uppman/F. Guarrera,
		A. Velis, C. Anthony, K. Adler cond.

| June 13 | *Tosca* (1) | B. Nilsson, C. MacNeil, F. Corena, |
| | | F. Molinari Pradelli cond. |

| June 17 | *La bohème* (1) | L. Amara, C. Boky, D. Cossa, G. Tozzi, |
| | | F. Corena, J. Behr cond. |

MACERATA — ARENA SFERISTERIO

| July 4 | *Turandot* (3) | B. Nilsson, A. Cannarile Berdini, |
| [July 8, 11] | | A. Zerbini, F. Mannino cond. |

VERONA — ARENA

July 18	*Carmen* (7)	M. Dunn/A. Lazzarini, M. Chiara/A.
[July 23, 26, 29,		Cannarile Berdini, P. Cappuccilli, P. De
Aug 1, 9, 15]		Palma, G. Foiani, E. Zilio (Mercedes), G.
		Zancanaro (Morales), O. De Fabritiis cond.

VIENNA — STAATSOPER

Oct 25	*Don Carlo* (9)	G. Janowitz, S. Verrett, N. Ghiaurov,
		E. Waechter, M. Talvela, E. Gruberova
		(Tebaldo), J. Blegen (Heavenly Voice),
		H. Stein cond.

MUNICH — MEETING HALL OF GERMAN MUSEUMS
Dec 13   Concert   N. Santi cond.
                Rigoletto: Questa o quella
                Andrea Chénier: Improvviso
                L'africana: O paradiso
                Tosca: Recondita armonia
                Le Cid: Ô souverain (Massenet)
                Mefistofele: Giunto sul passo estremo (Boito)

BELGRADE — NATIONAL THEATER
Dec 16   *Carmen* (1)   B. Calef, R. Bakocevic, J. Gligorievic,
                                                  D. Miladinovic cond.

Dec 19   *La bohème* (1)   R. Bakocevic, M. Pez-Galer, K. Krstic, G.
                                                  Giurgevic, F. Maksimovic, B. Babic cond.

BERLIN — [Recording session]
                Carmen   A. Moffo, H. Donath, P. Cappuccilli,
                (in the original language)   J. Van Dam (Zuniga), L. Maazel cond.
                                                   (Orchestra and Chorus from Berlin's
                                                   Deutsche Oper)

1971

NEW YORK — METROPOLITAN OPERA HOUSE
Jan 8   *Ernani* (2)   M. Arroyo, S. Milnes, B. Giaiotti/
[Jan 16]   E. Flagello, T. Schippers cond.

Jan 11   *Lucia di Lammermoor* (1)   R. Peters/G. Robinson, M. Manuguerra,
                                                   B. Giaiotti, C. Franci cond.
                                                   [First act only, then replaced by John Alexander]

Jan 14   *Andrea Chénier* (1)   G. Tucci, C. MacNeil, M. Dunn, N. Castel,
                                                   F. Cleva cond.

PHILADELPHIA — ACADEMY OF MUSIC
Jan 26   *Carmen*   R. Resnik, N. Stokes, R. Fredericks,
                                                   A. Guadagno cond.

NEW YORK — METROPOLITAN OPERA HOUSE
Feb 27   *Werther* (10)   C. Ludwig/R. Elias/R. Crespin, J. Blegen/
[Mar 4, 9, 12, 18,   G. Robinson, J. Reardon, D. Cossa,
22, 27, 31,   N. Castel, F. Corena, A. Lombard/
Apr 7, 12]   M. Rich cond.

Apr 3   *La bohème* (2)   J. Pilou, J. De Paul, W. Walker, G. Tozzi/
[Apr 15]   J. Diaz, F. Cleva cond.

BOSTON — JOHN B. HYNES CIVIC AUDITORIUM (MET SPRING TOUR)
Apr 23   *Werther* (1)   R. Crespin, J. Blegen, C. Anthony,
                                                   D. Cossa, F. Corena, A. Lombard cond.

CLEVELAND — PUBLIC AUDITORIUM (MET SPRING TOUR)
Apr 27   *Werther* (1)   R. Crespin, J. Blegen, C. Anthony,
                                                   D. Cossa, F. Corena, A. Lombard cond.

Apr 30   *Aida* (1)   M. Arroyo, I. Dalis, M. Sereni, E. Flagello,
F. Cleva cond.

ATLANTA — CIVIC CENTER (MET SPRING TOUR)
May 6   *Werther* (1)   R. Elias, J. Clements, J. Reardon,
C. Anthony, A. Lombard cond.

MEMPHIS — MUNICIPAL AUDITORIUM (MET SPRING TOUR)
May 11   *Werther* (1)   R. Elias, J. Clements, J. Reardon,
C. Anthony, F. Corena, J. Behr cond.

DALLAS — STATE FAIR MUSIC HALL (MET SPRING TOUR)
May 15   *Aida* (1)   L. Amara, I. Dalis, M. Serini, E. Flagello,
F. Cleva cond.

MINNEAPOLIS — NORTHROP AUDITORIUM (MET SPRING TOUR)
May 21   *Werther* (1)   R. Elias, G. Robinson, J. Reardon,
C. Anthony, J. Behr cond.

DETROIT — MASONIC TEMPLE AUDITORIUM (MET SPRING TOUR)
May 24   *Werther* (1)   R. Elias, G. Robinson, J. Reardon,
C. Anthony, J. Behr cond.

May 28   *Aida* (1)   M. Arroyo, I. Dalis, M. Sereni, C. Siepi,
F. Cleva cond.

NEW YORK — METROPOLITAN OPERA HOUSE (JUNE FESTIVAL)
May 31   *Aida* (1)   M. Arroyo, G. Bumbry, M. Serini, C. Siepi,
F. Cleva cond.

June 5   *Tosca* (2)   G. Bumbry, P. Glossop, P. Plishka/
[June 12]   F. Corena, J. Levine cond.

June 9   *La bohème* (1)   R. Kabaivanska, C. Boky, M. Manuguerra,
J. Macurdy, R. Gibbs, J. Behr cond.

MACERATA — ARENA SFERISTERIO
July 4   *La bohème* (3)   L. Maragliano, E. Ferracuti, G.G. Guelfi,
[July 7, 10]   N. Zaccaria, F. Mannino cond.

HAMBURG — STAATSOPER
Oct 10   Gala concerts (2)
[Oct 16]   (with scenery and costumes)
     La bohème (finale of Act I)   M. Freni, N. Santi cond.
     Aida [finale of the opera]   I. Ligabue, F. Cossotto, N. Santi cond.

HAMBURG
Oct   Requiem Mass (1)

Oct 22   *Aida* (1)

JAPAN — CONCERT TOUR
Oct 29   Tokyo   Koseinenkin Kaikan
Nov 1   Osaka   Festival Hall
Nov 5   Tokyo   Hibiya Kokaido
Nov 8   Tokyo   Koseinenkin Kaikan
Nov 12   Tokyo   Hibiya Kokaido

[Programs of five concerts]   A. Ventura piano and cond.
Una lacrima (Donizetti)
La serenata (Tosti)
Sogno (Tosti)
La fanciulla del West: Ch'ella mi creda
I te vurria vasà! (Di Capua)
A la Barcillunisa (Favara)
Rigoletto: La donna è mobile
Vaghissima sembianza (Donaudy)
Venezia no! (Tortorella)
Macbeth: Ah, la paterna mano
The World Is Mine Tonight (Posford)
Tu ca nun chiagne (De Curtis)
Lu tradimiento (Donizetti)
Caro mio ben (Giordani)
E canta il grillo (Billi)
L'Arlesiana: È la solita storia del pastore
Jota (De Falla)
L'ultima canzone (Tosti)
Tosca:Recondita armonia
Because (D'Hardelot)
'A vucchella (Tosti)
I Lombardi alla Prima Crociata: La mia letizia infondere (Verdi)
Dicitencello vuie (Falvo)
Turandot: Nessun dorma
O sole mio (Di Capua)
Rigoletto: Questa o quella
Andrea Chénier: Improvviso
L'africana: O paradiso
La bohème: Che gelida manina

SEOUL (KOREA)
Nov 15   Concert   A. Ventura piano
                 Sogno (Tosti)
                 Lu tradimiento (Donizetti)
                 La fanciulla del West: Ch'ella mi creda
                 La conocchia (Donizetti)
                 Amore e morte (Donizetti)
                 Rigoletto: La donna è mobile
                 Venezia no! (Tortorella)
                 Una lacrima (Donizetti)
                 Tu ca nun chiagne (De Curtis)
                 Silenzio cantatore (Lama)
                 E canta il grillo (Billi)
                 L'ultima canzone (Tosti)
                 'A vucchella (Tosti)
                 O sole mio (Di Capua) [ritornello]

BELGRADE — NATIONAL THEATER
Nov/Dec   *Norma*   R. Bakocevic

PARMA — TEATRO REGIO
Dec 29   *Norma* (1)   C. Deutekom, F. Mattiucci, M. Mazzieri,
                                                   A. Votto cond.

1972

NEW YORK — METROPOLITAN OPERA HOUSE

Jan 21
[Feb 7, Mar 8]
La forza del destino (3)
L. Price/G. Cruz Romo, J. Forst/N. Casei,
M. Sereni/K. Paskalis, E. Flagello/C. Siepi/
J. Hines, F. Corena, M. Veltri/J. Behr cond.

Feb 1
[Feb 11, 14, 19,
24, Mar 4, 13]
Werther (7)
R. Crespin/R. Elias, C. Boky, J. Reardon/
D. Cossa, F. Corena, A. Lombard/M. Rich/
J. Behr cond.

Apr 4
[Apr 12, 22]
Don Carlo (3)
M. Caballé, M. Dunn/G. Bumbry,
R. Merrill/S. Milnes, G. Tozzi,
C. Siepi, J. Macurdy, F. Von Stade
(Tebaldo), F. Molinari Pradelli cond.

Apr 22
Gala performance
Otello: Già nella notte densa [duet from Act I] with Teresa Zylis-Gara,
K. Böhm cond.
[in honor of Sir Rudolf Bing]
(with other artists)

June 6
[June 15, 21]
Don Carlo (3)
G. Tucci/E. Ross, F. Cossotto/N. Rankin/
G. Bumbry, R. Merrill, G. Tozzi/
R. Raimondi, J. Macurdy, F. Von Stade
(Tebaldo), F. Molinari Pradelli cond.
[Verdi Festival]

June 9
La forza del destino (1)
G. Tucci, R. Merrill, J. Macurdy,
F. Von Stade, M. Veltri cond.

June 24
Aida (1)
E. Ross [first act only]/M. Arroyo,
G. Bumbry, A. Colzani, R. Raimondi,
F. Molinari Pradelli cond.

VERONA — ARENA

July 15
[July 21, 28,
Aug 5, 9]
Ernani (5)
I. Ligabue/V. Gordoni, P. Capuccilli,
R. Raimondi/I. Vinco, O. De Fabritiis cond.

Aug 15
[Aug 19]
Aida (2)
L. Maragliano, V. Cortez/L. Bordin Nave,
G. Mastromei, A. Ferrin, G. Foiani,
O. De Fabritiis cond.

NEW YORK — METROPOLITAN OPERA HOUSE

Oct 23
[Nov 1, 7, 18]
Aida (4)
G. Tucci, G. Bumbry/L. Chookasian,
R. Merrill, B. Giaiotti, G. Tozzi,
F. Molinari Pradelli cond.

Nov 11
Roméo et Juliette (1)
A. Moffo, C. Anthony, J. Reardon,
P. Plishka, A. Lombard cond.

NEW ORLEANS

Nov
Concerts (2)
O leggiadri occhi belli (Anonymous)
Amore e morte (Donizetti)
Lu tradimiento (Donizetti)
R. Tebaldi, G. Parson piano

A la Barcillunisa (Favara)
Soave sogno (Bellini)
La bohème: O soave fanciulla [duet from Act I]
Sogno (Tosti)
La serenata (Tosti)
E canta il grillo (Billi)
L'ultima canzone (Tosti)
Tosca: Chi è quella donna bionda lassù [duet from Act I]

MEMPHIS — MUSIC HALL AUDITORIUM
Nov 27   Concert   R. Tebaldi, G. Parson piano

SAN ANTONIO — THEATER FOR THE PERFORMING ARTS
Dec 6   Concert   R. Tebaldi, L. Smith piano

COLUMBUS
Dec 10   Concert   R. Tebaldi, G. Parson piano

WASHINGTON (D.C.) — PERFORMING ARTS SOCIETY
Dec 15   Concert   R. Tebaldi, G. Parson piano

PHILADELPHIA — ACADEMY OF MUSIC
Dec 20   Concert   R. Tebaldi, G. Parson piano
              O leggiadri occhi belli (Anonymous)
              Amore e morte (Donizetti)
              Se (Denza)
              Lu tradimiento (Donizetti)
              Soave sogno (Bellini)
              La conocchia (Donizetti)
              La bohème: O soave fanciulla [duet from Act I]
              La serenata (Tosti)
              Sogno (Tosti)
              'A vucchella (Tosti)
              L'ultima canzone (Tosti)
              Tosca: Chi è quella donna bionda lassù [duet from Act I]
              Tu ca nun chiagne (De Curtis)

1973

MIAMI — DADE COUNTY AUDITORIUM
Feb 10   *Carmen* (2)   J. Davidson, A. Maliponte, N. Treigle,
[Feb 17]   E. Buckley cond.

MIAMI — MIAMI BEACH THEATER
Feb 14   *Carmen* (1)   J. Davidson, A. Maliponte, N. Treigle,
                                         E. Buckley cond.

FORT LAUDERDALE
Feb 20   *Carmen*

NEW YORK — METROPOLITAN OPERA HOUSE
Mar 1   *Aida* (1)   M. Arroyo, G. Bumbry, M. Manuguerra,
                                         R. Raimondi, F. Molinari Pradelli cond.

LISBON — TEATRO DE SÃO CARLOS
Mar 18   *Tosca* (3)   R. Bakocevic, S. Bruscantini,
                                         O. De Fabritiis cond.

NEW YORK — METROPOLITAN OPERA HOUSE

Mar 31   *Roméo et Juliette* (1)   C. Boky, D. Cossa, C. Anthony,
J. Macurdy, M. Rich cond.

Apr 7   *Tosca* (3)   D. Kirsten/L. Amara, T. Gobbi, F. Corena,
[Apr 14, 20]   C. F. Cillario cond.

BOSTON — JOHN B. HYNES CIVIC AUDITORIUM (MET SPRING TOUR)

Apr 24   *Tosca* (1)   L. Amara, T. Gobbi, F. Corena,
C. F. Cillario cond.

CLEVELAND — PUBLIC AUDITORIUM (MET SPRING TOUR)

Apr 30   *Tosca* (1)   D. Kirsten, T. Gobbi, F. Corena,
C. F. Cillario cond.

May 5   *Aida* (1)   L. Amara, F. Cossotto, G. Sarabia,
J. Macurdy, F. Molinari Pradelli cond.

MEMPHIS — MUNICIPAL AUDITORIUM (MET SPRING TOUR)

May 15   *Macbeth* (1)   G. Bumbry, S. Milnes, R. Raimondi,
F. Molinari Pradelli cond.

DALLAS — STATE FAIR MUSIC HALL (MET SPRING TOUR)

May 18   *Macbeth* (1)   G. Bumbry, S. Milnes, R. Raimondi,
F. Molinari Pradelli cond.

MINNEAPOLIS — NORTHROP MEMORIAL AUDITORIUM (MET SPRING TOUR)

May 21   *Macbeth* (1)   G. Bumbry, S. Milnes, G. Tozzi,
F. Molinari Pradelli cond.

May 24   *Tosca* (1)   G. Bumbry, T. Gobbi, F. Corena,
C. F. Cillario cond.

MILAN — RAI [Televised production]

May 25   *Andrea Chénier*   C. Casapietra, P. Cappuccilli,
C. Anghelakova, L. Roni, E. Lorenzi,
B. Bartoletti cond.

DETROIT — MASONIC TEMPLE AUDITORIUM (MET SPRING TOUR)

May 28   *Tosca* (1)   G. Bumbry, T. Gobbi, F. Corena,
C. F. Cillario cond.

June 1   *Aida* (1)   G. Cruz Romo, N. Rankin, R. Merrill,
P. Plishka, F. Molinari Pradelli cond.

NEW YORK — METROPOLITAN OPERA HOUSE (JUNE FESTIVAL)

June 7   *Tosca* (2)   G. Bumbry, T. Gobbi, F. Corena/R. Best,
[June 12]   C. F. Cillario cond.

June 18   *Cavalleria rusticana* (1)   E. Ross, G. Sarabia, J. Forst,
C. F. Cillario cond.

June 23   *Aida* (1)   G. Cruz Romo, N. Rankin, A. Colzani,
J. Macurdy, F. Molinari Pradelli cond.

CINCINNATI — MUSIC HALL
July 7   Concert   R. Tebaldi, A. Guadagno cond.
                                                     (Cincinnati Symphony Orchestra0
                    Rigoletto: Questa o quella
                    L'africana: O paradiso
                    La bohème: O soave fanciulla [duet from Act I]
                    Le Cid: Ô souverain (Massenet)
                    Tosca: Chi è quella donna bionda lassù [duet from Act I]

PHILADELPHIA — TEMPLE UNIVERSITY FESTIVAL
July 12   Concert   R. Tebaldi, L. Tung cond.
                                                     (Pittsburgh Symphony Orchestra)
                    Rigoletto: Questa o quella
                    L'africana: O paradiso
                    La bohème: O soave fanciulla [duet from Act I]
                    Le Cid: Ô souverain (Massenet)
                    Tosca: Chi è quella donna bionda lassù [duet from Act I]

LISBON — TEATRO DE SÃO CARLOS
Sep 8   *Carmen* (3)   V. Cortez, Z. Saque, S. Bruscantini,
                                                     O. De Fabritiis cond.

LONDON — ROYAL ALBERT HALL
Oct 9   Concert   R. Tebaldi, G. Jephtas piano
                    La serenata (Tosti)
                    La conocchia (Donizetti)
                    Sogno (Tosti)
                    Lu tradimiento (Donizetti)
                    Soave sogno (Bellini)
                    Amore e morte (Donizetti)
                    La bohème: O soave fanciulla [duet from Act I]
                    Le Cid: Ô souverain (Massenet)
                    L'ultima canzone (Tosti)
                    Occhi turchini (Denza)
                    Tosca: Chi è quella donna bionda lassù [duet from Act I]
                    Tu ca nun chiagne (De Curtis)
                    'A vucchella (Tosti)

VIENNA — GESELLSCHAFT DER MUSIKFREUNDE
Oct 14   Concert   R. Tebaldi, G. Jephtas piano
                    La serenata (Tosti)
                    La conocchia (Donizetti)
                    Lu tradimiento (Donizetti)
                    Sogno (Tosti)
                    Soave sogno (Bellini)
                    Amore e morte (Donizetti)
                    La bohème: O soave fanciulla [duet from Act I]
                    Le Cid: Ô souverain (Massenet)
                    Occhi di fata (Denza)
                    Ouvre ton coeur (Bizet)
                    Tosca: Chi è quella donna bionda lassù [duet from Act I]
                    L'ultima canzone (Tosti)
                    Tu ca nun chiagne (De Curtis)
                    'A vucchella (Tosti)

MANILA — NEW MUSIC CENTER
Oct 23   Concerts (2)   R. Tebaldi
[Oct 27]

MANILA — ARANETA COLISEUM
Oct 31   Concert   R. Tebaldi, T. Mori cond.

JAPAN/KOREA — CONCERT TOUR
Nov 7   Tokyo   Bunka Kaikan
Nov 10   Osaka   Festival Hall
Nov 14   Seoul   Sports Palace
Nov 17   Seoul   Sports Palace
Nov 21   Tokyo   NHK Hall
Nov 24   Mito   Ibaragi Kenritsu Bunka Center

[Program for six concerts]   R. Tebaldi, T. Mori/K. Sato cond.
                Il Canto (Donizetti)   (Tokyo only: Tokyo Philharmonic Orchestra)
                Ouvre ton coeur (Bizet)
                Tosca: Recondita armonia
                Il Guarany: Sento una forza indomita [duet]
                Macbeth: Ah, la paterna mano
                Una lacrima (Donizetti)
                O leggiadri occhi belli (Anonymous)
                Noche feliz (Posades)
                Tosca: Chi è quella donna bionda lassù [duet from Act I]
                Occhietti amati (Falconieri)
                Soave sogno (Bellini)
                Rigoletto: La donna è mobile
                Otello: Già nella notte densa [duet from Act I]
                Werther: Pourquoi me réveiller
                Mignon: Elle ne croyait pas (Thomas)
                Peer Gynt: Solveig's Song
                Jota (De Falla)
                La bohème: O soave fanciulla [duet from Act I]

HONG KONG — THE HONG KONG ARTS CENTER
Nov 27   Concert   R. Tebaldi, S. Hall Ieung piano
                Una lacrima (Donizetti)
                La conocchia (Donizetti)
                Sogni d'infanzia (Bellini)
                Lu tradimiento (Donizetti)
                Tosca: Chi è quella donna bionda lassù [duet from Act I]
                Sogno (Tosti)
                I Love Thee (Chapman)
                Le Cid: Ô souverain (Massenet)
                La bohème: Che gelida manina...O soave fanciulla [duet from Act I]

NEW YORK — METROPOLITAN OPERA HOUSE
Dec 10   *La bohème* (5)   E. Tarrés, M. Niska, M. Manuguerra/
[Dec 26, Jan 1, 10,   D. Cossa, J. Hines, R. Christopher,
28, 1974]   L. Seegerstam cond.

1974

PALM BEACH
Feb 12   Concert   R. Tebaldi

NEW YORK — METROPOLITAN OPERA HOUSE
Feb 16   *La bohème* (3)   M. Caballé/L. Amara/T. Zylis-Gara,
[Feb 20, Mar 19]   M. Niska/E. Moser, D. Cossa/M. Sereni,
                                                J. Macurdy/P. Plishka, L. Seegerstam cond.

NEW YORK — BROOKLYN COLLEGE
Feb 23   Concert   R. Tebaldi, E. Kohn piano

MIAMI — DADE COUNTY AUDITORIUM
Feb 26   Concert   R. Tebaldi, E. Kohn piano

BOSTON — JOHN B. HYNES CIVIC AUDITORIUM (MET SPRING TOUR)
Apr 27   *Turandot* (1)   E. Ross, E. Moser, J. Macurdy, R. Goodloe,
                                    A. Velis, C. Anthony, G. Otvos cond.

DETROIT — MASONIC TEMPLE AUDITORIUM
May 2   *Turandot* (1)   E. Ross, E. Moser, J. Macurdy, R. Goodloe,
                                    A. Velis, C. Anthony, G. Otvos cond.

LONG ISLAND — POST COLLEGE
May 5   Concert   R. Tebaldi, E. Kohn piano
              O leggiadri occhi belli (Anonymous)
              Soave sogno (Bellini)
              La conocchia (Donizetti)
              Lu tradimiento (Donizetti)
              Occhi di fata (Denza)
              Sogni d'infanzia (Bellini)
              La bohème: O soave fanciulla [duet from Act I]
              Rigoletto: La donna è mobile
              Silenzio cantatore (Lama)
              Tu ca nun chiagne (De Curtis)
              Tosca: Chi è quella donna bionda lassù [duet from Act I]

ATLANTA — CIVIC CENTER (MET SPRING TOUR)
May 9   *Turandot* (1)   E. Ross, E. Moser, J. Macurdy, R. Goodloe,
                                    A. Velis, C. Anthony, G. Otvos cond.

MINNEAPOLIS — NORTHROP AUDITORIUM (MET SPRING TOUR)
May 25   *Turandot* (1)   E. Ross, E. Moser, J. Macurdy, R. Goodloe,
                                    A. Velis, C. Anthony, G. Otvos cond.

NEW YORK — METROPOLITAN OPERA HOUSE (JUNE FESTIVAL)
May 28   *Turandot* (3)   M. Lippert, T. Zylis-Gara/A. Moffo/
[June 5, 14]   L. Amara, J. Macurdy, R. Goodloe,
                                    A. Velis, C. Anthony/N. Castel,
                                    G. Otvos cond.

VIENNA (VA) — WOLF TRAP FARM PARK (MET TOUR)
June 19   *Turandot* (1)   E. Ross, L. Amara, P. Plishka, R. Goodloe,
                                    A. Velis, N. Castel, G. Otvos cond.

VIENNA — GESELLSCHAFT DER MUSIKFREUNDE
June 28   Concert   R. Tebaldi, E. Kohn piano
              Toglietemi la vita ancor (Scarlatti)
              Vaga luna che inargenti (Bellini)
              Arianna: Lasciatemi morire (Monteverdi)
              Torna vezzosa fille (Bellini)
              Io chiedo al ciel
              Mille cherubini in coro (Melichar)
              Rigoletto: La donna è mobile
              Macbeth: Ah, la paterna mano
              Aida: Già i sacerdoti adunansi [duet from Act IV]
              Core 'ngrato (Cardillo)
              L'ultima canzone (Tosti)
              La bohème: O soave fanciulla [duet from Act I]

MACERATA — ARENA SFERISTERIO
July 13   *Carmen* (4)   G. Bumbry, W. Vernocchi, F. Bordoni,
[July 18, 21, 27]   O. De Fabritiis cond.

CLEVELAND — PUBLIC AUDITORIUM (MET FALL TOUR)
Sep 20   *Turandot* (1)   E. Ross, T. Zylis-Gara, J. Morris,
        R. Goodloe, A. Velis, C. Anthony,
        A. Erede cond.

NEW YORK — METROPOLITAN OPERA HOUSE
Sep 24   *Turandot* (9)   E. Ross/N. Tatum/I. Bjoner, T. Zylis-Gara/
[Sep 30, Oct 4, 12,   L. Amara/A. Maliponte, J. Morris/
15, Nov 2, 6,   J. Macurdy, R. Goodloe, A. Velis,
Dec 13, 28]   C. Anthony, A. Erede cond.

Nov 14   *Roméo et Juliette* (4)   A. Maliponte, C. Anthony, J. Morris,
[Nov 23, 29,   L. Carlson, H. Lewis cond.
Dec 7]

Dec 23   *Cavalleria rusticana* (1)   G. Bumbry, M. Baldwin, A. Colzani,
        J. Nelson cond.

1975

MIAMI — DADE COUNTY THEATER
Jan 18   *Roméo et Juliette* (2)   C. Boky, M. Ewing, H. Thompson,
[Jan 25]   J. Reardon, J. Diaz, C. Anthony,
        E. Buckley cond.

MIAMI — MIAMI BEACH THEATER
Jan 22   *Roméo et Juliette* (1)   C. Boky, M. Ewing, H. Thompson,
        J. Reardon, J. Diaz, C. Anthony,
        E. Buckley cond.

BOSTON — JOHN B. HYNES CIVIC AUDITORIUM (MET SPRING TOUR)
Apr 26   *Roméo et Juliette* (1)   J. Blegen, C. Anthony, D. Cossa, R.T. Gill,
        M. Rich cond.

DETROIT — MASONIC TEMPLE AUDITORIUM (MET SPRING TOUR)
Apr 29   *Roméo et Juliette* (1)   J. Blegan, C. Anthony, D. Cossa, R.T. Gill,
        M. Rich cond.

May 3   *La bohème* (1)   K. Ricciarelli, R. Shane, W. Walker,
        G. Tozzi, L. Seegerstam cond.

ATLANTA — CIVIC CENTER (MET SPRING TOUR)
May 7   *Roméo et Juliette* (1)   J. Blegen, C. Anthony, D. Cossa,
        J. Macurdy, H. Lewis cond.

May 10   *La bohème* (1)   K. Ricciarelli, R. Shane, W. Walker,
        G. Tozzi, L. Seegerstam cond.

MEMPHIS — MUNICIPAL AUDITORIUM (MET SPRING TOUR)
May 14   *Roméo et Juliette* (1)   J. Blegen, C. Anthony, D. Cossa,
        J. Macurdy, H. Lewis cond.

DALLAS — STATE FAIR PARK AUDITORIUM (MET SPRING TOUR)
May 17   *La bohème* (1)   K. Ricciarelli, R. Shane, W. Walker,
        G. Tozzi, L. Seegerstam cond.

MINNEAPOLIS — NORTHROP AUDITORIUM (MET SPRING TOUR)
May 21   *La bohème* (1)   K. Ricciarelli, R. Shane, W. Walker,
                                         G. Tozzi, L. Seegerstam cond.

May 24   *Roméo et Juliette* (1) J. Blegen, C. Anthony, D. Cossa,
                                         J. Macurdy, H. Lewis cond.

OSAKA — FESTIVAL HALL (METROPOLITAN OPERA TOUR)
June 5   Concert

TOKYO — NHK HALL (METROPOLITAN OPERA TOUR)
June 7   *La bohème* (1)   D. Kirsten, M. Costa, W. Walker, M. Smith,
                                         L. Seegerstam cond.

TOKYO — FESTIVAL HALL (METROPOLITAN OPERA TOUR)
June 10   *La bohème* (1)   A. Maliponte, M. Costa, W. Walker,
                                         M. Smith, L. Seegerstam cond.

OSAKA — FESTIVAL HALL (METROPOLITAN OPERA TOUR)
June 13   *La bohème* (1)   D. Kirsten, M. Costa, W. Walker, M. Smith,
                                         L. Seegerstam cond.

VIENNA (VA) — WOLF TRAP FARM PARK (MET TOUR)
June 23   *La bohème* (2)   R. Scotto, M. Costa, J. Reardon, J. Diaz/
[June 28]   J. Morris, L. Seegerstam cond.

WASHINGTON (DC)
June   Concert

VERONA — ARENA
July 12   *Carmen* (7)   V. Cortez/G. Bumbry/C. Gonzales,
[July 17, 20, 25,   E. Mauti Nunziata/W. Vernocchi,
29, Aug 2, 7]   T. Krause/G.G. Guelfi/G. Fioravanti/
                                         G. Byagian, R. Giovaninetti cond.

Aug 15   *Turandot* (2)   D. Mastilovic/H. Janku, A. Novelli,
[Aug 21]   G. Casarini, G. Zecchillo, G. Patanè cond.

TORRE DEL LAGO (LU) — OPEN-AIR THEATER
Aug 10   *La bohème* (2)   A. Maliponte, G. Santelli, A. Romero,
[Aug 13]   M. Mazzieri, N. Sanzogno cond.

1980

MADISON (NJ) — FAIRLEIGH DICKINSON UNIVERSITY
June 8   Concert
                "L'ultima canzone" (Tosti)
                "A la Barcillunisa" (Favara)

1981

NEWARK (NJ) — SYMPHONY HALL
Apr 25   Concert   K. Barlow, V. Zeani, F. Tagliavini,
                Pecché (Pennino)   N. Rossi Lemeni, J. Hines,
                L'ultima canzone (Tosti) A. Silipigni cond./piano

'O marenariello (Gambardella)
E canta il grillo (Billi)
I te vurria vasà (Di Capua)
Silenzio cantatore (Lama)
A la Barcillunisa (Favara)

HOLMDEL (NJ) — GARDEN STATE ARTS CENTER
July 9   Concert   A. Silipigni cond./piano
                La fanciulla del West: Ch'ella mi creda
                La Serenata (Tosti)
                Le Cid: Ô souverain (Massenet)
                Pecché (Pennino)
                Otello: Niun mi tema
                L'ultima canzone (Tosti)
                Occhi di fata (Denza)
                Sogno (Tosti)
                E canta il grillo (Billi)
                A la Barcillunisa (Favara)
                Mamma mia che vo' sapè (Russo/Nutile)
                Core 'ngrato (Cardillo)

STOCKHOLM — Televised performance: Evening concert in honor of Birgit Nilsson
Nov   L'ultima canzone (Tosti)

It is always difficult to trace the real, complete chronology of a career, and Franco Corelli's is not an exception, even though it presents the undoubted advantage of having totally developed in the great theaters.

The weak points in every chronology are above all the concerts, which are held in unforeseeable places, and are sometimes practically impossible to trace. This difficulty, together with the unresponsiveness of some (even if, luckily, only very few) theaters, causes inevitable gaps in my work in spite of thoroughly committed research.

I am grateful to everybody who sent the editor additions, elaborations, and corrections that were possible to document, and I would like to thank all of them now.

Particular thanks are due to Alberto Bottazzi, who, years ago, passed along to me some booklets containing the Annals of the Metropolitan in which such a large part of Franco Corelli's career was documented. He was the first to stimulate me in the idea of tracing a systematic chronology.

GILBERTO STARONE

Index to the Chronology

Discography

edited by Gilberto Starone

Complete Operas and Selections
(*) *indicates a performance recorded "live"*

ADRIANA LECOUVREUR — Francesco Cilea
With: Magda Olivero, Giulietta Simionato, Ettore Bastianini
Cond.: Mario Rossi
Naples (Teatro di San Carlo), Nov. 28, 1959 — "Live" recording
*MRF Records — MRF 47 (2 LP)
*Replica Editoriale Sciascia — RPL 2454/56 (3 LP)
*Historical Opera Performance Editions — HOPE 246 (3 LP)
*IGI 249 (2 LP)
*Morgan Records — MOR 5901 (3 LP)
*Melodram — MEL 43 (3 LP)
*Fonit Cetra "Documents" — DOC 19 (3 LP)
*Melodram — CDM 27009 (2 CD)

ADRIANA LECOUVREUR — Francesco Cilea
With: Renata Tebaldi, Biserka Cvejic, Anselmo Colzani
Cond.: Silvio Varviso
New York (Metropolitan Opera), Feb. 9, 1963
*Great Opera Performances — G.O.P. 56 (2 LP)
Opera Phoenix — PX 502 (2 CD)

AGNESE DI HOHENSTAUFEN — Gaspare Spontini
With: Lucille Udovich, Dorothy Dow, Francesco Albanese, Enzo Mascherini,
Anselmo Colzani, Gian Giacomo Guelfi
Orchestra and Chorus of the Maggio Musicale Fiorentino
Cond.: Vittorio Gui
Florence (Teatro Comunale), May 9, 1954 — "Live" recording
*Fonit Cetra "Documents" — DOC 72 (3 LP)
*Melodram — CDM 27055 (2 CD)

AIDA — Giuseppe Verdi
With: Antonietta Stella, Fedora Barbieri, Anselmo Colzani, Mario Petri
Cond.: Vittorio Gui
Naples (Teatro San Carlo), Nov. 24, 1955 — "Live" recording
Bongiovanni "The Golden Age of Opera" — GAO 116/17 (2 CD)

AIDA — Giuseppe Verdi
With: Maria Curtis Verna, Miriam Pirazzini, Gian Giacomo Guelfi, Giulio Neri,
Athos Cesarini
Orchestra and Chorus of the Radiotelevisione Italiana
Cond.: Angelo Questa
Turin (RAI), 1956

Fonit Cetra — LPC 1262 (3 LP)
Fonit Cetra — LPS 3262 (3 LP stereo)
Fonit Cetra — CDO 29 (2 CD)

AIDA — Giuseppe Verdi
With: Gabriella Tucci, Irene Dalis, Cornell MacNeil, Giorgio Tozzi
Cond.: George Schick
New York (Metropolitan Opera), Mar. 3, 1962 — "Live" recording
(Date documented in the Metropolitan Opera Annals)
*Stradivarius — STR 1011/13 (3 LP)
*Great Opera Performances — G.O.P. 33 (3 LP)

AIDA — Giuseppe Verdi
With: Birgit Nilsson, Grace Bumbry, Mario Sereni, Bonaldo Giaiotti
Orchestra and Chorus of the Teatro dell'Opera of Rome
Cond.: Zubin Mehta
Rome (Teatro dell'Opera) July 1965
EMI — 3 C 165-0084/0086 (3 LP stereo)
EMI — 7632292 (2 CD)

AIDA — Giuseppe Verdi
With: Maria Callas
Cond.: Georges Prêtre
"Pur ti riveggo" (Duet, Act Three)
Paris (Sala Wagram), June 1964
EMI (unpublished)

AIDA — Giuseppe Verdi
With: Leontyne Price, Elena Cernei, Sherrill Milnes, Jerome Hines
Cond.: Zubin Mehta
New York (Metropolitan Opera), Mar. 13, 1966 — "Live" recording
Great Opera Performances — G.O.P. 733 (2 CD)

ANDREA CHÉNIER — Umberto Giordano
With: Renata Tebaldi, Ettore Bastianini, Elisabeth Hoengen (Contessa), Hilde Konetzni
(Madelon), Renato Ercolani (Incredibile), Kostas Paskalis (Fleville)
Cond.: Lovro Von Matacic
Vienna (Staatsoper), June 26, 1960 — "Live" recording
Morgan Records — MOR 6003 (3 LP)
*Fonit Cetra — CDE 1017 (2 CD)
Fabbri Editori — OP 10 A/B (2 CD)

ANDREA CHÉNIER — Umberto Giordano
With: Antonietta Stella, Mario Sereni, Anna Di Stasio, Stefania Malagù, Piero De Palma,
Paolo Montarsolo
Orchestra and Chorus of the Teatro dell'Opera of Rome
Cond.: Gabriele Santini
Rome (Teatro dell'Opera), June/July 1963
EMI — AN 128-130 (3 LP)
EMI — RLS 910/13 (3 LP stereo)
EMI — CDS 749060 8 (2 CD)
EMI — CDS 5652872 (2 CD)

ANDREA CHÉNIER — Umberto Giordano
With: Montserrat Caballé, Dino Dondi
Cond.: Anton Guadagno
Philadelphia (Academy of Music), Apr. 5, 1966
*Historical Recordings Enterprises — HRE 386 (2 LP)

LA BATTAGLIA DI LEGNANO — Giuseppe Verdi
With: Antonietta Stella, Ettore Bastianini, Marco Stefanoni
Cond.: Gianandrea Gavazzeni
Milan (Teatro alla Scala), Dec. 4, 1961 — "Live" recording
*Robin Hood Records — RHR 520 (2 LP)
*MRF Records — MRF 109 (2 LP). Includes "Corelli Concert"
*Melodram — MEL 430 (2 LP)
Morgan Records — MOR 6103 (3 LP)
Myto Records — MCD 89010 (2 CD)

LA BOHÈME — Giacomo Puccini
With: Mirella Freni, Edith Martelli, Sesto Bruscantini, Raffaele Arié, Renato Cesari
Cond.: Carlo Felice Cillario
Chicago (Lyric Opera), Oct. 1965 — "Live" recording
*Legendary Recordings — LR 195 (2 LP)

LA BOHÈME — Giacomo Puccini
With: Renata Tebaldi, Anneliese Rothenberger, Frank Guarrera, Jerome Hines,
Fernando Corena
Cond.: Fausto Cleva
New York (Metropolitan Opera), Dec. 14, 1965 — "Live" recording
*Magnificent Editions — ME 101 (2 LP)
Bongiovanni "The Golden Age of Opera" — GAO 107/8 (2 CD)

LA BOHÈME — Giacomo Puccini
With: Renata Tebaldi, Clarice Carson, John Darrencamp
Cond.: Anton Guadagno
Philadelphia (Academy of Music), Dec. 2, 1969 — "Live" recording
Legato Classics — SRO 821 (2 CD)

LA BOHÈME — Giacomo Puccini
With: Montserrat Caballé, Maralin Niska, Dominic Cossa, John Macurdy, David Holloway
Cond.: Leif Segerstam
New York (Metropolitan Opera), Feb. 16, 1974 — "Live" recording
*Great Opera Performances — G.F.C. 021/22 (2 LP)

CARMEN (It.) — Georges Bizet — Selections
With: Giulietta Simionato, Sena Jurinac, Ugo Savarese
Cond.: Arthur Rodzinski
Naples (Teatro di San Carlo), Dec. 19, 1953 — "Live" recording
*Historical Recordings Enterprises "Edizione Lirica" — EL 001 (2 LP)

CARMEN (It.) — Georges Bizet
With: Giulietta Simionato, Mirella Freni, Gian Giacomo Guelfi, Loretta Di Lelio
Cond.: Pierre Dervaux
Palermo (Teatro Massimo), Feb. 8, 1959 — "Live" recording
*Stradivarius — STR 1003/5 (3 LP)
*Great Opera Performances — G.O.P. 30 (3 LP)
Great Opera Performances — G.O.P. 727 (2 CD)

CARMEN (It.) — Georges Bizet
With: Giulietta Simionato, Renata Scotto, Ettore Bastianini
Cond.: Francesco Molinari Pradelli
Verona (Arena), July 1961 — "Live" recording
Bongiovanni "The Golden Age of Opera" — GAO 118/19 (2 CD)

CARMEN (It.) — Georges Bizet — Selections
With: Pia Tassinari, Margherita Benetti, Gian Giacomo Guelfi
Cond.: Arturo Basile
Turin (RAI), Dec. 15, 1961 (Date stamped on the vinyl of the record)
Cetra — LPC 55020 (1 LP)
Myto Records — MCD 953.132 (1 CD)

CARMEN (Fr.) — Georges Bizet
With: Leontyne Price, Mirella Freni, Robert Merrill
Vienna Philharmonic Orchestra and Chorus of the Vienna Opera
Cond.: Herbert Von Karajan
Vienna, Nov. 1963
RCA Victor — LDS 6164 (3 LP stereo)
RCA Victor — VKS 45477 (3 Audiocassettes, stereo)
RCA Victor — GD 89199 (2 CD)
RCA Victor — GD 60190 (1 CD selection)
Lyrica — LRC 01013 (3 CD)

CARMEN (Fr.) — Georges Bizet
With: Anna Moffo, Helen Donath, Piero Cappuccilli, José Van Dam (Zuniga)
Orchestra and Chorus of the Deutschen Oper di Berlin
Cond.: Lorin Maazel
Berlin, 1970
Eurodisc "Cetra" — LPS 3276 (3 LP stereo)
Eurodisc "Cetra" — GD 69147 (2 CD)

CAVALLERIA RUSTICANA — Pietro Mascagni
With: Victoria De Los Angeles, Adriana Lazzarini, Mario Sereni
Orchestra and Chorus of the Teatro dell'Opera of Rome
Cond.: Gabriele Santini
Rome (Teatro dell'Opera), 1962
EMI — 3 C 165-00007/00008 (2 LP)
EMI — CMS 7 63967 2 (2 CD)

CAVALLERIA RUSTICANA — Pietro Mascagni
With: Giulietta Simionato, Gabriella Carturan, Gian Giacomo Guelfi
Cond.: Gianandrea Gavazzeni
Milan (Teatro alla Scala), Dec. 7, 1970 — "Live" recording
*Historical Recordings Enterprises — HRE 413 (3 LP). Includes PAGLIACCI (RAI, Feb. 12, 1954)
*Fonit Cetra "Documents" — DOC 58 (4 LP). Includes L'AMICO FRITZ with Mirella Freni and Gianni Raimondi (same evening performance)
Fonit Cetra — CDE 1041 (3 CD). Includes L'AMICO FRITZ with Mirella Freni and Gianni Raimondi
*Compagnia Generale del Disco — CGD Hunt 564 (1 CD)
Arkadia — HP 564 (1 CD)

CAVALLERIA RUSTICANA — Pietro Mascagni
With: Grace Bumbry, Nedda Casei, Frank Guarrera
Cond.: Leonard Bernstein
New York (Metropolitan Opera), Jan. 8, 1970
Melodram — CDM 27095 (3 CD). Includes PAGLIACCI (Met, Apr. 11, 1964)

DON CARLO — Giuseppe Verdi (Selections, with the entire tenor part)
With: Maria Curtis Verna, Irene Dalis, Mario Sereni, Jerome Hines
Cond.: Nino Verchi
New York (Metropolitan Opera), Apr. 15, 1961 — "Live" recording
With: Leonie Rysanek, Nicolai Herlea, Irene Dalis, Giorgio Tozzi, Hermann Uhde

Cond.: Kurt Adler
New York (Metropolitan Opera), Mar. 7, 1964 — "Live" recording
*Great Opera Performances — G.O.P. 21 (2 LP)
Great Opera Performances — G.O.P. 739 (2 CD) (Selections with the entire tenor part)

DON CARLO — Giuseppe Verdi
With: Raina Kabaivanska, Oralia Dominguez, Louis Quilico, Nicolai Ghiaurov, Nicola Ghiuselev
Cond.: Anton Guadagno
Hartford (Bushnell Memorial Auditorium) — "Live" recording
Melodram — CDM 27511 (3 CD)

DON CARLO — Giuseppe Verdi
With: Raina Kabaivanska, Oralia Dominguez, Louis Quilico, Nicolai Ghiaurov, Nicola Ghiuselev
Cond.: Anton Guadagno
Philadelphia (Academy of Music), Oct. 25 1966 — "Live" recording
*Impresario Editions — IE 3001 (3 LP)

DON CARLO — Giuseppe Verdi
With: Gundula Janowitz, Shirley Verrett, Edita Gruberova (Tebaldo), Eberhard Waechter, Nicolai Ghiaurov, Martti Talvela, Judith Blegen (Heavenly Voice)
Cond.: Horst Stein
Vienna (Staatsoper), Oct. 1970 — "Live" recording
*Legendary Recordings — LR 163 (3 LP)
*Morgan Records — MOR 7003 (3 LP)
*Legato Classics — SRO 514 (3 CD)
*Legendary Recordings — LR 1028 (3 CD)

DON CARLO — Giuseppe Verdi
With: Montserrat Caballé, Grace Bumbry, Sherrill Milnes, Cesare Siepi, John Macurdy
Cond.: Francesco Molinari Pradelli
New York (Metropolitan Opera), Apr. 22, 1972 — "Live" recording
Foyer — 2-CF 2092 (3 CD)

ERACLE — Georg Friedrich Händel
With: Elisabeth Schwarzkopf, Fedora Barbieri, Ettore Bastianini, Jerome Hines
Cond.: Lovro Von Matacic
Milan (Teatro alla Scala), Dec. 29, 1958 — "Live" recording
Historical Recordings Enterprises — HRE 304 (3 LP)
Historical Opera Performances Editions — HOPE 239 (3 LP)

ERNANI — Giuseppe Verdi
With: Leontyne Price, Mario Sereni, Cesare Siepi
Cond.: Thomas Schippers
New York (Metropolitan Opera), Apr. 10, 1965 — "Live" recording
*Great Opera Performances — G.O.P. 10 (2 LP)
*Great Opera Performances — G.O.P. 702 (2 CD)
Memories — HR 4370/71 (2 CD)
Hofman Music — 27025/26 (2 CD)

ERNANI — Giuseppe Verdi
With: Ilva Ligabue, Piero Cappuccilli, Ruggero Raimondi
Cond.: Oliviero De Fabritiis
Verona (Arena), July 15, 1972 — "Live" recording
Bongiovanni "The Golden Age of Opera" — GAO 131/32 (2 CD)

LA FANCIULLA DEL WEST — Giacomo Puccini
With: Gigliola Frazzoni, Tito Gobbi, Nicola Zaccaria
Cond.: Antonino Votto
Milan (Teatro alla Scala), Apr. 4, 1956 — "Live" recording
*Historical Recordings Enterprises — HRE 278 (3 LP)
*Great Opera Performances — G.O.P. 28 (2 LP)
*Legato Classics — SRO 506 (2 CD)

LA FANCIULLA DEL WEST — Giacomo Puccini
With: Dorothy Kirsten, Anselmo Colzani
Cond.: Anton Guadagno
Philadelphia (Academy of Music), Nov. 10, 1964 — "Live" recording
Melodram — CDM 27081 (2 CD)

FAUST (Fr.) — Charles Gounod
With: Joan Sutherland, Nicolai Ghiaurov, Monica Sinclair, Robert Massard
The London Symphony Orchestra — The Ambrosian Opera Chorus
and The Choir of Highgate School
Cond.: Richard Bonynge
London, May 1966
Decca — MET 327/330 (4 LP)
Decca — SET 327/330 (4 LP stereo)
Decca — 421240-2 (3 CD)

LA FORZA DEL DESTINO — Giuseppe Verdi — Selections
With: Gian Giacomo Guelfi
Cond.: Arturo Basile
"*La vita è inferno all'infelice;*" "*Morir! Tremenda cosa;*" "*Giunge qualcuno, aprite*"
Turin (RAI), Nov. 27, 1956 (Date stamped on the vinyl of the record)
Cetra — LPC 55017 (1 LP)
Myto Records — MCD 953.132 (1 CD)

LA FORZA DEL DESTINO — Giuseppe Verdi
With: Renata Tebaldi, Oralia Dominguez, Ettore Bastianini, Boris Christoff, Renato Capecchi
Cond.: Francesco Molinari Pradelli
Naples (Teatro di San Carlo) Mar. 1958 — "Live" recording
*Historical Recordings Enterprises — HRE 206 (3 LP)
Bongiovanni "The Golden Age of Opera" — GAO 151/53 (3 CD)
Melodram — CDM 70102 (3 CD)

LA FORZA DEL DESTINO — Giuseppe Verdi
With: Eileen Farrell, Joann Grillo, Anselmo Colzani, Ezio Flagello
Cond.: Anton Guadagno
Philadelphia (Academy of Music), Apr. 14, 1965 — "Live" recording
*Legendary Recordings — LR 170 (3 LP)

LA FORZA DEL DESTINO — Giuseppe Verdi
With: Gabriella Tucci, Joann Grillo, Ettore Bastianini, Giorgio Tozzi
Cond.: Nello Santi
New York (Metropolitan Opera), Feb. 6, 1965 — "Live" recording
*Great Opera Performances — G.O.P. 14 (3 LP)
*Great Opera Performances — G.O.P. 706 (2 CD)

LA FORZA DEL DESTINO — Giuseppe Verdi
With: Leontyne Price, Louise Pearl, Robert Merrill, Jerome Hines, Fernando Corena
Cond.: Francesco Molinari Pradelli
New York (Metropolitan Opera), Mar. 9, 1968 — "Live" recording
Myto Records — MCD 945.112 (2 CD)

LA GIOCONDA — Amilcare Ponchielli
With: Eileen Farrell, Nell Rankin, Mignon Dunn, Robert Merrill, Giorgio Tozzi
Cond.: Fausto Cleva
New York (Metropolitan Opera), Mar. 31, 1962 — "Live" recording
(Date Documented in the Metropolitan Opera Annals)
*Estro Armonico — E/A 045 (3 LP)

LA GIOCONDA — Amilcare Ponchielli
With: Renata Tebaldi, Biserka Cvejic, Mignon Dunn, Cornell MacNeil, Cesare Siepi
Cond.: Fausto Cleva
New York (Metropolitan Opera), Sep. 22, 1966 — "Live" recording
*Stradivarius — STR 1023/25 (3 LP)
*Great Opera Performances — G.O.P. 37 (3 LP)

GUERRA E PACE — Sergei Prokofiev
With: Rosanna Carteri, Fedora Barbieri, Mirto Picchi, Ettore Bastianini, Anselmo Colzani, Italo Tajo
Orchestra and Chorus of the Maggio Musicale Fiorentino
Cond.: Arthur Rodzinski
Florence (Teatro Comunale), May 26, 1953 — "Live" recording
*Fonit Cetra "Documents" — DOC 77 (3 LP)

LUCIA DI LAMMERMOOR — Gaetano Donizetti
With: Roberta Peters, Matteo Manuguerra, Bonaldo Giaiotti
Cond.: Carlo Franci
New York (Metropolitan Opera), Jan. 11, 1971 — "Live" recording
Bongiovanni "The Golden Age of Opera" — GAO 125 (1 CD — selections). Includes
  CONCERTO DI CANZONI POPOLARI ITALIANE. Cond.: Anton Guadagno
New York (Carnegie Hall), Mar. 20, 1968 — "Live" recording
Lago/Mayer: "*La biondina in gondoleta;*" Ostelli/Pignarelli: "*La Montanara;*" Cesarini:
"*Firenze sogna;*" Arona/Drovetti: "*La campana di San Giusto;*" Tortorella: "*Venezia no!;*"
Rascel: "*Arrivederci Roma;*" Murolo/Tagliaferri: "*Piscatore 'e Pusilleco;*" Califano/Cannio:
"*'O surdato 'nnammurato;*" De Curtis: "*Tu ca nun chiagne;*" Tosti: "*'A vucchella;*" Silvestri:
"*'Na gita a li castelli*"

MESSA DI REQUIEM — Giuseppe Verdi
With: Gwyneth Jones, Grace Bumbry, Ezio Flagello
Cond.: Zubin Mehta
Los Angeles (Philharmonic Auditorium), Nov. 14, 1967 — "Live" recording
*Legendary Recordings — LR 125 (2 LP)
Legendary Recordings — LR 1026 (2 CD)

NORMA — Vincenzo Bellini — Selections
With: Maria Callas, Elena Nicolai, Boris Christoff
Cond.: Antonino Votto
Trieste (Teatro Verdi), Nov. 19, 1953 — "Live" recording
Historical Recordings Enterprises — HRE 283 (2 LP)
*Timaclub — (1 LP — selezione)
Melodram — CDM 26031 (2 CD)

NORMA (Act I) — Vincenzo Bellini
With: Maria Callas, Miriam Pirazzini, Giulio Neri
Cond.: Gabriele Santini
Rome (Teatro dell'Opera), Jan. 2, 1958 — "Live" recording
*Voce Records — VOCE 8 (1 LP)
*G.F.C. 008/9 (2 LP). Includes selections from TOSCA with Maria Callas, Tito Gobbi
*Melodram — CDM 16000 (1 CD)

NORMA — Vincenzo Bellini
With: Anita Cerquetti, Miriam Pirazzini, Giulio Neri
Cond.: Gabriele Santini
Rome (Teatro dell'Opera), Jan. 4, 1958 — "Live" recording
*Great Opera Performances — G.O.P. 722 (2 CD)

NORMA — Vincenzo Bellini
With: Maria Callas, Christa Ludwig, Nicola Zaccaria
Orchestra and Chorus of the Teatro alla Scala di Milan
Cond.: Tullio Serafin
Milan (Teatro alla Scala), Sep. 1960
EMI — QCX 10430/32 (3 LP)
EMI — SAX 27334 (3 LP stereo)
EMI — 3-081 7630002 (3 CD)
EMI — 081 7630912 (1 CD — Selections)

PAGLIACCI — Ruggero Leoncavallo
With: Mafalda Micheluzzi, Tito Gobbi, Mario Carlin, Lino Puglisi
Orchestra and Chorus of the Radiotelevisione Italiana
Cond.: Alfredo Simonetto
Milan (RAI Television), Feb. 12, 1954
*Historical Recordings Enterprises — HRE 413 (3 LP). Includes CAVALLERIA RUSTICANA
    (Milan — Teatro alla Scala, Dec. 7, 1963)
Historical Recordings Enterprises — HRE 1001-2 (1 CD)
*Great Opera Performances — G.O.P. 4 (3 LP). Includes PAGLIACCI with Marilyn Horne,
    Mario Del Monaco, Ettore Bastianini
*Legato Classics — SRO 515 (1 CD)

PAGLIACCI — Ruggero Leoncavallo
With: Lucine Amara, Tito Gobbi, Mario Zanasi, Mario Spina
Orchestra and Chorus of the Teatro alla Scala di Milan
Cond.: Lovro Von Matacic
Milan (Teatro alla Scala), June/July 1960
EMI — QCX 10407/08 (2 LP)
EMI — SAXQ 7303/04 (2 LP stereo)
EMI — 3C 293-00525/26 (2 Audiocassettes)
EMI — CMS 7 639672 (2 CD)

PAGLIACCI — Ruggero Leoncavallo
With: Lucine Amara, Anselmo Colzani, Franco Ghitti
Cond.: Nello Santi
New York (Metropolitan Opera) Apr. 11, 1964 — "Live" recording
Melodram — CDM 27095 (3 CD). Includes CAVALLERIA RUSTICANA.(Met, Jan. 8, 1970)

POLIUTO — Gaetano Donizetti
With: Maria Callas, Ettore Bastianini, Nicola Zaccaria, Piero De Palma
Cond.: Antonino Votto
Milan (Teatro alla Scala), Dec. 7, 1960 — "Live" recording
*BJR Recordings — BJR 106 (2 LP)
*MRF Records — MRF 31 (2 LP)
*Rodolphe Productions — RP 12715 (2 LP)
Estro Armonico — E/A 006 (2 LP)
*C.G.D. 52 (2 LP)
*Melodram — CDM 26006 (2 CD)
*C.G.D. Hunt 520 (2 CD)
Arkadia — HP 520 (2 CD)
Hofman Music — 28003/04 (2 CD)

ROMÉO ET JULIETTE (Fr.) — Charles Gounod
With: Gianna D'Angelo, Agostino Ferrin, Peter Gottlieb
Cond.: Anton Guadagno
Philadelphia (Academy of Music), Apr. 14, 1964 — "Live" recording
Historical Recordings Enterprises — HRE 1011-2 (2 CD). Includes selections with
    Jeannette Pilou (Oct. 24, 1967)

ROMÉO ET JULIETTE (Fr.) — Charles Gounod
With: Jeannette Pilou, Justino Diaz, Charles Anthony, John Reardon
Cond.: Francesco Molinari Pradelli
New York (Metropolitan Opera), Oct. 16, 1967 — "Live" recording
*Great Opera Performances — G.O.P. 51 (2 LP)
Great Opera Performances — G.O.P. 737 (2 CD)

ROMÉO ET JULIETTE (Fr.) — Charles Gounod
With: Anna Moffo, Louis Sgarro
Cond.: Anton Guadagno
Hartford (Bushnell Memorial Auditorium), Dec. 15, 1967 — "Live" recording
*Lyric Distribution Incorporated — ALD 1065 (2 Audiocassettes)

ROMÉO ET JULIETTE (Fr.) — Charles Gounod
With: Mirella Freni, Robert Cardona, Henri Gui, Xavier Deprez, Eliane Lublin
Orchestra and Chorus of the National Opera Theater of Paris
Cond.: Alain Lombard
Paris, July/Aug. 1968
EMI-CAN 235/7 (3 LP)

TOSCA — Giacomo Puccini
With: Zinka Milanov, Gian Giacomo Guelfi
Cond.: Alexander Gibson
London (Royal Opera House Covent Garden), July 1, 1957 — "Live" recording
*Unique Opera Records — UORC 157 (2 LP)
*Legato Classics — SRO 511 (2 CD)
Legato Classics — LCD 102 (2 CD)

TOSCA — Giacomo Puccini
With: Renata Tebaldi, Anselmo Colzani
Cond.: Mario Parenti
Livorno (Teatro La Gran Guardia), Oct. 21, 1959 — "Live" recording
Foné "Work in Progress" — 93 F 15 (2 CD)
Legato Classics — LCD 171 (2 CD)

TOSCA — Giacomo Puccini
With: Leontyne Price, Cornell MacNeil
Cond.: Kurt Adler
New York (Metropolitan Opera), Apr. 7, 1962 — "Live" recording
*Teatro Dischi — TD 101 (2 LP)
Myto Records — MCD 925.70 (2 CD). Includes selections from LUCIA DI
    LAMMERMOOR (Met, Jan. 11, 1971)

TOSCA — Giacomo Puccini
With: Maria Callas, Tito Gobbi, Andrea Velis
Cond.: Fausto Cleva
New York (Metropolitan Opera), Mar 19, 1965 — "Live" recording
Estro Armonico — E/A 013 (2 LP)
Historical Recordings Enterprises — HRE 275 (2 LP)
*Melodram — MEL 450 (2 LP)
*Melodram — CDM 26030 (2 CD)

TOSCA — Giacomo Puccini
With: Virginia Gordoni, Attilio D'Orazi
Cond.: Giuseppe Morelli
Parma (Teatro Regio), Jan. 21, 1967 — "Live" recording
Bongiovanni "The Golden Age of Opera" — GAO 127/27 (2 CD)

TOSCA — Giacomo Puccini
With: Birgit Nilsson, Dietrich Fischer-Dieskau, Alfredo Mariotti
Orchestra and Chorus of the Accademia Nazionale di Santa Cecilia of Rome
Cond.: Lorin Maazel
Rome, July 1966
Decca — SET 341/42 (2 LP stereo)
Decca — 440.051 (2 CD)

IL TROVATORE — Giuseppe Verdi
With: Antonietta Stella, Giulietta Simionato, Ettore Bastianini
Cond.: Oliviero De Fabritiis
— "Live" recording
Rodolphe Productions — RPAC 132752 (1 CD, selections)

IL TROVATORE — Giuseppe Verdi
With: Leontyne Price, Irene Dalis, Mario Sereni, William Wildermann
Cond.: Fausto Cleva
New York (Metropolitan Opera), Feb. 4, 1961 — "Live" recording
Myto Records — MCD 917.51 (2 CD). Includes PAGLIACCI. (Met, Apr. 11, 1964, selections)

IL TROVATORE — Giuseppe Verdi
With: Mirella Parutto, Fedora Barbieri, Ettore Bastianini, Agostino Ferrin
Cond.: Oliviero De Fabritiis
Berlin (Theater Der Westens), Oct. 1, 1961 — "Live" recording
*Melodram — MEL 50 (3 LP)
Datum — DAT 12313 (2 CD)

IL TROVATORE — Giuseppe Verdi
With: Leontyne Price, Giulietta Simionato, Ettore Bastianini, Nicola Zaccaria
Cond.: Herbert Von Karajan
Salzburg (Festspielhaus), July 31, 1962 — "Live" recording
*Morgan Records — MOR 6201 (3 LP)
*Paragon — DSV 52025 (3 LP)
*Movimento Musica — MM 03018 (3 LP)
*Movimento Musica — 012.001 (2 CD)
Historical Recordings Enterprises — HRE 287 (3 LP)
*Melodram — MEL 710 (3 LP)
*Lyric Distribution Incorporated — ALD 1075 (2 Audiocassettes)
*Rodolphe Productions — RPC 32482/83 (2 CD)
*Arkadia — ARK 7 (3 LP)
Arkadia — KAR 228 (2 CD)

IL TROVATORE — Giuseppe Verdi
With: Antonietta Stella, Fiorenza Cossotto, Ettore Bastianini, Ivo Vinco
Cond.: Gianandrea Gavazzeni
Milan (Teatro alla Scala), Dec. 7, 1962 — "Live" recording
*Legendary Recordings — LR 188 (2 LP)
*Claque — GM 2013/14 (2 CD)
Melodram — CDM 27068 (2 CD)

IL TROVATORE — Giuseppe Verdi
With: Gabriella Tucci, Giulietta Simionato, Robert Merrill, Ferruccio Mazzoli
Orchestra and Chorus of the Teatro dell'Opera of Rome

Cond.: Thomas Schippers
Rome (Teatro dell'Opera), July/Aug. 1964
EMI — AN 151-3 (3 LP)
EMI — RLS 916/3 (3 LP stereo)
EMI — COM 7 63466-2 (1 CD — Selections)
EMI — CMS 7 63640-2 (2 CD)

TURANDOT — Giacomo Puccini
With: Maria Luisa Nache, Mafalda Micheluzzi, Antonio Cassinelli
Cond.: Mario Parenti
Livorno (Teatro La Gran Guardia), Oct. 6, 1960 — "Live" recording
Foné "Work in Progress" — 93 F 16 (2 CD)

TURANDOT — Giacomo Puccini
With: Birgit Nilsson, Anna Moffo, Bonaldo Giaiotti
Cond.: Leopold Stokovski
New York (Metropolitan Opera), Mar. 4, 1961 — "Live" recording
*Melodram — MEL 448 (2 LP)
Historical Recordings Enterprises — HRE 299 (3 LP)
Memories — HR 4535/36 (2 CD)
Datum — DAT 12301 (2 CD)

TURANDOT — Giacomo Puccini
With: Birgit Nilsson, Galina Vishnevskaya, Nicola Zaccaria
Cond.: Gianandrea Gavazzeni
Milan (Teatro alla Scala), Dec. 7, 1964 — "Live" recording
*Historical Recordings Enterprises "Edizione Lirica" — EL 003 (3 LP)
*Nuova Era — 013.6318/19 (2 CD)
Memories — HR 6318/19 (2 CD)

TURANDOT — Giacomo Puccini
With: Birgit Nilsson, Renata Scotto, Bonaldo Giaiotti, Guido Mazzini, Piero De Palma,
Franco Ricciardi, Angelo Mercuriali
Orchestra and Chorus of the Teatro dell'Opera of Rome
Cond.: Francesco Molinari Pradelli
Rome (Teatro dell'Opera), June/July 1965
EMI — AN 159-61 (3 LP)
EMI — RLS 921/3 (3 LP stereo)
EMI — CMS 7693272 (2 CD)

TURANDOT — Giacomo Puccini
With: Birgit Nilsson, Mirella Freni, Bonaldo Giaiotti
Cond.: Zubin Mehta
New York (Metropolitan Opera), Dec. 3, 1966 — "Live" recording
*Great Opera Performances — G.O.P. 17 (2 LP)
Great Opera Performances — G.O.P. 756 (2 CD)
Arkadia — MP 479 (2 CD)

GLI UGONOTTI — Giacomo Meyerbeer
With: Joan Sutherland, Giulietta Simionato, Fiorenza Cossotto, Nicolai Ghiaurov,
Wladimiro Ganzarolli, Giorgio Tozzi
Cond.: Gianandrea Gavazzeni.
Milan (Teatro alla Scala), June 7, 1962 — "Live" recording
*MRF Records — MRF 18 (3 LP)
*Fonit Cetra "Documents" — DOC 34 (3 LP)
*Great Opera Performances — G.O.P. 2 (3 LP)
*The Golden Age of Opera — EJAS 246 (3 LP)
Morgan Records — MOR 6202 (3 LP)
*Great Opera Performances — G.O.P. 701 (3 CD)
*Melodram — CDM 37026 (2 CD)

LA VESTALE — Gaspare Spontini
With: Maria Callas, Ebe Stignani, Enzo Sordello, Nicola Rossi Lemeni
Cond.: Antonio Votto
Milan (Teatro alla Scala), Dec. 7, 1954 — "Live" recording
*Melodram — MEL 419 (3 LP)
Estro Armonico — E/A 009 (2 LP)
Raritas — OPR 405 (2 LP)
*Melodram — CDM 26008 (2 CD)
Great Opera Performances — G.O.P. 54 (2 LP)
Great Opera Performances — G.O.P. 741 (2 CD)

WERTHER (Fr.) — Jules Massenet
With: Rosalind Elias, Fernando Corena, John Reardon, Dominic Cossa
Cond.: Alain Lombard
New York (Metropolitan Opera), Mar. 27, 1971 — "Live" recording
Melodram — CDM 27088 (2 CD)

FRANCO CORELLI A PARMA
Parma (Teatro Regio): 1961-1971 — "Live" recording
Operatic Selections:
    NORMA — Vincenzo Bellini
    With: Cristina Deutekom, Franca Mattiucci
    Cond.: Antonino Votto
    Parma, Dec. 29, 1971

    TOSCA — Giacomo Puccini
    With: Virginia Gordoni, Attilio D'Orazi
    Cond.: Giuseppe Morelli
    Parma, Jan. 21, 1967

    IL TROVATORE — Giuseppe Verdi
    With: Ilva Ligabue, Adriana Lazzarini, Mario Zanasi
    Cond.: Arturo Basile
    Parma, Jan. 1, 1961
Myto Records — MCD 924.64 (1 CD)

FRANCO CORELLI A PARMA — II
Parma (Teatro Regio): 1961-1971 — "Live" recording
Operatic Selections:
    LA FORZA DEL DESTINO — Giuseppe Verdi
    With: Radmila Bakocevic, Franco Federici
    Cond.: Fulvio Vernizzi
    Parma, Dec. 26, 1967

    NORMA — Vincenzo Bellini
    Cristina Deutekom, Franca Mattiucci, Maurizio Mazzieri
    Cond.: Antonino Votto
    Parma, Dec. 29, 1971

    IL TROVATORE — Giuseppe Verdi
    With: Ilva Ligabue, Adriana Lazzarini, Mario Zanasi
    Cond.: Arturo Basile
    Parma, Jan. 1, 1961

    TOSCA — Giacomo Puccini
    With: Virginia Gordoni, Silvio Maionica, Virgilio Carbonari
    Cond.: Giuseppe Morelli
    Parma, Jan. 21, 1967
Myto Records — MCD 944.108 (1 CD)

Recitals

78 RPM
Accompanied by the Symphonic Orchestras of the RAI (Radiotelevisione Italiana)

FRANCO CORELLI — Recital
Puccini — TURANDOT: *"Non piangere Liù;"* *"Nessun dorma"*
Cetra — AT 0411

FRANCO CORELLI — Recital
Cilea — ADRIANA LECOUVREUR: *"L'anima ho stanca;"* *"La dolcissima effige"*
Cetra — AT 0412

FRANCO CORELLI — Recital
Puccini — LA FANCIULLA DEL WEST: *"Ch'ella mi creda;"* *"Or son sei mesi"*
Cetra — AT 0413

FRANCO CORELLI — Recital
Puccini — TOSCA: *"Recondita armonia;"* *"E lucevan le stelle"*
Cetra — AT 0408

FRANCO CORELLI — Recital
Donizetti — LA FAVORITA: *"Una vergin, un angiol di Dio;"* Puccini — LA FANCIULLA DEL WEST: *"Ch'ella mi creda"*
Cetra — AT 0469

45 RPM

FRANCO CORELLI — Recital
Orchestra conducted by Arturo Basile
Puccini — TOSCA: *"Recondita armonia;"* *"E lucevan le stelle;"* Puccini — TURANDOT: *"Non piangere Liù;"* *"Nessun dorma"*
July 6, 1956. (Date stamped on vinyl of the record)
Cetra — EPO 0326

FRANCO CORELLI — Recital
RAI Symphonic Orchestra conducted by Alfredo Simonetto
Donizetti — LUCIA DI LAMMERMOOR: *"Tombe degli avi miei;"* Verdi — RIGOLETTO: *"La donna è mobile;"* Verdi — I LOMBARDI ALLA PRIMA CROCIATA: *"La mia letizia infondere"*
Turin (RAI), Jan 16, 1957 (Date stamped on vinyl of the record)
Cetra — EPO 0327

FRANCO CORELLI — Recital
Verdi — UN BALLO IN MASCHERA: *"Ma se m'è forza perderti;"* Giordano — FEDORA: *"Amor ti vieta;"* Puccini — LA FANCIULLA DEL WEST: *"Ch'ella mi creda"*
Cetra — EPO 0328

FRANCO CORELLI — Recital
Giordano — FEDORA: *"Mia madre, la mia vecchia madre...Vedi io piango"*: Leoncavallo — PAGLIACCI: *"Recitar...Vesti la giubba;"* *"No, pagliaccio non son"*
Cetra — EPO 0340

FRANCO CORELLI — Recital
Verdi — AIDA: *"Se quel guerrier io fossi...Celeste Aida"*
Cetra — EPO 0348

FRANCO CORELLI — Recital
Leoncavallo — PAGLIACCI: *"Recitar...Vesti la giubba;"* *"No, pagliaccio non son"*
Cetra — SPO 1005

FRANCO CORELLI — Recital
Mascagni — LODOLETTA: *"Ah, ritrovarla;"* Mascagni — CAVALLERIA RUSTICANA:
"Addio alla madre"
Cetra — SPO 1006

FRANCO CORELLI — Recital
RAI Symphonic Orchestra conducted by Arturo Basile
Massenet — WERTHER: Duet, Act One (with Loretta Di Lelio); Giordano — FEDORA: *"Mia madre"*
Turin (RAI), Jan. 21, 1957 (Date stamped on vinyl of the record)
Cetra — SPO 1007

FRANCO CORELLI — Recital
Giordano — ANDREA CHÉNIER: *"Un dì all'azzurro spazio;"* *"Come un bel dì di maggio"*
Cetra — SPO 1010

FRANCO CORELLI — Recital
Massenet — WERTHER: *"Ah, non mi ridestar;"* Verdi — IL TROVATORE: *"Ah! sì, ben mio"*
Cetra — SPO 1012

FRANCO CORELLI — Recital
Bellini — NORMA: *"Meco all'altar di Venere;"* Verdi — LA FORZA DEL DESTINO: *"O tu che in seno agli angeli"*
Cetra — SPO 1013

FRANCO CORELLI — Recital
RAI Symphonic Orchestra conducted by Gian Stellari
Buzzi/Peccia: *"Lolita;"* Lara: *"Granada"*
Turin (RAI), Nov. 22, 1955 (Date stamped on vinyl of the record)
Cetra — SP 5

FRANCO CORELLI — Recital
RAI Symphonic Orchestra conducted by Alberto Bonocore
Pennino/De Flavis: *"Pecché;"* Liberati/Piccinelli: *"Cancion moresca"* (From the ballet *"L'ultima amante di Don Giovanni"*)
Turin (RAI), Dec. 30, 1955 (Date stamped on vinyl of the record)
Cetra — SP 16

FRANCO CORELLI — Recital
Orchestra conducted by Franco Ferraris
Cairono/Lysel: *"Pourquoi fermer ton coeur;"* Denza/Paris: *"Si tu m'amais"*
Jan. 9, 1962 (Date stamped on vinyl of the record)
La Voce del Padrone — VdP 7RO 3131

33 RPM (LP) and Compact Disc (CD)

FRANCO CORELLI — Recital
RAI Symphonic Orchestras conducted by Arturo Basile/Fulvio Vernizzi
Puccini — LA FANCIULLA DEL WEST: *"Ch'ella mi creda;"* *"Or son sei mesi"*: Puccini —
TOSCA: *"E lucevan le stelle;"* *"Recondita armonia;"* Donizetti — LA FAVORITA: *"Una vergin, un angiol di Dio;"* Puccini — TURANDOT: *"Non piangere Liù;"* *"Nessun dorma;"* Cilea —
ADRIANA LECOUVREUR: *"L'anima ho stanca;"* *"La dolcissima effige"*

Turin (RAI), Jan. 11, 1955 (Date stamped on vinyl of the record)
Cetra — LPV 45005 (1 LP)

FRANCO CORELLI — Recital
Puccini — TOSCA: *"Recondita armonia;"* Puccini — MADAMA BUTTERFLY: *"Amore o grillo;"* *"Addio, fiorito asil;"* Puccini — MANON LESCAUT: *"Fra voi belle;"* Puccini — TURANDOT: *"Non piangere Liù;"* *"Nessun dorma;"* Puccini — LA FANCIULLA DEL WEST: *"Or son sei mesi;"* *"Ch'ella mi creda"*
Cetra — LPV 45021 (1 LP)

FRANCO CORELLI — Recital
RAI Symphonic Orchestras conducted by Angelo Questa/Arturo Basile/Alfredo Simonetto
Verdi — AIDA: *"Celeste Aida;"* IL TROVATORE: *"Ah! sì ben mio;"* *"Di quella pira;"* ERNANI: *"Come rugiada al cespite;"* RIGOLETTO: *"La donna è mobile;"* OTELLO: *"Esultate;"* LA FORZA DEL DESTINO: *"O tu che in seno agli angeli;"* IL TROVATORE: *"Deserto sulla terra;"* I LOMBARDI ALLA PRIMA CROCIATA: *"La mia letizia infondere"*
Turin (RAI), Feb. 6, 1957 (Date stamped on vinyl of the record)
Cetra — LPC 55018 (1 LP)
Cetra — LPO 2044 (1 LP; technical reconstruction, 1979)

FRANCO CORELLI — Recital
RAI Symphonic Orchestra conducted by Arturo Basile
Mascagni — CAVALLERIA RUSTICANA: *"Addio alla madre;"* Bizet — CARMEN: *"Il fior che avevi a me tu dato;"* Massenet — WERTHER: *"Ah, non mi ridestar;"* Giordano — ANDREA CHÉNIER: *"Improvviso;"* Leoncavallo — PAGLIACCI: *"No, pagliaccio non son;"* Giordano — ANDREA CHÉNIER: *"Come un bel dì di maggio;"* Mascagni — LODOLETTA: *"Se Franz dicesse il vero;"* Leoncavallo PAGLIACCI: *"Recitar;"* Giordano — FEDORA: *"Amor ti vieta;"* Boito — MEFISTOFELE: *"Giunto sul passo estremo"*
Turin (RAI), Apr. 5, 1957 (Date stamped on vinyl of the record)
Cetra — LPC 55019 (1 LP)
Cetra — LPO 2078 (1 LP; technical reconstruction, 1981)

FRANCO CORELLI — Recital
RAI Symphonic Orchestras conducted by Arturo Basile/Umberto Cattini
Bellini — NORMA: *"Meco all'altar di Venere;"* Puccini — MADAMA BUTTERFLY: *"Addio, fiorito asil;"* Puccini — MANON LESCAUT: *"Tra voi belle;"* Boito — MEFISTOFELE: *"Dai campi, dai prati;"* Verdi — RIGOLETTO: *"Questa o quella;"* Verdi — SIMON BOCCANEGRA: *"Sento avvampar nell'anima"*
Turin (RAI), Feb. 10, 1958 (Date stamped on vinyl of the record)
Cetra — LPV 45020 (1 LP)

THE YOUNG CORELLI — His First Recitals (1956-1959)
RAI Symphonic Orchestras conducted by Arturo Basile/Alfredo Simonetto/Fulvio Vernizzi
Verdi — I LOMBARDI ALLA PRIMA CROCIATA: *"La mia letizia infondere;"* ERNANI: *"Come rugiada al cespite;"* IL TROVATORE: *"Deserto sulla terra,"* *"Ah! si ben mio,"* *"Di quella pira;"* RIGOLETTO: *"La donna è mobile;"* LA FORZA DEL DESTINO: *"O tu che in seno agli angeli;"* AIDA: *"Celeste Aida;"* OTELLO: *"Esultate!;"* Puccini — TOSCA: *"E lucevan le stelle;"* TURANDOT: *"Non piangere Liù,"* *"Nessun dorma;"* Mascagni — CAVALLERIA RUSTICANA: *"Mamma, quel vino è generoso"*
Palladio "Enterprise" — PD 4136 (1 CD)

CANZONI NAPOLETANE
Orchestra conducted by Franco Ferraris
Cardillo: *"Core 'ngrato;"* De Curtis: *"Senza nisciuno;"* Tortorella: *"Addà turnà;"* D'Annibale: *"'O paese d'o sole;"* Pennino: *"Pecché;"* Bellini: *"Fenesta ca lucive;"* Tagliaferri: *"Pescatore 'e Pusilleco;"* De Curtis: *"Tu, ca nun chiagne;"* Di Capua: *"I te vurria vasà;"* De Curtis: *"Torna a Surriento"*

Recording session: London, Oct. 1961
EMI — QALP 10322 (1 LP)

CANZONI NAPOLETANE N. 2

Orchestra conducted by Franco Ferraris
Falvo: "*Dicietencello vuje;*" Falvo: "*Guapparia;*" Lama: "*Silenzio cantatore;*" De Curtis: "*Voce 'e notte!;*" Gambardella: "*'O marenariello;*" Tagliaferri: "*Passione;*" Di Capua: "*'O sole mio;*" Cannio: "*'O surdato 'nnamurato;*" Tosti: "*A vucchella*": Valente: "*Torna!;*" Cioffi: "*'Na sera 'e maggio;*" Valente: "*Addio mia bella Napoli*"
Recording session: London, Dec. 1961
EMI — QALP 10360 (1 LP)

LA VOCE DI FRANCO CORELLI

Orchestra conducted by Franco Ferraris
Giordano — ANDREA CHÉNIER: "*Improvviso;*" Donizetti — LA FAVORITA: "*Spirto gentil;*" Puccini — TOSCA: "*Recondita armonia;*" Bellini — I PURITANI: "*A te o cara;*" Puccini — MANON LESCAUT: "*Donna non vidi mai;*" Cilea — ADRIANA LECOUVREUR: "*L'anima ho stanca;*" Puccini — TURANDOT: "*Nessun dorma;*" Meyerbeer — GLI UGONOTTI: "*Bianca al par di neve alpina;*" Giordano — ANDREA CHÉNIER: "*Come un bel dì di maggio;*" Puccini — TOSCA: "*E lucevan le stelle;*" Ponchielli — LA GIOCONDA: "*Cielo e mar*"
Recorded in 1962
EMI — QALP 10364 (1 LP)
EMI — ASDQ 5319 (1 LP stereo)
EMI — CDM 7692362 (1 CD), (Title: FRANCO CORELLI)

ARIE E CANTI RELIGIOSI

Orchestra and chorus conducted by Raffaele Mingardo
Stradella: "*Pietà Signore;*" Schubert: "*Ave Maria;*" Händel — SERSE: "*Ombra mai fu;*" Tortorella: "*Ave Maria;*" Wagner: "*L'ange;*" Verdi — MESSA DI REQUIEM: "*Ingemisco;*" Anonimo: "*Adeste Fideles;*" Bach/Gounod: "*Ave Maria;*" Mozart: "*Ave Verum Corpus;*" Rossini — PETITE MESSE SOLENNELLE: "*Domine Deus;*" Bizet: "*Agnus Dei;*" Franck: "*Panis Angelicus*"
Milan, Jan. 4 and 20, 1964 (Dates stamped on vinyl of the record)
EMI — QALP 10377 (1 LP)
EMI — 7243 5 68887 22 (1 CD)

MELODIE E CANZONI

Orchestras conducted by Raffaele Mingardo/Franco Ferraris
Lara: "*Granada;*" Donaudy: "*Vaghissima sembianza;*" De Curtis: "*Ti voglio tanto bene;*" Cairone; "*Mon ciel c'est toi;*" Pedrazzoli: "*Il canto della rinuncia;*" Grieg/Chapman: "I Love Thee;" D'Hardelot: "Because;" Mingardo: "*Carrettieri*" (canto popolare); Berrafato: "*Tu lo sai;*" Cairone: "*Pourquoi fermer ton coeur;*" Tortorella: "*Mammina mia;*" Serrano: "*Te quiero*"
Oct. 27 and Nov. 3, 1967 (Dates stamped on vinyl of the record)
EMI — QELP 8145 (1 LP)

TEBALDI AND CORELLI "GREAT OPERA DUETS"

Orchestre de la Suisse Romande conducted by Anton Guadagno
Puccini — MANON LESCAUT: "*Tu, tu amore*" (Duet, Act Two); Verdi — AIDA: "*Già i sacerdoti adunansi*" (Duet, Act Four); Cilea — ADRIANA LECOUVREUR: "*Ma dunque è vero*" (Duet, Act Two); Ponchielli — LA GIOCONDA: "*Ma chi vien...Oh! La sinistra voce*" (Duet, Act Two); Zandonai — FRANCESCA DA RIMINI: "*No, Smaragdi, no!...Inghirlandata di violette*" (Duet, Act Three)
Recorded in 1973
DECCA — SXL 6585 (1 LP)

METROPOLITAN OPERA GALA HONORING SIR RUDOLF BING

Recital with other artists
Soprano Teresa Zylis-Gara

Orchestra conducted by Karl Böhm
Verdi — OTELLO: "*Già nella notte densa*" (Duet, Act One)
New York (Metropolitan Opera), Apr. 22, 1972 — "Live" recording
*Deutsche Grammophone Gesellschaft — DGG 2530 260 (1 LP stereo)

FRANCO CORELLI "THE PRINCE OF TENORS"
Volume 1
Arias from: RIGOLETTO, LE CID, LA BOHÈME, L'AFRICANA, LA FANCIULLA DEL WEST,
UN BALLO IN MASCHERA, DON CARLO, CARMEN
*Legendary Recordings — LR 123 (2 LP) — "Live" recording

FRANCO CORELLI "THE PRINCE OF TENORS" Volume II
Arias from: AIDA, ERNANI, RIGOLETTO, OTELLO, IL TROVATORE, I LOMBARDI ALLA
PRIMA CROCIATA, LA FAVORITA,NORMA, UN BALLO IN MASCHERA, MEFISTOFELE,
SIMON BOCCANEGRA, FEDORA, MADAMA BUTTERFLY, ADRIANA LECOUVREUR,
LA FANCIULLA DEL WEST, LODOLETTA, PAGLIACCI, WERTHER, CARMEN — *Canzoni*.
*Legendary Recordings — LR 198 (2 LP) — "Live" recording

CONCERT
(In memory of Martin Luther King)
With: Montserrat Caballé, Bonaldo Giaiotti
Orchestra conducted by Alfredo Silipigni
Verdi — MACBETH: "*Ah, la paterna mano;*" Massenet — LE CID: "*Ô souverain;*" Meyerbeer
— L'AFRICANA: "*O paradiso;*" Giordano — ANDREA CHÉNIER: "*Vicino a te*" (Duet, Act
Four); Tosti: "*'A vucchella*"
New York, Apr. 7, 1968 — "Live" recording
*MRK (1 LP stereo)
*Legato Classics — LCD 101 (1 CD), Title: GALA OPERATIC CONCERT
Melodram — CDM 28051 (2 CD)

THE DEFINITIVE FRANCO CORELLI COLLECTION
Arias from: DON CARLO, AIDA, ERNANI, LE CID, ANDREA CHÉNIER, LA GIOCONDA,
LA BOHÈME, WERTHER, PAGLIACCI
*Historical Recording Enterprises — HRE 352 (3 LP) — "Live" recording

THE BEST OF FRANCO CORELLI "LIVE"
Arias from: TURANDOT, PAGLIACCI, ERNANI, LA GIOCONDA, TOSCA, AIDA, LA
FANCIULLA DEL WEST, WERTHER, CAVALLERIA RUSTICANA, ANDREA CHÉNIER,
ROMÉO ET JULIETTE, IL TROVATORE
*Legendary Recordings — LCR 5001 (Audiocassette) — "Live" recording

LIVE — 25 VOCI CELEBRI DELLA LIRICA — FRANCO CORELLI
Bizet — CARMEN: "*Il fior che avevi a me tu dato*" (1/16/56); Meyerbeer — GLI UGONOTTI:
"*Bianca al par di neve alpina;*" "*Dove vo? A soccorrer gli amici*" (Duet, Act Three, with
Giulietta Simionato) (5/28/62); Massenet — WERTHER: "*Ah non mi ridestar*" (3/15/55);
Donizetti — POLIUTO: "*D'un'alma troppo fervida;*" "*Sfolgorò divino raggio;*"
"*Donna!...Malvagio!*" (Duet, Act Three, with Maria Callas) (12/7/60); Verdi — LA BATTAGLIA
DI LEGNANO: "*O magnanima e prima;*" "*È ver, sei d'altri?*" (Duet, Act One, with Antonietta
Stella) (12/7/61); Verdi — DON CARLO: "*Io l'ho perduta;*" "*Dio che nell'alma infondere*"
(Duet, Act One, with Mario Sereni); "*Io vengo a domandar grazia*" (Duet, Act Two, with
Maria Curtis Verna) (4/15/61); Giordano — ANDREA CHÉNIER: *Improvviso*" (1956); Cilea
— ADRIANA LECOUVREUR: "*La dolcissima effige*" (1/17/56); Puccini — TOSCA: "*Recondita
armonia;*" "*Mario!...Son qui!*" (Duet, Act One, with Leontyne Price) (4/7/62); Puccini —
TURANDOT: "*Non piangere Liù*" (with Anna Moffo and Bonaldo Giaiotti) (3/4/61); Puccini
— LA FANCIULLA DEL WEST: "*Or son sei mesi*" (1955)
*Melodram — MEL 099 (2 LP) — "Live" recording

CONCERTO MARTINI & ROSSI
With: Rosanna Carteri
Orchestra Sinfonica della RAI of Milan conducted by Oliviero De Fabritiis
Cilea — ADRIANA LECOUVREUR: "*La dolcissima effige;*" Bizet — CARMEN: "*Il fior che avevi a me tu dato*"
Milan, Jan. 17, 1956 — "Live" recording
*Fonit Cetra — LMR 5014 (1 LP)
Fonit Cetra — CDMR 5014 (1 CD)

FRANCO CORELLI — Recital
Orchestras conducted by Arturo Basile/Alfredo Simonetto/Umberto Cattini
Bellini — NORMA: "*Meco all'altar di Venere*" (with Athos Cesarini); Verdi — ERNANI: "*Come rugiada al cespite;*" Verdi — UN BALLO IN MASCHERA: "*Ma se m'è forza perderti;*" Boito — MEFISTOFELE: "*Dai campi, dai prati;*" Verdi — SIMON BOCCANEGRA: "*Sento avvampar nell'anima;*" Giordano — FEDORA: "*Mia madre;*" Puccini — MADAMA BUTTERFLY: "*Addio fiorito asil;*" Cilea — ADRIANA LECOUVREUR: "*La dolcissima effige;*" Puccini — LA FANCIULLA DEL WEST: "*Or son sei mesi*"
Fonit Cetra — LPO 2079 (1 LP; technical reconstruction, 1981)

TENOR POT-POURRI
Various artists
Verdi — LA FORZA DEL DESTINO: "*Le minacce, i fieri accenti*"
With: Gian Giacomo Guelfi (recording by Fonit Cetra)
Bongiovanni — BG 1110 (1 CD)

FRANCO CORELLI
Orchestras conducted by Lorin Maazel/Anton Guadagno/Richard Bonynge
Puccini — TOSCA: "*Recondita armonia;*" "*E lucevan le stelle;*" Zandonai — FRANCESCA DA RIMINI: "*No, Smaragdi, no*" (Duet, Act Three, with Renata Tebaldi); Ponchielli — LA GIOCONDA: "*Ma chi vien?...Oh! La sinistra voce*" (Duet, Act Two, with Renata Tebaldi); Gounod — FAUST: "*Rien! En vain j'interroge...Salut! O mon dernier matin;*" "*Quel trouble inconnu...Salut! demeure chaste et pure;*" Puccini — MANON LESCAUT: "*Tu, tu amore?*" (Duet, Act Two, with Renata Tebaldi); Cilea — ADRIANA LECOUVREUR: "*Ma dunque è vero?*" (Duet, Act Two, with Renata Tebaldi)
Registrazioni 1966, 1967, 1973
DECCA — GRV 19 (1 LP stereo)

THE SENSATIONAL FRANCO CORELLI
Verdi — RIGOLETTO: "*Questa o quella;*" Giordano — ANDREA CHÉNIER: "*Improvviso;*" Meyerbeer — L'AFRICANA: "*O paradiso;*" Puccini — LA BOHÈME: "*Che gelida manina;*" Puccini — LA FANCIULLA DEL WEST: "*Ch'ella mi creda;*" Massenet — LE CID: "*Ô souverain;*" Favara: "*A la Barcillunisa;*" Di Capua: "*'O sole mio;*" Cardillo: "*Core 'ngrato;*" De Curtis: "*Tu, ca nun chiagne;*" Tosti: "*'A vucchella*" (Tokyo 11/8/71 — Conductor and pianist, Alberto Ventura); Denza: "*Occhi di fata;*" Bellini: "*Soave sogno;*" Verdi — RIGOLETTO: "*La donna è mobile;*" Monterverdi — ARIANNA: "*Lasciatemi morire;*" Verdi — OTELLO: "*Già nella notte densa*" (Duet, Act One, with Renata Tebaldi) (Tokyo 11/21/73 — Conductor, Tadashi Mori); Puccini — TURANDOT: "*Non piangere Liù*" (1964 — Conductor, Donald Vorhees); Verdi — IL TROVATORE: "*Ah! sì, ben mio*" (Duet, Act Two, with Leontyne Price); "*Di quella pira*" (1962 — Conductor, Herbert Von Karajan)
*Legendary Recordings — LR 1001 (1 CD) — "Live" recording
*Melodram — CDM 16503 (1 CD) — "Live" recording

FRANCO CORELLI — BIOGRAPHIES IN MUSIC (1955/1970)
Leoncavallo — PAGLIACCI: "*Un grande spettacolo a ventitré ore;*" "*Eh! Eh! Vi pare?...Un tal gioco;*" "*Ma poi ricordatevi;*" "*Recitar!...Vesti la giubba;*" "*Vo' il nome dell'amante tuo*" (1955); Massenet — WERTHER: "*Pourquoi me réveiller*" (1955); Bizet — CARMEN: "*Il fior che avevi a me tu dato*" (1956); Puccini — LA FANCIULLA DEL WEST: "*Una parola sola!...Or son sei mesi;*" "*Per lei soltanto...Ch'ella mi creda*" (4/4/1956); Puccini — TOSCA: "*Recondita*

armonia;" "Vittoria! Vittoria! L'alba vindice appar" (with Zinka Milanov and Gian Giacomo Guelfi); *"E lucevan le stelle"* (7/1/1957); Bellini — NORMA: *"Svanir le voci...Meco all'altar di Venere...Me protegge"* (1/4/1958); Giordano — ANDREA CHÉNIER: *"Improvviso;" "Il mio nome mentir...Io non ho amato ancora;" "Come un bel dì di maggio"* (1958); Cilea — ADRIANA LECOUVREUR: *"Perché? Sincero amor...La dolcissima effige"* (with Magda Olivero); *"L'anima ho stanca"* (11/28/1959); Donizetti — POLIUTO: *"Sfolgorò divino raggio"* (1960); Giordano — ANDREA CHÉNIER: *"Sì, fui soldato"* (1961); Verdi — LA BATTAGLIA DI LEGNANO: *"O magnanima e prima"* (1961); Verdi — IL TROVATORE: *"Deserto sulla terra;" "Mal reggendo all'aspro assalto"* (1961); Verdi — IL TROVATORE: *"Il presagio funesto...Ah! sì, ben mio;" "Manrico?...Di quella pira"* (7/31/1962); Verdi — AIDA: *"Se quel guerrier io fossi!...Celeste Aida"* (1962); Meyerbeer — LES HUGUENOTS: *"Plus blanche"* (in Italian) (6/7/1962); Ponchielli — LA GIOCONDA: *"Ed or scendete a riposarvi...Cielo e mar!;" "Deh! Non tremar"* (1962); Mascagni — CAVALLERIA RUSTICANA: *"Oh Lola, ch'hai di latti la cammisa;" "Comare Lola...Viva il vino spumeggiante"* (with Gabriella Carturan); *"Compar Alfio, lo so che il torto è mio;" "Mamma, quel vino è generoso"* (with Maria Grazia Allegri) (12/7/1963); Puccini — TURANDOT: *"Non piangere Liù"* (with Galina Vishnevskaya and Nicola Zaccaria); *"No, no, principessa altera;" "Nessun dorma"* (12/7/1964); Bizet — CARMEN: *"La fleur que tu m'avais jetée;" "Tu me dis de la suivre"* (with Marilyn Horne) (1965); Verdi — ERNANI: *"Mercé, diletti amici...Come rugiada...O tu che l'alma adora"* (1965); Verdi — LA FORZA DEL DESTINO: *"La vita è inferno all'infelice...O tu che in seno agli angeli"* (1965); Verdi — MACBETH: *"O figli, o figli miei...Ah, la paterna mano"* (1968); Massenet — LE CID: *"Ô souverain"* (1968); Meyerbeer — L'AFRICANA: *"Mi batte il cor...O paradiso"* (1968); Verdi — DON CARLO: *"Io l'ho perduta!...Io là vidi il suo sorriso"* (1970) *Cantabile — BIM 702 (2 CD) — "Live" recording

FRANCO CORELLI — Recital 1
Donizetti — POLIUTO *"D'un'alma troppo fervida;" "Sfolgorò divino raggio;" "Donna!... Malvagio!"* (with Maria Callas); Verdi — LA BATTAGLIA DI LEGNANO: *"O magnanima e prima;" "È ver, sci d'altri?"* (with Antonietta Stella); Giordano — ANDREA CHÉNIER: *"Improvviso;"* Cilea — ADRIANA LECOUVREUR: *"La dolcissima effige;"* Puccini — TOSCA: *"Recondita armonia;"* Puccini — TURANDOT: *"Non piangere Liù;"* Meyerbeer — GLI UGONOTTI: *"Bianca al par di neve alpina;" "Dove vo? A soccorrer gli amici"* (with Giulietta Simionato) — Massenet — WERTHER: *"Ah, non mi ridestar;"* Bizet — CARMEN: *"Il fior che avevi a me tu dato"*
(Selections from the album *"Voci Celebri della Lirica"* — MEL 099)
*Melodram — CDM 16503 (1 CD) — "Live" recording

FRANCO CORELLI SINGS NEAPOLITAN SONGS
(Selections taken from two LPs of Neapolitan Songs, QALP 10322 and QALP 10360)
EMI Angel — CDC-7 478352 (1 CD)

FRANCO CORELLI — OPERA ARIAS
Verdi — IL TROVATORE: *"Ah! sì, ben mio;" "Di quella pira;"* Verdi — AIDA: *"Se quel guerrier io fossi...Celeste Aida;"* Mascagni — CAVALLERIA RUSTICANA: *"Mamma, quel vino è generoso;"* Puccini — TURANDOT: *"Nessun dorma;"* Gounod — ROMÉO ET JULIETTE: *"L'amour! Oui, son ardeur...Ah! Lève-toi soleil!;"* Leoncavallo — PAGLIACCI: *"Recitar!...Vesti la giubba;"* Giordano — ANDREA CHÉNIER: *"Colpito qui m'avete...Un dì all'azzurro spazio;" "Credo a una possanza arcana;" "Sì, fui soldato;" "Come un bel dì di maggio;"* Bellini — NORMA: *"Meco all'altar di Venere...Me protegge, me difende"*
(Selections taken from the complete operas, EMI)
EMI — CDC-7 47851 2 (1 CD)

MONTSERRAT CABALLÉ & FRANCO CORELLI "In concert" — 1968
*Historical Recordings Enterprises — HRE 400 (1 LP stereo)

DOROTHY KIRSTEN & FRANCO CORELLI "In concert" — 1965
Arias and duets from TOSCA, LA FANCIULLA DEL WEST, MACBETH, LA BOHÈME
*Historical Recordings Enterprises — HRE 432 (1 LP)

THE UNFORGETTABLE DUO: RENATA TEBALDI AND FRANCO CORELLI
Arias and duets from ADRIANA LECOUVREUR, ANDREA CHÉNIER, OTELLO, LA BOHÈME, LE CID, MANON
*Legendary Recordings — LR 117 (1 LP) — "Live" recording

THE UNFORGETTABLE DUO: RENATA TEBALDI AND FRANCO CORELLI
Verdi — OTELLO: "*Già nella notte densa*" (Duet, Act 1); Massenet — LE CID: "*Ô souverain;*" Cilea — ADRIANA LECOUVREUR: "*La dolcissima effige*" (Duet, Act One); Puccini — LA BOHÈME: "*O soave fanciulla*" (Duet, Act One) (Recorded: Tokyo, Nov. 1973); Puccini — MANON LESCAUT: "*Oh, sarò la più bella...Tu! Tu! Amore tu!*" (Duet, Act Two) (Recorded in 1966); Puccini — LA BOHÈME: "*Sono andati?*" (Duet, Act Four and Finale of the Opera) (Recorded in 1965); Giordano — ANDREA CHÉNIER: "*Ecco l'altare...*" (Duet, Act Two); Act Four, complete (Recorded in 1966)
*Legendary Recordings — LR 1027 (1 CD) — "Live" recording

VIRGINIA ZEANI & FRANCO CORELLI — "GALA CONCERT 1981"
Orchestra conducted by Alfredo Silipigni
Pennino: "*Pecché;*" Tosti: "*L'ultima canzone;*" Gambardella: "*'O marenariello;*" Billi: "*E canta il grillo;*" Di Capua: "*I te vurria vasà;*" Lama: "*Silenzio cantatore;*" Favara: "*A la Barcillunisa*"
*Legendary Recordings — LR 152 ST (1 LP) — "Live" recording

FRANCO CORELLI — OPERATIC DUETS
Various Orchestras and Conductors — "Live" recording
With: Zinka Milanov (TOSCA), Maria Callas (POLIUTO), Giulietta Simionato (GLI UGONOTTI), Grace Bumbry (CARMEN), Leontyne Price (LA FORZA DEL DESTINO), Renata Tebaldi (OTELLO), Fiorenza Cossotto (IL TROVATORE), Gabriella Tucci (AIDA), Montserrat Caballé (LA BOHÈME), Licia Albanese (ANDREA CHÉNIER)
*Legendary Récordings — LR 186 (2 LP)

FRANCO CORELLI / ETTORE BASTIANINI
Duets from LA FORZA DEL DESTINO
Cond.: Nello Santi
New York (Metropolitan Opera), Feb. 1965 — "Live" recording
*PCL 1002-1 (1 LP)

CORELLI AND BASTIANINI "TOGETHER" — Great Verdi Scenes
IL TROVATORE: "*Di geloso amor sprezzato*" (Finale, Act One); "*Il balen del suo sorriso;*" "*Di quella pira*"
With: Leontyne Price
Cond.: Herbert Von Karajan
Salzburg, 1962

LA FORZA DEL DESTINO: "*La vita è inferno...O tu che in seno agli angeli;*" "*Solenne in quest'ora;*" "*Morir, tremenda cosa...Urna fatale...Egli è salvo;*" "*Ne gustare m'è dato*" (Finale, Act Three); "*Invano Alvaro*"
Cond.: Nello Santi
Metropolitan Opera, 1965

OTELLO: "*Niun mi tema*"
Cond.: Alfredo Silipigni
Newark, 1981
*Legendary Recordings — LR 167 (1 LP) — "Live" recording

A FESTIVAL OF SONG — "Legendary Operatic Voices Sing Light Music"
Various Singers
*Legendary Recordings — LR 142 (5 LP)

I GRANDI DELL'OPERA — VOLUME 1
Various Singers
Verdi — AIDA: "*Celeste Aida*"
*International Joker Production — SM 1353 (1 LP)

FIRESTONE PRESENTS YOUR CHRISTMAS FAVORITES — VOLUME 3
With: Roberta Peters, Gordon MacRae, Martha Wright
Firestone Orchestra and Chorus directed by Joe Harnell
Franck: *"Panis Angelicus;"* Adam: "O Holy Night"
*Firestone — SLP 7008 (3 LP stereo)
Firestone — MLP 7008 (3 LP mono)

THE BEST OF FRANCO CORELLI
Orchestras conducted by Franco Ferraris/Raffaele Mingardo
Di Capua: *"'O sole mio;"* Di Capua: *"I te vurria vasà;"* Puccini — TOSCA: *"Recondita armonia;"* *"E lucevan le stelle;"* Händel — SERSE: *"Ombra mai fu;"* Schubert: *"Ave Maria;"* Ponchielli — LA GIOCONDA: *"Cielo e mar;"* Puccini — TURANDOT: *"Nessun dorma;"* Bizet: *"Agnus Dei;"* Gambardella: *"O marenariello;"* De Curtis: *"Torna a Surriento;"* De Curtis: *"Voce e notte;"* Chapman: "I Love Thee;" Lara: *"Granada"*
Capitol Records — SPAO 9703 (1 LP)

FRANCO CORELLI SINGS GRANADA AND OTHER ROMANTIC SONGS
Capitol Records — SP 8661 (1 LP)

In MARIA CALLAS *"D'Art et d'Amour"*
Paris (Salle Wagram), June 1964
Cond.: Georges Prêtre
Verdi — AIDA: *"Pur ti riveggo"* (Duet, Act Three)
EMI — CD57 54103 (2 CD)

FRANCO CORELLI — 1957/1970
Various Orchestras and Conductors — "Live" recordings
Selections from the operas: ANDREA CHÉNIER, LUCIA DI LAMMERMOOR, CARMEN, LA GIOCONDA, TOSCA, NORMA, MESSA DI REQUIEM
Melodram — CDM 26520 (1 CD)

CONCERT
Munich (Meeting Hall of German Museums), Dec. 13, 1970 — "Live" recording
Cond.: Nello Santi
Verdi — RIGOLETTO: *"Questa o quella;"* Giordano — ANDREA CHÉNIER: *"Un dì all'azzurro spazio;"* Meyerbeer — L'AFRICANA: *"O Paradiso;"* Puccini — TOSCA: *"Recondita armonia;"* Massenet — LE CID: *"Ô souverain;"* Boito — MEFISTOFELE: *"Giunto sul passo estremo"*
Melodram — CDM 16521 (1 CD)

FRANCO CORELLI — RITRATTO 1955/1965
Various Orchestras and Conductors — "Live" recordings
Selections from the operas: GLI UGONOTTI, ERNANI, LA BATTAGLIA DI LEGNANO, IL TROVATORE, CARMEN, POLIUTO, WERTHER, TURANDOT, TOSCA, ADRIANA LECOUVREUR, ANDREA CHÉNIER
Memories — HR 4204/05 (2 CD)

MARIA CALLAS AND FRANCO CORELLI — OPERATIC DUETS
Various Orchestras and Conductors — "Live" recordings
Selections from the operas: NORMA, POLIUTO, AIDA
Palladio "Enterprises" — PD 4170 (1 CD)

FRANCO CORELLI CONCERT
Vienna (Gesellschaft der Musikfreunde), Oct. 14, 1973 — "Live" recording
With: Renata Tebaldi
Piano: Gordon Jephtas
Tosti: *"La serenata;"* Donizetti: *"La conocchia;"* Donizetti: *"Lu tradimientu;"* Tosti: *"Sogno;"* Bellini: *"Soave sogno;"* Donizetti: *"Amore e morte;"* Puccini — LA BOHÈME: *"O soave fanciulla;"* Massenet — LE CID: *"Ô souverain;"* Denza: *"Occhi di fata;"* Bizet: *"Ouvre ton coeur;"* Puccini — TOSCA: *"Chi è quella donna bionda lassù;"* Tosti: *"L'ultima canzone;"* De Curtis: *"Tu ca nun chiagne;"* Tosti: *"'A vucchella"*

New York (Philharmonic Hall), Apr. 7, 1968 — "Live" recording
With: Montserrat Caballé and Bonaldo Giaiotti
Cond.: Alfredo Silipigni
Verdi — MACBETH: "*Ah, la paterna mano;*" Massenet — LE CID: "*Ô souverain;*" Meyerbeer — L'AFRICANA: "*O Paradiso;*" Giordano — ANDREA CHÉNIER: "*Vicino a te;*" Tosti: "*'A vucchella*"
Great Opera Performances — G.O.P. 757 (2 CD)

OMMAGIO A FRANCO CORELLI — 1955/1972
Songs, Concerts, USA and RAI, Duets and Opera Arias
Massenet — WERTHER: "*Ah, non mi ridestar;*" Puccini — LA FANCIULLA DEL WEST: "*Or son sei mesi;*" Giordano — ANDREA CHÉNIER: "*Un dì all'azzurro spazio;*" Cilea — ADRIANA LECOUVREUR: "*L'anima ho stanca;*" Bizet — CARMEN: "*Il fior che avevi a me tu dato;*" Puccini — TOSCA: "*E lucevan le stelle,*" "*Amaro sol per te*" (with Lisa Della Casa); Mascagni — CAVALLERIA RUSTICANA: "*Brindisi,*" "*Addio alla madre;*" Di Capua: "*I te vurria vasà;*" Puccini — TURANDOT: "*Non piangere Liù;*" D'Annibale: "*'O Paese d'o sole;*" Verdi — UN BALLO IN MASCHERA: "*Teco io sto*" (with Régine Crespin); Puccini — LA BOHÈME: "*O soave fanciulla* (with Dorothy Kirsten); *Tre canzoni napoletane* (medley); Franck: "*Panis Angelicus;*" Adam: "*O Holy Night;*" Massenet — LE CID: "*Ô souverain;*" Verdi — I LOMBARDI ALLA PRIMA CROCIATA: "*La mia letizia infondere;*" Puccini — TOSCA: "*Recondita armonia;*" Cardillo: "*Core 'ngrato;*" Di Capua: "*I te vurria vasà;*" Tosti: "*L'ultima canzone,*" "*'A vucchella,*" Verdi — MACBETH: "*Ah, la paterna mano;*" De Falla: "*Jota;*" Puccini — LA FANCIULLA DEL WEST: "*Ch'ella mi creda;*" Verdi — IL TROVATORE: "*Di quella pira*" (encored); Di Capua: "*'O sole mio;*" Posford: "The World Is Mine Tonight;" De Curtis: "*Tu ca nun chiagne;*" Verdi — RIGOLETTO: "*Questa o quella;*" Giordano — ANDREA CHÉNIER: "*Un dì, all'azzurro spazio;*" Meyerbeer — L'AFRICANA: "*O Paradiso;*" Puccini — LA BOHÈME: "*Che gelida manina;*" LA FANCIULLA DEL WEST: "*Ch'ella mi creda;*" Massenet — LE CID: "*Ô souverain;*" Di Capua: "*'O sole mio;*" Cardillo: "*Core 'ngrato;*" De Curtis: "*Tu ca nun chiagne;*" Tosti: "*'A vucchella;*" Verdi — OTELLO: Duet, Act One (with Teresa Zylis-Gara)
Great Opera Performances — G.O.P. 760 (2 CD)

FRANCO CORELLI: THE GOLDEN YEARS 1962-1966
Various Orchestras and Conductors — "Live" recordings
De Curtis: "*Tu ca nun chiagne;*" Denza: "*I te vurria vasà;*" Mascagni — CAVALLERIA RUSTICANA: "*Addio alla madre;*" *Tre canzoni napoletane* (medley); Torelli: "*Tu lo sai;*" Mascagni — CAVALLERIA RUSTICANA: "*Brindisi,*" "*Addio alla madre;*" Puccini — TURANDOT: "*Non piangere Liù;*" LA BOHÈME: "*O soave fanciulla*" (with Dorothy Kirsten); Giordano — ANDREA CHÉNIER: "*Vicino a te*" (with Renata Tebaldi); Verdi — UN BALLO IN MASCHERA: "*Teco io sto*" (with Régine Crespin)
Englewood (New York), Mar. 18, 1962 — "Live" recordings
Piano: Alberta Masiello
Bizet — CARMEN: "*Il fior che avevi a me tu dato;*" Lama: "*Silenzio cantatore;*" Denza: "*I te vurria vasà;*" Tagliaferri: "*Pescatore 'e Pusilleco;*" Di Capua: "*'O sole mio;*" De Curtis: "*Tu ca nun chiagne;*" Giordano — FEDORA: "*Amor ti vieta;*" Tosti: "*'A vucchella;*" Puccini — TOSCA: "*Recondita armonia;*" LA FANCIULLA DEL WEST: "*Ch'ella mi creda*"
Legato Classics — SRO 812 (1 CD)

Audiocassettes and Compact Discs within Opera Collections

I GIOIELLI DELLA LIRICA (Longanesi Periodici)

N. 23: Donizetti — POLIUTO (Selection) (1 LP)
With: Maria Callas, Ettore Bastianini
Cond.: Antonino Votto

N. 63: Verdi — LA BATTAGLIA DI LEGNANO (Selection) (1 LP)
With: Antonietta Stella, Ettore Bastianini
Cond.: Gianandrea Gavazzeni

N. 72: Verdi — AIDA (Selection) (1 LP)
With: Gabriella Tucci, Cornell MacNeil
Cond.: George Schick

LIRICA (Fabbri Editori)

N. 16: Puccini — TURANDOT (Selection) (1 Audiocassette)
With: Lucille Udovich, Renata Mattioli, Plinio Clabassi
Cond.: Fernando Previtali

OPERA VIVA (Armando Curcio Editore)

N. 1: Verdi — IL TROVATORE (Selection) (1 CD)
With: Leontyne Price, Giulietta Simionato, Ettore Bastianini
Cond.: Herbert Von Karajan

N. 26: "Bonus" — FRANCO CORELLI (1 CD) Enclosed

Verdi — IL TROVATORE: *"Ah! sì ben mio...Di quella pira"* (12/7/1962); Verdi — LA BATTAGLIA DI LEGNANO: *"O magnanima e prima;"* *"È ver? Sei d'altri?"* (Duet, Act One, with Antonietta Stella) (12/7/1961) Puccini — TOSCA: *"Recondita armonia"* (4/7/1962); Puccini — TURANDOT: *"Non piangere Liù"* (3/4/1961); Donizetti — POLIUTO: *"D'un'alma troppo fervida;"* *"Sfolgarò divino raggio;"* *"Donna! Malvagio!...Nell'alma la grazia"* (Duet, Act Three, with Maria Callas) (12/7/1960) Meyerbeer — GLI UGONOTTI: *"Non lungi dalle torri...Bianca al par;"* *"Dove vo? A soccorrer gli amici"* (Duet, Act Four, with Giulietta Simionato) (5/28/1962) Massenet — WERTHER: *"Ah! non mi ridestar"* (3/15/1955) Bizet — CARMEN: *"Il fior che avevi a me tu dato"* (1/16/1956).

OPERA ITALIANA (Armando Curcio, Editor)

N. 8: Verdi — IL TROVATORE (Complete Opera) (2 CD)
With: Leontyne Price, Giulietta Simionato, Ettore Bastianini
Cond.: Herbert Von Karajan

Tapography — Live Recordings

compiled and edited by Federico Rota

Note: The list which follows includes those live tapings whose existence it was possible to ascertain, and whose inclusion (together with the official recordings) was the basis for critical considerations of Franco Corelli's art which have been made in the text of this book. Naturally, the choice cannot attempt to include all such recordings in existence. We will be grateful to any collectors who would like to notify us of the existence of material that would fill in the gaps.

ADRIANA LECOUVREUR
Naples — Nov. 28, 1959
New York — Feb. 9, 1963
New York — Apr. 19, 1969
Cleveland — May 2, 1969
Dallas — May 15, 1969

AGNESE DI HOHENSTAUFEN
Florence — May 6, 1954

AIDA
Naples — Nov. 24, 1955
New York — Mar. 3, 1962
Cleveland — Apr. 21, 1964
New York — May 1, 1964
Cleveland — May 1, 1965
New York — Mar. 13, 1966
New York — Dec. 14, 1966
Cleveland — Apr. 28, 1967
Philadelphia — Feb. 20, 1968
Cleveland — Apr. 30, 1971
New York — May 31, 1971
New York — June 24, 1972
Verona — Aug. 15, 1972
Verona — Aug. 19, 1972
New York — Mar. 1, 1973

ANDREA CHÉNIER
Naples — Mar. 3, 1957
Naples — Nov. 29, 1958
Milan — Jan. 20, 1960
Vienna — June 26, 1960
Venice — June 19, 1961
New York — Nov. 17, 1962
Philadelphia — Apr. 5, 1965
New York — Feb. 5, 1966
New York — Mar. 22, 1966
New York — Jan. 14, 1971

LA BATTAGLIA DI LEGNANO
Milan — Dec. 7, 1961

LA BOHÈME
New York — Feb. 29, 1964
Atlanta — May 15, 1964
Chicago — Oct. 22, 1965
New York — Dec. 14, 1965

New York — Apr. 12, 1969
Cleveland — Apr. 29, 1969
Philadelphia — Dec. 2, 1969
New York — Apr. 15, 1971
New York — June 9, 1971
Macerata — July 4, 1971
Macerata — July 7, 1971
New York — Feb. 16, 1974
Torre del Lago — Aug. 10, 1976
Torre del Lago — Aug. 13, 1976

CARMEN
Naples — Dec. 30, 1953
Palermo — Feb. 3, 1959
Verona — Aug. 2, 1961
Philadelphia — Apr. 3, 1962
New York — June 11, 1968
New York — June 14, 1968
Verona — July 23, 1970
Verona — Aug. 1, 1970
Philadelphia — Jan. 26, 1971
Lisbon — Sept. 8, 1973
Macerata — July 13, 1974
Verona — July 8, 1975
Verona — July 12, 1975

CAVALLERIA RUSTICANA
Milan — Dec. 7, 1963
New York — Mar. 28, 1964
New York — Feb. 7, 1970
New York — June 18, 1973
New York — Dec. 23, 1974

DON CARLO
New York — Apr. 15, 1961
New York — Mar. 7, 1964
Philadelphia — Oct. 25, 1966
New York — Feb. 14, 1970
Vienna — Oct. 25, 1970
New York — Apr. 4, 1972
New York — Apr. 22, 1972
New York — June 6, 1972
New York — June 15, 1972
New York — June 21, 1972

ERACLE
Milan — Dec. 29, 1958

ERNANI
New York — Nov. 22, 1962
New York — Apr. 10, 1965
New York — Nov. 14, 1965
New York — Jan. 8, 1971
Verona — July 15, 1972
Verona — July 21, 1972
Verona — July 28, 1972
Verona — Aug. 9, 1972
LA FANCIULLA DEL WEST
Trieste — Dec. 3, 1955
Milan — Apr. 4, 1956
Naples — Feb. 9, 1957
San Diego — Nov. 10, 1965
Los Angeles — Nov. 13, 1965
New York — Jan. 8, 1966

LA FORZA DEL DESTINO
Naples — Mar. 15, 1958
New York — Feb. 6, 1965
Philadelphia — Apr. 14, 1965
Parma — Dec. 26, 1967
New York — Mar. 9, 1968
Cleveland — Apr. 30, 1968
New York — Jan. 21, 1972
New York — Feb. 7, 1972
New York — Mar. 8, 1972

LA GIOCONDA
New York — Mar. 31, 1962
Philadelphia — Feb. 18, 1964
New York — Sep. 22, 1966
Philadelphia — Oct. 18, 1966
New York — Oct. 22, 1966
New York — Nov. 14, 1966
New York — Nov. 23, 1966
Atlanta — May 1, 1967
New York — Nov. 22, 1967
New York — Dec. 2, 1967

GIULIO CESARE
Rome — Dec. 26, 1955

GUERRA E PACE
Florence — May 26, 1953

LUCIA DI LAMMERMOOR
New York — Jan. 11, 1971

MACBETH
Memphis — May 15, 1973
Dallas — May 18, 1973

NORMA
Trieste — Nov. 19, 1953
Rome — Jan. 2, 1958
Rome — Jan. 4, 1958
Parma — Dec. 29, 1971

PAGLIACCI
New York — Apr. 11, 1964

POLIUTO
Milan — Dec. 7, 1960

ROMÉO ET JULIETTE
Philadelphia — Apr. 14, 1964
New York — Sep. 27, 1967
New York — Oct. 16, 1967
Philadelphia — Oct. 20, 1967
Hartford — Nov. 15, 1967
New York — Nov. 25, 1967
New York — Mar. 28, 1968
New York — Nov. 30, 1968
New York — Apr. 18, 1970
New York — Mar. 31, 1973
New York — Nov. 29, 1974
New York — Dec. 7, 1974
Miami — Jan. 25, 1975

TOSCA
London — June 27, 1957
London — July 1, 1957
Naples — Mar. 6, 1958
Livorno — Oct. 21, 1959
New York — Feb. 6, 1962
New York — Apr. 7, 1962
Cleveland — Apr. 23, 1963
New York — Mar. 22, 1964
Boston — Apr. 18, 1964
New York — Mar. 19, 1965
New York — Apr. 3, 1965
Detroit — May 29, 1965
New York — Jan. 25, 1966
Parma — Jan. 21, 1967
New York — Feb. 7, 1968
Pasadena — Mar. 2, 1968
New York — Apr. 13, 1968
New York — Apr. 18, 1968
New York — Oct. 4, 1968
New York — June 13, 1970
New York — June 5, 1971
Lisbon — Mar. 18, 1973
New York — Apr. 20, 1973

IL TROVATORE
Parma — Jan. 1, 1961
New York — Feb. 4, 1961
Salzburg — July 31, 1962
Milan — Dec. 7, 1962
New York — Feb. 1, 1964
New York — Feb. 24, 1964
Cleveland — Apr. 20, 1964
Chicago — Oct. 9, 1964

TURANDOT
Monte Carlo — Feb. 28, 1960

Livorno — Oct. 4, 1960
Livorno — Oct. 6, 1960
New York — Mar. 4, 1961
Naples — Jan. 13, 1962
New York — Feb. 24, 1962
Milan — Dec. 7, 1964
New York — Feb. 1, 1965
New York — Feb. 14, 1965
New York — Oct. 3, 1966
New York — June 6, 1970
Macerata — July 4, 1970
Boston — Apr. 27, 1974
New York — May 28, 1974
New York — June 14, 1974
New York — Oct. 4, 1974
New York — Dec. 28, 1974
Verona — Aug. 15, 1975
Verona — Aug. 21, 1975

GLI UGONOTTI
Milan — May 28, 1962

LA VESTALE
Milan — Dec. 7, 1954

WERTHER
New York — Feb. 27, 1971
New York — Mar. 27, 1971
New York — Mar. 31, 1971
New York — Mar. 13, 1972

MESSA DI REQUIEM
Los Angeles — Nov. 14, 1967

CONCERTS
RAI — Feb. 17, 1956
Newark — Apr. 1962
New York — Mar. 25, 1965
Cleveland — Mar. 17, 1966
New York — Apr. 16, 1966
Philadelphia — Dec. 15, 1966
Cleveland — Dec. 10, 1967
New York — Mar. 20, 1968
New York — Apr. 7, 1968
Munich — Dec. 13, 1970
Hamburg — Oct. 10, 1971
Tokyo — Oct. 29, 1971
Tokyo — Nov. 8, 1971
Tokyo — Nov. 12, 1971
New York — Apr. 22, 1972
New Orleans — Nov. 2, 1972
Philadelphia — Dec. 20, 1972
Cincinnati — July 7, 1973
Philadelphia — July 12, 1973
London — Oct. 9, 1973
Vienna — Oct. 14, 1973
Tokyo — Nov. 21, 1973
Vienna — June 28, 1974
Newark — June 8, 1980
Newark — Apr. 25, 1981
Newark — July 9, 1981

Videography

compiled and edited by Gilberto Starone, Mark Schiavone and Stephen R. Leopold

Note: The materials listed here are those whose existence we have been able to directly document. Some of them were available to the public in the era of videorecording, others circulated only among collectors, and others are still unavailable.

Complete Operas

PAGLIACCI — Ruggero Leoncavallo, Sep. 26, 1954
With: Mafalda Micheluzzi, Tito Gobbi, Lino Puglisi
Orchestra and Chorus of the RAI di Milan
Cond.: Alfredo Simonetto
Bel Canto Society; Legato Classics

TOSCA — Giacomo Puccini, Sep. 24, 1955
With: Renata Heredia Capnist, Carlo Tagliabue, Vito De Taranto
Orchestra and Chorus of the RAI of Milan
Cond.: Antonino Votto
Bel Canto Scoiety

CARMEN (It.) —Georges Bizet, June 13, 1956
With: Belen Amparan, Anselmo Colzani
Orchestra and Chorus of the RAI of Milan
Cond.: Nino Sanzogno
Bel Canto Society

LA FORZA DEL DESTINO — Giuseppe Verdi, March 15, 1958
With: Renata Tebaldi, Ettore Bastianini, Boris Christoff, Oralia Dominguez, Renato Capecchi
Orchestra and Chorus of the Teatro di San Carlo of Naples
Cond.: Francesco Molinari Pradelli
Bel Canto Society; Legato Classics

ANDREA CHÉNIER — Umberto Giordano, Nov. 29, 1958
With: Antonietta Stella, Ettore Bastianini, Miriam Pirazzini
Orchestra and Chorus of the Teatro di San Carlo of Naples
Cond.: Franco Capuana
Not yet available

TURANDOT — Giacomo Puccini, Dec. 23, 1958
With: Lucille Udovich, Renata Mattioli, Plinio Clabassi
Orchestra and Chorus of the RAI of Milan
Cond.: Fernando Previtali
Bel Canto Society; Legato Classics

IL TROVATORE — Giuseppe Verdi, Parma, Jan. 1,1961 (Date of Broadcast: May 1, 1961)
With: Ilva Ligabue, Adriana Lazzarini, Mario Zanasi, Salvatore Catania
Orchestra and Chorus of the Teatro Regio of Parma
Cond.: Arturo Basile
Not yet available

ANDREA CHÉNIER — Umberto Giordano, May 25, 1973
With: Celestina Casapietra, Piero Cappuccilli
Orchestra and Chorus of the RAI of Milan
Cond.: Bruno Bartoletti
Bel Canto Society

Miscellaneous Appearances

THE ED SULLIVAN SHOW (Televised variety show) New York
Jan. 28, 1962: *"Tu ca nun chiagne"*
Feb. 3, 1963: *"I' te vurria vasa"*
Apr. 5, 1964: CAVALLERIA RUSTICANA: *"Addio alla madre"*
Apr. 17, 1966: LA BOHÈME: *"O soave fanciulla"* (with Dorothy Kirsten)
Sep. 18, 1966: ANDREA CHÉNIER: *"Vicino a te"* (with Renata Tebaldi)
Nov. 20, 1966: *"Tu ca nun chiagne," "O prima amore,"* and *"Torna a Surriento"*
Mar. 3, 1968: *"Tu lu sai"*
All appearances available from Bel Canto Society without Ed Sullivan's introductions

THE BELL TELEPHONE HOUR (Televised variety show) — New York
Mar. 16, 1962: TOSCA: excerpts with Lisa Della Casa
Mar. 25, 1964: UN BALLO IN MASCHERA: *"Teco io sto"* (Duet, Act Two, with Régine Crespin)
Not yet available

THE VOICE OF FIRESTONE
Jun. 3, 1963: Excerpts from CAVALLERIA RUSTICANA ; Neapolitan songs; and TURANDOT:
"Nonpiangere, Liu"
VAI (Video Artists International)

RAI — 1963?
Italian song, first shown in U.S. on UMBERTO LANDI'S CONTINENTAL MINIATURES,
New York, 1966
Not yet available

STORIA DELL'OPERA — 1963?
Participation in a broadcast in six installments given by Lauretta Masiero. (RAI)?
Not yet available

OPERA CONCERT — Munich, Dec. 13, 1970
Program: Verdi —RIGOLETTO: *"Questo e quella;"* Giordano — ANDREA CHÉNIER:
"Improvviso;" Meyerbeer — L'AFRICANA: *"O paradiso;"* Puccini —TOSCA: *"Recondita armonia;"* Massenet —LE CID: *"Ô souverain;"* Boito — MEFISTOFELE: *"Giunto sul passo estremo."*
Not yet available

CONCERT IN NHK TV — Tokyo, Oct. 31, 1971
Program: Verdi — RIGOLETTO: *"Questa o quella;"* Giordano — ANDREA CHÉNIER:
"Improvviso;" Meyerbeer — L'AFRICANA: *"O paradiso;"*Puccini — LA BOHÈME: *"Che gelida manina;"* LA FANCIULLA DEL WEST: *"Ch'ella mi creda;"* *"'O sole mio"* (Di Capua);
"Core'ngrato" (Cardillo); *"Tu ca nun chiagne"* (Di Curtis); *"'A vucchella"* (Silvestri)
Cond.: Alberto Venturi (also on piano)
Bel Canto Society

GALA PERFORMANCE IN HONOR OF SIR RUDOLF BING — New York, Apr. 22, 1972
Verdi — OTELLO: *"Già nella notte densa"* (Duet, Act One, with Teresa Zylis-Gara)
Orchestra of the Metropolitan Opera of New York
Cond.: Karl Böhm
Not yet available

CONCERTI DI GALA — Hamburg, Oct. 10, 1973
Puccini — LA BOHÈME (Aria and Finale of Act One, with Mirella Freni); Verdi — AIDA
(Finale of the Opera, with Ilva Ligabue and Fiorenza Cossotto) (With sets and costumes)
Cond.: Nello Santi
Bel Canto Society

CONCERTO CON RENATA TEBALDI — Tokyo, Nov. 21, 1973
Program: *"Il Canto"* (Donizetti); *"Ouvre ton coeur"* (Bizet); Puccini — TOSCA: *"Recondita armonia;"* Gomez — IL GUARANY: *"Sento una forza indomita"* [duet]; Verdi — MACBETH: *"Ah, la paterna mano;"* *"Una lacrima"* (Donizetti); *"O leggiadri occhi belli"* (Anonymous); *"Noche feliz"* (Posades); Puccini — TOSCA: *"Chi è quella donna bionda lassù"* [duet from Act I]; *"Occhietti amati"* (Falconieri); *"Soave sogno"* (Bellini); Verdi — RIGOLETTO: *"La donna è mobile;"* OTELLO: *"Già nella notte densa"* [duet from Act I]; Massenet — WERTHER: *"Pourquoi me réveiller;"* Thomas — MIGNON: *"Elle ne croyait pas"* (Thomas); Grieg — PEER GYNT: *"Solveig's Song;"* *"Jota"* (De Falla); Puccini — LA BOHÈME: *"O soave fanciulla"* [duet from Act I]
Tokyo Philharmonic Orchestra
Cond.: Tadashi Mori
Bel Canto Society

FRANCO CORELLI CONCERT — Newark, N.J., Apr. 25, 1981
Program: *"Pecché"* (Pennino); *"L'ultima canzone"* (Tosti); *"'O marenariello"* (Gambardella); *"E canta il grillo"* (Billi); *"I te vurria vasà"* (Di Capua); *"Silenzio cantatore"* (Lama); *"A la Barcillunisa"* (Favara) with Klara Barlow, Virginia Zeani, Ferruccio Tagliavini, Nicola Rossi Lemeni, and Jerome Hines
Cond.: Alfredo Silipigni (also on piano)
Bel CantoSociety

INCONTRO CON FRANCO CORELLI — RAI, July 1980
Not yet available

FRANCO CORELLI — LIPSINE GARDEN SHOW, German TV, 1980?
Bel CantoSociety

BIRGIT NILSSON BIRTHDAY —Stockholm, Nov. 1981
Program: Excerpt from TURANDOT (Puccini); *"L'ultima canzone"* (Tosti)
Bel Canto Society

GRANDI VOCE E FRANCO CORELLI — RAI, Jan. 1983
For the series I GRANDI DELLA LIRICA
Cond.:Guido Guarnera
Bel Canto Society

FRANCO CORELLI TRIBUTE — RAI, 1993
Highlights from previous Corelli broadcasts: Puccini —TOSCA (1954); Leoncanvallo — PAGLIACCI (1955);Giordano — ANDREA CHÉNIER (1973)
Legato Classics

For information about the availability of these videos, contact the following sources:

Bel Canto Society, 11 Riverside Drive, Dept. ST, New York, NY 10023
Legato Classics, 18 Madison Ave., Hicksville, NY 11801
Video Artists International, P.O. Box 153, New York, NY 10023

Filmography

TOSCA — Cinemascope. Regia di Carmine Gallone (1956)
With: Franco Corelli, Frances Duval, Afro Poli, Vito De Taranto
With the voices of: Maria Caniglia, Gian Giacomo Guelfi, Vito De Taranto
Orchestra and Chorus of the Teatro dell'Opera of Rome
Cond.: Oliviero De Fabritiis
Bel Canto Society

Bibliography

ENCYCLOPEDIAS

Note: We are listing only those encyclopedias and works that have been directly consulted. [ref. "Voice," "Franco Corelli"]

Dictionnaire des chanteurs de l'Opéra de Paris du XVII siècle à nos jours — Albatros, Paris 1982

Dizionario enciclopedico della musica e dei musicisti — Fabbri, 1978

Dizionario Enciclopedico Universale della Musica e dei Musicisti — UTET, Turin

Enciclopedia della musica Ricordi — Ricordi, Milan 1963

Grande enciclopedia della musica classica — Armando Curcio Editore, Rome

Grande enciclopedia della musica lirica — Longanesi Periodici, Milan

Kutsch, K.J., and Leo Riemens — *Grosses Sängerlexikon*, Francke Verlag, Bern and Stuttgart

Le grandi voci — Istituto per la Collaborazione Culturale, Rome 1964

La musica — UTET, Turin 1968

The New Grove Dictionary of Music and Musicians — Macmillan Publishers Ltd., London 1980

La nuova enciclopedia della musica Garzanti — Garzanti, Milan 1983

BOOKS

Note: Only the books that were directly or indirectly utilized in the text appear on the following list. We are therefore excluding texts of general reference, whether of music history or vocal technique. Biographies or autobiographies have been listed only when they were expressly cited in the text.

— *Il Teatro Lirico Sperimentale di Spoleto nel suo primo ventennio*, Rome 1966

Bing, Rudolf — *5000 Nights at the Opera*, Doubleday & Co., Garden City, N.Y., 1972.

Caputo, Pietro — *Cotogni, Lauri Volpi e...*, Bongiovanni, Bologna, 1980

Celletti, Rodolfo — *"I cantanti"* in *La Fenice*, Milan 1972

Celletti, Rodolfo — *Memorie di un ascoltatore*, Il Saggiatore, Milan 1985

Celletti, Rodolfo — *Pavarotti — 25 anni per la musica*, Ruggeri, Bologna 1986

Celletti, Rodolfo — *Storia del belcanto*, 2nd ed., La Nuova Italia, Florence 1986

Celletti, Rodolfo — *Il teatro d'opera in disco 1950-1987*, 3rd ed., Rizzoli, Milan 1988

Celletti, Rodolfo — *Voce di tenore*, Idealibri, Milan 1989

Downs, Joan — "Franco Corelli" in Herbert H. Breslin, ed., *The Tenors*, Macmillan Publishing Co., New York 1973

Herman, Robert — *The Greater Miami Opera 1941-1985*, Miami 1986

Hines, Jerome — *Great Singers on Great Singing*, Doubleday & Co., Garden City (N.Y.) 1982

Lauri-Volpi, Giacomo — *Misteri della voce umana*, Dall'Oglio, Milan 1957

Lauri-Volpi, Giacomo — *Voci parallele*, 3rd ed., Bongiovanni, Bologna 1977

Leoni, Edilio — *Un medico e un teatro*, Electa, Rome 1987

Marinelli, Carlo — *Opere in disco*, Discanto, Fiesole 1982

Marinelli, Carlo — *Faust e Mefistofele*, Quaderni dell'I.R.T.E.M. n. 3, Treviso 1986

Merkling, Frank, John Freeman and Gerard Fitzgerald — *The Golden Horseshoe*, The Viking Press, New York 1965

Montale, Eugenio — *Prime alla Scala*, Mondadori, Milan 1981

Morini, Mario, ed. — *Umberto Giordano*, Sonzogno, Milan 1986

Nathen, Alex — *Primo uomo: Grosse Sänger der Oper*, Basilius Press, Basel-Stuttgart 1963

Paoletti, Pier Maria — *Quella sera alla Scala*, Rizzoli, Milan 1983

Pasi, Mario — *Maria Callas: la donna, la voce, la diva*, International Music of Italy, Milan 1981

Prawy, Marcel — *Die Wiener Oper*, Verlag Fritz Molden, Vienna 1969

Ricci, Walter — *I casti divi*, Gammalibri

Rosenthal, Harold — *Great Singers of Today*, Calder & Boyers, London, 1966

Schiavo, Remo — *Stelle dell'Arena*, Panda Edizioni, Verona 1988

Segalini, Sergio — *Meyerbeer: diable ou prophète?*, Beba, Paris 1985

Sguerzi, Angelo — *Le stirpi canore*, Bongiovanni, Bologna 1978

Sguerzi, Angelo — *Le stirpi canore, Vol. II*, Bongiovanni, Bologna, 1988

Stinchelli, Enrico — *Le stelle della lirica*, Gremese, 1986

Vishnevskaya, Galina — *Galina, una storia russa*, Frassinelli 1984

PRESS SOURCES

Articles, reviews and chronicles were used from the following press sources:

Daily Papers
(in alphabetical order referencing place of publication)

ITALY: *Il corriere adriatico* (Ancona); *Il corriere mercantile* (Genoa); *Il corriere del pomeriggio* (Genoa); *La gazzetta del lunedì* (Genoa); *Il lavoro nuovo* (Genoa); *Il corriere della sera* (Milan); *Il corriere d'informazione* (Milan); *Il giorno* (Milan); *La notte* (Milan); *Il mattino* (Naples); *La gazzetta di Parma* (Parma); *L'avanti* (Rome); *Il messaggero* (Rome); *Il tempo* (Rome); *L'unità* (Rome); *La stampa* (Turin); *Stampa sera* (Turin); *L'Adige* (Trento); *Il gazzettino* (Venice); *L'arena* (Verona)

ABROAD: *Diario de noticias* (Lisbon); *O seculo* (Lisbon); *Minneapolis Tribune* (Minneapolis); *St. Paul Dispatch* (Minneapolis); *The New York Herald Tribune* (New York); *The New York Journal-American* (New York); *The New York Times* (New York); *Il progresso italo-americano* (New York); *Le Figaro* (Paris); *Le Monde* (Paris); *The Evening Bulletin* (Philadelphia)

Reviews
(in alphabetical order)

ITALY: *Amica, Candido, Il corriere del teatro, Discoteca HI-FI, Epoca, L'Espresso, L'Europeo, Grand Hotel, Mondo lirico, Musica, Musica d'oggi, Musica e dischi, Musica e dossier, Oggi, L'Opera, Radiocorriere TV, Rassegna melodrammatica, La Scala.*

ABROAD: *The Gramophone, High Fidelity, Musical America, The New York Times Magazine, Opera, Opera International, Opera News.*

Index

Photo Credits

Mark Schiavone: 4, 7, 9, 11-13, 20, 21, 24, 26, 27, 39, 41, 42, 50, 53, 54, 59, 60, 67, 68, 71, 85, 94, 97, 98, 102, 106-111, 113-119; Bill Park: 5, 14, 36, 103; Irifoto: 6; Troncone (Naples): 15; Marina Boagno: 16, 52, 89; Opera News/Metropolitan Opera Guild, Inc.: 17, 18, 19, 31-35, 100, 105; Erio Piccagliani/ La Scala—Opera News/Metropolitan Opera Guild, Inc.: 22; Erio Piccagliani/La Scala— Bill Park: 23; La Scala: 25, 40, 51, 72; Mark Schiavone/Marion Rahman: 28, 61; Reale (Rome): 29; Fayer (Vienna): 30, 55, 46; Erio Piccagliani/La Scala: 37, 43, 45, 48, 56-64, 70-77, 79, 80, 83, 84, 86, 87, 90-92; Villani Bologna: 38, 44; Bill Park/Louis Mélançon, New York, N.Y.: 47; Archiv Salzburger Festspiele: 65; Irifoto (Verona): 66; Louis Mélançon/Opera News/Metropolitan Opera Guild, Inc.: 69; Capitol Records, Inc./Erio Piccagliani: 78; La Scala: 81, 82, 93, 96; Louis Mélançon, New York, N.Y./Bill Park/ Metropolitan Opera Association, Inc.: 88; Louis Mélançon/Metropolitan Opera Association, Inc.: 95, 99, 101; Louis Mélançon/ Opera News/Metropolitan Opera Guild, Inc.: 104; Angel Records/Mark Schiavone: 112.

Thanks

We would like to thank the following entities and institutions, and their respective representatives, who have allowed us access to documents, or facilitated that access.

ITALY: Ufficio Stampa del Teatro alla Scala di Milan (Patrizia Biffi); Istituzione Teatro Lirico Sperimentale "A. Belli" di Spoleto (Claudio Lepore); Dipartimento Relazioni Esterne del Teatro Regio di Turin (Bruna Martinotti e Massimo Martino); Civico Museo Teatrale "C. Schmidl" di Trieste; Archives of "L'Arena" di Verona (Felice Gattamelata e Maria Rita Ferro); Archives of "Il Gazzettino di Venezia" (Daniela Zamburlin); Biblioteca Civica di Verona (Silvana Morandi); Biblioteca Civica di Milan (Giovanna Colombo); Archivio del Centro Produzione RAI di Rome; Ufficio dello Stato civile del Comune di Ancona; Ufficio dello Stato Civile del Comune di Osimo.

Particular thanks go to the personnel of the Biblioteca del Conservatorio "Giuseppe Verdi" of Milan for its useful and cordial assistance.

FRANCE: Archives of the Opéra de Paris; Théâtre de l'Opéra di Nice (Louis Rossi).

PRINCIPALITY OF MONACO: Archives of the Société des Bains de Mer of Monte-Carlo.

MALTA: Teatro Manoel of La Valletta (Miss J. Portelli).

SPAIN: Asociaciòn Bilbaina de Amigos de la Opera of Bilbao (Mikel Viar).

GERMANY: Staatsoper of Hamburg (Suzanne Litzel); Deutsche Oper of Berlin (Barbara Hering and Gisela Thielicke); Library of the State Theater of Bonn (Alef); Deutsche Oper am Rhein of Dusseldorf; Opera Theater of Dortmund (Monika Pichler); Niederasachsiche Staatssheater of Hannover (Sabine Hammer); Bayerische Staatsoper of Munich (Barbara Wagner-Galdea); Staatstheater of Stuttgart (Monika Weng-Gebhardt).

UNITED STATES: Lyric Opera of Chicago (Al Chiccit, Jr.); Houston Grand Opera (Ava Jean Mears); Dallas Opera (Jonathan Pell); Los Angeles Opera (Allen Gardner); Archives of the Metropolitan Opera of New York (Michael Vocino); San Francisco Performing Arts Library & Museum (Barbara R. Geisler, Lee G. Mosley, Margaret K. Norton); Seattle Opera (Cindy Miller); Metropolitan Opera Guild (Kay Long, Louise Guinther).

We should like to thank besides the following people who have contributed in various ways to the realization of this book.

ITALY: *Cassano Magnago:* Mario Vicentini; *Crema:* Gianfranco Caravaggio; *Milan:* Maria Grazia Andreoli, Sergio Baratelli, Carlo Bergonzi, Margherita Bianchi, Oreste Braccini, Joseph Buttigieg, Rodolfo Celletti, Dantina Chiesi, Jilou Combel, Graziano Corelli, Bianca Dal Molin, Roswita Krull, Silvia Labò, Giancarlo Lenzi, Mario Morini, Daniela Pistoia, Luciano Pituello, Mario Roversi, Sauro Sili, Anna Setti, Emanuela Velludo, Gianfranco Villa; *Parma:* Claudio Dal Re, Odoardo Stocchi; *Rome:* Giulio Andreotti, Carlo Belli, Gina Guandalini, Marco Rossi, Sandro Rinaldi, Enrico Stinchelli, Gabriella Tucci; *Turin:* Giorgio Gualerzi, Angelo Quattrocchi, Vincenzo Quattrocchi; *Trieste:* Gianni Gori; *Venice:* Giuseppe Pugliese; *Verona:* Barbara Dompieri, Gianni Zatachetto; *Voghera:* Norma and Pierino Girani.

A particular word of thanks is due to Liliana and Ubaldo Corelli, siblings of the artist, for their cordial welcomes and precious encouragements.

ABROAD: *Antwerp* (Belgium): Gerda De Keyser; *Athens, Texas* (U.S.A.): Bill Park; *Philadelphia* (U.S.A.): Jerry S. Leonard; *Lisbon* (Portugal): Francisco Moita; *Salzburg* (Austria): Chiara Gerini.

Finally we would like to express our thanks to the artists (singers, orchestra conductors, stage directors) and all the various people connected to the opera world who have kindly consented to meet with us, and to remember their impressions and episodes of their professional contacts with Franco Corelli.

We would like to lay particular stress on the fact that, although contributions may have been cited more or less diffusely throughout the text, depending on the way the narrative was unfolding, all were equally important in enabling us to form a complete picture of our subject's personality.

Contributors' names are listed chronologically, according to the time they were interviewed: Anselmo Colzani and his kind wife Ada; Maestro Giampiero Tintori; Magda Olivero; Luisa Maragliano and Maestro Tristano Illersberg; Maestro Michelangelo Veltri; Adriana Maliponte; Jeannette Pilou; Elena Nicolai; Lucia Kelston Ferraris and Maestro Franco Ferraris; Maestro Argeo Quadri; Antonietta Stella; Birgit Nilsson; Laura Carol and Gian Giacomo Guelfi; Maestro Francesco Molinari Pradelli and his kind wife Bianca Maria; Maestro Ottavio Ziino; Anita Cerquetti and Edo Ferretti; Gigliola Frazzoni; Raoul Grassilli; Giuseppe Negri; Fedora Barbieri; Carlo Perucci; Giulietta Simionato; Piero De Palma; Renata Tebaldi; Maestro Carlo Franci; Maestro Gianandrea Gavazzeni; Luigi Oldani; Mirella Freni; Grace Bumbry; Adriana Lazzarini.

Marina Boagno and Gilberto Starone

Additional Thanks

In addition to all the people who, in various ways have helped me to realize this work, and are mentioned elsewhere in this book, I think I should thank several people in particular by name.

Thanks to my sons, Pier Giovanni and Michelangelo, who, their youth notwithstanding, have helped me in many different ways with their musical advice, with computer software, with typing, with the correction of galley proofs, and with patient support in so many small details during the three years of my research.

Thanks to Federico Rota, a fan, a collector, and a friend, without whose interventions at crucial times I might never have been able to write this book. And thanks to fate, fortune or the arcane powers that led to our meeting in the most incredible of circumstances.

Thanks to Gilberto Starone, my indispensable collaborator, and still very dear friend, who helped me and supported me in my work in all possible ways, whose generosity was so unsparing that he could reconcile one of the most cynical of cynics with human nature.

Now that the American edition of my book is about to be printed, I would like to thank Ms. Jane Howle of Baskerville Publishers for her kindness to me and her dedication to this work.

I also want to thank two American friends, whose efforts and enthusiasm all of us have to thank for the American edition of this book. They are Bill Park, who has for many years assisted my research in the United States, and Mark Schiavone, one of the "old faithful" among the Corelli fans, and one of my dear friends, even if we have never personally met, who strongly believed in this venture and finally made it possible.

Marina Boagno, September, 1966